…TRODUCTION TO
…ORATE STRATEGY

Also by Richard Pettinger

Introduction to Management
Introduction to Organisational Behaviour
Preparing and Handling Industrial Tribunal Cases
Managing the Flexible Workforce

INTRODUCTION TO CORPORATE STRATEGY

Richard Pettinger

MACMILLAN
Business

First published 1996 by
MACMILLAN PRESS LTD
Houndmills, Basingstoke, Hampshire RG21 6XS
and London
Companies and representatives
throughout the world

ISBN 0–333–61104–7 hardcover
ISBN 0–333–61105–5 paperback

A catalogue record for this book is available
from the British Library.

10 9 8 7 6 5 4 3 2 1
05 04 03 02 01 00 99 98 97 96

Copy-edited and typeset by Povey–Edmondson
Okehampton and Rochdale, England

Printed in Great Britain by
Mackays of Chatham PLC
Chatham, Kent

Contents

List of figures, tables and boxes

Figures

Tables

Boxes

Preface

The current state of the commercial and social environment has caused the questioning of every form of business and public service practice hitherto accepted. Patterns of consumption, the global nature of trade, production expertise and organisation practices have all become subject to scrutiny and inquiry in recent years. There are few, if any, safe and protected markets or spheres of activity. In particular the success of the Japanese and the other countries of the Pacific Rim – Taiwan, Malaysia, Korea, Indonesia and the Philippines – in penetrating and holding global markets has caused organisations in the West to rethink their entire approach to product excellence, delivery, durability and price, and to revolutionise their approach to customers and consumers, and hitherto accepted concepts of quality, satisfaction and value. This is also true for the education, health and other services provided by societies, both in respect of their content, in the ways in which they are delivered and also who is to be responsible for them. Parts of this are within the control of organisations and their managers; much of it indeed creates opportunities for change, development, growth and advancement. Some of it, however, is clearly outside this control and a key ingredient for effectiveness lies in the ability to understand this and to create successful directions and operations within these constraints. Recent events that have contributed to this have included the collapse of the USSR in 1989, the Gulf War of 1991, the currency crisis of 1992, the enlargement and ordering of the EC; and all have placed significant limitations on the ways in which business and public services are conducted.

This is the broad context in which corporate strategy is studied. Strategy and direction emerge from examinations and analyses of the environment at large and in the particular parts where the conduct of activities is envisaged; and from the creation and development of organisations and expertise that are capable of pursuing these activities. It is, therefore, a process based on series and patterns of decisions, interactions and forces.

More specifically, corporate strategy is concerned with matching organisational capability and capacity with the demands and restraints of the markets to be served and the pressures of the wider environment. Within this broad statement some basic principles of effective strategy can be identified. Clarity of purpose and direction, absolute standards of honesty and integrity, and high levels of confidence and respect are found in all successful organisations. There are particular requirements also in the establishment of product and service quality, and in dealings with both customers and the community. There are also certain requirements in the creation of organisation forms, style of management, and attitudes and approaches to the staff employed to carry out the work. Finally, high levels of expertise are required to translate this into practice, providing successful and effective activities.

The ability to view the organisation and its activities strategically – to take this overview and the longer perspective that this implies, and to relate this to the desired outcome of activities – is therefore a distinctive and critical part of the expertise for managers. Determining the purpose and direction of the organisation, the means by which this is to be achieved and the measures of success and failure to be accorded rests with the Chief Executive, top management and directors. Implementation, however, is the responsibility of everyone if a direct relationship between strategy, operations and activities is to be achieved. Everyone therefore needs to understand the organisation's purpose and direction. All need to know where they fit into the wider scheme and what their contribution is. They must understand the interrelationship between all these interacting forces and the particular business activities and functions. They must also be integrated into the monitoring, evaluation and review processes that are devised in order to measure progress and, where necessary, to take remedial action.

The academic base on which corporate strategy is studied is derived from two main standpoints: extensive studies of great numbers of organisations in all fields of activity; and the assessment of those features, principles and qualities that ought to be present in successful organisations. The outcome of this has been a transformation of the approach taken to the field of corporate strategy.

It is apparent that there is a direct relationship between clear and unambiguous purpose understood by all concerned and organisation success and effectiveness. Clearly everyone is involved; strategy is not the exclusive remit of a coterie of directors. Neither is strategy exclusively concerned with planning: this is rather the means by which resources are allocated and controlled in the pursuit of the desired direction. Management and supervision must engage in a broader field than merely the completion of the day's work; there is a strategic context to be found in the organisation and direction of operations and activities. This in turn is critical to the effective ordering and scheduling of these activities; it provides a different context from that traditionally regarded as the best form of practice; and it has direct implications for the design of organisations and the ordering of work practices and schedules which in turn affect everyone and everything involved. This reinforces the point made earlier that strategy is a process rather than a linear series of activities and events. It involves the direction, management and control of these interacting forces and functions, and an acknowledgement of the strengths, capabilities and limitations of the organisation in its dealings with its markets and environment.

It follows from this that the ability to think strategically is required of all managers and that they must be trained and developed in this critical feature of their expertise. There are concepts, techniques and tasks to be learned; a body of contemporary and historic material to be studied so that these lessons can be taught and assimilated; and quality, skills and expertise to be developed in the field. The outcome of this is an understanding of the range, scale and complexity of the tasks of strategic management: that this is a professional activity based on this body of knowledge and expertise; that a critical function of this consists of the ability to understand and manage the strategy process; and that it applies to a greater or lesser extent to all managers.

The book introduces and addresses each of these themes. Four key elements may also be identified: analysis, formulation, development and implementation. This is the basis on which distinctive aspects of the process are then addressed: the adoption of a unique generic position; the means by which this is enhanced; the abilities and qualities needed to compete; and the context of the particular sectors in which activities are contemplated. The softer, less precise forces and elements are then considered, including ethics, key players, confidence, development and wider perceptual and behavioural influences on organisations, customers and environment. Strategy implementation is presented using the themes of achieving commitment to purpose, assessing that which is possible and feasible given the various constraints that exist on all activities, and devising suitable sub-strategies for the conduct and harmonisation of distinctive sets of activities. There is a separate chapter on the particular issues surrounding change. The final chapter is a short illustration and discussion of those factors that affect or are likely to affect the nature of activities in the future.

The text is illustrated throughout with figures, diagrams, examples and illustrations. These reinforce the matters for consideration and give constant pointers and sources of reference for general discussion and for developing a deeper understanding of these issues. At the end of each chapter are questions for discussion and assignment work. Some of these address the material of the particular chapter, while others require this material to be developed through additional research on the part of the reader.

As to the terminology used, the following is a useful introduction. The word 'organisation' denotes anybody, in any sector of commerce, business or public service; 'company', 'firm', 'authority', 'hospital', 'school' and so on are used where a more precise definition is required. 'Policy', 'strategy', 'purpose' and 'direction' are used more or less interchangeably as are 'product', 'service' and 'offering'. 'Management' is normally used as a general statement of responsibility or definition of executive function. However, the aim has been to avoid as far as possible the use of management course and business school jargon.

The book is intended for students on undergraduate, diploma and masters' courses at universities and colleges, and for those following part-time or open courses of study leading to recognised management qualifications. It is also a useful general reader for those seeking to broaden their general understanding of the field of organisation strategy. Its specific value is as an introduction to the range and complexity of qualities, concepts, skills and attributes necessary in the formulation of policy and direction; it is therefore most likely to appeal to those on business, public policy and strategic management courses. It also has general value as an introduction to the background and environment in which organisation direction and choice is based and the processes behind this. More generally still, it is a useful introduction to the interactive processes between organisations and their environment which must be understood if success is to be achieved.

RICHARD PETTINGER

Acknowledgements

Many people have helped in and influenced the preparation of this book. I am indebted to the staff and students of University College London, especially John Andrews, Barbara Young, Victor Torrance, Bev Nutt, David Kincaid and Ram Ahronov of the Bartlett; and to Andrew Scott and Graham Winch of the University's Management Centre. I am also grateful to Paul Griseri of the London Guildhall University; and to Roger Cartwright of the Management Centre at Oxford College of Higher Education. Jane Powell and Stephen Rutt at Macmillan have been a constant source of strength and support. I am also very grateful to Kelvin Cheatle; Jonathan Rice; Anthony Impey; Mark Genney; Stephen Frank; and to Rebecca Frith for typing and editing the manuscript.

RICHARD PETTINGER

CHAPTER 1

Introduction: The Context and Background of Effective Strategy

Introduction

Corporate strategy is concerned with directing and guiding the inception and growth of organisations, and the changes that occur as they conduct their activities. A clearly articulated and accurate strategy is at the core of all successful commercial and public activities. Indeed, where success is not forthcoming, this is often because this clarity is missing.

Strategy is concerned with reconciling the need for organisational stability and continuity in a turbulent commercial and public service world. Conflicting demands for resources must be reconciled; the use of different resources – capital, premises, technology, information and expertise – harmonised.

The long term future of the organisation must be secured. This is possible only if good-quality products and services are made available at the right price, quality, volume and location for those who are to use and consume them. This has to be seen in the context of the current range and state of activities, and also of past history, traditions, triumphs and disasters.

It is also much easier to assess success and failure if purpose, aims and objectives are expressed clearly and understood by all concerned. This extends beyond the organisation's employees to customers, clients and consumers and indeed, to the wider community and environment; for example, people will pay top prices for a commodity that is known or perceived to have high quality and value, but will be less keen to do so if this is not clear (whether or not it is present).

Moreover, the commercial and public service world is competitive. For everything there is always the option to refuse. Everything must therefore carry a basic value and utility otherwise people will go elsewhere. This applies as much to the satisfaction of needs – health care, education, energy supply, food and transport – as it does to the fulfilment of wants (for example, designer clothes, fast cars, perfumes).

This is the background against which all organisations decide and determine their activities. It is the basis for deciding the size scope and scale of activities. These must be matched and harmonised with the environment, resource and expertise capacity and capability. They must also accord with the expectations and values of everyone involved and affected.

The purpose of this chapter is therefore to introduce the scale and scope of corporate strategy as it applies to all commercial business and public sectors, and not-for-profit activities.

Definition

A range of definitions of corporate strategy is given in Box 1.1. A useful summary of these is:

> The strategy of an organisation is the definition and implementation of its purpose.

For this to be successful, there are elements which must be present; there are rules that must be followed; and sources of strategy to be found.

Elements

Clarity of purpose

Everything about any organisation stems from the purpose for its existence. If this is not clear, everything else is clouded also. The plans and policies that are devised, the activities related to strategic development and implementation and the operations, work methods and practices devised in pursuit of this will also lack focus, direction and therefore purpose.

BOX 1.1 Authoritative Definitions of Strategy

H. I. Ansoff defined strategy as 'a set of decision-making rules for the guidance of organisational behaviour'.

Richard G. Hamermesh distinguished between different levels of strategy:

- corporate strategy – the determination of the businesses or sectors in which a company will compete and the allocation of different resources among those businesses and sectors;
- institutional strategy – the basic character and vision of a company or organisation and its leadership;
- business strategy – determination of how a company will compete in a given business and position itself among its competitors.

C. Roland Christensen says that strategy is 'the study of the functions and responsibilities of senior management, the crucial and critical problems that affect success in the total enterprise and the decisions that determine the direction of the organisation and shape its future.'

Kenneth R. Andrews believes corporate strategy is to be the 'pattern of decisions in a company which determines, shapes and reveals its objectives, purposes and goals; which produces the principal policies and plans for achieving these goals; which defines the business that the company intends to be in, and the sort of organisation that it intends to be in pursuit of this.'

Vision

Organisation and strategic vision is a necessary precursor for organisation success. The vision of an organisation is its shining light, the star by which to steer, the illuminator of the path (see Box 1.2). It is a combination of visualisation, enthusiasm, ambition, and a commitment to work.

It is usually articulated by the creator of the organisation, or by those who are energising or championing particular initiatives and projects (see Box 1.3). It is often their all-consuming passion, their professional and operational reason for being. As with all visions and visionaries, the matter is approached with zeal, fervour, dynamism and energy; it is the impact of this on those who are to be caught up in the initiative or project that determines its success.

BOX 1.2 Vision

This approach is easy to identify in organisations such as Virgin, The Body Shop, Mary Kay Cosmetics and Amstrad. The energy is provided by strong creators and entrepreneurs, people who invest their heart and soul, as well as their business and strategic capabilities, in getting the organisation up and successful. Each case may be illustrated by one example taken from it.

Virgin Atlantic was created by Richard Branson in the 1980s as a top quality niche airline to fly between London, the USA and the Far East. To promote this Branson created a distinctive image based on quality and identity with the passenger, and reinforced this himself by constantly keeping himself and therefore the company in the public eye.

The Body Shop was created by Anita Roddick as an ethically and environmentally sound cosmetics empire. The products were made from organic sources, drawn from emerging nations, and for which fair prices and formal trading relations were established.

Mary Kay Cosmetics was created by Mary Kay Ash as a successful organisation based on the 'eternal principle'. This is articulated by Mary Kay Ash as 'Do unto others as you would have them do unto you.' It permeates throughout all dealings with all the people with whom the organisation comes into contact: staff, agents and franchisees, customers and clients, as well as the wider community.

Alan Sugar was so determined to get his Amstrad range of low-cost personal computers off the ground and successful that he engaged in personal promotional campaigns in order to ward off the adverse publicity which was generated about his products by larger companies in the sector.

In each case the end result has been the creation of an organisation of strong image, identity and, above all, profitability.

BOX 1.3 Vision: The Body Shop

INSPIRED
by the knowledge of other cultures we make
EXCLUSIVE
products to our own original recipes
COMMITTED
to fairer trading and the environment, we bring you
THE BODY SHOP

BOX 1.4 Business Policy

Once an organisation has established its direction it can then determine the manner and approach that it intends to take to pursue this. Statements of policy indicate this, outlining what will and will not be done in such pursuit. These statements reflect standards of behaviour attitudes and values, integrity and any strong beliefs held by those responsible for direction.

For example:

- a retail chain may only sell goods under its own name, it may concentrate its buying in domestic markets, it may set its own standards of product safety regardless of what legislation exists;
- a company that owns and publishes newspapers may not interfere with editorial freedom;
- an armaments company may not sell to regimes that do not follow certain standards of conduct towards its people;
- a cosmetics company may not sell products whose testing involves cruelty or suffering to animals;
- a furniture factory may not use wood products from tropical rainforests.

The mix of examples is intended to illustrate both the positive and the negative. These cover operational, social and ethical issues; and all indicate absolute standards of performance, behaviour and approach.

Commitment

Effective organisation strategies carry a 'commitment to achieve', in whatever terms this is to be measured: financial gains and profits; effectiveness and quality of service; or a combination of the two (see Box 1.5).

This is also reflected in the volume, quality and nature of resources used; the ways of working adopted; the shared values, management and operational styles drawn up in support of this; and any distinctive moral or ethical stance that is also taken up.

BOX 1.5 Commitment: The Corporate Mission of British Airways

A Company Aiming 'To be the best'

The corporate mission of British Airways is: to be the best and most successful company in the airline industry.

The company's seven corporate goals are:

Safe and secure	To be a safe and secure airline.
Financially strong	To deliver a strong and consistent financial performance.
Global leader	To secure a leading share of air travel business worldwide with a significant presence in all major geographical markets.
Service and value	To provide overall superior service at good value for money in every market segment.
Customer drive	To excel in anticipating and quickly responding to customer needs and competitor activity.
Good employer	To sustain a working environment that attracts, retains and develops committed employees who share in the success of the company.
Good neighbour	To be a good neighbour, concerned for the community and the environment.

Source: *BA Company News*, Spring 1994.

BOX 1.6 Customers and Clients

The customers and clients of organisations are those who avail themselves of its products and services. A finer distinction may also be drawn as follows: the customer is the one who pays for the offering; the client is the one who uses it. The two may be the same (the driver who both pays for and uses the petrol for the car), or they may not be (the parent buys toys, the child uses them).

This also applies to public services and the not-for profit sector. In each case, continual focus on the client groups in question is critical to their effective operation, maximisation and optimisation of what are invariably scarce resources.

BOX 1.7 Stakeholders and Interested Parties

Stakeholders or interested parties of an organisation are those affected by it and those who affect it. They hold varying types of degrees of influence and interest in it, its products and services, its ways of working, its standards and outcomes, its successes and its failures. They are as follows.

1. The staff: everyone who works for and in the organisation and who is therefore dependent upon it for their income and spending power and, to a greater extent, for their standard and style of living. This also applies in some measure to sub-contractors and other retainers, and to potential staff. It also covers trade unions and professional associations, and any others who have representative interests in it.
2. The communities in which the staff live and work and in which the organisation operates. All organisations have a basic general association within their communities. They provide work and resources for the community and also therefore triggers to other economic activities within it.
3. Social customers: for example, charities, schools and hospitals which may approach the organisation for sponsorship and support for social, educational, charitable or other worthy causes.
4. Shareholders: the investors of money in an organisation in the expectation and anticipation of returns.
5. Other financial interests including backers, contributors, bankers, other loan-makers, venture capitalists, sponsors, city institutions and stock markets.
6. Suppliers of components and raw materials: these have a vested interest in the success of the organisation in focus, both in terms of continuity of this particular sphere of business and also in the gaining of a wider reputation for those components and raw materials as they are used successfully, effectively and profitably in its own pursuits.
7. The community sectors and markets in which the organisation offers its products and services for sale.

8. Distributors and agents who rely on their own position between the organisation in question and the end users of the products or services for their own existence.
9. Government departments and agencies with whom the organisation comes into contact. Clearly, while the nature and extent of this involvement varies between organisations, at the very least this means legal and financial compliance.
10. Trade, market, and employers' federations and associations that are active in the particular field.
11. Competitors and offerers of alternative products and services, substitutes and competition for the organisation in question. These must be considered as stakeholders in this regard insofar as very few sectors or niches operate in complete isolation or insulation from others. As we shall see elsewhere, the continuity of competition in a particular sector is an opportunity as well as a burden; the converse is also true: the loss of a competitor in a sector may not only lead to greater opportunities for those remaining in it, but may destabilise it.
12. Lobbyists, vested interest groups and other influential groups related to the location of activities, the nature of activities, the ways in which those activities are carried out, the marketing of them, and the distribution of them. This may also include addressing wider questions of ethics, morality and social values.

The point to recognise is the relative position of each in given sectors of operation. Not all carry the same influence; conversely, one may carry overwhelming influence. They often have conflicting interest. It is a critical part of the strategy formation process that the range of stakeholders and their relative influence and the extent and nature of the impact of this influence upon the strategy is recognised.

Customers and clients

All effective organisation strategies place customers and clients at their core: without customers and clients there is no need for the organisation or its activities (this also applies to internal strategies and organisation systems, subsystems and procedures). The following must be addressed:

- the nature, locations, volume of the customer and customer bases;
- their needs and wants in regard to the organisation's range of offerings;
- where this range exists on the scale of a customer's priorities;
- the distinctive advantages held by these offerings in relation to those of competitors;
- reputation, confidence and loyalty to the organisation among its customers;
- financial elements.

This can be summarised as: let us commit ourselves to long term service and satisfaction of our customers, remembering that if we do not they will go elsewhere.

■ Timescale

A clear recognition and evaluation is required of what is truly to be achieved over different periods of time. This has to be measured in terms of steadiness, permanence and transience. It is a function of the nature and type of investment in which the organisation is engaged. It also reflects the nature of returns required by the organisation's different stakeholders, and the conflicts inherent in these that must be recognised and reconciled (for example, the capacity to reconcile demand for high wages on the part of the staff, high levels of dividend demanded by shareholders, high share price demanded by stock market investors).

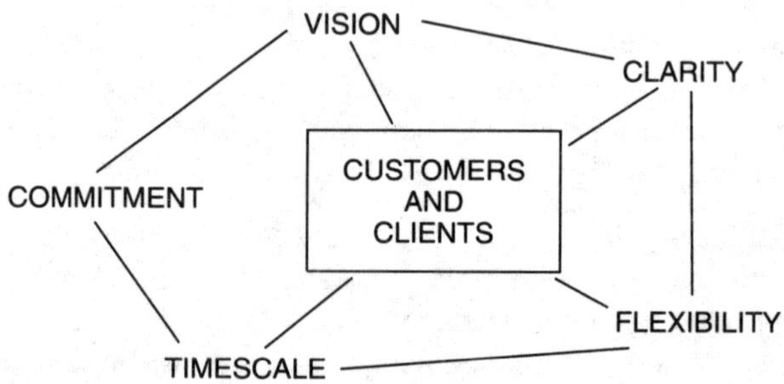

Purpose: to indicate and illustrate the relationship of these elements with each other, and to place the customers and clients at the centre of the picture at the outset.

Figure 1.1 Elements of strategy

■ Language

Clarity (or otherwise) of purpose is reflected in the actual words used in the articulation of strategy. The greater the clarity of articulation, the greater the likely clarity of purpose. The converse is also true: where the strategic purpose is not easy to read, follow or understand, because the organisation has not fully grasped its own purpose.

This clarity of language is needed across the board in dealings with staff, customers, clients, the wider public and community. It is reinforced by the standpoint adopted to each of these groups, of openness or otherwise, of honesty and directness or otherwise, or of commitment or abdication.

Language must also be seen in general terms as the oil of the business processes and systems used, both in the internal operating and staff management systems, and in the external marketing activities, public relations and customer and commercial interfaces.

■ Flexibility and dynamism

Strategy is a continuous and dynamic process, not a single event; neither is it cast in tablets of stone. Part of the true clarity of purpose is the reconciliation of the ability to respond to customer demand with the capacity for recognising and evaluating the opportunities that exist. It is therefore necessary to establish a permanent organisation which can accommodate this flexibility.

Peters calls this the 'simultaneous loose-tight properties'. This is the capacity for allowing latitude to staff departments and divisions to seek out commercial opportunities without deflecting from the absolute standards, qualities, focus and direction of the organisation. It is the capacity to include a measure of dynamism within this stated direction.

■ Soft and hard

□ *Soft*

This is the recognition of the standards and quality of treatment expected on the part of the staff and customers of the organisation and its communities. These elements are general standards of honesty, openness, forthrightness, trust and decency.

□ *Hard*

This is the profit motive. The case is absolute that profitable business is only possible if the soft elements referred to above are in place. Customers will not deal with organisations that are found to be dishonest, closed and untrustworthy. This also applies to the complete range of public services. Where it is impossible to avoid dealing with such bodies they will be approached with trepidation and with the certainty on the part of customers that they are to receive a less than full service or to be treated with duplicity.

Business strategies are only successful if profit is made as the result. A core obligation to all the stakeholders of the organisation is to remain in business, to continue and to improve. In public service terms the equivalent is effectiveness. This again is a reflection of the core obligation to stakeholders (in this case to provide high quality and effective services to those demanding them).

In the 'not-for-profit' sector the equivalent is effectiveness again: in resource-gathering and utilisation; and also in the generation of commitment to the cause or the matter in hand.

Change

Strategies change and evolve according to the need to remain competitive; according to changes in people's perceptions, needs and wants; and as the result of technological advances. Strategy is therefore a multi-dimensional process, not a linear function.

The rules of strategy

From this, a set of rules may be identified.

The golden rule is the placing of a customer at the centre of all activities and the recognition of this on the part of all those who work in the organisation, in whatever function.

The others are:

- continuity, permanence and sustenance (investment) that reflect the commitment of the organisation to its purpose;
- replacement and re-investment elements, technology, marketing, staff, expertise, premises, capital and consumables;
- the setting of absolute standards of policy, ethics and morality and the creation of shared values and common beliefs in support of this;
- the devising of a suitable culture, style and way of working that both reflects and harmonises the nature of the staff, the nature of the markets, the necessary ways of working and the nature of the actual offerings;
- the capacity to quantify and qualify the returns that are made for success, failure, areas of strength and weakness and improvement;
- recognition that the process is imperfect, set in an imperfect and changing world and carried out by imperfect people;
- recognition that qualities of enthusiasm, commitment, energy, vitality, drive and ambition are required by everybody concerned;
- recognition that loyalty is required by staff, markets and communities to the organisation, and by the organisation to its customers, staff and communities;
- continuous reference to distinctive expertise, competence and technology;
- continuous reference to reputation and confidence;
- constant attention to improvements in all areas and activities;
- the theme of doing unto others as you would have them do unto you; an absolute regard and respect for all the stakeholders involved.

Sources of strategy

These are the distinctive competence, expertise and technology possessed by the organisation, together with its ability to combine these in ways that are suitable for the production of outputs that the public wishes to buy, use or consume (or, in public service terms, that public groups require).

It is necessary to identify opportunities, customer bases, market sectors and niches where the outputs produced can be successfully, effectively and profitably offered.

More generally, there is a combination of the identification of gaps in the market, and the demands of the community and society in general that have to be considered (see Figure 1.2). These must then be brought together in ways that allow for success and effectiveness to continue over a sufficient period of time.

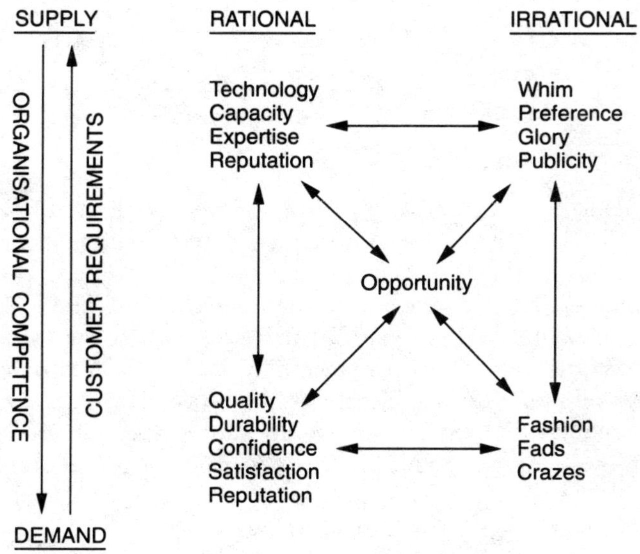

Purpose: an indication of the range, mixture and interaction of the components of strategy and direction.

Figure 1.2 Sources of strategy (1)

In simple markets and one-product or simple product range offerings there is an absolute time factor. There has to be a sufficient absolute time span available to render the exercise meaningful: it is exceedingly rare to be able to carry out a single operation on a short-run timescale in isolation. It is clearly possible to do this as part of a more complex or sophisticated portfolio of offerings, however. Fast moving consumer goods, foodstuffs, electrical clothing, fashion and seasonal goods mixes are all produced on this basis.

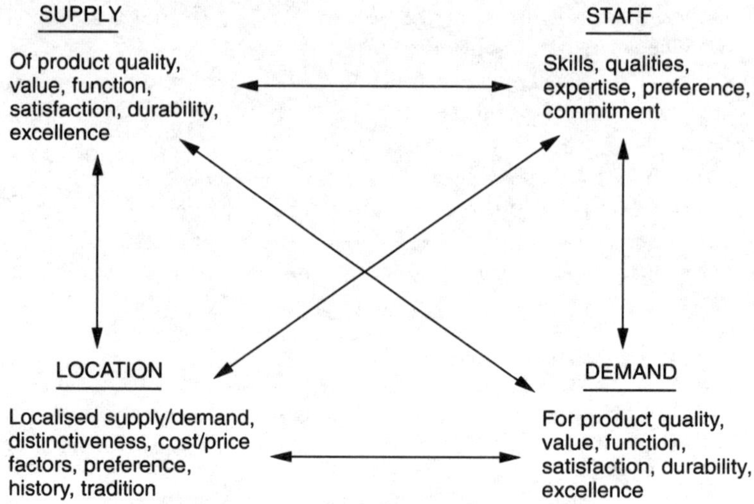

Figure 1.3 Matching opportunities with capabilities

It is also necessary to identify the levels of returns desired or necessary to support this on the timescales and frequency with which these returns are required.

The rationale outlined above is then tempered and limited by the human activities that go with it. This may at its most extreme be the whim of the entrepreneur or the chief person of the company ('I want to be a shipping tycoon', for example). This will clearly only be successful in commercial terms if the person in question then goes on to hire others of this distinctive expertise to work for him; however, the initial choice remains just that: choice. A similar position may be taken up around preferred location, technology used, or the desire to work with other particular individuals.

BOX 1.8 The Characteristics of the Customer and Client

The customers of organisations have the same characteristics the world over. They apply in all sectors whether personal consumers, industrial or commercial operations, public services or interdepartmental relationships within organisations. These characteristics are as follows.

Satisfaction Whatever is bought or purchased or is the outcome otherwise of a transaction, the customer expects satisfaction. This is true for any transaction in any situation. It is also true that as satisfaction is the expectation, no great positive result is achieved by the granting of it. Satisfaction is no more than the customer expects. Conversely, however, great dissatisfaction is generated by the failure to satisfy. The perceptions and memory of dissatisfaction also last much longer in the minds of the customer than those of satisfaction.

Examples In places where the UK Department of Social Security is held in low regard by its customers and clients, this is because it very seldom satisfies their needs, which are to be assessed for any benefits that may be due to them and to have them paid quickly. Dissatisfaction occurs where the assessment is not quick and where the benefits are not paid quickly or accurately. Because of the means of activity and the ways in which these are carried out, this is invariably the case.

Holiday companies and tour operators provoke great customer dissatisfaction through their processes of consolidation (that is, the practice of changing flight times and places, hotels and destinations in order that the airliner or hotel or resort in question is filled up).

British Rail and its operating companies receive complaints about the quality of their rolling stock, stations and facilities in direct proportion to the reality of the time-keeping of the trains. As the time-keeping gets worse so the volume of complaints about the other matters increases; during periods of good time-keeping, complaints in other areas decline.

Manufacturers produce items that are expected to fulfil the purposes of their clients. Product recalls are expensive and inconvenient and even if carried out at the manufacturer's expense cause clients to cast around for alternative sources of satisfaction.

Late deliveries also cause dissatisfaction. Clients will remember the one late delivery rather than the dozens that may have arrived on time or early.

Centrality

The customer is central and critical to all business activities. It follows from this that all customers expect high levels of focus and concentration on them. They do not wish to hear excuses (or, for that matter, perfectly valid reasons) why organisations are unable to meet their needs and wants. They do not wish to hear tales of computer crashes, hold-ups on motorways and freeways, inability to get particular parts, strikes and disputes or the bad weather. If these are contingencies that affect the organisation in question they must be in-built to the process of customer focus. When they occur they start to give general impressions of lack of focus: the customer is not the most important being in the eyes of the organisation.

Confidence and trust All customers must have confidence in those organisations with whom they conduct business. This extends to confidence in the strength and quality of the relationship between the parties, confidence in the products and services being delivered and received, confidence in the continuity, reliability and stability of the organisation with whom business is being conducted and of the situation in general.

Much of this aspect of the relationship with customers is perceptual and psychological. An understanding of this is therefore essential and attention must be paid to it. No effective relationship (whether in business or in any other sphere for that matter) exists without it.

Banks often foreclose on individuals and organisations because they are not confident that the difficulties being encountered can be resolved. Suppliers and sub-contractors run credit checks on contractor organisations to satisfy themselves of the extent of their creditworthiness. Organisations that become involved in accidents, disasters and tragedies experience a general loss of confidence and trust as a result even though in practice such organisations redouble their efforts to ensure that these occurrences will never happen to them again.

Benefits Customers do not buy products or services for themselves but rather for the benefits that they bring with them. The benefits of the offering of the organisation have therefore to be translated and presented in terms with which the customer identifies. These clearly vary between organisations and sectors. In general, the coverage includes price, quality, value, effectiveness, accessibility, relative utility, flexibility, switching (which is the ability to vary between products or suppliers) and the extent to which the offering in question is essential, desirable, marginal or peripheral. It also includes more general matters of confidence, trust and association indicated.

Understanding The ultimate key to the success of any strategy is the ability to translate this into identifying and satisfying the precise requirements of a sector or niche and its customers. Without different levels of understanding no effective business relationship can take place. An integral part of the strategy of any organisation must therefore be to generate full understanding of the needs, wants, beliefs, values and conceptions of the customer base. Those organisations that do this invariably provide satisfactory levels of service.

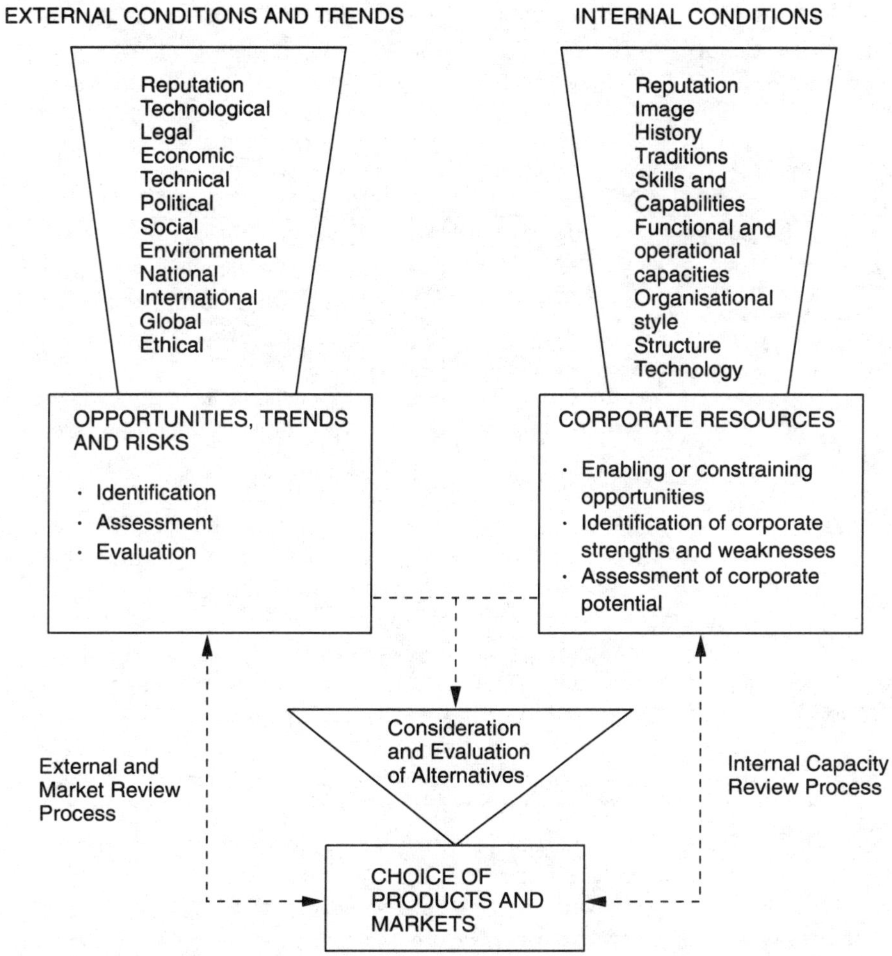

Figure 1.4 Sources of strategy (2): matching opportunities with capabilities and capacity

Opportunity

In practice, this occurs frequently. It happens either because the organisation in question is approached with an overtly viable proposition or because another sphere of activity opens up as the result of current involvement elsewhere. It may also occur because of pioneering and entrepreneuring/intrapreneuring on the part of those currently active. The opportunity becomes the starting point for another commercial route or journey. It may – and does – also occur from scratch. The Japanese presence in the car and electrical goods sectors of the

West was originally founded on the opportunity afforded by the lack of quality or reliability in the local outputs in these areas. This has now been fully developed by the other countries of the Pacific Rim.

Indicators of organisation strength	Indicators of business potential
• Market share	• Market size
• Marketing activities	• Market state: growth, maturity, decline
• Customer service	• Cyclical and seasonal factors
• Confidence and image	• Market structure
• Nature of operations	• Competition
• Financial structure, strength and resources potential	• Profitability
• Product range	• Entry and exit barriers
• Product potential	• Legal factors
• Quality, reliability, strength of products and services	• Social factors
• Managerial quality and expertise	• Ethical factors
• Technology – availability, usage, potential	• Other drives and restraints
• Distinctive expertise: availability, usage and potential	

Figure 1.5 Sources of strategy (3): matching strengths and capabilities with potential

BOX 1.9 The Brilliant Organisation

The 'perfect organisation' does not exist. However, it is possible to isolate characteristics that are present in any organisation which meet all the criteria proposed for the formulation and implementation of successful, effective and, above all, profitable strategies. These are:

- customers and their satisfaction are central to the whole way of working of the organisation;
- accurate assessment and establishment of market sectors, niches and segments that are to be served is carried out;
- every member of staff, whatever their function, understands and recognises the direction taken;
- clarity of vision and purpose and how this is to be achieved is established at the outset;
- staff must have a real stake in the organisation, possibly in terms of equity and profit share; certainly in terms of commitment and identity; they must also be committed to, and take pride in, all of the organisation's products and services, and must be highly motivated.

This is mirrored by the absolute commitment that organisations must have to the staff and their expertise, development and welfare. Staff must be highly valued and well paid and rewarded for what they do.

Organisation

The organisation must be quick and accurate in the delivery of its products and services. Effectiveness of resource utilisation means that anything which takes longer than necessary adds cost not value. It must be able to reconcile proactivity, dynamism, flexibility and responsiveness, with continuity and stability.

Culture

The culture of the organisation must be positive, infectious and all-pervasive. It must harmonise the staff and their qualities with the required activities, management and organisational style. Positive cultures also often help attract customers.

Improvement

This is constant and continuous and affects all aspects of the business, activities, equipment and technology, staff expertise and outputs. There is no limit to this: every improvement made adds value, satisfaction and quality, and therefore also adds to the organisation's total performance.

■ Non-rational elements

Having spent the previous pages taking the view that there is a rational approach to the formulation and development of strategy that should be adopted, it is now necessary to recognise that this does not always happen in practice. Many students of strategy go a stage further, holding the view that non-rational elements are essential in the march of progress of the business sphere (see Box 1.10).

BOX 1.10 Progress

There are two kinds of people in the world, the reasonable and the unreasonable. The reasonable person will accommodate and accept the world for what it is; the unreasonable person will expect the world to come into line with them.

Progress is therefore dependent upon the unreasonable person. (Shaw: *Man and Superman*)

Post It

It took the 'post-it', a simple note pad with a sticky strip, 12 years to come on-stream, 12 years for the development of something that is now taken completely for granted and which started out life as a hymn-book mark that would not fall out of the page when the book was opened.

This is the down side of championing, determination, and sheer courage in the pursuit of something in which the individual has faith. If all such products took 12 years to come on-stream no progress would ever be made.

The inspirational and creative elements are essential in the development of new products and services. Any organisation that wishes to create new products and services must invest in these activities and qualities if it is to be successful. This is almost a rational approach to the realm of creativity, and explains why organisations sponsor and encourage champions, experimenters, tryers and trialists, suggestion schemes, work improvement groups and quality circles. Similar approaches are taken to procedures, processes and structures, and to management development-type project work. The best organisations are capable of accommodating, assimilating and evaluating these elements in order to give them life and resources for as long as they merit.

Other facts must also be considered. The very nature of work, management, organisation and direction all have to be energised by irrational human beings. Translation of strategy, policy and direction into operations and actions may go right, or wrong, or differently for entirely human reasons. All organisations have their own life and the sub-currents, secondary and hidden agenda, and *realpolitik* that occur within them as a matter of course, and all affect operations, activities and performance.

There are also resource and time constraints, opportunity costs, opportunity gains, the prevailing wider and economic factors, the state of the markets served, actual (and invariably imperfect) levels of understanding of those markets.

Apart from these aspects there are factors present in all organisations that limit, corrupt, dilute, dissipate and destroy (and sometimes enhance) the rational approach. The pressure for quick results is a major factor, and is often at odds with the long-term nature of strategy and direction formulation and implementation.

■ Pressure groups and lobbies

These come from a variety of directions and include trade unions, professional bodies, professional and trade associations, other lobbies and action groups.

Their influence varies in different situations (see Box 1.11). However, it may be necessary to gain their support (or at least acquiescence) and, in order to do this, the ideal outcome of the proposed initiative may have to be diluted. Differences with trade unions have come about in the introduction of new technology and some have resisted this because they saw job, status or influence losses as the consequence. This also occurs when difficulties with experts and professionals arise. Again, the result is likely to be a dilution of the strategy in order to engage the support or acquiescence of these groups.

BOX 1.11 Barriers to Progress: Summary

Public policy	Dissident groups; vested interests; trade unions; professional bodies; lobbies (such as residents' groups, conservation bodies, popular associations); political opposition.
Public projects	Residents' groups and associations; political opposition; other social pressure groups (for example, environmental); conflicting demands for land (such as motorways, natural wildlife habitats); public inquiries.
Innovation	Those concerned with the old and the existing range of activities; those threatened by technological change; those under pressure to learn new skills and attributes; those on career paths in the existing ways.
Power and influence	Those who are set to lose this as the result of new directions: this includes divisional leaders and managers; managerial coteries; committee structures; trade unions; existing occupations; rewards delivered by the status quo.
Business policy	Initiatives at variance with current or traditional activities; changes in current and traditional activities; changes in standards and values.

■ Existing functions

Akin to this is the resistance of internal organisation functions, divisions and departments, invariably in response to changes in activities which are (or are seen to be) threatening to their own particular well-being. This may lead to the dilution of the ideal in order to gain the required acquiescence.

■ Overmighty departments, groups and subjects

These exist in sprawling and sophisticated organisations where there may not be the corporate will or structure to control them. This may go a stage further, to the point where the organisation actively depends on overmighty subjects to control these departments and divisions.

Particular current personal, professional, organisational and occupational expertise also often commands this level of influence.

■ Blocking

The ability to block or negate progress is also important. It is found in individuals who carry influence, especially in boards, groups and committees, through expertise, by weight of personality or an aura of decisiveness.

The secondary or sub-agenda of those who attach themselves to projects and strategies is also important. Top managers, directors and politicians often need triumphs: something that can be written up and broadcast in glowing terms in the global, national or sectoral media. At lower and operational levels, individuals require successes for their career résumés in the interests of their own advancement. They also need to be successful in terms of organisational and operational politics. They therefore pursue what is right in these terms, whether or not this is in the organisation's best interests.

BOX 1.12 Politicking

At the macro end of politics there is often no need to present a positive programme: simply to rubbish either the status quo or the opponent's offering in the field is enough. An example of this was the Community Charge (poll tax) introduced into the UK over the period 1986–91. The driving force behind it was the need to reform the property tax (domestic rates) structure which was inefficient, discredited and unpopular.

UK Community Charge 1986–91

Within minutes of its conception it could be demonstrated empirically that the Community Charge would not work, and that it would be both expensive and inefficient to collect.

However, because it was a political measure and because a substantial part of the opposition to it was political, the strategic purpose of what was envisaged quickly became obscured in the battle of wills that ensued in order to get the measure on to the statute book and operational in the community. This was exacerbated by the fact that the prevailing political opposition was determined to revert to the old system. Rather than a full consideration of the best way of raising this particular tranche of revenue, the battle that was enjoined was between the old and the new, between political big battalions. This all contributed to the detriment and decline of the public services that were to be funded by the measure.

BOX 1.13 The Bunker Mentality

This arises from a combination of high levels of expertise, insulation from the customer interface, high degrees of favour (on the part of organisations, chief executives and politicians) and a strong group identity (akin to a genuine people culture). Often designed as strategic think-tanks or research branches, their output is accepted at face value by their sponsors and commissioners; and because of the nature of these sponsors and commissioners, their policies get implemented.

Sometimes they are successful. Unless they are very carefully managed and maintained however, such groups develop their own view of the world which, although a variant of the real world, becomes the one that is adopted by the organisation.

The phrase originates from the group mentality that emerged in the bunker used by Hitler and his chiefs of staff and strategic and operational planners during the last days of the Third Reich. Unable to face the reality of the collapse of the Nazi Empire, they simply created their own version of the world, isolated from the real world, which they maintained in the bunker (the operations room) until the Russians invaded Berlin and destroyed it.

Favouritism and departmental, divisional and functional pecking order in the organisation (by accident or design) leads to resources and priorities following the requests and initiatives for these reasons rather than operational necessity. In such circumstances, it is impossible for all departments and functions to have any commonality of purpose. They become too busy fighting their own particular corner. It follows from this that other departments use their valuable time, effort, energy and resources in building up their own capacities to survive in the organisational *realpolitik*, rather than concentrating on their own core purposes. Ultimately, organisations create an atmosphere and structure of discrete departments surrounded on the one hand by their own defensive walls, and on the other using networks, the canteen culture and extramural relations when anything does need to be done. In such cases, no truly effective strategy is ever going to take place and much effort and resource is dissipated in the structural malfunction.

BOX 1.14 'It Cannot Be Done'

This is a phrase that is used by any of the groups or individuals to whom reference has been made in these pages. It easily gains a life and credence all of its own. It becomes an accepted norm and organisational received wisdom. Organisations may move away from ostensibly effective and profitable types and levels of activity that are well within their capacity, simply because influential persons and groups either cannot recognise them as such, or do not (for whatever reason) want them.

BOX 1.15 'It Must Be Done'

This is the driving phrase behind the triumph or expedient range of activities to which reference is made. The overwhelming need is for the issue to be instant, photogenic and media-friendly, so that those involved may have their moment of glory. Lesser versions of this occur lower down within organisations. The drive again is for internal public relations and pecking order coups that will lead to the raising of departmental, divisional or functional status of the aspect of the organisation that finds itself in the spotlight. This is often the explanation for the failure of public policy initiatives when they have been introduced before full pre-evaluation. It also explains in part the drive of some companies – especially in the chemical and drugs industries – in bringing products to market before they are fully tested and evaluated.

This is often overlooked, especially in public services and charitable activities. A lack of clear direction is often also to be found in niche offerings and departmental, divisional and individual initiatives in larger organisations. To avoid this, strategic and directional standpoints are much better seen in terms of the following:

- the products, services or offerings that are to be made and the volume and quality in which they are to be made;
- the total level of investment required;
- the market segments and niches to be served;
- the activities in which the organisation is to be engaged in their promotion;
- the style of operations and ways of working that are envisaged;
- the desired culture of the organisation;
- the means, methods and technology that are to be used to produce the offerings;
- the nature and quality of staff to be employed; the qualities required of them; the ways in which work is to be divided and jobs defined; the management structure and style chosen; the operational ways of working; systems and procedures adopted;
- the need to bring new offerings into the markets served;
- ethical considerations, defined in the widest terms, and including consideration of the ways in which the organisation interacts with staff, customers, community and the wider global business sphere;
- the profit motive in whatever terms this is defined (including high levels of effectiveness for public services).

If this is done then likely or certain areas of difficulty can be assessed at the strategy formulation (or pre-formulation) stage. For example, any proposed entry into high-tech market niches cannot be done on a shoestring, either in terms of production technology or staff. Operations in a public transport niche cannot be carried out without adequate reference to technology, replacement, maintenance and surface considerations, skills, qualities, and, above all, a mission to serve those requiring the transport services.

Lessons should also be learned from cases and examples of best and worst practice. Extensive studies have been carried out in recent years, concentrating especially on the following areas.

1. Emergent sectors, especially the Pacific Rim car and electrical goods industries that have a phenomenal track record of commercial success in their dealings with the West over the medium to long term and in taking market share from established and familiar organisations that hitherto produced, marketed and sold these items both successfully and profitably in their own countries.
2. Distinctive companies of high local profitability, reputation and regard. In the UK, examples of these are The Body Shop, the Virgin Group, Marks & Spencer and Co-Steel Sheerness. In the USA examples quoted extensively include Stew Leonard (supermarket), Millikens (textiles), WalMart (supermarket and department store chain), and Bethlehem Steel Inc.
3. Distinctive generic sectors – such as food retailing, cars, travel, media – in which many companies operate extremely successfully. The purpose of these studies is the identification of those properties present in organisations that compete in these areas, and the relationship between these and the success of their operations.
4. Segmentation and specialisation and the extent to which these are viable as organisation (rather than secondary or subsidiary) strategies, and other elements such as timescale and duration of these niches and the activities that are required to maintain and sustain them.
5. Permanence/transience: the extent to which the certainty of the state of the sector can be predicted. It is seen both in terms of the other elements indicated here, and where the priority to use or consume the particular offerings lies. This has particular importance on the one hand when deciding whether or not to invest in an experience, production/output technology and resources required. It also requires consideration when getting into fashionable and faddish sectors.
6. The absolute volumes of market sectors. Normally these are measured in terms of:

   (a) money: for example, this is an £*x* million sector/industry and so on;
   (b) volume: for example this sector consumers *y* tonnes of particular products per annum;
   (c) levels of investment required to become a sectoral player;
   (d) rates of return: for example, investors in this sector get z per cent return on their investment; or shares in this sector may be expected to rise by z per cent;
   (e) numbers of customers available.

   These can then be measured in relation to the number and size of other players in the given sector and the nature of the precise rate of return that they get. Analysis of the key players, especially the major players in terms of size, market share, volume of business contracted, profitability, rates and speed of returns, can also then be analysed.

7. Competitors: the extent, nature and prevalence of these and the nature of their offerings, whether absolute alternatives, close substitutes or part of the more general substitution processes discussed elsewhere; the extent to which differentiation is a major part of playing in the sector.
8. The state of the market itself: whether expanding, contracting, declining; young, mature, old; in need of rejuvenation; capable of being rejuvenated or re-energised; and the implications of this for the organisation concerned.
9. Analysis of public sector services against models of political drive, service creation and client demand.
10. Analysis of distinctive models of operation that exist at the public/national/critical sector crossroads. Two main models of this are nationalisation and privatisation. In addition, there are the beginnings of public/private cooperation in public services provision and in the putting out to contract of particular public activities.
11. Establishing specific criteria upon which to base the analysis and evaluation of strategy. While these clearly vary in detail between sectors, certain common and universal elements may be drawn out. Above all, these are elements relating to cost, price, quality, value, timescales, continuity, confidence and expectation to which constant reference is made throughout this book.
12. Questioning existing and traditional approaches to both direction and organisation. This includes the questioning of the format and structure of organisations, their ways of working, their targets and outputs.

A great volume of information and literature has emerged from this particularly over the period of the 1980s and 1990s. There are, however, few absolutes. No simple or distinctive sets of traits are found to exist in all organisations or sectors that are successful. No absolute performance targets can be created; they have to be seen in their own particular context. No absolute measures of price, quality, volume, value, cost, confidence, expectation or understanding exist. Again, these all have to be seen in particular contexts, and the nature and balance of these varies between sectors.

The main lesson to be drawn from this is the lack of absolutes and the recognition that this is an imperfect field in a rapidly changing global environment.

There are also other lessons. There is the necessity to establish the basis on which business is to be conducted, the fundamental ground rules by which the organisation in question is to exist. This is clearly a matter of individual creation. The fact that a successful operator in a given field has a certain structure, direction, shared values and vision does not mean that these can be copied by others to the same effect. The fact that it is possible to operate in a particular sector with a fair degree of certainty or that the sector itself is relatively permanent (such as food or transport, for example) is not an absolute guide to organisation success; other elements have still to be present.

Moreover, there exists in all organisations and activities the requirement and capacity for constant change and improvement. The development of effective strategy is the ability to recognise where these capacities lie in relation to the given organisation and the activities being carried out. It is necessary, if effective business strategies are to be designed and developed, that sub-strategies and operational activities with this change and improvement process in mind are constantly addressed.

The elements and rules, sources and opportunities indicated have all to be related individually to particular organisations and situations. No general blueprints exist for successful corporate strategies. The value of studying the field from as broad a perspective as possible is to generate awareness and understanding and to draw lessons and conclusions. These must then be applied and related to particular situations and not adopted piecemeal.

From this introduction and background, it is possible to indicate certain principles of corporate strategy which must be considered in all situations, however. These are:

- a clear basic position, understood by everyone concerned;
- support activities that relate to strategic positions and initiatives pursued by organisations;
- barriers to operations related to capital, technology and expertise (these also represent barriers to change and progress);
- other constraints (legal, social, political, economic, behavioural and ethical);
- the match of opportunities with resources, expertise, technology and capability;
- the mixture of cost, price, quality, volume and timescale adopted;
- the mixture of determination of direction with qualities of flexibility, dynamism, responsiveness and opportunism;
- organisation and management structure, culture and style;
- the nature and qualities of those who are to be employed and the jobs that they are to carry out; the interaction between the organisation and its environment; the nature of the business sphere; the nature of the market sectors in which activities are carried out; the ability to manage change;
- conflicting demands and priorities of different stakeholders, and their position relative to each other.

Much of the strategy process is concerned with reconciling and harmonising these conflicting and emergent factors and elements. These therefore form a substantial part of the material and content of the rest of this book.

BOX 1.16 Intuition

Great play is made of intuitive and inspirational elements of the strategy process. It is nearly all myth and legend.

It is possible to identify and define a professional or rational intuition that comes from knowing one's organisation, department, division or expertise to the level of being a true expert. All true expert 'intuition' is actually based on this.

This is not to be confused with guesswork or apparently inspired flashes of brilliance that are supposed to obviate the need for the hard-working and painstaking alternative. Two examples will suffice here.

The *Herald of Free Enterprise*

The first reports of the capsize of the *Herald of Free Enterprise* in March 1987 cited the fact that roll on/roll off car and freight ferries are inherently unstable: that is, if there is any sea movement, the cars and lorries roll around the car decks causing instability. This was broadcast by the UK news media on the first reports of the disaster in spite of the fact that the same reports ended up with precise descriptions of just how closely the cars and lorries were actually packed in together, and therefore could not have rolled around anyway (even had the sea been rough: it was calm at the time). This did not prevent those concerned from using their intuition and publishing this inaccurate report (which had to be pulped and re-written for subsequent bulletins).

Operation Barbarossa

Operation Barbarossa was launched by Hitler in June 1941. Fighting a mass global and resource-expensive war with the Western nations, Hitler grouped a massive army on the Polish–Russian border. He then ordered it to attack the USSR. There were initial spectacular advances across great swathes of agricultural land, and rapid territorial gains that went with them. However, a rational approach would nevertheless have required consolidation at each stage to ensure a continuity of fuel and supplies (apart from anything else).

The attack was based entirely on Hitler's personal intuition that the Russians were weak and inferior and would not and could not fight, and that now was the time to make this conquest.

Barbarossa is widely regarded by both military strategists and military historians as the turning point of the Second World War: the point at which the beginning of the end for Hitler commenced.

Strategy is nothing to do with making guesses of this sort.

Conclusions

The purpose of this introduction has been to indicate the background and context against which organisational activities are formulated. From this, a contextual framework for organisation strategies may be drawn up.

Strategy is concerned with identifying opportunities for successful and effective activities. These come either from the capabilities and expertise of the organisation, or from the actual and potential market demand, or a combination of both.

Strategy is concerned with the range, scale and scope of an organisation's activities and the boundaries within which it chooses to operate. It is also concerned with the ways in which the activities are conducted and the means by which they are controlled.

Strategy is concerned with matching the opportunities afforded to the organisation's capabilities and expertise. This, in turn, has implications for resource requirements: staff, finance, technology, premises and information.

Strategy is concerned with commitment to purpose. Once an opportunity has been identified and the decision taken to exploit it, some form of commitment – of resources and direction; of personnel; and also in terms of reputation and expectation – has been made.

Strategy is concerned with creating direction and understanding for all involved, so that everything which is carried out in the name of the organisation is positive and effective. This includes setting behavioural and ethical standards, as well as operational.

Strategy is – when effective and understood – the fountain, the energy and the direction of operations and activities; and it therefore creates both sub-strategies in its support, and patterns of operational and shorter-term decisions.

Strategy is a combination of continuous evolution with commitment and determination. This has clear implications for the creation of attitudes and values, as well as products, services and operations. It also indicates the range of expertise required in the area of strategy, among those responsible for the direction and guidance of organisations and their activities.

CHAPTER 2

Strategic Management in Practice

Introduction

The overall purpose of strategic management is to establish, assess, maintain and develop the organisation's position in its markets and activities. This implies a wide knowledge and awareness of and capacity for, assimilation and analysis, and this extends to all aspects of the organisation in the environment and community (see Figure 2.1). It requires the ability to take an overview of the purpose chosen and to assess this for suitability and effectiveness. From this the effective establishment of organisation direction emerges. This has then to be monitored and evaluated for success and effectiveness, and fine-tuned and adjusted as necessary and as progress is made. It must be capable of taking advantage of opportunities that come its way; and capable also of responding to crises and emergencies.

Strategic management designs, shapes and influences culture and style, staff motivation and morale, and is responsible for standards of the organisation's ethics, honesty, probity, personal behaviour and qualities, as well as operations and output.

Strategic management is the energiser of activities. It creates style, structures and cultures that enable the pursuit of excellent and effective activities. There is a negative to be considered; it is that wherever excellent and effective activities are not present there is inevitably some fault to be found.

It is essential also to recognise the position of the organisation in its own history and state of development. Much of the organisation's future is determined by the ways in which it views and comes to terms with its past and present. For example, a strong affinity with the past (e.g. a strong sense of the good old days) must be understood – and managed – if present and future activities are to be effective. This is critical to the effective strategic management of change and of establishing policy and direction in a changing and turbulent environment. Effective future strategy may not be formed in isolation from the past and present.

Top managers gain kudos and rewards for their organisation's successes and are accountable for the failures. This is viewed in hard terms (the effectiveness and profitability of the organisation), and in soft terms (the quality, expertise and commitment of the staff; the reputation of the organisation and its outputs – see Figure 2.1 – and the confidence of all stakeholders).

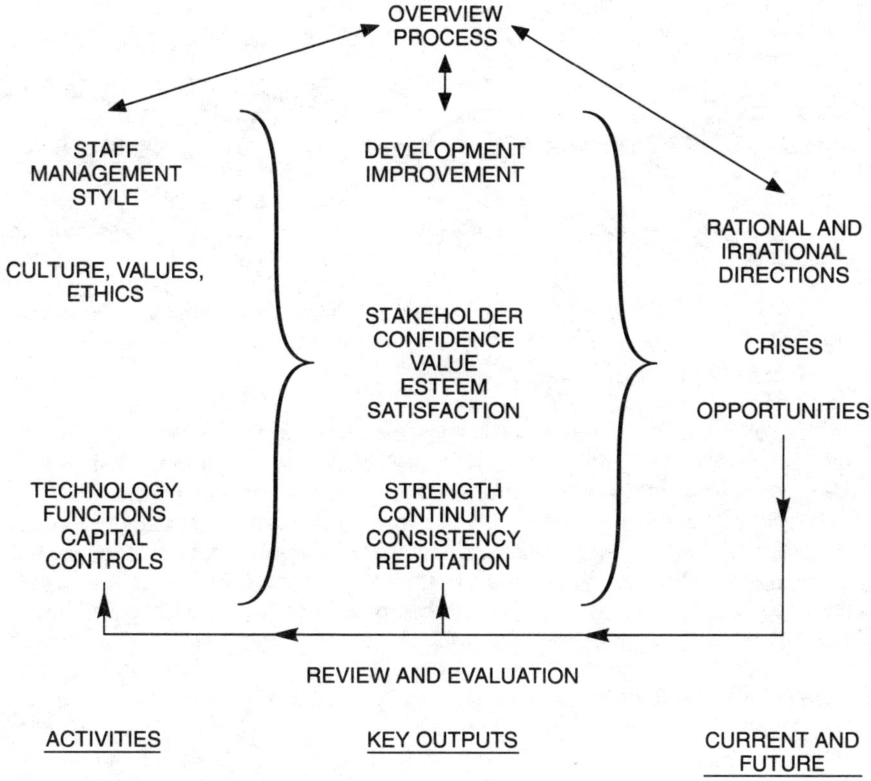

Figure 2.1 The complexity of strategic management

Whatever strategy is devised must be capable of implementation via the organisation's systems and procedures. Ideally these are designed with each other in mind. In practice it often works out that intended strategies are not fully realised because they are not suitable (wholly or partially) to the organisation's way of working and to its *realpolitik*.

Strategic management is concerned with the design of organisation purpose. It is, by implication, about the design of organisations suitable for the purpose, both in terms of strategy implementation and in relation also to the wider environment. It is concerned with securing achievements for the present and developing the organisation and its capabilities to ensure results for the future. General management cannot therefore be seen in isolation from operations but rather as their source. Above all, the returns on excellent strategic management are the rewards and successes achieved by high-performance, highly-effective and highly-profitable organisations.

BOX 2.1 The Military Comparison

It is almost traditional to find analogies of war in the introduction to chapters on strategy in business and management textbooks: for example, 'There are many similarities between military operations and running a business, and nowhere is this as striking as in the sphere of strategy' (M. G. Wright 1980).

Attractive though the proposition is superficially, it should be seriously doubted on two grounds. The first is that future war strategies are normally devised on the basis of past experiences rather than in the anticipation of the requirements of the future. For example, the trench warfare of the First World War was a derivation of the trench warfare carried out by the British in South Africa during the Boer War of 1899–1902. The Maginot Line was built along the Rhine by the French in the 1920s and 1930s to counter a possible future German invasion. Both were fundamentally flawed. The designers of the Maginot Line never considered that an invasion might come through Belgium, thus bypassing the large and sophisticated defences of the line. In the case of the First World War, nobody ever did get around to putting troops in places where the opposing armies were not.

The other ground for questioning the military concept of strategy is in the articulation of purpose. In consideration of empirical evidence, in most cases the purpose of military strategy is not articulated fully or accurately. It is for example difficult to believe that the strategic purpose of either party during the first World War was to get bogged down in trenches across north-eastern France and Belgium for 2½ years. Neither is it credible that the purpose of operation Barbarossa in 1943 was to lose an army of one million people, frozen to death in inadequate clothing and with equipment that was useless in that particular theatre of war (that is, the Russian winter). This was compounded by the commitments to other theatres of war on the part of Germany which made successful completion of operation Barbarossa impossible.

In each of these examples the operations took on lives of their own and the strategic focus was lost.

Moreover, the message is often not received by the staff, (the troops). For example, in R.C. Sherriff's play, *Journey's End*, the purpose of being in the trenches is 'to advance and win the war'. Clearly this is not a strategy. It might in some context be a general aim. In all circumstances, such a statement would require amplification, clarification and development.

The conclusion therefore is that the military analogy is limited in its usefulness and value as a template for the study of business strategy because overwhelmingly it sets such a bad example.

Strategic management is concerned with:

- establishing clear aims and objectives;
- establishing standards of performance and the means by which this is to be measured for success/failure;
- establishing and maintaining a high quality work force;

- developing the expertise, capacity and performance of the organisation.
- long-term effectiveness and success

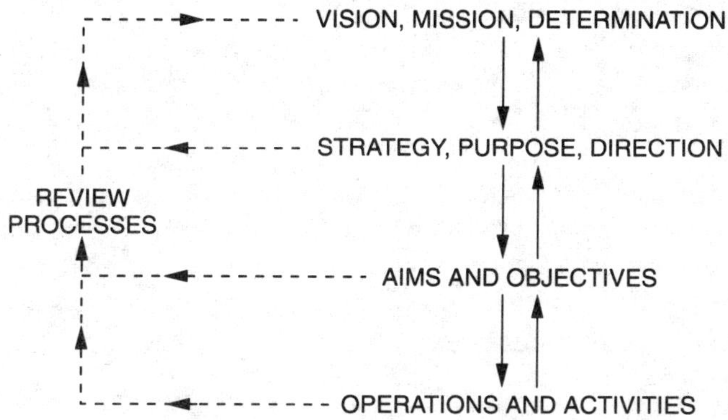

Purpose: Indication of the direct relationship between Strategy, Aims and Objectives, and of the range of review processes required.

Figure 2.2 Strategy, aims and objectives

Setting aims and objectives

The reason for setting clear aims and objectives is in order to give everybody concerned the clarity of purpose to which reference has already been made (see Box 2.2). This will be set at a variety of levels; the purpose must be to ensure that everybody is working towards the same ultimate goal: that is, the completion of a strategy which has been fully endorsed by the directors of the organisation and translated into purposes and activities for each of its functional areas. The basis of setting objectives is therefore to give a clear statement of direction to each department; to indicate courses of action that are to be taken; to indicate priority ranges; and to give measures of success or failure on which performance evaluation can subsequently take place. Without this no universal clarity of purpose exists. It also emphasises the counterpoint to the military strategy example given above.

BOX 2.2 Aims and Objectives

The text indicates the context for these and the barriers and constraints that must be addressed in the process. Only if this is accurate can truly precise targets and measures of expectation, performance and success be drawn up. These are in turn a reflection of capacity, achievement, stability and progress. It is also only possible to judge and evaluate performance accurately if this form of approach is adopted.

The following are useful examples.

1. 'To achieve a return on investment of 30 per cent by 31 December 1996' is very precise, easy to follow and understand; but is only valid if it has first been evaluated and judged as suitable and accurate.
2. 'To seek and achieve a return commensurate with expectations' is likely to be uncertain unless everyone understands what these expectations are, and when and how they are to be met (in which case this should be developed further).
3. To seek to maximise opportunities as and when they arise' is less precise still; it commits nobody to anything. The normal reason for aims and objectives to be produced in this way is a lack of clarity, direction or purpose at the top of the organisation.

Aims and objectives occur at different levels.

The corporate level	Reflecting the overall scope of the organisation; how it is to be run in structural and financial terms; and how resources are to be allocated to different operations and activities.
Competitive or business level	How the organisation is to compete in its different markets; which products and services should be developed and offered to the different markets; and the extent to which these meet customer needs in such ways as to achieve the organisation's objectives.
Operational levels	How the different functions of the organisation (production, marketing, sales and so on) contribute to corporate purpose and competitive activities.
Behavioural	Related to the general aura of well-being or otherwise; to the softer side of management; and customer and community satisfaction.
Confidence	The more general relationship between the organisation and its environment; the expectations of all stakeholders; and wider public coverage including media and stock exchanges.
Ethical	Meeting the standards enshrined in policy; general factors relating to acceptability; the ability to work in certain activities in certain locations.

Aims and objectives should be:

- specific: dealing with easily identifiable aspects of performance;
- measurable: devised in ways so that success and failure can be identified;
- achievable: striking the balance between maximising/optimising resources and output without setting standards so high that the targets are unattainable and therefore unvalued;
- recognisable: understood by everyone concerned;
- time constrained: so that a continuous record of progress and achievement may be kept.

■ Strategic performance targets and indicators

The composition of effective performance varies between sectors. It is a combination of specific measures of actual performance that is set in the context of the sector concerned and compared also with the opportunities forgone on the part of investors in the organisation in question. No real understanding of the success, failure, viability or otherwise of any organisation can be achieved unless accurate, measurable and achievable performance targets are drawn up. This is also true for the day-to-day operations; hence the need for performance indicators. Targets and indicators must be reliable, measurable and capable of being validated. They must be easily understood by all concerned. They should form the basis of general performance reviews over periods of time, and in reference to particular activities.

■ Performance targets

These are drawn up in the following ways.

□ *Earnings*

1. Earnings per employee, including all the employees of the business in question and not just the sales force, production line or other sharp end or front-line operators.
2. Earnings per customer, by which the total income over a period is measured against the customer base.
3. Earnings per offering, important especially where there are mixed or sophisticated ranges.
4. Earnings per outlet, in whatever terms the outlet is defined by the particular organisation (the office, the sales person, the department store, the airliner, the restaurant).
5. Earnings per square foot, of location, of individual premises or of total premises owned; or again this can be broken down and recalculated by office, store, airliner, ship, lorry and so on.

□ *Profit*

Each of the items above may also be re-presented as profit (per employer, per customer, per outlet, per offering and per square foot); again, this would be calculated over given periods of time.

□ *Returns on capital*

1. Earnings per share in organisations where share capital has been issued; and per partner (and therefore partnership fee) where this form of organisation exists.
2. Returns on total capital employed: share capital plus loans, debentures, creditors, premises and equipment.

BOX 2.3 Examples of Appropriate Performance Measures

1. Income/turnover/profits per square metre: retail, banking, brokerage, public air, sea and rail transport, mass and flow produced.
2. Income/turnover/profits per employee: retail, banking, transport, manufacturing (especially unit and batch), assembly.
3. Income/turnover/profits per customer: mail order, retail, in specific areas (such as toys), foodstuffs.
4. Income/turnover/profits per outlet: petrol stations, railway stations.
5. Volume sales per product: retail, mail order (subject to evaluation), petrol, basic foodstuffs, seasonal goods. This also applpies to product clusters and product ranges.
6. Density/frequency of usage: sports, health care, hotel facilities, public transport, cash points, commercial durables (such as copiers, fax).
7. Longevity of usage: private transport, consumer durables, furniture, white goods.
8. Quality/professional/absolute measures: public education, health and personal social services.
9. Speeds of response (absolute): emergency public services (police, fire, ambulance), private services such as car breakdown, disaster insurance, appliance repair.

BOX 2.4 Performance Targets

For the period 1993–4, the UK Scottish Office was required to meet the following target:

> 'That no more than 2.5 Category B prisoners per 1,000 be lost.'

Given that there were 3000 prisoners in this Category, the absolute requirement was that no more than 7.5 prisoners be lost in fact.

Nobody seemed to be able to explain how the target had been devised, who devised it, or why it was considered the right way of measuring this activity.

☐ *Volume*

The volumes of business conducted, and the quantities of products and goods moved may also be measured.

1. Sales/product/throughput per employee, again overall and by occupation, department or function.
2. Volume of goods sold per customer and per outlet.
3. Rate of volume turnover per outlet.
4. Volume of each offering turned over, and the rate at which this turnover occurs.

□ *Costs*

Cost targets may be appropriate in relation to earnings, profits and volumes, as indicated above, and also as part of any drive for constant improvement. In cases where these have been accurately targeted they will address premises and equipment costs, capital charges, administrative and bureaucratic overheads, working methods, personnel, marketing and distribution charges, purchasing, lease and rental. Accurate target costs per employee, per department, per square metre, per premises, may therefore be calculated.

□ *Productivity*

Productivity measures are introduced in context. They set norms and standards. They are a benchmark of progress. They are to be read in conjunction with effectiveness, profitability and volume targets, and also in conjunction with the earnings, profits, volume and cost targets outlined above.

Productivity measurement also indicates where improvements may be made. Capital investment, streamlining, or changes in ways of working may therefore come about as part of this.

□ *Comparisons*

Most organisations require some understanding of where they stand and how they operate in relation to other companies in their sector. From this, they may deduce whether there is any scope for improvement overall, or in particular activities. Or they may conclude that general competitive advantage is only to be gained by adopting strategies and methods radically different from the rest of the sector.

Comparisons are vital in the area of pricing and customer satisfaction; and the two are related. Customers may go to a top-quality operator and pay any price premium necessary rather than receive an inadequate offering at a lower price.

Comparisons may also usefully be made in the measurement of output, volume, profit margins and turnover, but care has to be taken that like is truly being compared with like. In 1993, for example, Honda UK declared a profit of £300 per car produced. This could be compared to the figure given by the exclusive Morgan Company of £2500 profit per car. However, they are not comparable operators. They do not serve the same market. Honda does not enjoy the price premium advantage that Morgan commands; Morgan does not enjoy (or seek) the global volumes of Honda.

Problems with comparisons also arise from taking comfort from general and bland statements such as: 'We are no worse than anyone else in the sector', or 'We are 10th out of a total number of companies measured in the sector'. (see Box 2.7). Such statements appear in industrial trade media and company annual reports. They should always be a trigger for further inquiry and assessment for the true meaning of the comparison. This should be related to: scope and scale of activities; size of organisation by capital, work force and technology; nature of specialisation and expertise; and accurate assessment of market sectors and segments. And ultimately, all organisations have to have their own distinctive capability to exist independently.

□ *Percentages and annual comparisons*

Organisations set themselves targets of 'increasing sales by a particular percentage in relation to last year's performance'; or 'increasing output volume by a particular percentage' or 'reducing costs by a particular percentage'. Invariably the benchmark is in relation to recent performance (usually the previous year or period). There is nothing inherently wrong with this approach provided that the criteria against which the previous year's targets were set and achieved remain valid for the current period. Where such measures fall down, and where organisations go badly wrong as a result, is when the percentages become the driving force, rather than the targets in the pursuit of which the percentages were struck and achieved.

More generally, percentages have a residual value in measuring progress against inflation, both general and sectoral; the opportunity costs forgone in investing elsewhere; and in the assessment of financial management targets: for example, interest on loans, depreciation of capital equipment, whether to buy or lease transport fleets and distribution outlets.

□ *Qualitative aspects*

Successful organisations are so because they get the qualitative aspects as accurate as the quantitative. Organisations set themselves such targets as 'to be the top quality operator in the field/sector/locality/profession'. Those that subsequently achieve this do so because they successfully translate the pursuit of this into measurable, achievable, recognisable and understandable targets (that is, translating the pursuit of quality into measures such as earnings per customer or increases in sales or profits). Additionally, accurate assessment is required of what the 'quality' words actually mean in the given situation (success, achievement, quality, top, high). This is a much greater problem where no particular clarity or agreement exists in the first place.

BOX 2.5 Performance Targets in Public Services

The main problem to be addressed lies in the establishment of a valid standpoint from which to measure the performance of these services. There is an initial difficulty in that the service outputs may not be apparent for very long periods of time (for example, it can take 20 years for a person to complete her education; and health and social care may be required by individuals for long periods also). This has to be reconciled with the immediate short-term needs, drives and directions of politicians and service managers. There are often historical bases, resource constraints and social pressures which have all also to be accommodated.

The knowledge, expertise, judgement, attributes and qualities of the public service manager become critical. These form the context in which 'broad' and 'narrow' perspectives on service performance can then be taken.

Broad The state of the work environment: the school, classroom, library, hospital ward, laboratory, prison; the availability, use, value, quality and appropriateness of equipment to service users and consumers; cleanliness, warmth and comfort; general ambience; professionalism of staff; currency of professional expertise; interaction of staff with consumers; prioritisation of activities; resource effectiveness, efficiency, adequacy and usage.

Narrow Application of absolute standards of service delivery; speed of response to consumers; nature and content of response to users; nature and volume of complaints, failures and shortcomings; attitudes of service users to providers (and vice versa); acceptance of professional responsibility and standards; acceptance of professional development.

The levels of aims, objectives and activities of the constraints around these that are indicated in the text remain the same. These require initial thought and specific translation into context for the given service, however. This in turn then becomes the basis of judgement and evaluation of performance. It is carried out by service experts and analysts (in the same way as commercial and business analysts and experts carry out the evaluation of company performance).

■ Service targets

The most effective means of establishing these are in terms of service quality and effectiveness, service reliability and service responsiveness. Again, having assessed in qualitative terms what these mean in regard to the service in question, they will be translated into measurable and assessable targets.

Department stores, travel companies, airlines and other retail, distribution and transport activities all establish their targets in these ways. There are also clear implications for the governors, directors and top managers of schools, colleges, hospitals, civil and social service providers.

Other service sector targets concern improvements in the areas already indicated and discussed of quality, effectiveness, reliability and responsibility.

Performance effectiveness

The following are all indicators of performance effectiveness:

- output targets – quality, volume and timescale considerations; quality control elements; reject rates and wastage;
- time usage, including down and slack time, overtime, maintenance and repair time;
- flexibility and responsiveness: for example, the ability to accommodate one-off orders, special deliveries, emergencies and crises;
- customer satisfaction, including the volume and nature of complaints; the reasons for gaining business at the expense of competitors and loss of business to competitors;
- workforce satisfaction and attitudes – the prevalence and extent of strikes, disputes, absenteeism, sickness and accidents; labour turnover; the general demeanour, happiness and commitment of the staff;
- communication and information systems, organisation structures and management style, and the general state of workplace relations;
- timetables, critical paths and other means of production and progress checking;
- control mechanisms, reporting systems, budgets and other financial and information checks and controls;
- the balance of activities and nature of relationships between primary support and control functions;
- the balance and nature of relationships between operations, functions and divisions and head office;
- the effectiveness of public relations and other customer, community and media relations efforts.

Sectoral norms and expectations

Each sector carries its own mix of expectations and norms in terms of rates of return and also the time period over which these returns are to be achieved. Judgements are made on organisational performance by stock markets, valuers, commentators and analysts, partly in relation to the extent to which the organisation lives up to these expectations.

Going rates

There are normal levels of performance established in each sector. Organisations that fail to meet these become targets for concern. Organisations that exceed these (especially those that greatly exceed them) become the focus also of interest and analysis. It is in response to cases such as this that the whole way of working of a sector becomes radically reviewed, and perhaps radically re-orientated.

BOX 2.6 Norms, Expectations and Going Rates

In extreme cases the high performer shifts the whole expectational frame for the sector. Japanese car and electrical goods companies brought hitherto unknown standards of output and quality to these sectors in Europe and North America in the 1970s, 1980s and 1990s. This resulted in the indigenous operators losing market share and having to respond through investment, training and development. It also became apparent that there was great scope for improvement in these sectors in Europe and North America. The Japanese initiatives transformed the general expectations of performance and value for money in the sectors. Not only, therefore, were the Western companies not seen to be performing, but indeed the customer base was turning away from them.

Opportunity costs

General measures of performance may be gained from making comparisons and judgements against the retail price index, interest rates and the performance of other sectors. Performance in one area that does not live up to these will cause those investing in it to question their continued involvement and may result in their moving this investment elsewhere, especially if it is apparent that better returns are certain.

Monitoring, evaluation and review

Monitoring, evaluation and review compares and contrasts strategic projections with the reality of activities. Targets are established so that they can be measured, assessed, validated and criticised by those with this responsibility.

Monitoring, review and evaluation is a process consisting of:

- a continuous watching brief;
- a series of regular reviews (for example, at the end of every week/month/quarter/year);
- reviews at the end of each critical path element and end phase, to be conducted at the conclusion of the matter in hand.

Table 2.1 Performance targets and indicators: Norweb plc

	31.12.92 (%)	*1.12.91** (%)
Restore electricity supply within 24 hours	99.41	99.10
Attend to repair NORWEB fuses within four hours	99.89	99.84
Provide most new supplies within five days	99.97	99.92
Send estimates of charges within ten days	99.73	99.29
Give two days' notice of planned interruption of supply	99.94	99.96
Visit or contact to explain voltage variations within ten days	94.55	100.00
Visit or contact to explain meter disputes within ten days	98.90	99.30
Change payment methods within ten days	99.79	99.92
Attend all appointments agreed with customer	99.95	99.91

* Figures represent 6 months' operation of the standards.

The lesson of precision is clear; the only target open to any subjective interpretation is the last. Matters for judgement and evaluation arise from whether these performance measures are correct, and whether the standards indicated are acceptable.

BOX 2.7 Objectives: A Training and Enterprise Council

First and foremost it aims to raise awareness of the need to improve the level of skills through training. It will also seek to make the county's business advisory and support services more effective, thereby strengthening essential resources for commerce and industry.

The TEC will work to:

- stimulate the growth of established local businesses;
- support the formation of development of small businesses;
- help individuals maximise their potential;
- attract appropriate new investment to enhance the local economy;
- help employers to raise awareness of the value of good training;
- improve the network of services for small businesses and provide easy access to specialist advice;
- improve career guidance for young people and to encourage closer links between schools and industry;
- help more people wishing to return to work;
- improve the relevance and quality of training;
- help the disabled and others with special needs achieve their full employment potential.

These are imprecise and bind nobody to anything. They require rewriting in terms that can be measured and assessed, monitored, reviewed and evaluated.

The outcomes of this review process are as follows.

1. Fine-tuning of both strategy and operations arise as the result of information gathered and judgements made from the constant process of review.
2. The development of organisation early warning systems and escape routes also occur in this way. This is the ability to see a potential problem early enough to nip it in the bud, while having the space at the same time to leave it until it is apparent that it is a real issue which must be faced. The same applies to opportunities that accrue as strategy unfolds. The continuous and regular review processes enable full discussion to take place and judgements to be made, to ensure that they are genuine opportunities and worth pursuing.
3. It enables assessment of the strategy/operational interface to take place and to identify operating problems and their impact (usually their limitations). These can then be fully evaluated and analysed. While operational factors can limit strategy, development and implementation, it also happens that some strategies take unreasonable or optimistic views of operating capacities.
4. Regular reviews highlight continuing and enduring problems and provide information for judgement and action. They may also indicate more serious matters related to organisation structure, culture and management style; or marketing, production, efficiency and effectiveness, purchasing and supply, transport and distribution. This enables each aspect to be fully evaluated in turn.
5. It also enables the assessment of the targets themselves to take place and of the extent to which operational, financial and timescale targets were measurable. These should be judged and evaluated whether or not they were met, or whether or not they were exceeded (the latter in particular is no cause for complacency, and often results from placing extremely low expectations on the activities in question).
6. Resources used are measured and monitored for both wastage and also effectiveness. Opportunities for better usage will become apparent as will situations where resources must be concentrated.
7. Review and evaluation enables all those concerned to get to know the organisation and its practices and activities better. It gives messages to the staff and to the stakeholders of continuing concern and active interest. It indicates a drive for knowledge and commitment on the part of the senior managers and directors of the organisation. It reinforces the culture of participation (and this is unlikely to be fully effective if all staff, or at least every department, are not somehow involved) and of mutual involvement and benefit. It reinforces any openness of communication that exists (and again, this openness must be present for the review process to be fully effective). It reinforces the general level of confidence that staff members have in the organisation, and its directorate and top management (and again there is a mutuality of confidence that is essential for business success).
8. It is part of the process of mapping strategy and direction of the organisation, the process of clarifying the organisation's purposes, its competitive and comparative positions, its performance, potential, capabilities and capacities.

The best and most effective processes of monitoring, evaluation and review are kept as simple and as streamlined as possible. They are strategy-orientated and problem- and action-orientated, rather than constitutional and procedural. Those involved must have clear targets to which to work. Section managers and supervisors and their staff have strategies, sub-strategies, procedures, operations and output monitoring as a critical part of their jobs and activities. Reporting relationships are devised that enable any issues to be quickly raised and resolved.

■ Effective staff

Everyone who works in any organisation is a key player and performer. Their contribution is vital. Where this falls short of ideal, the total performance of the organisation is adversely affected. Everyone concerned is entitled to equality of treatment, to have a high value placed on their work, and to personal respect and esteem.

This contribution shapes and influences both the devising and implementation of strategy, and also the operations and activities undertaken. The need for high-quality staff in all jobs, occupations and activities is paramount. High-performing organisations pay attention to their entire workforce. Everyone who comes to work is inducted into the required ways of behaviour and attitude. They receive high-quality and continuous job training whatever their given occupation. Absolute standards of job performance are set and any shortfall in this becomes a matter for inquiry. There is a direct relationship between this approach to staff and high levels of business performance.

Strategic management is concerned with giving everybody the resources, equipment and training to do the job in hand; to continuously improve and develop all staff; to combine the discipline involved with carrying out the job in hand with giving the freedom to pursue projects and innovations (and obsessions); to reward staff for excellent performance and achievement; and to take remedial action where standards of performance can be improved.

BOX 2.8 Elements of Strategic Management

The following elements are present.

1. Organisational and environment analysis, to determine the opportunities that exist, and the capabilities required to meet them.
2. Critical factors: price, quality, value, volume and time.
3. Generic positions, based on price/cost; focus; and the ability and necessity to differentiate.
4. Strategic forms: expansion, contraction, offence, defence, acquisition and withdrawal.

5. Processes and activities: segmentation, competitive positioning and the identification of barriers to activities.
6. Performance measurement: in both quantifiable and qualifiable terms.
7. Sectoral factors: matters for consideration in the specific terms of manufacturing, production, distribution, and commercial and public services.
8. Ethics: social and other pressures and limitations.
9. Key players and key performers.
10. Behavioural and perceptual factors and elements.
11. Factors relating to the development and implementation of strategy, and the harmonisation and coordination of directed efforts.
12. Change as a constant factor.

The pattern of industrial, commercial and public service staffing used to consist of organising those involved into hierarchical and functional specialisms: dividing work, creating supervisory and management structures, distinctive areas of expertise and boundaries and spheres of influence and operation. This created order, certainty and permanence. It was widely perceived to be efficient. Levels of satisfactory performance could be achieved over long periods of steady-state activity. It provided opportunities and career paths for those who sought them.

This approach has been transformed. Orderly patterns of work are still necessary, as is functional and technological expertise. The issue is to translate this into effective performance (rather than efficient structuring). The best organisations have added further dimensions to work, and these apply to all levels of staff and functions. Where successful it has been possible to remove layers of general supervision as well as sophisticated control functions (see Box 2.9).

BOX 2.9 Dimensions of Effective Staff

Attributes

1. Commercial insight, organisation and market awareness.
2. The ability to work persistently and autonomously.
3. The use of innovative and creative faculties.
4. The ability to work within a changing and turbulent environment.
5. Analytical skills, the ability to solve problems.
6. Stamina and staying power.
7. The ability to harmonise with people at all levels and from different backgrounds, and with different expertise.
8. Understanding of customers' needs and wants.
9. Ability to work on own initiative.
10. Acceptance of responsibility and accountability.

Behavioural Qualities

1. High levels of motivation, moral and commitment.
2. High levels of identity and confidence between organisation and staff.
3. Acceptance of responsibility for one's own sphere of activities.
4. Acceptance of responsibility for developing one's own sphere of activities.
5. The determination to progress, develop, innovate and change.
6. Understanding the relationship between individual, group and organisation performance.
7. Sharing the rewards of success.
8. High levels of trust and respect.
9. Honesty and integrity.
10. Customer respect.

Attitudes

1. Equality of treatment and opportunity.
2. Flexibility, creativity, dynamism, responsiveness.
3. Positive rather than negative.
4. Continuous improvement and development.
5. Change as an opportunity rather than a threat.
6. Confidence.
7. Customer satisfaction.

Expertise

1. Potential as well as current expertise.
2. The obligation of staff to seek development.
3. The obligation of organisations to provide continuous development and improvement.
4. The application of distinctive expertise to all situations required.
5. The application and harnessing of all expertise (personal and peripheral, as well as functional, core and expert).
6. Variety and innovation.
7. Enrichment and enlargement of work.

The result is to reposition the relationship between organisation and employee from a traditional alienative/calculative involvement to a combination of partnership and participation. This is based on much higher levels of mutual understanding and general commitment; the approach is only successful where information and communication are given and received freely and without harm or prejudice.

It applies to all staff, whatever their job or function. The emphasis is on the distinctive value of every contribution. If there is no value there is no contribution; nobody is employed in any capacity unless there is a real and high-value job to be done (see Box 2.16).

The level of mutual commitment is very high. It may be summarised as 'high levels of work (value and quality) for high levels of reward'. It places obligations on both staff and organisations to deliver their particular part; and, if one or other is not forthcoming, the bond is broken.

It also concentrates on distinctive expertise for all staff, whether front line, support, administrative or managerial. To levels of expertise and qualification are added personal and professional commitment, and the attitudes and attributes indicated in Box 2.9.

The result is a high-value positive and creative working environment. Clearly possible in small and medium-sized enterprises, the approach is also one of the foundation stones of the Japanese multi-national corporation. It is applied as successfully in diversified and decentralised organisations (for example, The Body Shop, Interlingua, F International, Nissan) as in those that are concentrated and centralised (for example, the Virgin Group, United Airlines, Marks & Spencer). Above all, it enables the resources that would otherwise be used in administrative processes, supervisory structures and dispute resolution to be freed up to concentrate on customer service and satisfaction (see Box 2.10).

BOX 2.10 Nike

Unless new employees are capable of assimilating Nike expectations of centred hard work and caring, creative thought, Nike will stagger under the weight of a jet-setting, self-centred, arrogant – and average – middle management who aggrandise themselves on a past they were not a part of, instead of striving for future successes in which they can share. (Christensen, 1986, p. 664)

The onus on senior and general management is to create the conditions for this and to ensure that they continue. It is a matter of organisation policy. It requires a distinctive and complex attitude to measures of success and failure; appraisal and measurement of performance; and timescales. It is not enough to drive everything towards short-term gain. The long-term future must be ensured. Short-term performance represents a path towards long term success. This will permeate into departmental and divisional sub-strategies and lead to the creation of effective means of handling and resolving problems and crises.

This is only effective where it is reflected in reward patterns and the incentives and drives by which top levels of performance are encouraged. A long-term view will never be taken where rewards are issued for short-term performance. Egalitarian attitudes and values will not be created where divisive attitudes exist and where status, differential, importance and reward are issued on any basis other than performance.

BOX 2.11 Qualities of Excellence: Intrapreneuring

One way of establishing the qualities required in all excellent staff is to adapt the 'intrapreneurship' model. Intrapreneurs are 'entrepreneuring individuals working within organisations'. The purpose of the approach is to foster a combination of the following qualities and attributes among all categories of staff:

- the innovator or transformer, turning original vision into creative action;
- the designer, showing ability and awareness to harness the potential of markets previously not tapped;
- leadership and dynamism in every sphere;
- the change agent, seeking both new opportunities in new fields and also new opportunities in existing fields and for existing products;
- the animator who brings things to life, giving them energy and direction;
- the adventurer, discovering new territory and pioneering;
- the champion who adopts particular projects and products as her cause and makes it her business to get them to market;
- the hero or heroine: people to whom others within the organisation can look up.

The purpose is to get general managers to think of all people in terms of their potential rather than their limitations; how the potential might be unlocked; the conditions and form of organisation necessary; and the rewards to be gained, for both staff and organisation.

BOX 2.12 Villains

The array of villains that organisations use to draw upon includes unions, suppliers, rogue customers, other larger-than-life characters in their own ambit, politicians, the law and the personnel and finance functions. They are used to best advantage by organisations in particular circumstances as part of the mechanism of culture generation, myth and legend formation. They are misused when they become excuses or whipping posts for general and genuine shortcomings.

The idea of the 'common enemy' can also be used to great advantage when circumstances permit. A common identity is identified against whom the whole organisation can unite. It is most often a competitor, market, niche or sector; it may also, again, be unions, politicians or the law.

BOX 2.13 Fallen Idols

Problems arise with both the concept and creation of champions and heroes when they fall from grace. They exhibit the same foibles and failings as everyone else.

People who have been perceived as such include the following pair:

- Hugh Scanlon, who was the Communist leader of the engineering union in the UK in the 1960s and 1970s (he later accepted a peerage);
- Freddy Laker, who set out to break what he described as the multi-national stranglehold on the London–New York air routes in the 1970s; he went bankrupt in 1981.

General examples are to be found in all organisations.

- the local union representatives who urge resistance to redundancies in the face of excellent severance terms, and then are among the first to accept them;
- the maverick who receives promotion and then reverts to corporate executive type, and goes out of his way to restrict the activities of other mavericks;
- the strong union representative who crosses the floor to accept a managerial post (ie: the poacher turned gamekeeper).

In all cases the result is invariably a combination of disappointment, disenchantment and anger on the part of the others in the organisation.

The Chief Executive

Chief Executives form the links between purpose and action, strategy and operation, direction and execution. They give a personal identity to the organisation, both internally to staff, and also externally to customers and the community.

BOX 2.14 Chief Executives and Identity

The following forms of relationship between Chief Executives and staff may be identified.

Strongly positive	The Chief Executive is a powerful, dominant, dynamic or public figure, as with The Body Shop, McDonald's, Wendy and the Virgin Group.

Strong internal	For example, P&O, Boots and Marks & Spencer. In these cases, the presence of a Chief Executive is less public; they may even be virtually unknown outside their own organisation, but nevertheless the internal identity is very strong.
Weak internal or caucus	There is little impact on the wider organisation and its staff. This is prevalent throughout public service sectors, and some multi-nationals, especially where operations are diverse.
Inert	The Chief Executive has no wide positive influence. The relationship consists of a void. This is normally translated into operational uncertainty, divergence from objectives (which were probably not clear or accurate in the first place), and varying standards of activity. It is a fertile breeding-ground for overmighty subjects and alternative and canteen cultures, with all the negative effects that these bring to organisations and their operations.
Negative	This arises where there is a mutual antagonism between the Chief Executive and the rest of the organisation, brought about by a lack of mutual regard, respect and confidence. The usual cause of this arises from the appointment of the Chief Executive on false premises. It may also arise because the Chief Executive lacks basic directorial or managerial capability.

They are the organisation's guides. They shape, direct and energise its purpose and strategy. They embody the vision and values of the organisation, setting the standards for all to follow. They are 'the prow of the ship', the leading part and point of the organisation. They are adept at dealing with the media, and are the key player in public relations activities.

The Chief Executive is the hub of organisation culture. Chief Executives cannot expect staff to accept and respect high standards of commitment, motivation and behaviour if they do not do so themselves.

The Chief Executive is the personal leader and point of corporate identity, attitudes and ethics for the staff. He is responsible for the design, direction, activities and standards adopted in the pursuit of organisation purpose. He sets the final seal of approval on this and is ultimately responsible and accountable.

The task is complex and requires the following capabilities:

- mental toughness and agility, intellect and intelligence;
- stamina;
- the ability to take a global view;
- the appointment of capable aides and advisers;
- the ability to deal effectively with people from all areas;

- knowledge and understanding of the business sphere at large and of their given sector in particular;
- the ability to energise and harmonise resources, staff and stakeholders.

Chief Executive Officers who exhibit these qualities are highly prized and valued. They are also capable of being translated from one field to another, provided that the particular distinctive knowledge and expertise can be acquired.

The Chief Executive acts as the organisation's helmsperson, taking on the role of steering the organisation along its strategic path. Good Chief Executives see opportunities and obstacles that may arise.

The Chief Executive acts as the corporate monitor-evaluator, a constant general watching brief on all operations and activities.

BOX 2.15 Chief Executives and Public Relations

Alistair Morton, the Chief Executive of Eurotunnel, has been both architect and instrument of the public relations activities conducted by the organisation in support of its critical tasks of gaining and maintaining public confidence, gaining and maintaining backing and finance for the project and developing a highly complex working relationship with both banks and contractors. This he has then melded into an effective and continuing aura of public confidence in the project itself. In his own field he is a major authority.

He has also conducted a great range of general activities in support of the Channel Tunnel project. He has been a media panellist, pundit and interviewee. He has addressed conferences and seminars for both the construction industry and the management circuit.

Anita Roddick carries out similar public relations functions in pursuit of gaining a high-quality, distinctive and ethical reputation for The Body Shop. As well as appearing on media panels, and taking part in interviews, she has produced (and has been the subject of) television and radio programmes for the business and management sectors. The organisation has commissioned its own biography, *The Body Shop Story.*

Richard Branson has also taken this role extremely seriously. He has been involved in a number of high-profile activities, heavily covered by the world's news media. He took part in a balloon crossing of the Atlantic Ocean. He organised the Blue Riband crossing of the Atlantic Ocean, in a Sea Cat catamaran, which did indeed capture the trophy awarded to the ship holding the record for the fastest sea crossing of the Atlantic. He regularly appears on business television and radio programmes.

He is also courted as a general celebrity by chat show hosts and is regarded as good general media material. He used to visit the Virgin record stores on a regular basis before they were sold off by his company. He is to be found regularly serving food and drinks to the customers on his airline.

Everything considered here is regarded as a central part of the Chief Executive Officer's functions. It is sound expert business practice. It is instrumental in energising business and organisations. It is good internal public relations, part of the fountain of myths, stories and legends. It builds confidence, and thus continuity, and thus increased confidence.

Other qualities that Chief Executive Officers need to possess are as follows.

1. **Energy:** the willingness to put body, heart and soul into the organisation, its drives and purposes, and its activities.
2. **Faith:** based on a combination of knowledge of the field and the nature of the activities to be conducted, balanced with customer and market expectations.
3. **Vision:** the view of the world as it is to be when the organisation is successfully established.
4. **Success:** the burning drive and ambition is to succeed in all spheres of activity.
5. **Reality:** a hard understanding of the business sphere; however, faith, vision, energy and the burning desire to succeed are not in themselves guarantees of success. Neither is hard work, which must be effective and targeted.
6. **A bias for action:** generating new ideas, projects and initiatives.

■ Developing the human resource

All structures and styles are subject to constant evolution. The onus here is to ensure that this is always positive. It has to be geared to the advancement of the organisation, its products, services, and management and staff qualities. Organisations will strike a balance between growing and developing their own future managers; developing present managers for improved current and potential future performance; and taking in new blood, energies, talents and ideas. Organisations will invest in their own growth and improvement through all forms of development activity. Many organisations institutionalise and integrate this into learning cultures, seeing organisation development as a core strategic activity.

All organisations get the work forces that they deserve. Any organisation that has a history of industrial troubles and disputes has failed to convince its work force either of the importance of their contribution, or of their value to it. Organisations that have morale problems can invariably trace these back to the style of management adopted, its lack of clarity of direction, bad communications and decision-making processes. They can trace the institutionalisation of such troubles and problems to the emergence of vested interests and overmighty subjects which prosper, again as we have seen, in these situations.

Other organisations invest in the development of a strong positive culture among the staff. Members understand where they stand, what the expectations of them are, what their obligations to the organisation are, and the opportunities afforded by it for them. Industrial relations in its traditional form is unknown. There is a single identity generated, a standard for conformity. Organisations invest resources in staff and job training for development, induction, standard and attitude formation. Organisations are able to pass on a proportion of the resources that would otherwise have been spent on human resource management structures in the form of increased compensation, benefits and salaries to all the staff. Procedures are simple and clear, easy to understand and operate. Managers are trained to solve problems, not institutionalise them. The organisation will in all cases support a manager's view, provided that it is in keeping with standards and philosophies, and that the person in question has not exceeded his boundaries of operation.

Any potential member of staff can then make much more of an informed choice (rather than a guess) as to whether or not they wish to work for this organisation. Any actual staff member is able to work with a much fairer degree of certainty as to where they do stand, and what the relationship is between themselves and their organisation. In general terms, again, all of this will tend to reinforce the certainty of direction of the organisation. If all staff in all operations and departments know where they are going, there is easily identified both a mutual confidence and interest (dependent, of course, upon the correctness and effectiveness of the strategy and direction that is to be followed) that is itself so much more straightforward than where such direction is either lacking, or is not overtly apparent.

BOX 2.16 Management and Staff: Toshiba

At Toshiba, positive staff relations are based on a recognition that in employing somebody a relationship has been entered into. Management expects commitment to the company in return for treating every employee as a valued member. Staff are selected for their enthusiasm, idealism, attention to detail and expertise, as well as for their commitment. All are given the title production employee, which allows flexibility.

There is no job grading and evaluation scheme. Every employee is expected to wear a company issue blue jacket at work and to eat in the same restaurant. Each working day begins with a five-minute meeting to discuss problems, ideas and solutions. There are also monthly meetings of the whole manufacturing department, addressed by the production director, and six-monthly meetings of the whole company, addressed by the managing director. Employees are trained to be quality-conscious and self-checking. Production figures and quality level performance are freely displayed. The result is a low staff turnover, low absenteeism, minimal lateness, a cheerful work force and production on target.

The belief that each person should feel important has brought Toshiba excellent production results.

This is reinforced at induction by a message from the organisation's President to the following effect:

> If you come to work for this company, we are delighted to have you along. You are exceptional, you are valuable, you are essential. There are no spare bodies at this company, there is no excess capacity. Therefore when you join us we expect you to be here and we expect you to work. If you cannot accede to these expectations, or if you are the sort of person who has a lot of time off, you should question whether this is the right company for you.

The result of all this is that the organisation has negligible self-certificated absence rates, excellent output, strong staff identity, high motivation and morale, and an archetype culture of continuous improvement.

BOX 2.17 Staff Management: Other Examples

Nissan has underpinned its operations in the UK and USA with extensive selection, induction, orientation and job training programmes before turning on the production lines and processes. This is viewed by the company as an essential, integral part of the investment necessary to produce top quality cars. In the UK, the company transformed ex-miners, ex-dockers and ex-steelworkers into a top quality and highly flexible work force in pursuit of this. The organisation's production output per head is the highest of any car manufacturer in the EU.

The Body Shop staff are required to work on environmental projects in their own time as part of their work contract and commitment to the organisation. Anybody who does not agree to do this is not employed. It effectively adds an extra half-day to the working month. It also reinforces both the values of the organisation, and the identity required of the staff. It reinforces finally the level of commitment required to the organisation (which is very high).

The Boots Company puts all its departments or store staff through a nationally validated programme of induction and job training. Everyone is required to take part. The purpose is to set standards, and to ensure that all staff have the same basis on which the reputation of the organisation is to be built. The programme also opens up other opportunities for the staff to identify and, where possible, pursue career opportunities, operational development, and supervisory studies.

The programme reflects the value and importance placed on the staff by the organisation. It is a recognition that without top-quality people on the floor of the shops, top-quality service to customers is not possible.

Because the programme is validated, if a staff member does leave the organisation for any reason, they have a qualification to take with them, a proof of competence to be demonstrated to potential employees.

In each of these cases there is a direct relationship between the attitude, approach and value placed on the staff by the organisation, and the levels of business, profit and reputation generated.

Change agents and change catalysts

Change agents and catalysts may either be external or internal. Externals are brought in when organisations require transformations, shake-ups, refocusing, or re-orienting. These include expert and statutory bodies, as well as consultants with distinctive expertise. The value of the pronouncement of the expert body or consultant is normally to give a view that is acceptable to everyone concerned.

They may also be used to recommend specific courses of action (which may be unacceptable, or perceived to be so, if they were purely internal initiatives) and hired to resolve specific problems. They are used on each aspect of the organisation's operations, activities, attitudes and values. They may be asked to address its direction and strategy. The main point here is the accuracy and effectiveness of the contract between organisation and external consultant. This must have the purpose of ensuring an accurate recognition of the issues to be faced, and a clear remit to tackle them.

More generally, derived benefits from both expert bodies and more general consultations arise from the knowledge and perspective that the organisation and its top managers are sufficiently concerned with either direction or performance to call in experts with a view to remedying the situation.

BOX 2.18 Use of Consultants

The relationship between organisation and consulting body must be carefully drawn up, whether it is a statutory body or a management consultancy.

In either case, the organisation loses a measure of control of the outcome. A consultant may come up with an unpalatable truth. In the latter case the general management consultant's view is likely to be addressed to managers of strategy, functional operational or business concerns. The organisation and its directors are at liberty, more or less, to receive the views of the consultant and to pursue their recommended course of action or not.

In the case of the statutory body, the organisation has placed itself at the mercy of a nationally acknowledged expert body, and one which carries the equivalent of statutory force. Not only has the organisation lost the measure of control of the situation referred to above, it is also under much greater pressure to implement that which is recommended. If a work force dispute or grievance subsequently blows up, or if there is in future an accident or an emergency, the bodies conducting any inquiry arising will want to know what the expert advice was that was given, whether it was followed, and, if not, why not.

These points therefore illustrate the critical nature of the relationship, contract or agreement. Countless organisations have given general briefs to consultants and have subsequently received expensive surveys, reports and presentations which conclude that 'more work needs to be done in this area'.

If the project required is large and complex, a tendering process is often considered. If speed is the main criterion, this will be the key quality sought in the consultation. Whatever is required as the outcome will be specified in the agreement drawn up, whether this is advice, illustration, recommendation, or implementation of any proposed changes.

■ Internal

Key appointments act as agents for change: for example, where the organisation makes a high-profile appointment in an area where it seeks to improve its performance. They may, for instance, appoint an equal opportunities director who is a top operator in her field, with the purpose of giving the organisation a boost in the area; the result is that a specific particular value is placed on equality of opportunity. Similar appointments may be made in all key spheres of activity.

Organisations also appoint key players on fixed-term contracts with specific briefs and remits, specific tasks, precise measures of success and failure. As an example, many UK public services, local authorities and health service organisations do this for Chief Executive and Chief Officer appointments.

The approach may be varied in the creation of project teams and groups for specific purposes. Persons are seconded to teams while the project is in hand, returning to their previous duties when it is completed.

The championing approach may also be used. This is where someone, or a department (or an *ad hoc* group) is given a general brief or responsibility to pick up a particular issue and pursue it to see where it leads (or some other equivalent, vague, remit). Success in this context is certain to depend upon the championing qualities of the person, department or group commissioned. Another variation on this is to be found in the style of drawing up broad rather than narrow job descriptions.

BOX 2.19 Job Descriptions: The Case of the Invisible Job

C. B. Handy (1993) identified this phenomenon. The job holder in question came from a highly structured and regulated organisation to a small entrepreneurial outfit. When he asked what his job description was, he was told that one did not exist. When he asked what his job was, the reply was as follows:

> We want you out in the field looking for opportunities. We want ideas and projects from you. We have hired you because we respect and value your judgement in the field.

The effective pursuit of a remit such as this can only be contemplated if organisations have the flexibility of culture, structure and operations to accommodate the infinite range of 'ideas and projects' to which reference is made.
Source: Handy (1993).

Internal departments and functions are also often used as change agents, most commonly for finance and human resource personnel.

☐ *Finance*

The drive for change is likely to arise through a combination of budgeting reform, changes in financial targets or reporting methods, or more general financial restructuring.

☐ *Human resource personnel*

This arises from changes in any of the human activities at the workplace, including industrial relations, staff management, terms and conditions of employment, human resource maintenance (that is, occupational health, welfare, health and safety), organisation development, and implementation of new procedures and practices. This function is also certain to be involved in restructuring activities and programmes of cultural change.

Any department or function may be used as a change agent. Organisations can, and do, take these opportunities at the time of market change, production and technology, innovations, relocation. All business and all public services are currently being conducted in a volatile and turbulent environment. Effective agents of change are essential to ensure that opportunities are maximised. It is also clear that there are catalysts and agents of change to be found everywhere. It is essential to recognise these, and the opportunities and potential that they afford.

BOX 2.20 Rogues as Change Agents

Brief mention should be made of the organisation's rogues in this context. 'Rogues' are to be found among the range of larger-than-life characters in large and sophisticated organisations. They come in all the forms indicated. They are champions, obsessives, fringe operators, overmighty subjects.

They hold positions of power and influence in 'the informal organisation' networks and canteen cultures. They may be trade union officials. They may hold positions of influence in staff leisure clubs. They may already have myths and legends growing up around them.

They often hold a great deal of informal general respect and influence. Their opinion is valued by other members of staff. It may not be possible to persuade the staff to a point of view if the rogue is not persuaded first. They often have a great deal of negative influence: that is, they can mobilise forces that are resistant to change.

More generally, the extent and prevalence of networks, the informal organisation, and the canteen culture, must be considered by any organisation wishing to identify its barriers and opportunities for change. Any strategic approach to change must include consideration of this in turn as a key and core function (see also elsewhere).

■ Conclusion

This chapter has discussed strategic management in terms of the nature of organisation performance, and human performance and capability. It has paid particular attention to the roles and function of the Chief Executive Director, performance requirement and measurement, and the human factor, which all interact with each other.

It is essential to recognise the effects of this interaction. Strategy and direction must be designed with the nature of those responsible for its implementation in mind. Strategy, key players, and the human resource at large must be harmonised. If this is not possible, one or other needs to be amended.

If the proposed direction is truly correct for the organisation but cannot be accommodated by those concerned at present, then processes of culture and structure change, re-orientation, training and development have to be undertaken in advance. This may also include the replacement of some of the key characters discussed.

Matters will also be considered from the opposite point of view. Changes in personnel or culture may not be feasible in the situation in which the organisation is operating. In this case the strategy and direction have to be moderated in order to accommodate the drives of the business, the constraints imposed by those involved, and the ways in which they work. Changes in these matters then become considerations for the future, to be addressed by those responsible as part of the process of strategy development. Ultimately, however, no organisation may remain rigid and unchanging. Those responsible for its direction must ensure that both the organisation and its staff are developed and progress. This chapter has illustrated the context for this and the issues to be addressed in this part of the strategy process.

Work assignments and discussion questions

1. Discuss the view that extremely high levels of organisation performance can only be achieved and sustained as the result of: attracting top-quality, expert and committed staff; paying and rewarding them well; and requiring them to continually train and develop.
2. (a) Why is Richard Branson regarded as a successful company Chairman/Chief Executive?
   (b) How, when and where should the performance of a chief executive be measured? By whom should this be carried out?
3. Outline the main principles upon which a style of management should be founded and state the circumstances under which these may be diluted, compromised or abandoned.
4. (a) What are the merits and demerits of introducing a figure into an organisation purely as a catalyst for change?
   (b) What are the components of the balance to be achieved between growing and developing talent and potential from within, and obtaining new staff via the employment market?

CHAPTER 3

Strategic and Environmental Analysis

Introduction

The outcome of all analyses should be an accurate establishment of the organisation's strengths and capabilities, the commercial and operational advantages to be gained from the proposed activities and the wider general pressures and constraints that may be present. The models and methods explained address each of these.

There is a range of general factors and pressures to be taken into account.

Organisation

This includes:

- nature of current and proposed activities;
- market share, both current and envisaged;
- position in current and potential markets (for example, largest player, most distinctive player, degree of specialisation);
- customer base, both current and envisaged, and the impact of new activities on existing;
- position in the value chain;
- images of the organisation and regard in which the organisation is held;
- access, use and potential of technology and skills;
- capital strength, access to capital;
- cashflow and volume of business conducted;
- financial structure and resources;
- product portfolios and life cycles, new products, research and development activities;
- managerial expertise;
- ability to attract and retain staff and expertise.

Commercial and operational attractiveness

This includes:

- market size, both current and envisaged;
- market locations, both current and envisaged;

- market state: growth, maturity, decline; steady/turbulent;
- market structure;
- market profitability;
- the state of other players in the sector;
- entry and exit barriers;
- current and envisaged state of sectoral technology;
- images and regard in which the sector is held;
- barriers to activity (for example, competition for supplies, components, raw materials; availability of outlets).

Environmental considerations

This includes:

- regulation of activities;
- general perceptions of the organisation and its activities;
- legal restraints and factors;
- social issues and the relationship of the organisation with its locations and communities;
- availability of staff in these locations;
- ethical factors, especially concerning the nature of activities, relations with staff and the community; ethical and social pressures;
- behavioural and perceptual restraints;
- political factors;
- general aspects of stability, turbulence and uncertainty.

This provides a basis for consideration of proposed directions. It is not an end in itself. It sets useful boundaries for the more specific inquiries indicated below.

Means and methods of strategy analysis

The purpose here, therefore, is to ensure that what is done is kept under regular and constant review as part of the drive by the organisation to maximise its outputs, and also in order to be able to see any problems as they become apparent. The process of analysis should be both rigorous and streamlined; the purpose is to highlight issues that are of importance with the purpose of rigorously assessing, evaluating and discussing them. Any particular matters arising can then be prioritised for action. They may be accepted or rejected at their face value. They may also be used as the basis for further research and analysis.

Strengths, weaknesses, opportunities, threats: SWOT analysis

The purpose of conducting a SWOT analysis is to help organisations to learn, to clarify issues, to identify preferred and likely directions and to conduct a general and quick analysis of their current position.

In SWOT analyses issues are raised, highlighted and categorised under four headings (see Figure 3.1).

Example: Virgin Cola

Strengths	**Weaknesses**
• Virgin name • Generic product • Profile of Chief Executive Officer • Public confidence in other Virgin offerings • Reputation of Virgin group and name	• Strength of competitors' and existing brands • Confidence of public in existing brands
• Failure of this product may cause questioning of other offerings	• Size of generic markets • Developments and advances into soft drinks (and other foodstuffs)
Threats	**Opportunities**

The purpose is to give a quick and highly visual analysis of an organisation, situation, product or service. It then becomes the basis of more detailed analysis and evaluation.

Figure 3.1 SWOT analysis model

Strengths. Things that the organisation and its staff are good at and do well and that they are effective at; that they are well known for; that make money; that generate business and reputation; that generate confidence and understanding in the marketplace; that cause customers to come back for repeat business; that cause other organisations to try to learn from them; those matters on which the organisation has built its past reputation.

Weaknesses. These are the things that the organisation is bad at; the things that it does badly; the things that are ineffective; the things that the organisation is notorious for. It also includes consideration of those elements that cause it to make losses; that cause hardships, disputes, grievances and complaints; that should generate business but do not; and the raising and clarification of issues that have caused business to be lost and elements of bad reputation to be gained.

Opportunities. These are the directions which the organisation could profitably take for the future that may arise because of strengths or the elimination of weaknesses. This involves a consideration of the environment from the widest and most creative possible standpoint.

Threats. Threats arise from competitors, from strikes and disputes, from resource and revenue losses, from failing to maximise opportunities or to build on successes. They also arise from complacency, organisational and strategic lack of rigour, and from the erosion of margins due, for example, to rising cost levels.

In general, opportunities and threats are manifestations of the relationship between the external environment and the forces that work in it. Strengths and weaknesses are candid assessments of those areas of activity which the organisation is currently good and bad at.

The analysis is carried out in the form of a brainstorming and creative discussion. It is an effective means of gathering and categorising information, of illustrating and illuminating particular matters and of generating a great deal of interest in the organisation and its activities very quickly. The result of such an exercise should be to provide the basis on which a more detailed analysis can be conducted.

Social, technical, economic, political: STEP analysis

The purpose of STEP analysis (see Figure 3.2) is also to help organisations learn. However, the material that arises from a discussion such as this is likely to be much more concerned with the analysis of the wider strategic situation, the organisation in its environment and more global concerns.

Social	**Technological**
• Population • Lifestyle • Spending patterns • Social attitudes and values • Prejudices • Segmentation	• Education and training • Technological advance and invention • Obsolescence • Potential • Energy
• Legal factors • Sector regulation • Political pressures • Green issues • Governmental stance	• Confidence • Spending patterns • Propensity to spend • Inflation • Fixed and variable costs incurred
Political	**Economic**

Purpose: a quick and highly visual representation of the external pressures present, and their potential for limiting and enhancing proposed activities.

Figure 3.2 STEP analysis model

Social. This is to do with the social systems in place at the workplace, departmental and functional structures, work culture, attitudes, organisation and working methods; it also includes both formal and informal aspects of the organisation. In external terms, this is the relationship between the organisation and its environment as regards the nature and social acceptability of its products and services and the ways in which it does business; consideration is also given to the impact of marketing, promotion and public relations activities; and the general regard with which the organisation is held in its markets, communities and the wider environment.

Technological. This relates to the organisation's technology and the uses to which it is put, and also its potential uses; to the technology that is potentially available to the organisation and others operating in the given sector; to the technological advances that are present or envisaged elsewhere in the sector and the opportunities afforded by these to the organisation in question.

Economic. This concerns the financial structure, objectives and constraints placed upon the organisation. This relates to both the external (that is, the levels of profit and turnover generated and the extent to which this is viable and able to sustain current and envisaged levels of activity) and the internal financial position (means of financial controls, budgeting systems, budgets and financial management and practices). It also considers the market position, general levels of economic activity, the competition for the offerings made by the organisation and the commercial prospects and potential of the products and services offered.

Political. This consists of assessing the internal political systems, sources of power and influence, key individuals, key groups of staff, key departments, key managers and key executives; questions of management style, human resource management and industrial relations issues; general levels of motivation and morale.

Externally, it considers particular factors in the establishment of markets, by-products, vocation, ethics and values. There may also be political and legal constraints placed upon the activities of the organisation in question, especially where it is trading in places other than its own indigenous locality. Again, this is a starting point only, and the information thus raised must be further analysed and evaluated. The purpose is to establish in some detail the background against which particular product, service and offering initiatives take place already and may do in the future. It also highlights any wider concerns or issues that may in turn require attention; in particular, it may highlight matters over which the organisation has no control. Finally, a full STEP analysis will probably consider wider general directions and likely initiatives taken by governments in regard to social, technological, economic and political issues.

■ Industry structure analysis

This is based on Porter's five elemental forces of competition model (see Figure 3.3). It considers the following.

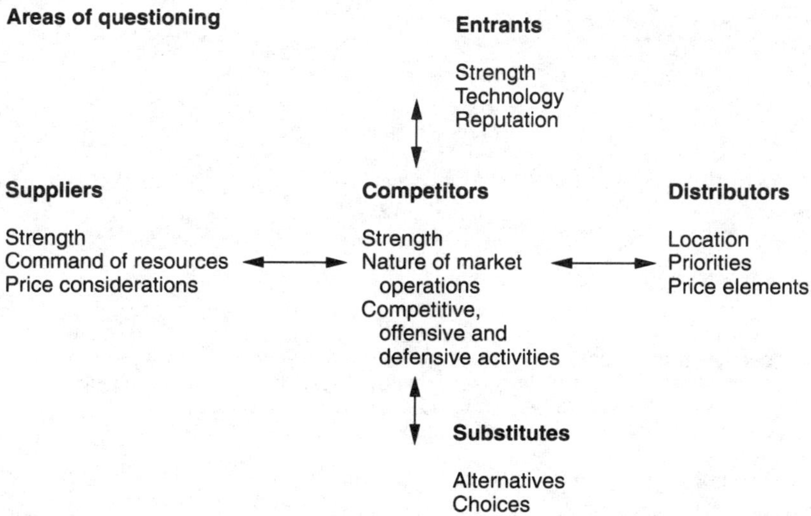

Figure 3.3 Industry structure analysis

1. The industry competitors, those at the centre of the model. This includes a consideration of the nature and extent of rivalry among those organisations currently operating in the field and the implications of this for the future. This may include consideration of the extent of differentiation activity, the prospect of price wars and impacts and implications for profit margins. It may also include questions related to the capacity of the sector (both in terms of existing levels of business and future potential).
2. The nature and extent of the bargaining power of suppliers and buyers. This includes the extent to which they may be able to withdraw or flood the market (on the supplier side); and the propensity and pressure to buy (on the buyer side).
3. The extent and nature of actual and potential substitution processes. Part of this will include the more detailed competitor analysis, discussed below.
4. The nature of potential entrants, and any distinctive advantages they would, could or might bring to the sector.

■ Competitor analysis

This involves assessing the other players in the field, including initiatives that they may take to promote their own strategic advantage, and also to measure the likely responses to such initiatives on the part of others in the sector and of the organisation in question. The components of a competitor analysis are as follows (see also Figure 3.4).

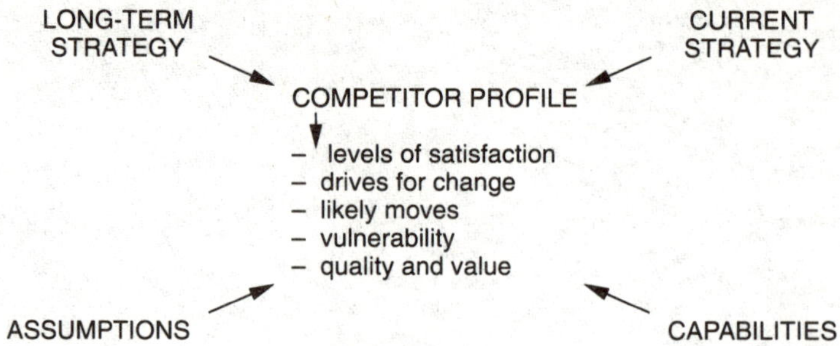

This process is similar to the Industry Structure Analysis, but is addressed to each individual company in the sector. It is questioned from the point of view of its corporate strategy; business strategy; capabilities and assumptions.

The result is a profile of each player against which the position of the organisation in question can be measured.

Figure 3.4 The components of a competitor analysis

1. The strategy of the competitor.
2. The driving and restraining forces that are placed upon it.
3. Its current business operations, capacities, strengths and capabilities.
4. Its current marketing operations and activities; confidence, reputation and images; the processes and effets of differentiation.
5. Assumptions held about the competitor.
6. Assumptions held about the industry itself.
7. Detailed profiles of each competitor in regard to assessing their current satisfaction with their current position; their likely moves and responses to competitive moves; their positions in the market in question; and the extent to which they are under- or over-stretched, the extent to which they are operating at under or over capacity.

What is required is a detailed discussion, to be devised and conducted on a sectoral, corporate and organisational basis. Once assessed and evaluated, the outcome is normally a presentation to the top management/directorate on the subject of the analysis itself, and the results, conclusions and recommendations that arise. The purpose is to illustrate and highlight the strengths and opportunities present in the rest of the field and to draw any lessons that are there to be learned from other players in the sector.

Product life cycles analysis

A useful way of looking at the offerings of organisations is to see them in terms of the life cycle (see Figure 3.5). The general hypothesis is that all products have a finite life and that within this they are born, they grow, develop and mature, finally reaching old age and (eventually) obsolescence.

INTRODUCTION	GROWTH	MATURITY	DECLINE	RENEWAL
• Interest	• Value	• Value	• Obsolescence	• Value
• Anticipation	• Potential	• Confidence	• Loss of confidence	• Confidence
• Expectation	• Demand	• Loyalty	• Loss of loyalty	• Altered perceptions
• Supply	• Strength	• Knowledge	• Knowledge	• New expectations
	• Confidence	• Acceptance	• Rejection	• New markets
			↓ DEATH	

The model indicates the regeneration, renewal and extension of the profitable life of the product concerned, and its relationship with successful marketing activity.

Figure 3.5 Product life cycles

In most cases, however, the process is more complex. It takes a great deal of invention, research and new product development activity to bring an item into being, and for each that is successful there are many that fail. Assuming that the product is intrinsically useful and valuable to a range of consumers in some way, the life cycle may be influenced at each stage. At the point of youth and adolescence, for example, growth may be accelerated by effective marketing or other differentiation activities (or, conversely, growth may be retarded or the product killed off altogether if the activities in question are poor, ineffective or inappropriate).

At the point of maturity, it may be differentiated for the purpose of gaining access to as many different sectors and segments as possible: for example, washing powder and washing-up liquids are based on a universal detergent formula. The detergent itself is differentiated by scent, concentration, packaging and advertising. It can therefore be offered across virtually the entire social segment range. However, people who buy Persil, say, would never dream of buying Radion because of this process of differentiation. (This is in spite of the fact that the products are essentially the same.)

Marketability	Durability	Productive ability
• Distribution	• Value	• Technology
• Price	• Breadth of market	• Knowledge
• Image	• Depth of market	• Skills, expertise
• Quality	• Potential of market	• Materials, supplies
• Value	• Elasticity of market	
• Public perceptions	• Locations of market	
• Design	• Substitutes	
• Packaging	• Threats	
• Appearance		

Figure 3.6 Selecting profitable products and services

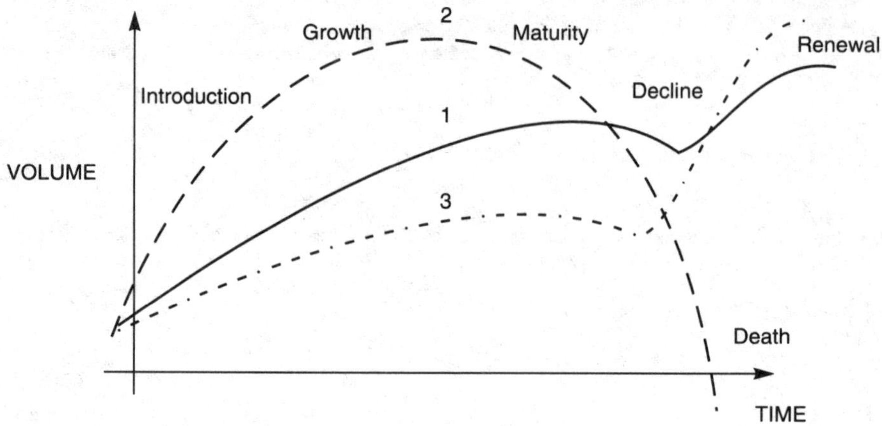

Products 1 and 3 are rejuvenated; Product 2 is killed off.

Figure 3.7 Product life cycle illustration

At maturity and old age, products may be regenerated or rejuvenated. Again, this is likely to be achieved through repackaging, re-presentation or the offering of a range of new benefits not hitherto considered or offered. For example, the filofax was a well established diary format that enjoyed steady but unspectacular commercial success in the 1960s and 1970s as a useful and effective continuous forward planner. It was transformed in the early 1980s through the generation of its perception, and subsequent adoption, as a fashion and status accessory. The word filofax is now a part of the English language and the item that it describes is much more widely recognised and used.

Some products and offerings give the appearance of living on and on. Coca Cola, for example, is subject to constant re-presentation, rejuvenation and image strengthening through the nature of the marketing and wider strategic activities conducted in its support (though its logo and distinctive packaging remains the same).

Items in the products portfolio may also feed off each other. Coca Cola is reinforced by the healthy and light (and therefore, in the 1990s, fashionable and desirable) images of the Diet Coke range. Diet Coke draws its inherent strength from the Coca Cola name, of which it is an offshoot.

Volkswagen, the German car manufacturer, for years had only one main offering, the Beetle. The product lasted so long that people were inclined to use the company name (Volkswagen) rather than the model name (Beetle). The company introduced a diversified range of cars from the 1960s onwards and the foundation of the success of this was built on the consistency achieved by the long history of the Beetle.

Some products also have a decline phase. This may be for a variety of reasons. Examples of this are loss of competitive advantage over, and vulnerability to, substitutes. Technological advances may render a particular product obsolete. Fashion changes may render it passé. In some cases this part of the cycle is quick and irretrievable: for example, the Sinclair C5 was initially hailed as a marvellous invention but it very quickly lost any reputation as the result of its extreme vulnerability when used on the roads.

In other cases this process is long and slow, but a steady decline nevertheless; such a process may or may not be retrievable. The sea cruise sector of the holiday industry is an example of this. The general volume of global passenger travel by sea declined in favour of the speed, convenience and availability of air travel. At the same time the sea cruise sector lost its ability to support itself as a top-quality and fully exclusive offering. From the decline of these two areas of activity arose the current sea cruise industry with its various niche and segment offerings that include: school and educational; packages; European, Asian, Caribbean, world; luxury; and economy.

Other factors that influence the product life cycle concept include the following.

Seasonal Sales of summer clothes peak in the spring and early summer. They are given an additional fillip through the use of such marketing activities as the late bargain or the end of season sale.

Locational The association of offerings with places. Again, taking the clothing example, the differentiation is achieved through the display of place names or the names of sports clubs on the offerings themselves.

Personal Again, taking clothing as an example, the generation of product association with particular persons. The Garibaldi and Macintosh coats are early and well-established examples of this, and both words have found their way into the general language. Variations on the theme that are in contemporary usage can be found, for example, through the association of tweeds with a country lifestyle. The casual wear sector includes various offerings that have the names or pictures of sports, music and film stars on them.

Ethical An example of this was the generation in the mid- to late 1980s of the environmental imperative as a marketing advantage. The retail petrol sector generated the lead-free market. This is currently the largest niche in the sector.

A wide range of phosphate-free domestic and household detergents, washing powders and cleaning products was also developed.

General familiarity	This is where the existing level of confidence and reputation is used either to give new products of the organisation their initial launch or to boost or regenerate them. This is especially important in the travel and package holiday sectors where the success of a particular package is likely to be dependent, in the UK at least, upon the ability to get the national travel agency chains to offer and promote it. It is the general familiarity of, and confidence in, the agency that is critical to the initial success of the offering.

The product life cycle is therefore a concept rather than absolute fact. It is a useful shorthand for both organisational strategists and operational managers. It is an indicator of the general state of a given product. It is a pointer (not a prescription) for assessment and analysis that may lead to specific activities subsequently being undertaken. It also helps to enable assessment of the product portfolio and the relative merits of each item within it (which again may indicate the necessity for changes and developments or not, and lead to actions being taken).

Against this must be weighed the uncertainties inherent in the concept as discussed. Products can and do take off extremely quickly, catching everyone involved by surprise. They also can die off just as quickly. They are subject to the vagaries of consumer fashion and fad. In commercial markets and mixed economies in general, there are the real and behavioural elements of price, value and quality to be taken into account. Demand for non-essential offerings is invariably transient. Demand for generic homogenous items, whether essential (such as food and clothing) or desirable (such as cars and electrical goods), is highly differentiated. The creation of a truly rational product life cycle model is therefore virtually impossible.

BOX 3.1 The Life of Products: The Fire Allegory

The Match: initially a bright light but essentially small and not long-lasting. They are only individually useful as a complement or starter for something else. In order to be inherently useful, they must come in large volumes.

The Bonfire: this requires initial effort if it is to be successful. The efforts are concentrated on the structure, the nature of the material and that which is added to ensure that it starts. It then requires regular top-ups to ensure that it has sufficient fuel to keep it going. If it is fed and tended it can be kept going virtually indefinitely. If the wrong fuel is added, it quickly dies down.

The Roaring Fire: it lasts for a relatively short time. It is both visually pleasing and highly useful (that is, it gives off warmth and comfort). It can be maintained as such by the regular addition of the correct fuel and lasts for a very long time if this is done correctly; conversely it dies down very quickly if it is neglected or if insubstantial or inappropriate fuel is added.

The Glow: this is the result of successful roaring fires. A long steady warmth is exuded. This eventually declines and dies if it is not tended; there are specific ways in which the glow should be tended if it is to be maintained or if it is to be encouraged to flare.
The Flare: a larger and improved version of the match. This blazes very brightly and also very briefly. It is highly useful for the short time of its life. Again, however it is useful over the long term only as part of a pack or collection. It is nevertheless sufficiently bright to illustrate and illuminate the wide picture.
The Damp Squib: this is a failure, invariably for operational rather than behavioural reasons. Perceptually and intuitively it is sound: it looks and feels as if it should work. It exhibits all of the qualities and appearance of near equivalents that have been known to work. It is only at the point of ignition that the failure becomes apparent. A variation is where it works, but does not fully live up to expectations.

■ Product portfolio analysis

The term 'product portfolio' is used to describe a range and mixture of offerings (see Figure 3.8). There are, as always, sectoral norms and considerations to be taken into account. In general, the portfolio will normally include a range of new and existing offerings, well-established and profitable lines, household names, and other brand or organisation leaders and flagships. In general also, it is likely to include failures: items that are becoming obsolete, mature and ageing. The organisation is likely to have ideas and products being piloted and tested, or undergoing other 'morning star' activities. The purpose of this is to ensure that new ideas currently under test eventually take their place as major organisation offerings. It is also a general part of the maintenance of organisation steadiness, stability, longevity and, above all, profitability.

Two models of product portfolios may usefully be studied. First, Peter Drucker categorised the products of an organisation under the following headings.

1. Today's breadwinners: the major current contributors to the organisation's success and profitability.
2. Tomorrow's breadwinners: those items that show promise and about which there is a good measure of positive response.
3. Specialities: those items that have limited, distinctive market niches.
4. Products under development: that is, the seed corn for future successes.
5. Failures.
6. Yesterday's breadwinners: the mature and ageing products that may be kept on because of their reputation or because of their impact upon today's and tomorrow's breadwinners.
7. Repair jobs: that is, products which have substantial commercial reality or potential, growth opportunities and continuing high levels of results but which are currently

going through crises of some form. Repairs will be undertaken in the expectation and anticipation of returns on them. Drucker stated that the repair element should normally be limited to one aspect only; if too many repairs were required it was likely that in any case the commercial potential would have been lost.

8. Unnecessary and unjustified specialities, either by direct unnecessary resource concentration or lack of commercial returns.
9. Investments in managerial ego, overmighty subjects and political triumphs.
10. Sleeping beauties: products or inventions whose time has not yet come and which are still asleep.

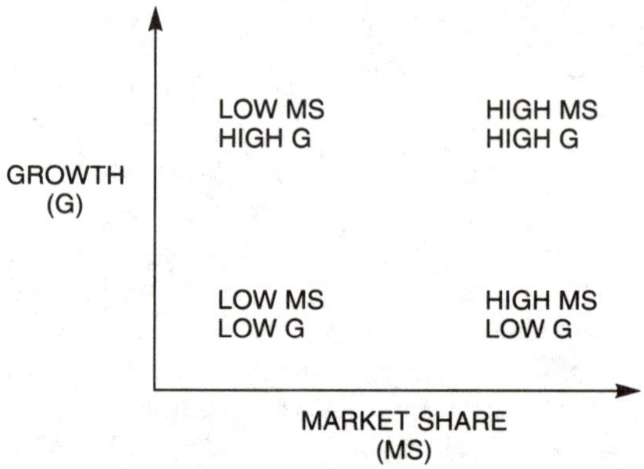

The model provides a means of placing the product range on the 'map' against the two criteria of market share and growth. This is a basis on which discussion, judgement and evaluation may be conducted and conclusions drawn.

Again, there are no right answers. For example, the 'low-low' may indicate an obsolete or ageing product; it may also indicate steady-state and stability; or a high-quality, high-price, high-value niche or specialism.

Figure 3.8 Product portfolios

□ *The Boston matrix*

The Boston Consulting Group devised the matrix indicated in Figure 3.9 as a simple and easy to use ready-reckoner of the state of the products of the organisation. The descriptions are as follows:

- the cash cow;
- the star;
- the question mark;
- the dog.

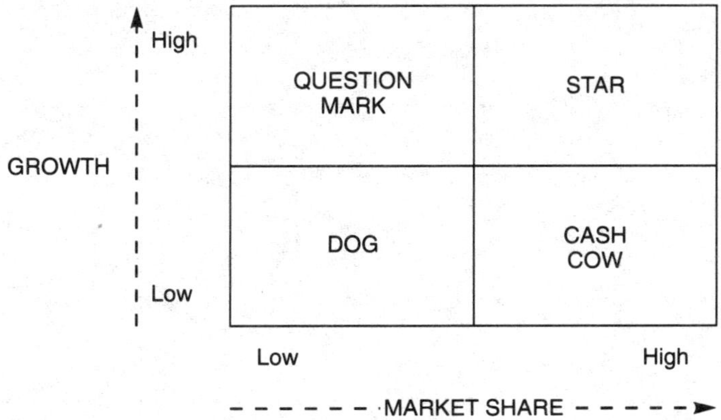

- Stars: high market share of high-growth market.
- Question marks: low share of high-growth market.
- Dogs: low share of low-growth market.
- Cash cow: high market share of low-growth market.

The purpose is the ability to assess and analyse the state of the product portfolio. It can be applied quickly and effectively and enable further strategic assessment to be made in terms of:

- dependency: the range of stars and cash cows in relation to the whole, and the length of time that they are likely to remain stars and cash cows;
- divestment: of dogs, and possibly also of question marks;
- question marks (sometimes also called problem children): the length of time that they have been question marks and the reasons for this;
- the likely future cash cows and stars, both from the company and the sector point of view.

Figure 3.9 The Boston Group matrix

In the case of both the Drucker model and the Boston matrix the overall purpose is the capability of organisations to compartmentalise and rationalise the range of their offerings. The purpose is also to establish the relative balance of the activities currently being undertaken and those projected for the future. A great benefit of both the models illustrated is their simplicity. Problems arise with them, however, in the actual classification of the given product ranges. This is especially true where there are additional agenda or imperatives. This occurs, for example, with product and project championing. It is also to be found in the interdepartmental or interdivisional politicking and rivalry (as explicitly illustrated in the Drucker model). It is also found where the organisation has invested heavily in ostensibly high prestige, high profitability undertakings which are showing clear signs of falling into the question mark or dog categories (or, in the Drucker classification, that of failure). This is compounded where there are problems also of product championing and interdepartmental infighting.

Company's competitive capabilities	*Prospects for sector profitability:* Unattractive	Average	Attractive
Weak	Disinvest	Phased withdrawal/ put on ice	Repackage Re-present
Average	Phased withdrawal	Custodial (proceed with care) Growth	Try harder
Strong	Cash generation	Growth Leader	Leader

This is a variation on the Boston approach. This sets the company's competitive capabilities against the projects for sector profitability in a three-by-three table. Each of the nine boxes contains a recommended strategy. It is designed to assess businesses and strategic business units. It may also be used to assess products, operations, staff qualities and capabilities and marketing activities.

Figure 3.10 The Shell Directional Policy Matrix

Within these constraints the benefit that accrues from the process is a clear representation of the activities. It gives a form of location for the product range. It illustrates both the opportunities to be seized and the areas for concern. This has then to be used for the general purposes of strategic development and analysis and as part of the colouring in of the backcloth to it. It has implications for directorial and managerial decision-making processes. It may finally indicate or imply the need for moves such as product or project cancellation, divestment, licensing; or, on the other hand, the commissioning of research, development and design of new products and the investigation and appraisal of new product opportunities.

■ Cost analysis

The analysis of cost is carried out with the purpose of establishing the nature and level of charges that accrue. This may be undertaken in regard to a total organisation; departments or divisions within it; or in relation to particular operations, activities and processes; or in regard to specific offerings. The primary purpose lies in the ability and necessity to establish exactly the costs incurred in activities. This in itself is not enough however; there is the usage of this information once it is known that is critical. Cost analysis is therefore an aid to strategic and general managerial decision-making. It is not a rigid set of rules and neither is it a substitute for strategic and managerial decision-making.

It is useful to consider the costs incurred in business and organisations as follows.

Fixed Costs (FC). These are those costs incurred that have to be met whether or not any business is conducted, any work done, any sales made, and any revenues accrued. FC include rent, rates, heating, lighting, other premises charges, equipment and capital charges, the costs incurred in staffing and any general financial charges and liabilities that are incurred in servicing these.

Variable Costs (VC). These vary with the volume of work actually carried out. They include raw materials, production processes, finishing, output, sales and energy charges that are incurred in the operational processes.

There are also grey areas between the two absolutes. The concepts of relatively fixed costs and relatively variable costs may be used in reference to variances in work load, the use of temporary and casual staff, consultants, agencies and other aspects of the peripheral work force.

Marginal Cost (MC). This is the cost that is incurred in producing one extra item of output (whatever the item of output may be). MC is on the range of nil to negligible if the extra item can be turned out within the existing way of working (that is, if there is effectively spare capacity to be taken up); at the other extreme, if the organisation is working to full capacity before the demand for the extra (or marginal) product is met, the MC includes all those charges incurred in its output: any overtime incurred by all those working on the process, capital investment or extra process technology that has to be installed. An understanding of this when taking extra work and accepting extra orders is essential.

The most important cost is the variable cost, in that as this constitutes the cost of given and particular activities, prices established and charges made will in general aim to at least cover these. Any income derived additional to this basic level makes a contribution to the fixed cost of the enterprise.

It is also important to recognise that FC may be varied over the medium to long term. Staffing levels and the staffing mix may be changed. Technology may be acquired or divested. A private company may be floated as a public limited company on the stock exchange and thus change the entire cost base and company rationale. Each of these examples come about only as the result of medium- to long-term strategy. They represent the cost basis on which business has to be conducted.

BOX 3.2 Some Notes on Costs

An understanding of the difference between fixed and variable costs is clearly essential concerning pricing policy. As stated in the text, in general the price charged will at least cover the variable cost and make a contribution to the FC. This contribution will clearly be as high as possible.

However, it ought to be recognised that the other extreme, that of absolute FC apportionment to each item sold or activity undertaken, often gives a charge level that is simply not warranted. This invariably leads to threats of market entry, undercutting and price wars. The apportionment of FC is, in any case, an imprecise activity. Levels of business are almost certainly not absolutely constant. Following this to its logical conclusion would result in charges rising as levels of business went down.

The following examples are from the travel sector. Airlines all offer standby tickets on the basis of late booking and subject to availability. From their point of view, it is better that they sell a £200 seat for £20 rather than not sell it at all, as the plane is travelling anyway. Further, the airline is likely to recoup additional income from on-board sales and duty-free goods; it may also attract and retain repeat business as the result of offering the standby fare in the first place.

The ships that sail between Dover and Calais have for years offered discounted day trips, often for as little as £1 per person, and sometimes for free. This is in the near certainty that they will make additional sales of duty-free goods, gifts, meals and bar offerings which command excellent returns. These tickets are offered subject to availability so that payers of premium fares are accommodated first; the fundamental basis remains the same as in the airline example, that it is better to have the passenger on board at a discounted rate than not to have them at all.

Cost benefit analysis

Cost benefit analysis is a straightforward ready-reckoner for the assessment of initiatives (and especially public sector projects). It identifies those elements that require further or more detailed consideration in advance of implementation. All the costs and charges that could possibly be incurred in such a venture are identified and then set against all the values or benefits that will be accrued through its completion.

The following areas are considered.

1. Action choices, the definition and meaning of the costs and benefits to be assessed.
2. Short, medium and long termism: the time periods over which costs are to be incurred and over which the results and benefits are to accrue. This has important implications for the position of backers.
3. Values. These are to be seen from both economic and income generation points of view and also in wider terms: integral to cost benefit analyses of public policy are notions of the value of the quality and style of life and the contributors to this – recreational, social and educational services and other leisure amenities, for example.
4. Priorities. Related to values are specific priorities; what is to be tackled first, why, the logic for this; and the opportunity costs.

BOX 3.3 Initiatives

A commercial example is the concept of loss leadership. An example from public service is the concept of regional aid, whereby resources are put into a hitherto depressed area for the purpose of kick-starting or pump-priming the local economy.

5. Initiatives and their wider impact and implications. This is a strategic discussion of consequences, costs and benefits.
6. Risk and uncertainty, and the nature and content of this in the particular context.
7. Strategic aspects and overviews in the consideration of products, projects, services and initiatives, and the benefits that they are to bring with them; again, this may be seen in terms of pump-priming and other knock-on effects.
8. Relative valuation, especially of different costs and benefits at the times, frequency, intervals at which they occur and how these are to be reconciled.
9. The balance between income and expenditure related in particular to values that accrue to those on different incomes; their relative importance to given or actual products and services; spending and consumption patterns and priorities; and their relative importance to different public services.

A model for detailed background analysis and evaluation of both products and services, both public and private, can then be drawn up. The widest possible constructs are placed on the given initiative. The more nebulous concepts of social and intangible costs and benefits are assessed. It features in the discussions of any major undertaking (especially in public sector or public services) as part of the target-setting, feasibility and initiative design stages.

■ Value analysis

The purpose of conducting a value analysis is to establish where the elements and activities that add value to the organisation's offerings lie; and conversely, where value is lost or deducted. Value analysis may be applied to products, services and offerings; all the departments, divisions and functions of an organisation; strategic and operational elements; purchasing, supply, input, process, output and distribution; and may also be seen in simple or complex terms.

If it is successfully and effectively carried out this analysis is a most useful tool. It enables clarification of strategy. It also enables focus and attention to be switched to those areas where value is being lost, or not maximised. Above all, it is a likely indicator of the points in operation where profits and losses are to be made.

□ *The value chain*

The value chain breaks an organisation down into its component parts. This is in order to understand the source of, and behaviour of, costs and actual and potential sources of differentiation. It also isolates and identifies the building blocks by which an organisation creates an offering of value to customers and clients. The concept was devised by Michael Porter as part of the process of analysis of organisations' competitive advantage. This hypothesis is that an understanding of strategic strength and capability has to start with an identification of value activities. These were identified as follows (see Figure 3.11).

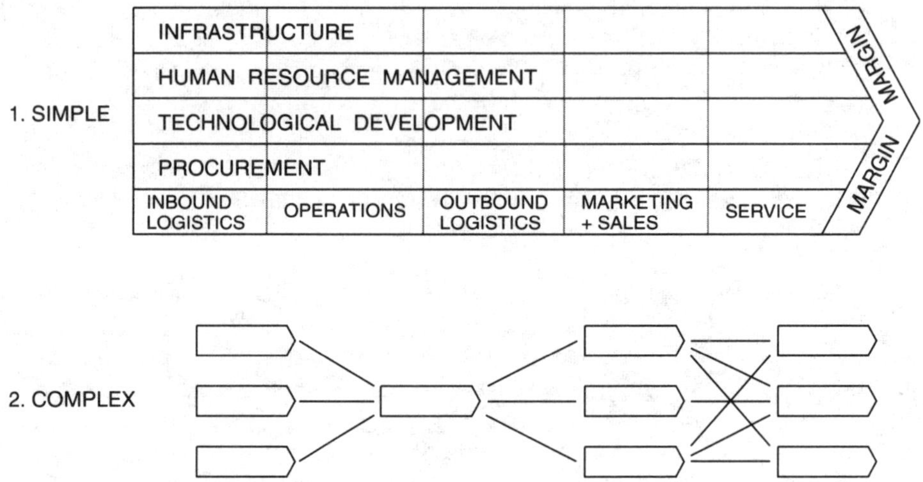

Figure 3.11 The value chain

Source: Porter (1981).

1. Inbound logistics: the activities concerned with receiving, storing and distributing components, supplies and materials that are to be used in the production of the output under consideration.
2. Operations which transform these various inputs into the product or service in question. This includes assembly, testing, packaging, production and assembly processes and procedures.
3. Outbound logistics: the collection, storage and distribution of the offerings in question to customers. For tangible products this includes warehousing, transport,

distribution, mail order, wholesaling. In the case of services, it is concerned with attracting people to the location at which the service is to be offered.

4. Marketing and sales: these provide the means whereby consumers are made aware of the product and service and are able to purchase it. This includes marketing and distribution activities.
5. Service: this covers all those activities which enhance or maintain the value of a product or service during the course of its useful life. This includes installation, repair, after-sales care, servicing, maintenance, the provision of spares and components, the capacity for overhauling; for such things as computer installations, it also includes training and familiarisation.

These primary activities are then seen in terms of the organisation's infrastructure: the basis, soundness and structure of the organisation in question; and also particular aspects of management and direction that Porter called the support activities (human resource management, technological development and advance, and procurement).

The value chain can be used at business unit level for clarity and accuracy. It can also be used in terms of the assessment of an organisation overall; of particular divisions and departments; and of a product process or activity. For greatest accuracy it should be used at the simplest possible level. It also gives a focus for organisation structuring and design, ensuring that any function, activity or system that is brought into play (whether primary or support) is seen from the point of view that what is to be done must be done with the overall purpose of adding value to the organisation's outputs.

The value chain can also be seen in terms of the complex model indicated in Figure 3.11. In such a case as this it is possible to trace the added value elements of a product right from the source of its primary resources and components through to its consumption by customers.

Finally, the model may usefully be translated into public service terms; measurement is in terms of effectiveness rather than profit.

□ *Other aspects of value analysis*

Value analysis takes place at a variety of levels. It involves addressing the ways in which value is added to and lost by organisations in the pursuit of their activities. It covers everything that is done: the primary activities of production, sales and marketing, and also the support functions of human resource, finance and administration. It also includes control functions, budgeting and cost centring.

Production and output activities are assessed for key and critical elements in the addition of value. It includes analysis of image, assembly, design, appearance, packaging and distribution. The product portfolio may also be analysed in this way, to assess the complexity of the value added process.

Manufacturing and distribution chains

This is where products and services are designed by one organisation, produced by another and sold on in blocks (wholesaled) to another and then offered for distribution to customers and markets by yet another.

Projects

A distinctive form of the whole process approach. These have to be analysed in terms of stated and desired outcomes and also in terms of the spin-offs and opportunities that accrue along the project implementation process.

Organisation analysis

This is carried out on a more general basis than the pursuit of activities indicated above. Its aim is a more fundamental assessment of wherein the value of the organisation lies, and which of its aspects and activities contribute to value and which do not. Reputation, confidence and expectations, past history and projected future are all considered. It is likely to include the establishment of points where interventions have to be made to increase the positive and mitigate the negative.

In conclusion, therefore, value is added at each stage of the process or at as many stages as possible if the product in question is to be successful. It is therefore clearly necessary to see each contribution to this in these terms. All functional and support activities should also be seen in this way; in particular this militates against the creation of expensive, extensive and sophisticated supervisory and control functions. Finally, the value added process should be seen in the context of the relationship between each of the range of products and offerings with the others; in many cases the offering of one enhances the value of the rest; very often also, one of the key components of the value added concept is in the range of offerings. Reducing the range of offerings just because one of them may not be particularly profitable often has a knock-on effect on the wider conception and total profitability.

BOX 3.4 Added Value: The Model Employer Concept

One of the reasons why The Body Shop is held in such high regard is that it is perceived to be both a model employer and a pillar of the community. It uses both of these in the pursuit of its direct business activities. The impression generated is therefore that this is an organisation which can be held in the highest possible regard. It is a model of corporate and social responsibility, setting the highest standards of ethical and honest business practice; it is also extremely profitable.

Each of these components adds to the total value of the organisation. If the organisation were to change any of these stances or the strong ethical image were to be lost there would be a dissipation and dilution of the nature of the business conducted and its profitability. It is noteworthy that whenever the business has had difficulties, the response has always been customer-focused rather than problem-oriented. This is all part of the process of maintaining and continuing these high standards. Without these, profitability would be lower.

■ Conclusion

Ideally the main outcome of these analyses is an information base for those responsible for organisational direction. This should consist of a full understanding of the wider environment and general pressures that exist, as well as the more specific aspects indicated.

It is important in the process of educating all managers (and especially top managers) to think strategically rather than operationally. All of the models indicated force managers to look beyond their operations, activities and areas of responsibility to the wider context, and from the short to the longer term. They also encourage creative and imaginative thinking and attitudes.

These activities also act as initial indicators of opportunities and threats. Areas of risk and uncertainty should start to become apparent, and points of stress and strain that may be created by following certain directions should also be indicated.

These activities are not ends in themselves. The key to successful strategic analyses lies in how the information gained is evaluated and used. Organisations must be able to translate this into effective activities based on their strengths of flexibility, dynamism, responsiveness and commitment.

■ Work assignments and discussion questions

1. Analyse the state of the market for petrol in the UK, using the SWOT and STEP models. What conclusions can be drawn from this? What are the likely effects on car companies, the oil companies, and consumers, of taxing motorway driving; doubling the price of crude oil; the production of medical evidence proving that both petrol and diesel fumes are a potentially lethal health hazard to car users?
2. Where would you place cigarettes in terms of product life cycle analysis, and on the Boston Matrix? What actions does this indicate for the companies concerned?

3. (a) Trace the progress of a bar of chocolate through the value chain, identifying the points at which value is seen to be added. What are the implications for a) consumers, b) manufacturers, c) distributors?
   (b) Repeat the exercise for the Boeing 747 (the Jumbo Jet).
4. What are the components of value for someone taking afternoon tea at the Ritz Hotel, London? What are the effects on this of (a) doubling the price and (b) opening the event up to coach parties of up to 50?

CHAPTER 4

Generic Strategies

Introduction

The purpose of this chapter is to introduce the basic idea that for any organisation to be successful, a distinctive strategic position must first be adopted.

The premise for this is that no organisation can serve an entire market, or sector, or segment for all time; that competition therefore exists; and that customers and clients always have a choice (at the very least, the choice to refuse or reject). Organisations have therefore to decide which parts of the market they are to serve and establish a distinctive basis as to how this is to be achieved.

Three distinctive positions are identified:

- cost leadership – the gaining of advantage through being the most efficient operator and competing in the market on the price advantage that is available as the result of this;
- focus or specialisation – the offering of a distinctive and often narrow range of products in a particular niche;
- differentiation – in which the basis of business success is founded on marketing and advertising, and image building activities, the purpose of which is to set the product apart from others in the sector and maintain the ability to sell at a premium price.

These are then related to:

- incremental approaches, or the gradual development of strategy;
- radical and transformatory approaches;
- offensive and defensive positions.

Models

Michael E. Porter

Porter (1985) defines three generic strategy models: cost leadership, focus, and differentiation. He argues that it is a prerequisite for long-term profitability and success that organisations choose their basic generic strategy from among this group. It enables an initial focus for organisation activities to be achieved. Too many organisations do not do this and therefore end up without any initial essential clarity of direction.

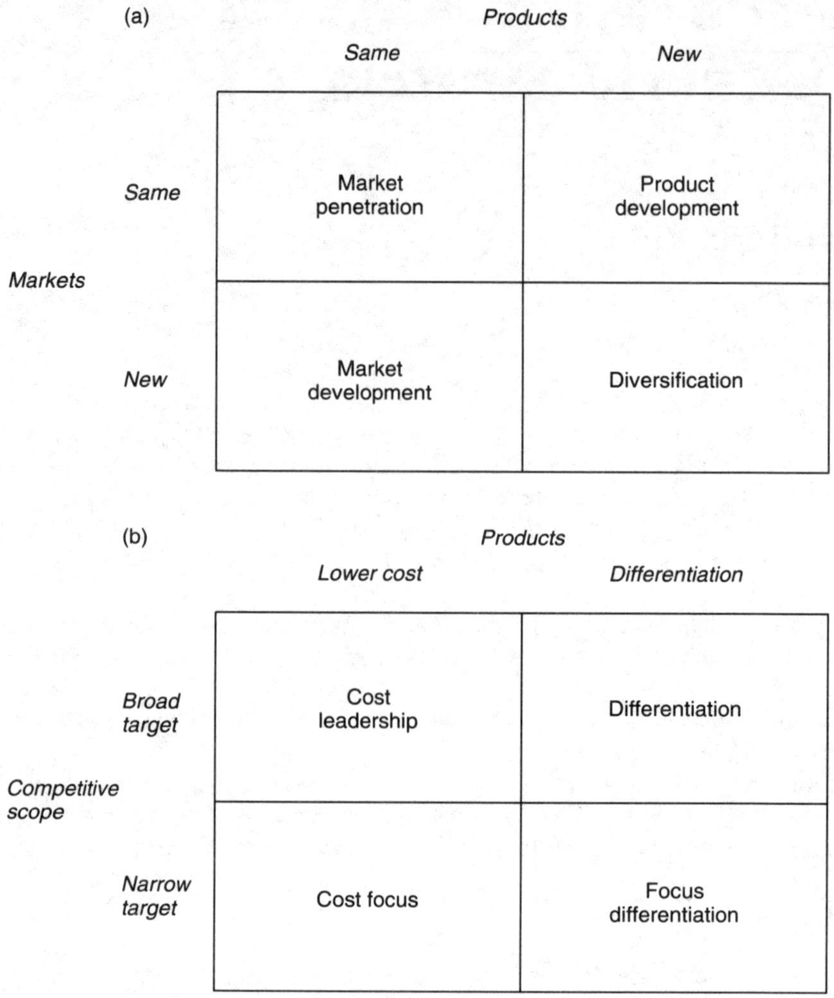

A simple illustration of the product/market expansion and diversification potentially available, and the strategic starting points relevant to these.

Figure 4.1 Product/market matrix of H. I. Ansoff

☐ *Cost*

Cost leadership is where the organisation concentrates on being the low-cost operator in its sector. In order to be able to do this it seeks out all sources of cost advantage. Organisation, production, marketing and distribution structures and strategies are all geared up to this key purpose. These firms are likely

Table 4.1 Contrasting views of the market

Issue	*Product-led*	*Market-led*
Definition of the market	Markets are arenas of competition where corporate resources can be profitably employed	Markets are shifting patterns of customer requirements and needs which can be served in many ways
Orientation to market environment	Strengths and weaknesses relative to competition: • cost position • ability to transfer experience • market coverage	Customer perceptions of competitive alternatives: • match of product features and customer needs • positioning
Identification of market segments	Looks for cost discontinuities	Emphasises similarity of buyer responses to market efforts
Identification of market niches to serve	Exploits new technologies, cost advantages, and competitors' weaknesses	Finds unsatisfied needs, unresolved problems, or changes in customer requirements and capabilities
Timescales	Fixed, stable	Fluid, flexible
Behavioural aspects	Reputation, image, confidence	Empathy, satisfaction
Competitive advantage	Expertise, quality	Flexibility, responsiveness

to offer standard, adequate and medium-quality products and services in markets where these are the key characteristics required. The extent of the firms' success depends on the levels of price that can be commanded in the pursuit of this. Premium price levels clearly lead to the prospect of high margins and high levels of financial success and performance. Moreover, if firms can achieve and sustain cost leadership, they will be good-to-high financial performers in the sector in question, provided that prices around the industry average can be sustained.

□ *Differentiation*

Differentiation strategies are those which seek a uniqueness or identity for their products in ways that are widely valued by buyers *other than price advantage*. This involves conducting marketing, promotions and public relations activities to give the organisation and its offerings a distinctive identity. Firms that can achieve and sustain differentiation are likely to be above-average performers in their sectors provided that the price premium more than covers the costs and charges incurred in 'being different'.

□ *Focus*

'Focus strategy' is the phrase used when the organisation concentrates on a segment or segments within a sector and seeks to serve them to the exclusion of the rest of the segment. This requires a basic concentration on identifying, anticipating and meeting the needs of the sector and ensuring that this is accurately completed. Focus is then usually based on product quality and certainty and continuity of relationship. (see Figure 4.2).

Both differentiation and focus strategies are discussed more fully below.

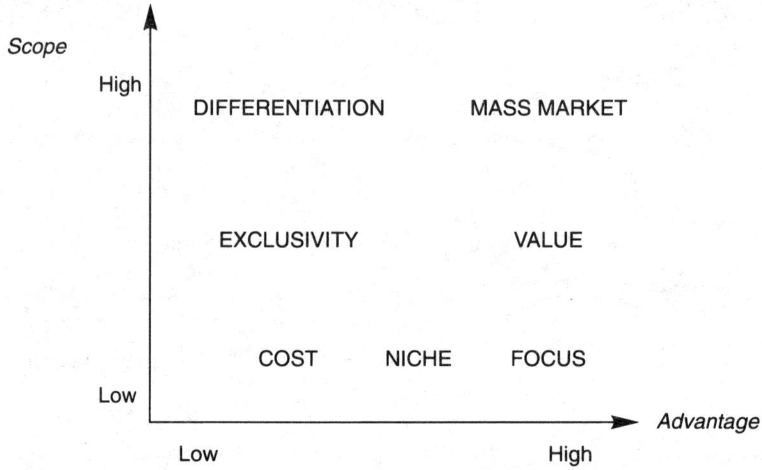

This is a version of Porter's generic strategies of cost leadership, focus and differentiation. It relates these in turn to the nature and scope of the market envisaged.

Porter's hypothesis is that one only of the generic strategies and positions should be chosen, and to fail to do this leaves the organisation with a lack of clarity of purpose, or unpositioned.

Figure 4.2 Competitive scope: competitive advantage model

■ Gerry Johnson and Kevan Scholes

Johnson and Scholes (1993) identified eight different points against two variables of **price** and **perceived added value.** They identify three strategy types within this.

□ *Price-based strategies*

Price-based strategies are those in which the leading determinant is price (route 1), but which may also have a value element (route 2 and 3). In routes 2 and 3 there is a cost imperative over the medium to long term. It is generally very unlikely that adequate margins would be achieved over such a period. As is indicated in Figure 4.3, there is a basic necessity to be cost leader in order to become involved successfully in such a strategy.

	Strategy	Needs/risks	
1.	Low price/low added value	Likely to be segment-specific	COST
2.	Low price	Price wars; need to be cost leader	
3.	Hybrid	Low-cost base; investment in technology and differentiation	DIFFERENTIATION
4.	Differentiation	Perceived added value	
5.	with price premium	Added value beats premium	
	• without price premium	Sectoral added value giving price premium	
	• Focus differentiation		
6.	Increased price/standard value	Risk loss of market share	FAILURE
7.	Increased price/low value	Monopoly	
8.	Low value/standard price	Immediate threat to market share	

Figure 4.3 Strategy, price and perceived added value

Source: Johnson and Scholes (1993).

□ *Value-added strategies*

Value-added strategies are those in which organisation resources and activities are concentrated in producing uniqueness or distinction in the offerings, as in the discussion of the Porter generic strategies above. This is achieved either through product/service improvement or through marketing activities.

The balance of price advantage with high perceived value added is called a hybrid strategy. They identify both the low-cost base and the capacity to invest and reinvest in sustaining the low price level and the differentiation activities as prerequisites to pursuing this strategy. Focused differentiation is the ability to concentrate on the value added elements and to charge a premium price for doing this (this compares with Porter's definition of differentiation of strategies).

□ *Failure*

Finally, failure strategies are defined. This is where situations are identified that cannot sustain normal levels of activities except where a monopoly or substantial extent of market domination exists. Even in such cases, these approaches are likely to be sustainable only while other operators bring out substitute products and alternative offerings, or where customers find alternative sources of satisfaction. In extreme cases – for example where there is a state monopoly and where there may be no possibility of normal commercial competition – pressure on the undertaking is likely to come from vested and public interest groups, and other lobbies. There may also be political questions.

Some initial conclusions may be drawn.

The generic strategy approach enables an initial assessment of likely directions, activities, investments, returns and margins to be identified, discussed and evaluated. It ensures that an initial defined and agreed position is taken up; this is the cornerstone of the strategy, the point from which progress is subsequently to be made. It indicates the extent of resource commitment that is implied: a high value or value added strategy clearly indicates a continuing commitment to differentiation activities and after-sales service, for example.

■ Cost and price

In practice, very few organisations in Western markets and economies are able to compete purely on price. There are nearly always other considerations, however minimal (especially time, volume, quality and value). Customers will not pay even the lowest of prices for products and services that do not afford basic levels of satisfaction. However, it is often highly profitable to charge premium prices for high quality and value, provided that customers are convinced that this is indeed what is on offer in return for the relatively high level of charges.

BOX 4.1 Differentiated Alternatives

This practice is a key feature of the food, clothing, car and consumer goods sectors. Supermarkets offer the same generic product range at a variety of different prices; the main difference is in the presentation and packaging (see the Tesco Value example in Box 4.13). Otherwise, the purpose is to provide a source of satisfaction to all customers rather than a limited range of products that might cause some people to go elsewhere.

Car companies produce both a standard specification and ranges of optional extras and accessories to get over this issue. The basic model comes at one price. Extra is charged for the accessories. The companies also bring out 'limited editions' (for example, the Ford Fiesta Festival, or the Peugeot 106 Key West and Key Largo). In each case the purpose is to generate additional sales without giving existing customers the feeling of having been somehow cheated because they bought a particular offering at a standard or premium price.

Coca Cola is packaged in different ways for different outlets. It is sold on draught from five and ten gallon drums in bars. It is sold in cans and multi-packs in bars also, and in shops and supermarkets. It is also packaged in 1-litre, 2-litre, 3-litre and 5-litre plastic bottles in shops and supermarkets. It is sold in half-litre and litre measures in plastic cups by McDonalds as part of their range of offerings. The price in the UK varied (199g) from 20p per litre (in the 3-litre supermarket bottle) to £3.00 per litre in public houses and bars (up to £1.80 per pint). In each case, because of the differentiation and packaging, the price is happily paid by consumers.

The value and quality elements may not be reduced unless the product is being taken into other sectors and niches. This clearly does happen from time to time. It is much more usual to bring out a differentiated alternative (see Box 4.1) or to engage in sales and discounts, rather than overtly reducing the value and quality of the offering in any way. This involves re-presentation and repackaging as well as the product itself. If customers perceive that they are receiving a reduced value offering they will tend to reject it.

At the other end of the spectrum, however, there are quality and value levels which are often not warranted. Customers gain a greater satisfaction from buying products that are of adequate, good, high or even excellent quality levels but which nevertheless clearly are not perfect. Any organisation that strives for the position of top-quality operator in the sector or to be the producer of near-perfect products for it must satisfy itself that it can recoup the costs incurred in the level of prices and charges that it then makes. It must satisfy itself that the sector is willing to sustain this level of quality.

The foundation of any successful organisation strategy lies in the initial choice and strength of the generic position. Everything else stems from this. The overall purpose is the creation and sustenance of a competitive and profitable position over the medium to long term, and this can only be achieved if everyone is clear about the initial direction.

Successful organisations also draw from elements of each of the points indicated. It may not be possible to be the cost leader, for example, but this does not prevent all organisations from seeking cost advantages and improvements wherever they may be found. Similarly, if an organisation is the cost leader, this does not prevent it from seeking differentiation, value or quality advantages.

■ Differentiation strategies

Differentiation is achieved through a combination of marketing, promotion, presentation and design with the purpose of giving the required image, properties, benefits, confidence and utilisation. Potential customers have therefore to be attracted towards the offerings under consideration and away from alternatives (the providers of which will be conducting the same processes).

For example, it is well documented (Clark, 1988) that smokers of cigarettes exhibit fierce brand loyalty, and yet cannot distinguish their brand from others without having the packets to choose from or the marque stamped on the cigarette. Coca Cola drinkers also retain loyalty to the brand in spite of the fact it is very difficult to tell different brands apart without the distinctive packaging. In these and similar cases, differentiation concentrates on reinforcing the brand loyalty as customers do not buy the products unseen. (Indeed, instead of asking for cigarettes over the counter customers ask for Benson & Hedges or Malboro, or whatever their particular brand is.)

Effective differentiation therefore attracts the attention of the potential customers and responds to their wants and needs (real, perceived or stated). If the customer 'needs' quality then this becomes the selling point of the product. If the customer 'needs' association with some preferred form of lifestyle, then this has to be reflected in the ways in which the product is offered. If the customers 'need' convenience, speed of delivery, ready access or easy payment terms, then in each case they will be satisfied only if these are produced. This also applies in transient, fastmoving, fashionable and faddish sectors. Special patterns, marques and logos on clothing, cars and household goods are distinctive – different – and therefore command interest and activity for a period. The difficulty is in sustaining this for any period of time in relation to a given offering and in comparison with other organisations making equivalent offerings on the same basis.

■ Differentiation and price

Porter (1985) makes the point that the mark of true differentiation is the ability to command a premium (that is top) price for the uniqueness (real or perceived) achieved. This is often gained over the short to medium term, and followed by a period of divestment when the items become obsolete. There is a more general price advantage when a sufficiently strong generic identity has been achieved. The customer base becomes stable and predictable over the medium term, and therefore there is a price premium commanded.

BOX 4.2 Differentiation and Price

The premise of Porter is criticised on the basis that it is possible to compete on both differentiation and price. It is certainly true that in some sectors there is a great range of different offerings of what is essentially the same commodity.

Example: Butter and Margarine

Butter and margarine are aids to cooking or else pleasant additions to the eating of bread, cakes, biscuits. The ranges of butters and margarine products are heavily differentiated. They are given distinctive packaging, marketing and promotional campaigns on the basis that according to which brand is chosen the purchaser will become sunny, happy, healthy, sexy, wealthy, well-dressed, stylish, thin or suntanned. There is also a range of prices that the consumer may choose to pay, and is therefore a balance of price, image, association and choice to be struck.

Porter is, however, clearly extremely strong when a sectoral view is taken. Where the butter or margarine simply represents an item in a supermarket shopping basket or trolley then differentiation is effectively achieved at the point of supermarket choice and not in relation to the individual product. Supermarkets therefore compete on a basis of differentiation and not price (whatever the slogan used by Sainsbury's 'Good food costs less at Sainsbury's', may actually say) in the pursuit of, and retention of, their customer bases. Price becomes a consideration only if the total grocery bill rises to an unacceptable level or is perceived to do so; and, when this occurs, it is used as a marketing (differentiation) aid by the supermarkets.

It is also necessary for differentiation strategies to concentrate on harder and more performance-related elements. Much of this has come about again as the result of the Japanese car, electrical and consumer goods revolutions of the period since 1970. These brought products to the Western consumer that were durable and reliable: the radio cassette, record or compact disc player that gave a high-quality sound; the car that started and travelled to its destination in all weathers. This caused the indigenous providers to have a hard look at the emerging fact that, given the choice between a stylish product and one that actually worked, the consumer would tend to choose the latter.

There are again behavioural considerations, especially in relation to reliability and confidence. Much of this relates to guarantees, delivery times, after-sales service and replacement and maintenance issues; and also to depreciation, obsolescence and length of useful and beneficial life. Consumers want to be well regarded for owning an item and to feel good about it themselves.

■ Focus strategies

These are based on the decision to operate in stated specific sectors and segments and niches within an industry. The emphasis is then placed either on cost focus, in which case the organisation sets out to achieve cost advantage in the sector in question; or differentiation focus, in which case it seeks a differentiated advantage in it.

☐ *Location*

Focus in this context is any point of concentration or specialisation. It may be a geographical area. Small and medium-sized companies in the building industry often do this, serving the building needs of a locality rather than travelling further afield in search of what might turn out to be a more profitable activity. The advantage that is gained and sustained is in the form of local reputation and confidence. The organisation makes a profitable living on this basis. Its repeat business comes from satisfied customers. Its new business comes on the basis of the local reputation thus generated.

☐ *Specialisation*

Component manufacture is another form of focus or specialisation. The items manufactured are then sold on to those organisations responsible for assembly of the finished products. The great opportunity with this type of focus is that as long as the product is of good quality and price and the supplying organisation is also reliable, in a stable market, steady-state and predictable levels of activity can be achieved profitably. The threat, on the other hand, is where one or more of these elements is missing. This is especially true of the stable market element: the supplying organisation may be both efficient and effective but is nevertheless dependent upon the continuing viability of the customer organisation. It may also be susceptible to market entry by organisations that operate in similar niches or that have similar technology and that have additional cost, delivery or reliability advantages.

If operating in this way, awareness of this is essential. Early warning systems are required so that any destabilisation that does occur is well signalled in advance. Organisations must also be aware of alternative outlets for the products in question, and alternative uses for their technology (ideally those that could be activated quickly if necessary).

☐ *Population and product concentration*

Other focus strategies concentrate on narrow and distinctive sectors: for example, the extremes of the price, quality and income brackets. Top-quality and exclusive niches exist in groceries (Fortnum & Mason); cars (Rolls-Royce); clothing (Armani); and air travel (Concorde). High-quality niches exist at levels below these in the same areas. Good quality groceries are sold by Marks & Spencer; high-quality cars are manufactured and sold by Mercedes and BMW; high-quality clothing is manufactured and sold by Gucci; and air travel under the auspices of exclusive travel groups, such as Kuoni, or in the first-class sectors of the major airlines. In all these cases, competitive advantage arises through concentration on quality and exclusivity.

At the bottom of the price, quality and exclusivity spectrum, niches also exist. Again, these are not mass markets but rather have their own form of exclusivity. Wholesale clubs, cash and carry operations and warehouse clubs in the food and fast moving consumer goods sectors (such as Costco) have opened up niches based on cost focus. Other examples of these are groceries at Kwik Save; cars by Lada and Skoda; clothing from Woolworths; air travel via discounted sales.

Success in any of these areas depends on the accuracy of focus and correct identification of the properties of the particular segments and niches.

BOX 4.3 One-Product Strategies (1)

This is a form of focus strategy whereby the organisation in question puts all of its eggs in one basket and pins its entire future prosperity on its faith in one product. Such approaches have been, and continue to be, spectacularly successful in certain areas. However, there are caveats to be considered. As stated in the text, the organisation that is wholly or heavily dependent upon one organisation to take the entire volume of a product, or a dominant volume of a product, is always at risk from a new entrant which can satisfy the customer organisation on all fronts and beat the existing supplier on one or more key elements. As an example of this Marks & Spencer insist absolutely on the quality standards of the products supplied to them. The pursuit and expectation of quality is the driving force of their key customer base. Suppliers that fall short on the quality side (and also on the regularity and reliability criteria) are not used again. Marks & Spencer, and all such organisations, are continually prospecting for new suppliers and sources of high-quality and reliable products regularly available. They will turn to these if let down by an existing supplier.

Some one-product strategies have come in other forms. The model T Ford was the world's first mass-produced car. It was the only model and came in only one colour: black. It was functional and available and it was the first of its kind. It transformed the automobile sector. However, it was not an end in itself, and when other makers came into the sector with different styles and designs of cars, the Ford company had to follow suit and extend its product range. In this case the one-product strategy was just the start.

The Coca Cola organisation was a one-product organisation for much longer than Ford. Even today the original product, 'the real thing' that comes in its distinctive red packaging with white lettering, is by far the organisation's most dominant product. There are alternative offerings, however: Cherry Cola, Diet Coke, Lilt and Fanta. The organisation also issues licences to manufacture to other soft drinks companies across the world, and commissions and sells clothing, fashion items, accessories and ornaments that carry its distinctive style and logo.

The Pepsi company has an equivalent approach and range, and has also recently diversified into low-calorie and diet drinks and high energy fitness/designer drinks.

The Guinness company relied heavily on sales of its dark extra stout beer for over 200 years. Again, however, it has diversified recently in this case by means of acquisition. It (controversially) acquired the Distillers Company the whisky organisation. It also owns Louis Vuitton Moet Hennessy, a French luxury goods, drinks and leisure group. It also has its own hotel chain and publishing companies.

Organisations that tread the one-product strategy have to be certain of continued confidence. Even organisations and brands as powerful and distinctive as those illustrated and discussed here have felt it necessary to increase the range of offerings, outlets and means of production in order to maintain their position. Furthermore, while the single products remain extremely powerful in their particular fields, each of the companies illustrated undertakes extensive marketing and promotional activity in their support.

BOX 4.4 One-Product Strategies (2): Defence Equipment

An illustration of the problems that can suddenly be faced by organisations that follow single-product or highly-focused strategies is to be found in the defence sectors of the West in the 1990s.

During the period since the Second World War and throughout the whole of the duration of the Cold War, the defence sector was of critical importance. As such, organisations that operated in it did so on the basis of stability and certainty that the governments of the West would be both receptive of their existing offerings and eager to commission new products.

At the end of the Cold War and with the collapse of the USSR many of these organisations suddenly found themselves without markets. Shipyards that specialised in the design and building of warships had to find new outlets for their expertise. So did those that built military aircraft or vehicles, radar and electronic guidance systems, munitions and ordnance. In all these cases the casting around for post-Cold War civilian and commercial markets has led to closures. In the commercial sectors in which they may have had transferable or related expertise, these were found to be either overstocked or else dominated by the new production techniques and cost advantages of the Pacific rim.

BOX 4.5 One-Product Strategies (3): Quality at McDonald's

The McDonald's fast food company has built its global reputation on the basis that wherever in the world the outlet is, the customer can be absolutely certain of the product range and quality on offer. This extends not only to the food and drinks but also to the ambience, cleanliness, speed and quality of service. It is true that the menu offered by McDonald's does change little by little over the years; there are also regional variations. However, the basic premise of quality, value and cleanliness remains; people are drawn into the organisation's outlets on this basis.

As with the one-product strategies illustrated in the first of these boxes, however, McDonald's engage in extensive promotional and advertising activities in order to support this. This advertising is a combination of ensuring a heavily localised flavour together with the universal value and quality that is on offer.

The generic basis may now be broadened.

Incremental strategies

The view of strategy as being incremental is popular with those who argue a rational approach to business and public service. The reasoning is that a genuine long-term strategy is actually impossible to achieve, given the sophisticated structure of organisations, their complexities and systems, and the turbulence and instability of markets.

The starting point for future strategies is therefore the position of the organisation today. The organisation moves forward in small steps or increments. As each of these steps is successful the next step becomes apparent. If a mistake is made it is easy to retrace the step and seek other directions from the previous position. The status quo and levels of performance are both taken as 'correct'. If costs are reduced or if profits have gone up in relation to last year, this is a 'good' general measure of performance. If costs have risen or profits declined in relation to the previous period this becomes 'a cause for concern'.

The opportunities arise from the fact that the organisation is moving slowly enough to recognise and evaluate those situations that present themselves as opportunities before rushing in headlong.

BOX 4.6 Chess

Competitive business is often compared to the game of chess.

In the game of chess your purpose is to check-mate your opponent's king. It is possible to work out in general terms how to do this and this remains the objective throughout the game. Your strategy will be moderated along the way, as responses have to be made to the moves of your opponent which are designed to check-mate your own king. It is also possible to enter into the game of chess with a general knowledge of how to play but no game plans or moves; what is to be done is dependent entirely upon responding to the initiatives of the opponent. Bureaucratic and sophisticated organisations may take equivalent views of their strategic position: that is, they will do nothing but respond to the initiatives of others in the field. If another player has a spectacular success then the incrementalist organisation will hope to have sufficient flexibility and resources available to follow it into the sphere of activities. It therefore adopts the follow-my-leader or second-in-the-field type of approach.

The consequences of the incremental approach centre on the fact that no genuine clarity of purpose is ever actually achieved. The purpose of the organisation is 'to see what happens'. The purpose of those working in it becomes to empty their in-trays, respond to orders, meet delivery schedules and bring new products on to the scene, but without any true understanding of the direction, rationale or logic behind them. Organisations that follow this line never assess whether they are making best, medium or worst use of their resources, but rather 'do what they do'. At no stage does the organisation truly articulate its purpose in terms of what it should be doing, why it should be doing it, how it should be doing it and what the range of outcomes could possibly be as the result of this.

The analogy of the chess game is inappropriate also. Even if a truly competitive situation could be found to exist between two organisations only (which is highly debatable in the first place), under no circumstances would they put all their resources on public display and respond in kind to each other's moves. To pursue the analogy for what it is worth as soon as one organisation found itself in trouble on the chess board it would find itself some football boots, boxing gloves or a racing car or even walk away from the chess game rather than continue in a struggle that it was certain to lose. In sophisticated differentiated markets the games analogy simply does not hold up. Business and organisation strategies require much more thought and expertise.

Increasingly, however, those organisations that have spent years following incrementalist approaches are having their patterns of behaviour, structures and norms shaken up. This is particularly prevalent in social services, central and local government, and health and education sectors where both strategic and operational emphases are being placed on efficiency and effectiveness, priorities and targets, rather than generalised offerings. Multi-national public limited company organisations are also becoming much more aware. The global banking sector, for example, has shaken out hundreds of thousands of functional and functionary jobs in the 1980s and 1990s.

However, it is important to acknowledge the extent and prevalence of current activities as influences on future strategy. Where organisations operate in these ways, moves to a more focused and directed strategic approach may take a long while, and need to be accompanied also by major restructuring and culture changes. These influences may be listed as follows.

1. The organisation's current range of activities and the ways in which these are carried out, technology used, controls that are used, the management style, the

budgeting processes and human resource, staff management and industrial relations approaches.

2. The size, complexity and sophistication of the organisation structure, its chains of command, communication and decision-making process, administration and support functions.
3. The prevailing ways of working in the organisation, its networks, its politics and the extent of the influence of particular managers and individuals within these ways of working. There should also be consideration of the balance and mix of what is done and the ways in which it is done. In many such organisations progress is only made as the result of negotiations and trade-offs between powerful and influential individuals and groups. Progress is therefore effectively limited to the extent to which such persons allow it to be made.
4. The attitudes and views of the organisation's backers and current client base, all of whom may be quite happy and satisfied with what is being achieved, and above all (as long as they are good) with the margins being achieved. This may also extend in more general terms to the communities in which the organisation exists. Indeed, its relative stability and overt lack of dynamism may give off very positive messages of comfort and confidence to all those who come into contact with it.
5. There is also a general perception in such situations that as long as the organisation is steady and stable it cannot be doing very much wrong (otherwise it would not be steady and stable). Until extremely recently in the UK, again, civil and public services, local government and the National Health Service used this as part of their strategy of attracting people to come and work for them. Those joining them did so on the basis that they forwent the excitement, dynamism and volatility of working in the private sector (and also, to an extent, the higher wage levels), in return for delivering a worthwhile service of value to the community in a steady-state organisation over a long period of time. A major attraction within this context was the job for life that was normally offered to those who came into the sector and the pension that was offered once retirement age was achieved.

There is therefore no doubt of the attractions of the comfort and orderly elements implied in this approach. They must, however, be balanced with genuine capability in a business sphere that is globally turbulent. Neither must structures, politics and current activities become the organisation's reasons for being. In cases such as these the great danger is that there is resistance to change or progress not because it is bad for the organisation but because it is bad for the status quo.

■ Radical strategies

These occur where the organisation decides to transform its ways of working and its total expectations of itself; it may also have decided to transform its image, markets and customer base. There may be a variety of reasons why this occurs. At the extreme there may be the need to escape from a sector or segment that has suddenly died or lost its profitability. This happened, for example, to large parts of the defence industries of the West following the end of the Cold War and the collapse of the USSR. It may also result from an organisation's realisation that the resources being used could be better used in a new or different sector; or re-organised to put them to better and more effective use in the service of the same sector; or radically to redesign the processes and structures used, although the outputs remain the same.

BOX 4.7 Radion

The radical approach may also apply to all aspects of the organisation's business. For example, Reckitt & Coleman's Radion washing powder and liquid was launched in the UK in the late 1980s. The strategy used to promote and advertise it focused on the role of the woman in washing the clothes, her need to get them clean and smelling nice for her husband and children, and her satisfaction in doing this. Moreover, the product was packaged in a bright red/orange container. It ran counter to the prevalent ethical notions of equality and mutual concern, and placed the woman firmly in the position of family servant. The bright garish packaging was in direct contrast to the green and environmentally concerned images being portrayed throughout the UK at the time. The product was spectacularly successful. Eighteen months after its launch it was the third best selling soap powder and detergent in the UK (after Persil and Daz).

This approach is also used in the management of the human resource and the associated style required. Japanese organisations coming to work in the West have brought with them notions of conformity, expectation, equality and single status at the workplace, and have demonstrated excellent results in relation to their Western counterparts. As a result of this experience and knowledge, many organisations are now addressing their highly complex and sophisticated human resource and industrial relations policies, procedures and structures with a view to simplification and streamlining, making them easier to understand and operate.

The willingness or need to adopt new production output or managerial technology may also lead to radical strategic approaches. Alongside this there are invariably staff management, human resource and industrial relations needs, and specific issues of retraining, re-organisation and restructuring. These may also occur as part of a general refocusing and re-organisation, or culture change, possibly in response to changes in the market or in order to remain competitive.

BOX 4.8 Effects of Radical Strategies

The excellence studies (e.g. of Peters and Waterman, Kanter, Lessem, and Goldsmith and Clutterbuck) are sprinkled with examples of where a radical approach to strategy has transformed the business of organisations. Peters in particular is fond of quoting successful examples from the steel and textile sectors which have succeeded and prospered way beyond the sectoral norms and expectations. The US Bethlehem Steel Company, for example, has 40 per cent of its share equity owned by the staff. Nissan USA is quoted as having an absenteeism rate of 0.25 per cent, and the Bethlehem Company 0.5 per cent. In all cases this has been achieved alongside internal strategies designed to gain the maximum commitment and involvement from the staff working in the organisations.

In general, any radical approach has to be seen in the highly rational context of results that are to be achieved. There are also specific issues related to the management of change (see Chapter 11). Staff, customers and clients, the business sphere, and the community must all be comfortable and confident in the proposed strategy. Furthermore it must be capable of integration into supply, distribution and value chains.

■ Offensive and defensive strategies

These terms are used to describe the play/response activities undertaken by organisations operating in the same sector and their competitive and strategic relations with each other.

□ *Offensive strategies*

These are undertaken in the pursuit of extending market share or dominance at the expense of other players in the sector. They may also be contemplated as one of the responses to be given to other offensive strategies in the sector: player A seeks to gain market at the expense of player B, so player B attacks player C, for example. The main features of offensive strategies are distinctive and aggressive marketing campaigns and the discrediting of the offerings of other players in the sector. Such strategies arise for a variety of reasons. They may be the result of overcapacity in the market or in response to new entrants or potential new entrants and alternative offerings. They may also be the result of a more general sectoral lack or loss of stability. Others arise again where a new player or potential entrant sees an opportunity (as with the Virgin Group in the international airline sector). Still others arise where a radically different approach to the existing sector is contemplated: for example, take-away food services have been transformed by the arrival of McDonald's, Burger King and Kentucky Fried Chicken.

They may also arise as the result of technology, volume or cost advantage, or from the control of supplies and raw materials, or outlets and the means of distribution in a sector.

□ *Defensive strategies*

These are undertaken in response to offensives by other players in the sector. In general, they involve one or more of the following. They may respond to the offensive activities of other players: for example, if the quality of one's operation is called into question the defensive response is to rebuild any loss of reputation for quality. They may also concentrate on other distinctive elements of their own offering. They may attack the attacker, either in kind by turning defence into offence, or on another front. They may attack the other players in the sector. The genesis of aggressive public relations and marketing campaigns may thus also be defensive as well as offensive.

Defensive strategies may also lead to price wars where, for example, the offensive option taken by player A to reduce her price leads to a larger cut by B which may lead to a further cut by A and then a further cut by B, and so on. This may in turn lead to market flooding or dumping, dependent upon the size and the capacities of the organisations involved. Charges like this have been levelled at oil producers at various stages over the period since 1977. The charge also has been made by the Western automobile and electrical goods sectors in response to the strategies of Nissan, Toyota, Mitsubishi, Panasonic, Sony and Sharp.

BOX 4.9 Defensive Strategy

One defensive response is not to respond. This strategy was adopted by the Republican incumbent President, Richard Nixon, during the 1971 US Presidential election campaign, in which he consistently refused to respond to criticisms of his administration made by his Democrat opponent, George McGovern. The Republican position was effectively not to campaign at all, but to allow their opponents to blow themselves out. It was highly effective and successful, and Nixon was returned to office.

Elsewhere organisations may ignore the offensive insofar as they continue to concentrate on their own strategy. If this is followed it is essential that a watching brief at least is kept on the offensive moves in question. Price-cutting may shift the whole range of margins hitherto available in the sector. Imaginative marketing may transform the image of the sector. Organisations must positively arrive at the judgement that they can maintain their position in spite of the offensive rather than merely hoping that they can. See Figure 4.4.

PRODUCT QUALITY

1. SPLIT LEATHER FOR RESISTANCE AND PROTECTION
2. POLYPAG FOR SOFTNESS, LIGHTNESS AND VENTILATION
3. ASYMMETRICAL EYELET STAY FOR THE BEST MAINTENANCE
4. SOFT PROTECTION WITH P.U. PIEDE FOR COMFORT FOR ACHILLES' HEEL
5. SPLIT LEATHER BACK COUNTER WITH CHEMI SHEET FOR HEEL MAINTENANCE
6. P.V.C. HEEL CUP FOR STABILIZATION
7. E.V.A. MIDSOLE FOR SHOCK-ABSORBING
8. THE RESISTANT RUBBER OUTSOLE OF HIGH DEGREE OF ABRASION
9. REMOVABLE CUP INSOLE FOR THE BEST CLEANNESS AND FITNESS
10. CALIFORNIA CONSTRUCTION FOR THE MAXIMUM OF FLEXIBILITY AND COMFORT

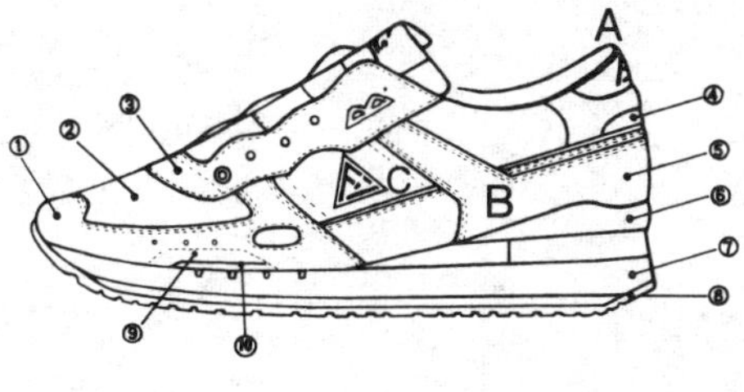

PRODUCT VALUE

A DISTINCTIVE STYLING

B COLOUR SCHEME AND MIXTURE

C LABEL AND LOGO
COMFORT; FASHION; COORDINATED WITH OTHER OFFERINGS.

PRICE RANGE: (UK) £4.99 (SUPERMARKETS)
£149.99 (REEBOK LEISURE FOR LADIES)

Figure 4.4 Price, quality, value: the trainer

In some sectors the offensive, defensive interaction is virtually entirely integrated into the differentiation and marketing processes. Thus, one supermarket chain may respond to price-cutting by a competitor by opening up a coffee shop or petrol outlet. One banking group may remove all charges from the personal accounts of its individual customers, while the others respond by doubling the number of cashpoints, therefore competing on convenience and not charges; or by doubling the limits on its credit cards, and therefore competing on behavioural rather than cost grounds.

Key factors

However the generic position is viewed, key strategic elements become apparent. These are price, time, quality, volume and value, and the ways in which they interact. Each is present in any product, service or activity although many clearly place their emphasis on one or two of these. However, people will not, for example, buy an item on price alone if there is no quality attached; and neither will they wait forever for the item of lowest price or highest quality to become available. This mix is therefore a function of the nature of demand in particular markets and sectors; and of the ways in which the organisations involved determine how these are to be supplied (see Figure 4.5).

In general, the result must be the ability to charge prices and price ranges that both cover costs incurred in the production of offerings and also make some contribution towards the other business expenses and charges.

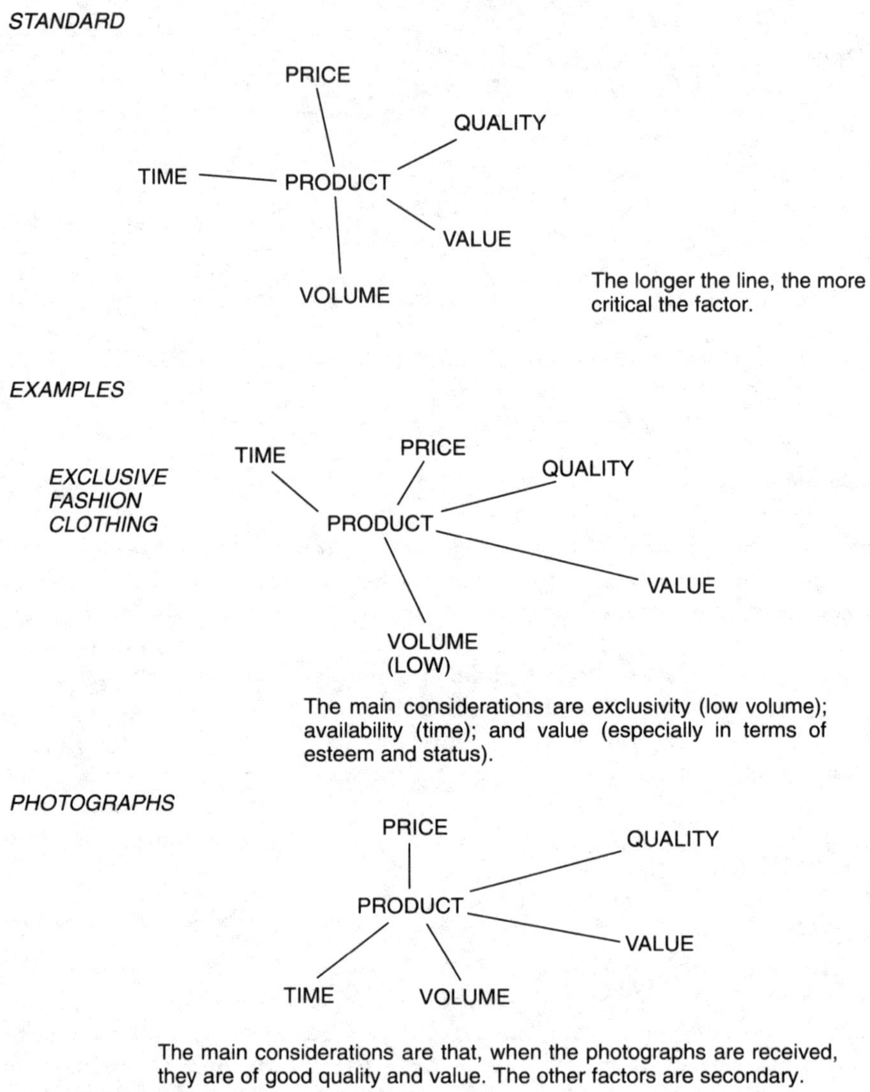

Figure 4.5 Critical factor mix

This mixture must also ensure that levels of income are maintained, consolidated and improved, and this comes about from understanding the patterns of spending and consumption of the customer base.

It is also necessary to understand the effects and opportunities of price and quality variations, and the shifts in the nature and volume of activities and consumption as these occur.

Pricing policies and strategies are therefore to be subject to the same rigorous analysis and evaluation as other aspects of the strategy process.

BOX 4.10 Price, Quality, Value, Time, Volume Illustrations and Examples

The Camcorder

This was introduced in the UK as an exclusive product in the early 1980s. It was heavy, cumbersome and expensive at £999.

It was followed up as an 'improved product' which was less cumbersome, easier to handle and at a price advantageous from the mid-1980s onwards, at £899.

This was followed by a range of midi and mini lightweight camcorders offered by all the major Japanese electrical goods companies from 1990 onwards. The price range initially was around £700, and then gradually drifted downwards, through £650, £600, £550, £500. For Christmas 1995 mini hand-held camcorders were available in major electrical goods retail chains from £199 up to approximately £799.

At each stage the market was increased through the combination of offering an improved and more convenient product at an ever more accessible price.

Sony/Aiwa

In 1990 Sony created the Aiwa marque as a differentiated range of electrical goods offered at (generally) lower prices than the Sony brand equivalent. The company took the view that there was market share to be gained by offering a range of products at lower prices but not by reducing the price of those offered under its own name. It therefore created a new name. As Aiwa is a Sony marque, however, it was unable to compromise on quality or the other aspects of value because of the overall loss of reputation that would probably ensue.

Apples

Apples are available at a multitude of outlets, at a large range of prices across the Western world. Examples of the price, quality, value, time and volume mix are:

- the offering of loose apples, both in and out of season, by greengrocers and aimed at those who would like to purchase from a specialist outlet and who are therefore prepared to pay a distinctive price level in return;

- the offering of apples both loose and pre-packed at supermarkets and large grocery stores, often at premium prices. It is usual for these outlets to have a choice of at least two varieties at different prices;
- the Marks & Spencer approach to offering apples, based on fruit appearance, uniformity and packaging, enabling the store to charge between 2 and 5 times the rate of each of the previous two examples.

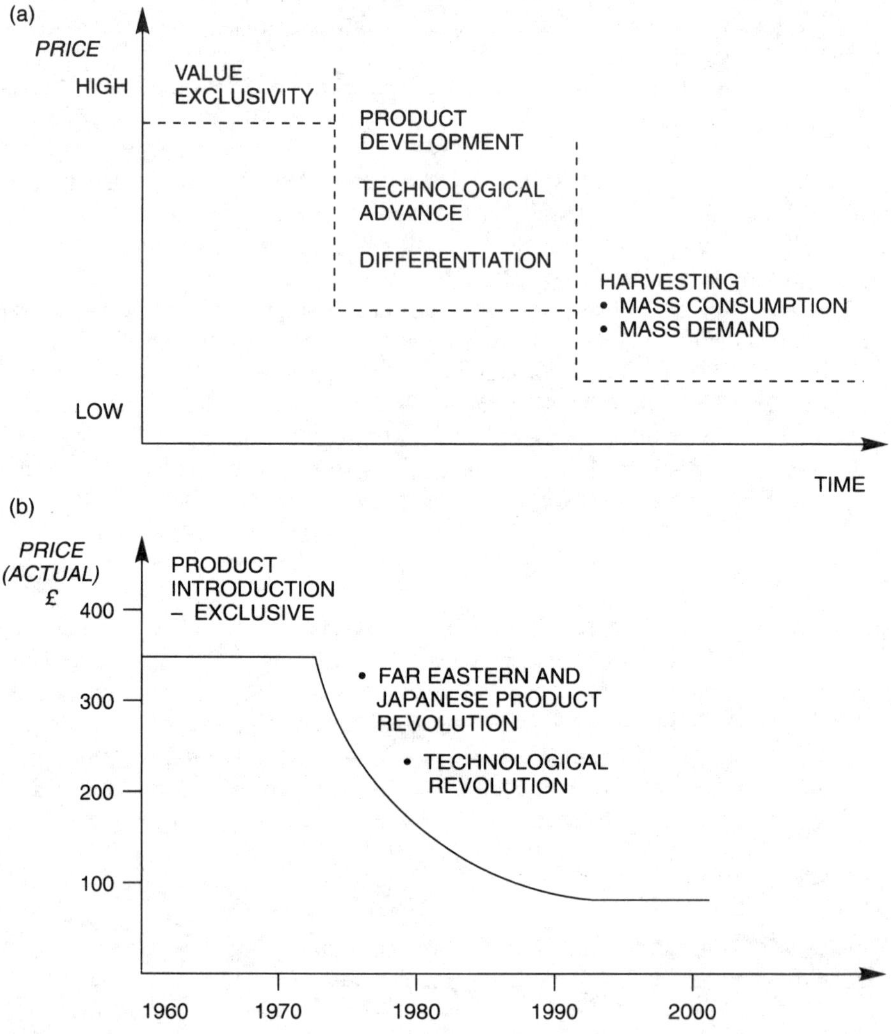

Figure 4.6 A model of product and market growth (example: colour televisions in the UK 1960–2000)

■ Price

In its simplest form the price charged for a product or service will be no lower than the organisation can bear in the interests of covering the full cost that it has accrued in getting the item on to the market. This must also be sufficient to generate enough revenue to meet its liabilities, generate a cash flow, pay wages and salaries, purchase new stocks of raw materials, advertise and promote, and distribute the offerings on to its markets.

□ *Maximisation/optimisation*

This is a reflection of the balance that must be struck between charging as high a price as possible (in order to maximise profits and ensure organisation continuity and general stakeholder satisfaction and confidence), and setting a lower level of charges that increase perceptions of value. Short- and long-termism, and the extent, continuity and length of the business relationship desired have all to be considered. Optimisation and maximisation should converge in the longer term.

□ *Elasticity of supply and demand*

The price of an offering inevitably reflects the extent to which alternatives and substitutes can be purchased elsewhere. The process of substitution is complex and requires wide assessment. Over-supply tends to lead to falls in price and over-demand to a rise.

However, organisations operating of either extreme are likely to take a more sophisticated view. High charges may tempt new entrants into the sector, leading to price wars. This may occur where lower prices charged by an established and successful operator of good reputation would have ensured its continuity for many years and made entry to the field by potential rivals that much more difficult.

Conversely, where there is over-supply, if the price comes down too far it may lead to bankruptcies in the sector. This leads to a realignment or rationalisation and, in extremes, to sector destabilisation.

Special consideration is given to primary sectors: for example, energy sources (especially electricity and fuel, including petrol). There are balances to be struck between the monopolistic/oligopolistic nature of the suppliers of this throughout the Western world, the price levels that the markets will stand and the moral element (which is discussed more fully below).

It is necessary finally to consider the position of the supplier of the key or rare component of an expertise or process on a purely commercial basis. Again, there is a clear propensity to charge premium rates for this, especially if the customer can pass these on to his customers in turn or to the final users.

☐ *Price leadership*

In this case the organisation promotes and enhances its general reputation on the price that it charges for its offerings. Everyone who purchases from the organisation does so in the full confidence that they are paying the lowest possible price in the sector.

Price advantage is never completely achieved at the expense of quality. The products and services must be basically good enough to attract purchasers. There are offerings that are so poor in quality that it is impossible to pitch the price low enough to sell; such offerings do not even satisfy the most transient, superficial or faddish of demands.

Moreover, for some goods and services there is an impression generated that if the price is too low, the offering will necessarily not be any good.

BOX 4.11 Perfume Wars

The relationship between price and value became important to the major UK perfume and fragrance companies in the winter of 1992. In the UK Superdrug, a retail chain, offered hitherto exclusive products at lower prices than the other retail outlets for them. At stake were the exclusivity and esteem elements of the traditional purchasers on the one hand; while, on the other, by bringing the price down the product range that was hitherto unattainable to other tranches and niches of society was suddenly available to them.

☐ *Price appearance*

This relates to the visual and behavioural aspects of the price charged.

A small commodity (foodstuffs, for example) appears better if the price charged is 99 pence or 99 cents rather than £1 or $1, because there is likely to be change given at the counter in return for payment, as well as the commodity itself. This is behaviourally very powerful and positive.

BOX 4.12 'Sail with the Mail for £1'

This promotion was offered by the *Daily Mail* and *Mail on Sunday* newspapers in conjunction with P&O European Ferries in January 1995. By collecting a certain number of tokens from the newspapers, people were able to purchase day-trip sea-crossing tickets from the UK to France, Belgium and Ireland for £1 (foot passengers), £10 (car and up to 5 passengers), and £49 (mini break of up to 5 days). Subsequently, the other ferry companies followed suit in conjunction with a variety of other newspapers.

The purpose behind the initiative was to increase sales of the newspapers and to fill the ships involved during what is usually their quiet season.

The attraction was the price and the price value mix offered. A sea-crossing for £1 represented an excellent purchase. The *Daily Mail* also doubled its offer by making the newspaper available at half price for the whole of January 1995.

This also increases the feeling of goodwill and satisfaction for the purchasers of the newspaper and the users of the ferry service. It also increases the opportunity for sales on board the ships, especially meals and duty-free goods. Because of the perception of great initial value, it increases the general propensity of customers to spend.

There is a general and related appearance of value in the charging of £399 or $399 for an airline ticket rather than £400 or $400. Again, part of this arises from the perception that change is to be offered, and partly also from meeting the more general expectation that this is what prices ought to look like.

It is also built into general marketing approaches of organisations that sell major purchases, either to other organisations or to individual consumers. For example, the advertising of cars refers to £7995 (rather than £8000).

□ *Price content*

This consists of the following.

1. **Whether the price is to be charged on a total or itemised basis.** For example, in the purchase of a television there are other matters to be considered: the aerial/dish/cable or other reception means to be considered; the tuning of the channels; initial and extended guarantees; trade-in and exchange policies. The price consideration is whether to charge a whole (and therefore relatively high) price which covers everything including the customer's peace of mind; or whether to go to the other extreme and to itemise everything separately; or whether to strike a point somewhere between the two extremes and sell the television as a package but with optional extras.
2. **The nature of the offering**, the price/value balance. Professional and technical services (for example, medicine, teaching, business consultancy, design) require a price high enough to convey the impression that they are indeed professional, as true experts charge high fees for their expertise. Similarly, people will impute or ascribe different values and qualities when choosing between cars on price. In the UK a £5000 new car implies certain levels and standards of travel; a £20000 new car a different level and standard of travel again.
3. **Expectations.** If customers pay a particular price, they expect a particular level of satisfaction. Where this is not met, complaints ensue. The cry 'I want my money back', is a clear indication above all that expectations have not been met. Conversely, reputations of organisations and their products and services grow where the consumer's expectations are exceeded.

4. **Satisfaction**, or why the offering has been bought, why the price has been paid. If satisfaction is not thought to be forthcoming, there is not a price low enough that can be successfully charged. Conversely people will pay well for high and excellent levels of satisfaction.
5. **The spending patterns of the market.** If one is supplying to those who use cash to purchase, then the offering or mix of offerings has to be priced within the volume of cash that is normally carried by the customers in question. The same is true of supplying to those who use credit or charge cards: the price range will be suitable for slotting into their purchasing patterns and powers.
6. **Sectoral expectations.** In sectors where there is a wide variety of offerings, choice of suppliers, or differentiation of a general generic or homogeneous product, there is usually established a broad price band. Anyone entering the market is therefore expected to conform to this, and to stake his position in the sector partly on the positioning of his price within the stated range. Anyone entering the market who sets their price above the stated range will invariably be differentiating in some other way. Anyone entering below the band may first have to convince the market sector in question that the version of the product that he has to offer is at least of an equivalent quality (or acceptable quality) in relation to the existing range of products.
7. **Economic rent.** This is the process of attaching particularly high prices to particular products and services based on a combination of excellence and quality, and rarity or scarcity value. This is applied to such matters as medical specialism (for example, pioneering surgery); business expertise (for example, Chief Executive); sport prowess (manifested through transfer and signing-on fees in football for example). Economic rent is also paid to those who control certain information, technology and expertise. It is also paid in respect of work in particular sectors such as defence, banking, and nuclear energy, weapons and research.

BOX 4.13 Price

In 1993 the Tesco supermarket chain effectively went into competition with itself when it launched its 'Value' range. This is a collection of basic popular and essential consumer commodities (for example, toilet rolls, bleach and sanitary towels) and foodstuffs (for example, milk, chips, ice cream). They are distinctively packaged, and they are also offered at a lower price than the company's own equivalent brands (for example, at the end of 1995 Tesco UHT skimmed milk was 40 pence per litre; Tesco Value UHT skimmed milk was 30 pence per litre). Since this initiative other chains have followed suit.

A previous UK initiative in the supermarket sector in this field was Shoppers Paradise. It offered lower prices in return for a 'no frills, no sophisticated merchandising' style of presentation. Organisation resources not spent on merchandising and presentation were passed on to the customers in the form of price cuts. The initiative was unsuccessful and failed.

The overwhelming reason was perceptual. Customers were put off by the 'no-frills' ambience. People felt that they were in surroundings with which they did not wish to be associated. There were implications of low quality attached to this. Above all, they were being associated with cheapness rather than value.

Other operators subsequently seeking this niche have had to consider this. Not only have they set out to be the price leader, but they have also had to satisfy the other customer and consumer expectations.

The American food and consumer goods giant Costco established its first UK operation near Lakeside in Essex in the UK in 1993. The organisation established its position on the basis of price leadership. It applied for and received warehouse rather than supermarket status in order to gain advantages and taxation and accommodation charges. On the basis of the Shoppers Paradise example above, people are even less likely to shop in a warehouse than a 'no-frills' supermarket. To get over this Costco addressed the other issues. The customers were required to join Costco to pay an association/affiliation fee before making any purchase. Features were made of the ease of access and the extensive car parking which was contrasted with the inadequate state of this elsewhere (and in particular the difficulties associated with getting into the car parks in the nearby Lakeside shopping complex). The overwhelming thrust was placed on value, not price. The notion of price leadership was allowed to emerge, and that of value was ceaselessly emphasised. In this way the organisation was able to gain its foothold.

□ *Loss leadership*

This is where products are sold at a price that does not cover production costs. The main reason for doing this is to encourage potential customers to come into the ambit of the organisation in question.

It is used by most commercial organisations that have a sophisticated and complex product portfolio or range of offerings. The cross-Channel ferry companies that operate between Dover and Calais offer low-cost day trips often for as little as £1 per ticket (see Box 4.12) because they know that they will subsequently gain on the sales of duty-free goods, meals and other merchandise, as well as offering a good-value excursion. There are well-indicated loss leaders at regular points throughout all large supermarkets and department stores, and they also make up the difference as their customers fill up their baskets with other lines. Behaviourally the propensity to spend is increased by the perception of the good-value purchase of the loss leader.

In international terms loss leadership in its extreme form is known as dumping. For example, multi-national or global organisations seek a foothold in a particular market or country, so the product is introduced at a phenomenal price advantage and the foothold is thus gained on price. However, it must be sustained on quality and value. If successful, the entrant gains market share at the expense of existing operators who may be driven from their traditional or indigenous markets or forced to devise strategies of their own to respond to this. The new entrant is then able to increase the prices and charges levelled (even more so if the indigenous operators do indeed exit from the market). Accusations of this form of 'entryism dumping' have been made regularly towards Japanese companies over the period since the 1970s in their dealings with the USA, Western Europe, Australia, New Zealand and South Africa. When Britain, France and Germany all had empires a variation on this form of dumping was created, whereby the Empire countries were forced to take a certain amount of products from indigenous producers at set prices. They were also restricted from shopping around for those products from other parts of the world.

From the standpoint of a supplying organisation that is a potential entrant to a new sector, loss leadership is attractive. However, it must be sustainable, and consideration may need to be given to the risk of setting a new and lower level of margin if those already in the field respond in kind and generate a price war.

□ *Skimming*

In business terms this is likened to the process of skimming the cream (the best bits?) off the top of a churn of milk. Normally the process is only sustainable for a short while. It consists of setting a high initial price to maximise income from a new product or offering range while there are no competitors. It is only possible if there are clear and distinguishable quality and value benefits for which customers are prepared to pay. In such cases the attention of potential entrants will inevitably be attracted. There are implications therefore about gaining market confidence and share as well as profits in the short term, and being able to bring the price down in the medium to long term without affecting viability and continuity. There is also a caveat in that early purchasers of a highly distinctive offering may resent the high price that they initially paid if the charges subsequently come down too far and too fast. This may lead to a general reduction or loss of regard or reputation. The instant camera is an example, both the one that takes photographs and then prints them off instantly, and also the 'use once and throw away' camera. In each case a high premium was charged initially for the novelty and convenience benefits. However, the technology was simple enough to permit a flood of followers into the field, and the price plummeted.

□ *Discounts*

Where discounts are being offered to end users – for example through retail outlets – the discount or sale must be able to sustain itself positively. There is no point in stating one price but in reality charging lower prices on all occasions. This also reduces scope for seasonal sale activities in that they become very difficult to distinguish from the steady state.

Discounts must also be seen to be fair to all customers and clients. Again, general questions about the ways in which business is conducted may be raised if some customers are known or believed to have received greatly favourable discounts and others have not.

Dominant customers can often insist on high levels of discount from suppliers. Clothes retailers insist on high levels of discount from garment manufacturers. Furniture retailers and do-it-yourself stores also gain large discounts in return for taking regular and high levels of product volume from suppliers, and placing them in prominent positions in their stores.

Where the suppliers have greater influence or bargaining power they are able to insist on returns for the discount. This may take the form either of the prime placement of the product in the outlet, or else it may be associated with the advertising and promotion activities of the retail outlet.

Some supplier organisations may insist that their product range does not go into seasonal sales as they fear that this may damage reputation and confidence. This is particularly true of the food sector (where many suppliers in any case produce flashed and other differentiated stock). It is also true of the *haute couture* sector of the clothing industry where discounting would reduce the brand exclusivity and reputation and might lead to losses in the existing general customer base.

☐ *Moral pricing*

Moral pricing constitutes balancing the ability to charge high prices for an offering by virtue of its nature (for example, electricity, gas, water; transport; drugs; defence equipment; restricted minerals, components or technology) with the taking of a moral, ethical or social view of the right level of charges that should be made. In each of the cases indicated high advantage rests with the supplier and substitution is not easy.

BOX 4.14 Utility Watchdogs and Price

Following the privatisation of gas, electricity, water, transport, and telecommunications industries throughout the world in the 1980s and 1990s, regulators/watchdog bodies were established with the purpose of monitoring their progress and performance as private monopolies or near-monopolies.

A key feature of this was (and remains) price regulation. On the face of it, the companies would otherwise be able to charge whatever they chose for their products and services to what are almost captive markets.

Formulae were therefore required which ensured a regular return for the companies and reflected the customer's ability to pay, together with a moral pricing element ensuring that charges did not go too high, thus eating into general standards of living. The general approach adopted was to break the price and service element down into its component parts – for example, line rental costs per call, maintenance, service and emergency, and equipment charges for telecommunications – and set charges for each that reflected encouragement to the consumers to use the service, while at the same time retaining a concept of 'value for money' based on historic levels of cost. Increases in charges were based partly on current rates of inflation and partly on 'low percentages'. They were subject to scrutiny by regulators and to examination and questioning by politicians, and this had to be balanced with giving shareholders an adequate rate of return for their investment.

Moral pricing therefore requires that the mixture of standpoints is adopted. It can be extended to housing and medical and education services, basic foodstuffs and clothing. There is also a requirement to take a wider view of the relationship between business and its communities.

□ *Geographical factors*

These have to be considered where the transport and distribution element is a significant proportion of the total price, especially where road, rail, air and sea transport fleets are required. It is compounded where the speed of distribution is also critical.

Geography is also important in the distribution of electricity through power cables, and water, oil, gas and chemical products through pipelines. The design, maintenance and upkeep of these is a significant price element.

Also important is the geographical nature of the market or community in question, especially where this is diverse and where lines of distribution and mobility are long. For example, there may be pressures to keep the price of cars low (and the reliability of them high) because such items are essential to support the quality of life that the community seeks to achieve for itself. This would then extend to the price of petrol and charges for maintenance and service. The same arguments would apply to public transport between isolated communities, such as island communities, and their mainlands and supply bases.

□ *After sales and guarantees*

These are meant to ensure that what is sold to customers has at least a measure of continuous capability and utility. In practice most organisations provide these services well in excess of the legal requirements, and any that do not have consequently to face an additional competitive burden. However, they do carry a price element.

Car companies that offer six-year anti-corrosion warranties, and double glazing firms that offer ten-year guarantees, may be faced with replacement costs in 5½ and 9½ years' time respectively.

■ Volume

This is important in this context because there is invariably an effect on the price, value and quality elements. Anything that becomes widely available by definition loses a measure of exclusivity, and may cease to command a premium price. Fashion leaders may deem the offering *passé* or obsolete, leaving it to the mercies of mass markets and other sectors.

□ *Supply and demand*

There is a general relationship between supply and demand in this context. At its simplest, limited supplies push up prices as consumers effectively go into an option mode. Decline in demand leads to the need to reduce price or re-present, repackage or rejuvenate the particular item, leading to attempts to open up new market sectors.

BOX 4.15 Location

The following are examples of using location as a statement of actual, perceived, inferred or implied quality and value:

- Devon clotted cream;
- Cornish, Jersey, Guernsey ice cream;
- Somerset cider;
- Kentish peg tiles.

These generally carry premium prices and the location is used as a marketing lever by the companies concerned.

British and Cyprus sherry, New Zealand butter and lamb, Argentine beef and English Brie cheese, all carry more general balances of price, quality and value expectations and implications.

Champagne, Burgundy and Bordeaux wines are all examples of using the place of origin as product description. The description may not be used to describe any near-equivalent offering which must instead be given its own name.

National and regional characteristics (both real and especially perceived) are also used in marketing and promotion campaigns for certain products: for example, Yorkshire beer (good, strong and honest); French food (good quality, exclusive, tasty and prestigious); Italian cars (stylish and macho); Japanese goods (durable, reliable and good value).

Supply and demand is affected by seasonal variations (ice cream sales increase in summer); annual life cycles (the main purchase of children's school books and equipment is in August and September); and annual events, such as the consumer boom in the weeks before Christmas, the January sales, and the new car boom in August in the UK related to the registration change. These factors determine production cycles in these sectors.

□ *Location*

This is considered from a variety of standpoints (see Box 4.15). An item may gain exclusivity because it is only available to a small range of outlets. It may be compatible with a distributor's existing range of offerings and lend itself to joint promotions, ventures or tie-ups. It may be a regional speciality, widely available in one part of the country only, or on sale elsewhere as a novelty or 'exclusive' and therefore at a premium price.

□ *Capacity*

This is assessed from two points of view: the capacity of the production technology, and the capacity of the market. It is clearly cost-effective to utilise production technology to the greatest possible extent, and to seek alternative outlets and configurations (for example, through packaging and differentiation) where existing market capacity is not great enough to take the volume (or potential volume) produced.

■ Value

Value is the combination of price with the anticipated or actual utility, satisfaction and benefits to be accrued from the purchase. Good value is obtained where high levels of satisfaction are gained in return for the purchase price; and bad value where this is not forthcoming.

The components of value in relation to given items are:

- length, frequency and intensity of usage (its 'useful life');
- depreciation/appreciation and resale aspects;
- maintenance, repair and replacement elements;
- feelings of esteem and worth that accrue from ownership and use;
- fashionable and faddish elements (important in clothing, cars and ranges of consumer goods);
- feelings of exclusivity, luxury, desirability;
- feelings at the end of the useful life or utility of the item (at the end of holidays, meals or social events for example);
- returns on investment, activity, energy and effort expended;
- particular demands and requirements of the individual customer.

Much that relates to this is therefore clearly perceptual; purchases made by different customers of the same item, for the same purpose, for the same price may result in widely differing levels of satisfaction and therefore value.

Much of this is also concerned with the relationship between anticipated and actual levels of satisfaction. This is a function of the ways in which offerings and their qualities of performance and identity are presented. To meet or exceed this is a function of high value.

■ Quality

Quality is the degree of excellence attributed to offerings. It is both absolute and relative.

□ *Absolute*

In absolute terms quality is a reflection of the products, performance, utility and longevity, general excellence and reputation. It is a reflection of the levels of profit and volume of sales generated. It is also a reflection of the organisation's commitment to its products, services and offerings. All of this is underpinned by the esteem in which staff and customers are held: it is very difficult to deliver high levels of service if there is no particular respect for either group.

Absolute quality goes wrong for two reasons: when either the quality is too low or too high. Where quality is inadequate, market share will be lost to those whose level is higher or at least satisfactory. Where quality is too high, the organisation is inevitably incurring costs in producing to a level of excellence that either the market does not require or which the price charged cannot recoup.

□ *Relative*

In relative terms the quality of a particular offering will take its place in the range of similar items available from different sources. Generally, part of this will involve establishing the required distinctive competitive position as price leader, as specialist, or as strongly branded or differentiated.

This is not an end in itself, however. There is no particular virtue in having the fifth highest quality in a 20-offering market, if people buying mainly on quality only go to the top two.

■ Time

Strategic management must be able to distinguish between concepts of long-, medium- and short-term time.

No timescales are prescribed for any of the periods. There are several reasons for this. To do so denies the variances that actually exist between all organisations and within all organisations in the pursuit of their own defined short-, medium- and long-term goals and objectives. There are sectoral variances that have to be considered: one person's long-term is another's instant. Matters relating to lead times must also be addressed: it takes much longer to get some activities and projects actually launched than others, while in some sectors public inquiries may be needed as the prerequisite to activities. Other products require extensive market research or testing. In public services there are political and procedural considerations that have to be accommodated before any actual work can take place.

Every sector, company, corporation and organisation, and the departments and divisions within them, will (if managed properly), have their own clear view of what constitutes short, medium and long term.

What is provided, therefore, is a framework for both direction and activity, and a conceptual approach for the study and evaluation of the work that is to be carried out. These may be distinguished as follows.

Short term: That which is achievable and measurable in precise terms. It will be precisely targeted, and subject to regular review, discussion of performance and operational appraisals. It will be subject also to in-depth scrutiny or resource utilisation efficiency and effectiveness. The deadline for the completion of the matter in question will be 'near at hand'.

Medium term: That which is clearly achievable and measurable, precisely targeted, and subject to regular review, and preview and monitoring as it unfolds. The approach here is likely to be more flexible than for the short term, without losing sight of the overall purpose, or desired and envisaged outcomes of the matters in hand. Again, the date will be a clearly recognised target.

Long term: The clearly articulated and presented vision of direction, the shape of things to come, and things that are getting underway or being researched or commissioned. These will include the design of new products and services, research into the requirements of the market or consumer segment served as to their needs and wants over the coming period, and their incorporation into strategy.

There are some specific points on these timescales related to the turbulent nature of the business sphere, together with technological advances, the opening up of new markets, and emergence of new economies. Any organisation that wishes to operate successfully must strike a balance between giving clarity of direction, and remaining flexible and responsive, and opportunist, in the light of the changes and developments that are certain to arise.

The need is to set realistic and achievable objectives within the time frame considered. Short-term objectives should be achievable using short-term resources and without diverting other resources away from longer-term activities.

The longer term represents the organisation's commitment to its own future. Japanese organisations have developed this to the extent that the markets which they serve have great all-round confidence that goods and technology will be developed. They are also to be relied upon to produce the next generation of products to a higher level of quality, reliability and accessibility.

☐ *The time-profit equation*

Performance has to be considered over periods that balance and reflect both the need to produce surpluses (profits) which satisfy those seeking rewards and returns from the organisation in return for their commitment to it (especially staff and shareholders), with the long-term needs of stability, continuity and confidence referred to above.

Ideally both will be satisfied, and one is not to be sacrificed for the other. In the UK especially, there has been an overwhelming history in the 1970s and 1980s to produce short-term results at the expense of investment for the future.

BOX 4.16 Short-Termism

Short-termism is applied to the process of achieving instant success: real, perceived and imagined.

Where there are operational pressures to reduce budgets and revenue expenditure, managers may be working in direct opposition to the stated aims, objectives and direction of the organisation in question.

Thus, for example, in UK National Health Service accounting terms, it is cheaper and more cost-effective to have hospital wards closed rather than open. The same applies to patient queues and waiting lists: it is cheaper to have patients off waiting lists than on them.

Sports clubs purchase short-term success at the expense of the long term. Professional clubs that buy in expensive players may win trophies in the short term. However, by doing this they are denying a place in the team to the player who is coming up through the club's own ranks; and if such players then leave the club, it must continue to buy in from outside in order to maintain its position. It thus generates for itself both a revenue shortage in this way, and also a capital shortage in that the stock of 'home-grown' players is allowed to run down.

Assets sales may also generate short-term revenue profits. These again must be seen against the long-term value of the assets in question. If it is a true divestment of something that the organisation is no longer interested in, or that is clearly revenue-consumptive, or is (in the opinion of the organisation's strategists) coming to the end of its useful life, then the sale at (almost) any price is the reflection of a clear opportunity. If, on the other hand, it is made on a point of expediency, it becomes effectively 'a sale of the family silver'; that is, a capital sale to raise current revenue.

☐ *Lead time*

This consists of the following.

1. **Development time**, the time taken to produce and test components of the proposed item and to bring them together to develop prototypes; and any technology that is necessary to produce these.
2. **Research time**, the time taken to establish measures of market size, availability and nature for the particular initiative; to decide and produce the actual product or service (again often in prototype or pilot test format); and to evaluate the initial impact, immediate and likely/possible/projected future results.
3. **Production time**, which covers all aspects of the manufacture of products, or the totality of the components of services.
4. **Delivery time**, which relates to access to goods and products, and accessibility and availability of services (including whether these are instantly available at the point of access, or whether appointments or booking systems are necessary).
5. **Distribution time**, which relates to the points and means of sales, location of outlets, and time taken to reach them by both suppliers and customers.
6. **Maintenance and repair time**, the amount of time taken to put right or service anything that goes wrong with the product or item in question.

Assessment of lead times should not therefore be seen as a linear process or in isolation from the other components of the proposed strategy or direction. It is an integral element of it. Accurate assessment will often also be an overriding element in the consideration of whether to proceed with an initiative, and this must be fully understood. This is especially true for those products and services that have long lead times.

There is also a cultural element. Lead times are inextricably linked to the expectation of results. Japanese companies take a long-term, almost eternal view of product and service development, and the lead time is whatever it takes (almost) to get a continuing range of offerings to customers.

The UK public services, by contrast, work hand to mouth, for instant results. Results must be achieved within budget and by the end of the current financial period. In these cases therefore the lead time element is determined by operational controls and not strategy.

BOX 4.17 Lead Time (1): Christmas Toys

Organisations supplying the Christmas toy market will do their best to have a range of new, interesting and novelty products on sale from the late summer onwards.

However, such organisations must also be able to respond instantly to a fad or fashion that suddenly erupts. If this happens the demand must be satisfied by

Christmas (not after), so that the customers (the parents) can purchase the goods for the clients or users (the children) before 25 December. Organisations that operate in these fields must therefore have the flexibility and the facilities for increasing both the production and distribution elements if this occurs. The relationship between capacity and time is therefore all important. Recent examples of these in the UK include the Teenage Mutant Hero Turtles in 1991 and Thunderbirds in 1992. In each case the owners of the patents managed to expand to a greater or lesser extent. In each case also sales were lost to close substitutes, copiers and imitators, that could be and were generated by quick response manufacturing outlets to fill the gaps. The range of merchandise and products included in each case – toys, dolls, films and videos, models, clothing, pictures, posters, books, stationery, pens and pencils, shoes, slippers and board and computer games. For something that truly catches the public imagination, the short-term opportunities and revenues to be gained are extremely high.

BOX 4.18 Lead Time (2): Defence Equipment

Organisations supplying the defence markets of the world work to long and often indeterminate lead times. The capacity of the equipment, whether offensive or defensive, whether weaponry or information, may and does take years to become apparent, and is subject to constant modification. Because of its nature, the whole sector is also subject to political pressures and variances.

Equipment and projects commissioned by one government may be delivered to its successor (or one of a number of subsequent successors, either following election in a democracy or a military coup elsewhere). Equipment and projects commissioned for one war or offensive (or defensive) capacity may not be delivered in time for it. Equipment commissioned as the latest and avant-garde approach to military strategy may be pedestrian and clumsy when finally delivered. General examples of this phenomenon can be found among the military hardware and technology that was commissioned by both sides in the Cold War of the 1970s and 1980s. The SS20 range of missiles of the USSR, the Trident nuclear submarine and weaponry programme of the USA and the UK, and the USA's Strategic Defence Initiative using laser defence technology were all designed with particular enemies in mind and a particular war in mind, and to ensure the continuity of mutual equality and capacity in what was after all a Cold War. When the USSR collapsed (because of economic rather than military pressures) in 1990, the weaponry became obsolete in regard to its particular purpose.

BOX 4.19 Lead Times (3): Sectoral Examples

Channel Tunnel

Part of the time planning of the period leading up to the opening of the Channel Tunnel in 1994 was taken up by the invention, design and commissioning of the equipment actually needed to bore the three tunnels.

Drugs

Organisations wishing to bring new drugs and cosmetics on to their markets must go through rigorous programmes, often on animals, and then finally on humans. The major drug and cosmetics companies of the Western world all keep banks of volunteers who agree to take part in product tests. These tests are an essential and legal prerequisite that must be completed before the drug or cosmetic goes on to the market.

Safety

Business premises in the Western world are subject to extensive health and safety, fire and emergency regulations. Inspections are carried out at the design, construction, commissioning, fitting-out and opening stages. In the UK no public, business or commercial premises may be opened until these inspections have been fully carried out, and certificated by the required authorities.

Public Services

In public services, there are often strong political forces which, unless properly evaluated and contained, exert great pressure to override time considerations wherever this is possible. They take on a variety of guises: the need of an influential politician to have a triumph; the need to meet (or give the impression of meeting) a manifesto commitment; the need to 'do something' (or at least to be seen to be trying to do it).

BOX 4.20 Funeral Insurance

In 1994 the UK Norwich Union Insurance Group of companies offered a funeral insurance plan. Premium rates were set according to the following criteria:

- the age of the customer;
- the lifestyle of the customer;

- the nature of the funeral required: whether secular or religious (and, if the latter, which religion or denomination); numbers of likely attenders; cremation or burial; number and type of cars to be provided; type of coffin; bearers; meal and refreshments, and so on;
- the memorial to be erected; the type of grave (if a burial); the type of plaque (if any) if a cremation;
- maintenance and upkeep over a period of time after the funeral; individual and family requirements.

Premium payments were to be made either annually or monthly, dependent upon customer requirements. In return for this, the next of kin of the deceased could safely leave everything in the hands of the company.

Many other insurance companies quickly followed suit and made similar offerings. The practice was also questioned on the grounds of ethical considerations by industry regulators and political watchdogs.

Conclusion

In practice, very few offerings are bought on one of the factors to the exclusion of all the others. For example, people generally will not travel for an item that is discounted hundreds of miles away, but the converse tends to be more true: people will pay a premium price for convenience (the shortening of the time factor).

As well as understanding, it is necessary to be able to apply this to the range of activities contemplated and conducted. Part of the process of organisational, environmental and directional analysis will therefore consist of establishing the basis of this mixture which is acceptable to the given sector. There is no point in seeking to compete on price if that is not critical to the consumers; there is no point in doubling the quality of a product if the existing range already more than meets the quality threshold.

Advantage can be gained, however, where improvements in any of these factors are genuinely sought by the customers and consumers, and as long as the rest of their expectations are not compromised. The main lesson here, therefore, lies in the ability to understand the price, quality, value and time mixture desired by those in the given sector and in the ability to meet this to best advantage.

An understanding of the basis on which business is to be conducted is therefore essential. The approach outlined and discussed enables a clarity of forethought to be established. It serves as a point of reference in the monitoring, evaluation and review processes. It enables organisations to address fundamental questions related to the consequences, obligations and implications of following particular paths, or entering and competing in given markets. It provides a basis for assessing the strategies of competitors both within the sector, and those who offer substitute and alternative products and services on its borders.

Organisations also seek other advantages in spite of their generic position. The broad brand leader will seek to optimise costs, but will not do this at the expense of the strength of the brand.

The cost leader seeks as high and positive a profile as possible. Again, this will not be at the expense of its position as cost leader. Indeed, part of its branding is likely to be on its distinctive position of cost/price advantage.

Focus and specialisation will seek cost and differentiated advantages, as long as by doing this the basic approach, especially the need for quality, can be maintained.

A successful generic approach can only be achieved if the ways in which the particular sector operates are fully understood and analysed. In sectors that operate largely on differentiation, the advantages of cost leadership can only be maximised if this is presented in acceptable ways. In specialised sectors, new entrants offering equivalent products at lower prices must be able to prove that they are also able to meet the quality, reliability and expectational aspects of the existing players.

The establishment of this position is not therefore an end in itself. Moreover, organisations that enter a sector on the basis of a high image differentiation may have this position eroded as others follow them and find other means of gaining advantage. Cost advantage may be wiped out if a competitor invests in production, technology and systems that supersede existing ways of working. For the organisation that specialises, the onus is also to provide a good, continuous, high-quality and customer-focused operation, bearing in mind that those taking the specialised products will themselves constantly be casting around for alternative sources of supply. This again underlines the need for a full assessment of the organisational and resource commitment involved as the result of the adoption of one of these positions. Without this, therefore, no effective foundation or direction for activities is likely to exist.

BOX 4.21 Generic Position: Sainsbury's

The following is part of a discussion held between David Sainsbury, Chairman of Sainsbury plc, the food retail chain, and Michael Porter, on the Thames television series, 'The World Turned Upside Down'(1987).

SAINSBURY: It seems to me that you do have customers who are interested only in price – in the food market it is quite a small bit, probably 10 per cent of the market. At the other end, you have people who are interested only in quality and will pay anything to get it. But the great majority of people are interested in both price and quality, which is summed up in the phrase 'really good value for money'. I think you can have a strattegy which is focused, as we are, absolutely on that middle range.

PORTER: David has shown me a model of a little truck which has the emblem of Sainsbury's on it. It says 'Good Food Costs Less at Sainsbury's'. I think that statement captures the positioning of Sainsbury's. Now the question is, can you be low cost and differentiated at the same time? If I read the slogan on the truck, it says good food costs less. So I would say, your quality is good but not unique. Your real strategy is low cost, and that's your real source of advantage. You're not trying both to beat your competitors on having better quality food than theirs and be lower in cost in supplying it.

Ultimately, if I read you correctly, you perceive your real advantage is going to be cost, but you are going to make sure your food is as good a quality as anybody else's . . . I wouldn't find better quality at Sainsbury's . . . The ultimate test of differentiation, to my way of thinking, is, do you command a premium price? How does Sainsbury's meet that test?

SAINSBURY: I think you can make superior profits if at the same time you can keep costs down, and have prices which are competitive, and get tremendous turnover. Then you get cost advantages which enable you to actually make superior profits without commanding a premium price, because you can have the lower price.

Source: 'The World Turned Upside Down' series Channel Four Television 1987.

■ Work assignments and discussion questions

1. What does the Sainsbury's example indicate about the company's generic position? What action would you recommend as the result of your conclusions?
2. Outline the relationship between cost leadership and price leadership.
3. What is the generic position of:
   (a) a village grocery store;
   (b) a publisher of railway magazines;
   (c) an exclusive restaurant.
   What are the main implications of adopting these positions? What would be the opportunities and consequences of shifting from this position to one of the others?
4. Why was the Superdrug company unsuccessful in its offensive strategy of October–December 1993, when it sought to undercut the perfume and fragrance market (see Box 4.11 above)?

CHAPTER 5

Competitive Activity

Introduction

In many organisations strategic processes and activities have bad reputations and low regard. The plans produced are so detailed, cumbersome, long and unreadable that nobody ever actually uses them or makes reference to them. It is therefore viewed as a waste of time and resources, carried out by persons in think-tanks or other elite committees, without reference to performance, production, outputs, quality, marketing or sales functions. Information, especially historic information, is analysed, and past gaps and discrepancies in performance highlighted in great detail. However, the information is not gathered or presented in ways useful to strategists or managers. A divergence is created between the 'strategy' and the reality of the organisation. The result of all this is to discredit the strategy processes. Organisations and their managers revert to operations rather than strategy as their reasons for being. Strategy is never discussed unless there is a crisis.

It is therefore clearly necessary to place a 'framework' around the process (see Figure 5.1). This consists of adopting a combination of purpose and activities targeted at particular markets, together with the processes devised and designed in their pursuit.

Competition

Competition is the process of striving against others to win or achieve something. Competition is both complex and sophisticated. The capability to compete is essential for the business of gaining customers and potential customers. This is the ability to satisfy that part of their wants and needs to the exclusion of others who are in direct competition. Restaurant owners want the customers coming to them rather than alternative locations, or choosing a take-away; or choosing to go to the cinema or theatre. It is also the organisation's capability to persuade customers to choose their product or activity in preference to those offered elsewhere.

Competition exists where there is choice. Choices are taken in varied and sophisticated ways, according to means, circumstances and preference, quite apart from any inherent or supposed nature and strength of the choices offered.

Competition has also to be seen as competing for scarce, limited and finite resources. It is therefore affected by levels of disposable income and the extent to which the offerings are essential, desirable, non-essential, luxury, general,

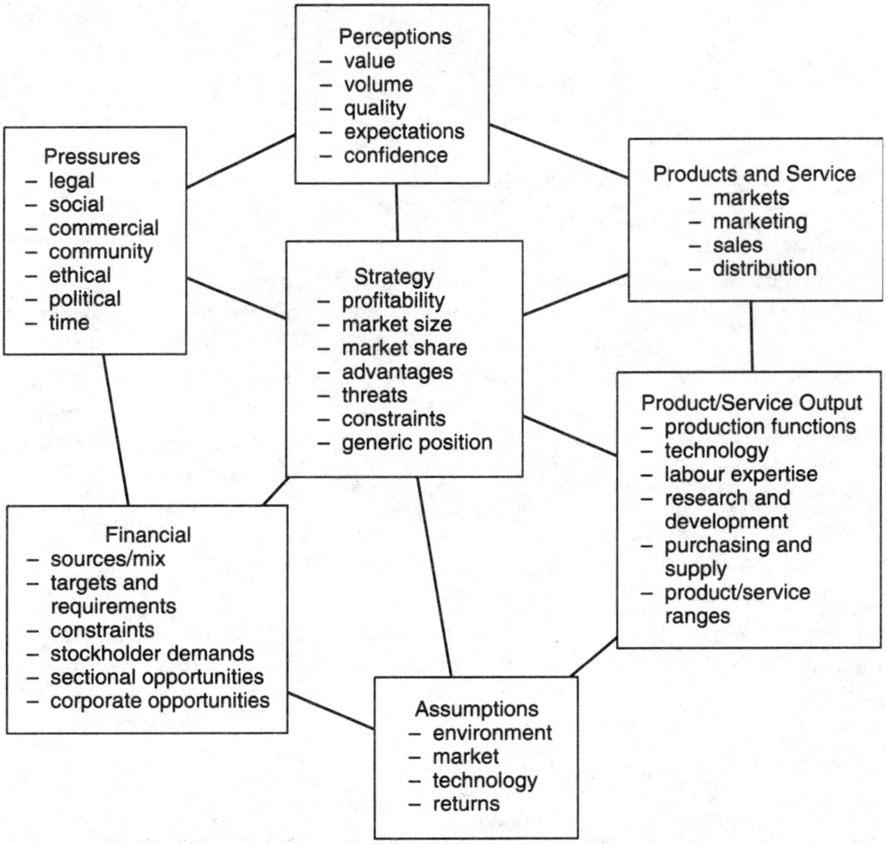

Figure 5.1 The competitive position

peripheral and marginal. Thus, for example, a travel agent that sells three to four holidays per annum to an affluent customer may find this cut back to one or two when general levels of prosperity fall; those customers that take only one holiday each year may do without this altogether; and the sector becomes prone to price wars, differentiation activities (especially extensive marketing and promotion) and the offering of top-ups (for example free luggage, free insurance, children go free). Competition has therefore to be seen also as variable, extensive and a continuous process, subject both to universal outside pressures and also to variations in the nature and level of those pressures.

■ Profit

Profit is whatever benefits the organisation in question, in whatever terms that is (and should be) measured. It is a function of the volume, quality and frequency of offerings sold. It is a function of income levels over periods of time. It is a function of the complexity, nature and sophistication of the products or offerings portfolio. It is the ultimate output of the generic strategy followed, the ultimate measure of its success or failure. It will be measured in terms of the rates of return achieved (over the sector and by absolute), in terms of opportunity cost (where else investors could have placed their money in order to get a return on it), and in terms of absolute percentages and percentage volumes achieved.

The public service equivalent is service effectiveness. This is measured in terms of the breadth and depth of the coverage of client groups, the level and quality of service offered and analyses of the costs and benefits mixture.

The time factor must be considered. This is the balance of short-, medium- and long-term performance and the related returns and implications. There is a balance to be struck between short-term gains, long-term stability and viability, levels of investment and the rates of return expected over the time periods by investors.

■ The competitive environment

The competitive environment is that in which competition takes place. Each competitive environment has its own distinctive elements under the following headings.

■ Degree of captivity

This is the extent to which the market – the meeting point between buyers and sellers – is captive because consumers have to buy from the particular suppliers; or the extent to which it is fluid (whereby anyone can supply the market and any consumer can go to anyone for their supplies).

□ *Expanding, static, stagnant or declining*

These elements may all be measured in terms of sales, financial and volume terms. They may also be measured in terms of the numbers of customers, and in terms of behavioural aspects such as reputation, perceptions of quality, general confidence and perceived benefits. In addition there may be dysfunction between the requirements of customers and the nature of the sector: for example, in much of the Western world health care provision is stagnant or declining, while at the same time demand for health care (in volume, variety, quality) is ever-increasing.

□ *Ethical and non-ethical*

This includes social, religious, environmental and civilisational concerns. It also includes the ethical aspects of some of the ground processes and research processes that are involved in product development (such as the use of animals in laboratory experiments). It may also be applied to entire sectors (such as defence and tobacco), and may apply to the use of women, children and animals in advertising and promotional campaigns.

□ *The nature of the entry and exit barriers*

These barriers consist of levels of capital investment; the nature, quality and volume of staff; the nature, quality and volume of technology; the location of markets; legal constraints; economies of scale; protectionism; the size of the market; access to distribution channels; the nature of the channels to be used; the loyalty of customers to existing players in the field (as where market entry is contemplated); the loyalty of customers to those organisations supplying substitute or alternative products; and the costs incurred in switching from the current to the proposed activities, either on one's own initiative or as the result of purchasing an operator in the field. Entry and exit barriers also have behavioural aspects relating to confidence and reputation.

□ *Legal constraints*

Certain markets and sectors have specific legal regulations and constraints. Governments may regulate the operations of organisations, requiring them to obtain licences for particular activities or to operate to particular standards in employment, marketing and production practices. They may require to be bonded or certificated in respect of quality assurance and standards of safety of product, operation or performance. There may be patent and copyright elements to the products in question that have also to be considered.

□ *Differentiation*

Differentiation activities occur in sectors with the purpose of generating either the reality or the illusion of difference, and the advantage of one product in regard to all others in the area.

□ *Volume of activities*

The features here are:

- the levels of income necessary to sustain the structure of the business (in actuality or as envisaged), and the technology, staff and support activities required;
- the levels of investment necessary to sustain, replace and update effective and profitable activities;
- the levels of income necessary to produce a rate of return acceptable to investors and stakeholders;

- the levels of income necessary to support crises, problems and contingencies;
- the levels of income necessary to support the desired quality of life for those responsible for the existence, success and direction of the business.

The service equivalent, especially in social and public services, and not-for-profit sectors is:

- the size of the client group or groups requiring the service;
- the level of investment necessary to sustain and support the level of service required, and its technology and expertise;
- the priority of the service in question relative to other demands for other services;
- the level of understanding of the constitution of public services by those responsible for structuring and delivering them.

Rivalry

Rivalry is the process by which a company establishes its position in its sector. It achieves this through competition, differentiation, competitive positioning, advertising campaigns and the building of reputation and confidence.

The following factors are to be considered.

1. The number and quality of the competitors in the sector. This includes the extent to which these are equivalent in size and capacity or, conversely, the extent to which the sector is dominated by one or two major players. It is also necessary to consider the extent to which the products and services that are offered by the sector are undifferentiated (that is, there is no particular brand loyalty or identity, or at least this is not the overriding factor).
2. The nature of sectoral growth, whether slow, steady, fast, positive or negative. Where sectors are steady, companies which wish to expand will precipitate price or differentiation wars. Where sectors are steady or declining (but not collapsing) there is the perception of high rewards that are to be gained by the winning or surviving players.
3. Exit barriers. Rivalry is especially intensive where exit barriers are high; that is, where the costs of withdrawing from a sector are greater than those of remaining in it even when market share and performance are being lost. Where this is the case companies will therefore remain in business in the sector because the costs of total withdrawal cannot be supported. Companies faced with this situation use it as an opportunity to seek other markets and also to engage in wider ranges of activities with the purpose of differentiating their offerings, generating new images and creating new strategies in support of them.

The mixture of these elements changes as the sector and market environment changes and as the marketing activities of all those involved have an effect. Where sectors are relatively stable the effects of intense rivalry ultimately mean that there will be company collapses, shake-outs, mergers and take-overs as weaker players go to the wall. This may also lead, over the medium to long term, to the destabilisation of the sector.

■ Buyer groups

Buyer groups have the greatest influence when they are in the position of being able to force down the prices that they pay to the supplier, or, conversely, they demand higher quality, better volume and better service from the supplier group, or else tighter delivery schedules. Buyer groups may also play off one supplier against the others.

The power and influence of buyer groups depends on the following.

1. The extent and nature of the entry barriers, especially where there are few critical entry barriers or switching costs on the part of suppliers. In these cases the buyers are able to approach anyone they choose.
2. Where products are undifferentiated, where there is little direct marketing activity, buyers also have greater influence.
3. Profit levels in the buyer's group; where this is low there is great pressure on the sector to lower its prices. As we have seen elsewhere in our discussion of the dependence and dominance spectrum, a powerful buyer group may be able to gain short term advantage. In the longer term this has to be considered from the widest possible standpoint.
4. Buyer groups may also consider the possibility of integrating backwards: that is, to establish or acquire their own supplies in order to maintain and develop security and stability of their operations.

■ Supplier groups

Supplier groups exert pressure on participants in a sector by raising prices or reducing the quality of products and services offered. They squeeze profitability out of any sector unable to recover its costs through price rises. Supplier groups are powerful, above all, they are dominated by a few companies. An example of this is oil, which is dominated by the major global players: Shell, BP, Texaco, Aramco, Gulf, Conoco and Exxon.

The supplier group is also powerful if the product is central to the expectations of buyers. It is compounded if the product is differentiated and buyers have particular brand loyalties and identities. It may be further compounded in industrial marketing if the product in question is a key component.

The supplier group is even more powerful if there are capital costs or legal elements present that act as entry barriers.

The supplier group may pose a threat to forward integration. It may seek to buy its way into the business of the sector concerned by establishing its own relationship with the ultimate clients and consumers of the product or services. The supplier group may be especially powerful if it is not dependent upon one sector to take the bulk of its products: that is, it produces a generic item that is heavily in demand by a variety of sectors (for example, car component manufacturers may be able to sell to all car companies, and also to aeroplane, ship and other builders).

■ Offering nature

This concerns the true nature of the products and services on offer; the functions that they serve; the range of benefits and attributes that they afford to purchasers; the potential or additional functions that they could also serve; and the ways in which they may be re-presented or repackaged.

■ Market nature

The true nature of the market or markets in which the products and services are offered. This includes considerations of expansion, contraction, stagnation, growth, maturity, saturation and decline. It also includes an assessment of the state of product and service life cycles and of the product portfolios.

It also includes: assessment of the niches being served; assessment of other niches that demand an equivalent range of benefits from similar offerings or different sources; studies of different locations. It also includes analysis of more general aspects of market expectations and levels of satisfaction (both required and actual).

■ Organisation assessment

This involves an assessment of the true nature of the organisation's competency, strengths and weaknesses together with an assessment of what truly distinguishes it and its products and services from the competition.

This activity is also required in terms of the competitors in the field, in order to assess what distinguishes each from the others in the sector. Finally, this requires an identification of the relative advantages of the organisation over its competitors and what the distinctive strengths and weaknesses of each player are.

■ Opportunities and concerns

This involves a full analysis and assessment of the opportunities and potential in the markets and sectors in which business is currently being conducted. It also includes assessing and continually investigating potential new areas of operation. The purpose here overall is to identify those areas where new, more profitable, more effective and better business could and should be carried out.

The wider concerns of the market must also be assessed. This includes the bases and standpoints upon which activities are carried out in the sector concerned. It also includes assessing the standpoints of wider environmental, ethical and moral concerns and the ways in which these should be addressed and tackled. There may also be proposed environmental, ethical or indeed legal constraints that are routed or proposed, and strategists of organisations must be able to assess and identify these in advance of their becoming reality. Finally, the wider concerns must also include a more general consideration of global trends and issues.

The competitive position is reinforced by:

- **segmentation**, the identification of particular population sectors with which to conduct business;
- **identification of entry and exit barriers**, the accessibility or otherwise of sectors and segments;
- **assessment of risk**, the measurement of likely success or failure in pursuit of activities.
- **The nature of the offerings:** the particular products and services offered for consumption.

■ Competitive positioning

This concept is applied both to organisations and to the elements of their product and offering ranges. Competitive position consists of a combination of the following.

1. The price, quality and value aspects of the product range or organisation in question. This includes the quality extreme (regardless of price) on the one hand, and the position of sector cost/price leader at the other extreme.
2. Distinctive factors: its design, appearance, functions and utility, durability (or disposability) and eventual obsolescence; and its extrinsic factors: levels of association and identity, the extent to which the design and appearance are fashionable, photogenic and otherwise presentable; its durability (or obsolescence) in fashion, lifestyle and perceptual terms.
3. The nature of differentiation, and the means by which this is achieved (advertising, marketing, branding, distribution).
4. The general strength and nature of the overall image and identity and the benefits to be drawn from this on the part of the organisation and of association with it on the part of the customer.
5. Other general perceptions on the part of the customer. These cover all aspects, both extrinsic and intrinsic. It may be summarised as the extent to which the want and need for the item under consideration has been positioned in the mind of the consumer or consumer group (and if it is an organisation's position that is under scrutiny, this is the extent to which confidence and willingness to do business with it has been generated in the mind of the consumer).
6. Confidence and reputation.
7. Extremities of quality, volume, price, value, access.
8. The essence of consistency, the creation and maintenance of this and the ability of the given product or organisation to sustain this.

The concept is important because of the nature of competition, and the increasing ability of global and high-tech organisations to enter what used to be thought of as safe or protected sectors.

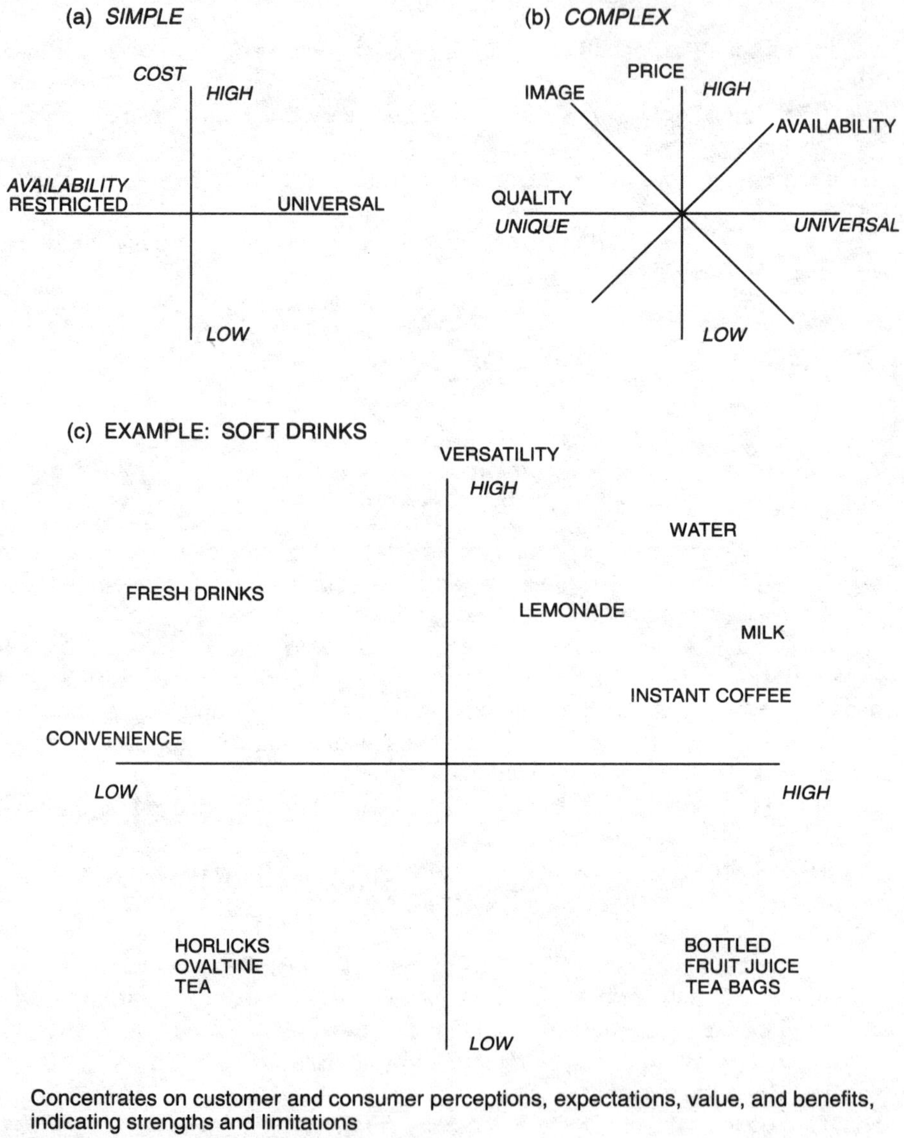

Figure 5.2 Market mapping analysis

Source: Randall (1992).

BOX 5.1 A Marketing View of Competitive Positioning

This may be considered in the following ways.

1. **First in the field/pioneering:** the opening-up of new markets, new outlets for existing products, new products for existing outlets. It may also arise resulting from the ability to take a fresh, original and creative approach to other activities (for example, through advertising or supplying other organisations). The rewards are very high if successful; similarly, the pioneering organisations carry a great burden of risk.
2. **Follow the leader:** resulting from the ability to recognise another's potential in a sphere of activities, and to follow them in. The great benefit of being second or third in the field is the ability to learn from mistakes (if any) of the first.
3. **Me-too** or **all-comers:** where the market is large and open, and where there are no particular barriers to entry. This occurs in large generic sectors – food, clothing, consumer goods – and is especially attractive where the sector is stable or expanding and where potential entrants are able to offer price, quality, value, volume and time advantages over existing players.
4. **Ethical stance:** where the organisation adopts strategies based on strong moral principles, and seeks opportunities based on this position, and where there is an attractiveness for this in the particular field.

BOX 5.2 High-Tech Extension

The Japanese electronics industry in the 1970s was able to develop its existing technology to produce accurate, fashionable, durable and highly desirable clocks and wrist watches that initially and almost instantly ruined the European (and especially Swiss) equivalent. The Swiss industry in particular was forced to respond in kind by investing in the levels and nature of technology that enabled it to generate all the tangible benefits afforded by the Japanese sector, alongside the status, traditional and intrinsic confidence and value elements that had hitherto been its strength. Alongside this, the Swiss, German and UK wrist watch manufacturers all generated exclusive top-quality, top of the range offerings, as distinct from the Japanese mass offerings. This was in order to differentiate them from the new standard offering, and therefore to maintain a measure of exclusivity in this sector. The top of the range offering was still available to those who still wanted the traditional and exclusive product.

Competitive positioning is a continuous process. In large, mature and global markets real improvements to products and services generated by one organisation are quickly copied by other operators. The entry into the mind of the consumer therefore becomes all-important. Having established the organisation or product under consideration in the required minds, in the desired way, this must then be nurtured and improved. The reinforcement and development of the quality, value and benefits afforded, attention to design, fashion, image and association are all integral to the success of this.

A critical part of the process of competitive positioning is the development of a theme of consistency for the given offering or organisation. This is driven by the reflective needs of the consumers for constancy and confidence. All things being equal, customers are much more confident and comfortable with an organisation or offering that has developed a consistency of image, quality, value and expectation (however this has been achieved).

The competitive position is therefore a matter of strategic rather than operational choice. Once established, it cannot easily be changed. Indeed, as we have seen elsewhere, it is much more usual for organisations to diversify and open up new activities in new sectors rather than to keep changing competitive position. This has to be seen in the context that the competitive position is subject to a continuous process of development and refinement; and that markets, sectors and segments in which the activities and operations take place are also constantly changing.

BOX 5.3 Competitive Positioning: Cars

The following is a simplified view of the competitive positioning of the operators in the UK car market. It is not fully comprehensive but is rather presented in this way to illustrate the point and concept. This illustration is from both the point of view of the operators and also the perceptions and requirements of the customers.

1. Price leadership: Skoda; also limited edition Ford Fiesta, Vauxhall Corsa, Kia Pride, Proton, Fiat Panda and Fiat Uno.
2. Extreme value for money: Skoda, Yugo, Lada, Kia.
3. Reliability: Nissan, Toyota, Hyundai, Volkswagen.
4. Fashion: Renault Clio, Peugeot 205, Ford Fiesta XR2, Morgan.
5. Opulence: BMW, Porsche, Mercedes, Jaguar.
6. Executive/occupational: BMW, Mercedes, Ford Scorpio, Ford Granada, Rover 900 Series.
7. Distinctive lifestyle: Volvo, Range Rover, Jaguar.
8. High performance: Porsche, Jaguar, top of the range and exclusive Toyota and Nissan models.
9. Safety: Volvo, Saab, Volkswagen, Ford (aspiring).

10. Consistency: Nissan, Toyota (this includes after-sales, service and bodywork guarantees), Ford and Vauxhall on the grounds of the longevity of the organisations in question and the general universal familiarity afforded by this.
11. Top quality: Rolls-Royce.
12. Fleet cars: Ford, Vauxhall, Peugeot (especially 306, 309 and 405), Nissan.
13. Small cars: Rover Group Mini and Metro, Nissan Micra, Peugeot 106 and 205, Ford Fiesta, Vauxhall Corsa, Kia Pride.

Notes

Position movements: examples. Skoda, since acquisition by the Volkswagen Group, has 'moved' from cheap to good value by virtue of design improvements, quality improvements and raised positive images and customer perceptions. Mercedes is trying to get into the family and commercial and fleet sectors as well as maintaining its exclusivity, it is using this exclusivity as part of the drive into these sectors. Ford is trying to extend into exclusive/executive sectors (both through improving its Scorpio and Granada model range and also through the acquisition of Jaguar). Vauxhall/General Motors is currently entering into the high-performance/high-fashion sectors through the development of the Colibri model range.

Indeterminate positioning: this occurs where a niche or niches have not been so far established. Thus the Renault Group, Audi, Fiat and Alfa all produce high quality cars. They have not, however, thus far established a strong competitive position in the UK market. In the case of Renault this is remarkable in view of the success of the Clio both as a competitor in the small car sector and as a fashion offering.

Salient features such as safety and performance are becoming less remarkable as all manufacturers seek to improve both the product itself and the strength of its competitive position in this regard. Thus, for example, Saab and Volvo are no longer the only 'safe' ranges of cars. From the point of view of performance Range Rover has imitators produced by many of the other main manufacturers (for example, the Renault Espace or Mitsubishi Shogun). There are also high performance cars in most of the model ranges of Ford, Vauxhall, Nissan, Toyota and the Rover Group.

■ The threat of entry and barriers to entry

The threat of entry depends on the extent to which there are barriers to entry. Threat of entry is greater the lower or less critical is the barrier to entry. The major barriers are as follows.

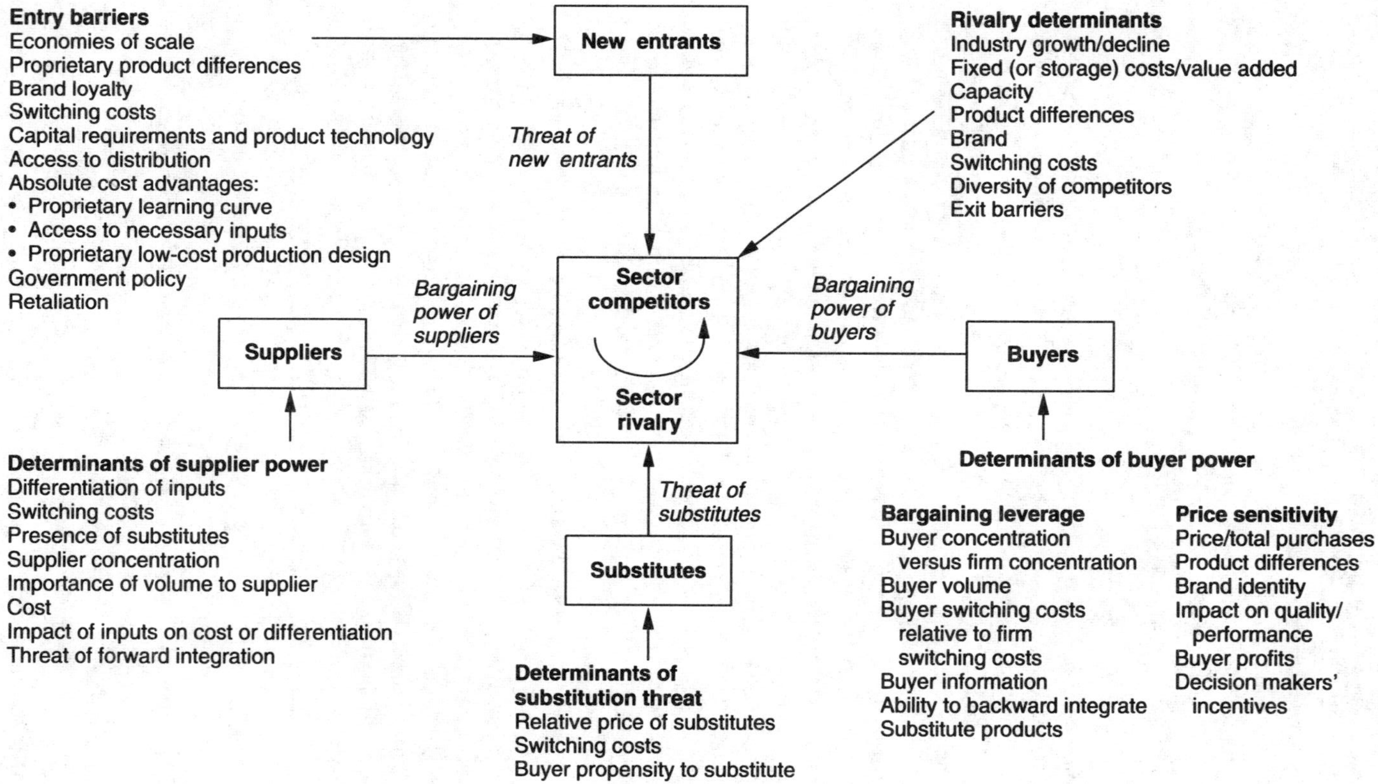

Figure 5.3 External pressures on the competitive position (a version of the Porter five-forces model)

Technology

This is the extent to which the necessary technology is available to potential market entrants. For many activities the technology to operate is universal and available on an open or commercial basis. The only issues are the financial ability to purchase it and the capability of staff to use it. In other sectors the technology is highly specialised or only available from a single supplier or few sources.

In capital project work the ability to operate in the field may depend upon having the capacity to first create the necessary technology. In order to build the Channel Tunnel, for example, Eurotunnel and its French partner had to be able to commission, design and build the tunnel boring machines before the tunnels themselves could be excavated.

Capital investment

This is the total level of investment necessary to gain access and the required foothold in the sector. The extent of capital required clearly varies between sectors. Account has also to be taken of payback times, return on capital employed and invested, opportunity costs, and alternative approaches.

In some sectors, partnership alternatives may be available while the market is being tested. For example, the ability to use distribution means and outlets of an existing operator (either on an experimental or short-term basis) might enable a potential entrant to test the viability of the market in question without having to engage in the capital investment necessary to create their own.

Staff and skills

This is the availability of the qualities and expertise necessary to operate in the chosen field. If it is an area of general activity (for example, retail distribution, production or operative work) these attributes may be found easily on the labour market. If there are high levels of economic rent to be paid for scarce or premium skills and knowledge, this in itself may constitute an entry barrier.

Conversely, the organisation may adopt the view that it is necessary to train staff in the required skills before opening. This approach was taken by Nissan, the Japanese car manufacturer at Washington in the north east of the UK and at Smyrna, Tennessee in the USA. The organisation retrained people who had previously been miners, shipyard workers and steelworkers, transforming them into highly skilled, advanced technology car production line operatives, before any commercial car production was undertaken.

Other cost barriers

These include the level of costs to be incurred as a continuous and commercial operator in the sector, and the consequent capacity of the organisation to sustain this. Cost premiums may be charged by both suppliers and distributors to new operators in a sector in order to cover their own uncertainties about them. This may be compounded if the new operator itself feels the need to bring its prices down simply in order to be able to gain an initial foothold. The new operator may thus find itself facing higher charges and reduced margins for the initial period of operation.

This may in turn generate a whole new set of commercial norms for the sector in question. Existing operators bring their charges and prices down, and the margins in the sector are reduced. The initial cost level, therefore, has to be borne over a much longer period of time; indeed, it may become the normal or accepted or essential way of working. An organisation which entered under one set of rules and norms may therefore find itself operating under another.

■ Familiarity barriers

New entrants may have to compete with the perceptions of permanence, quality and reliability of the established players in the field. To be able to do this successfully new entrants must take time and use the necessary resources to address the question of their own position in the sector and how to get over the barriers of familiarity. Closely related to this is the general question of confidence. In order to gain a foothold, a general aura of confidence in the capability and capacity of the new operator must be created. This has to be carried out both as part of the establishment of the new entrants as serious players in the field, and relative to other operators. In a relatively stable sector, or one in which key players have a long history of top-quality operation, this barrier to entry is high.

■ Other behavioural aspects

These are the more general norms and expectations of the sector and the ways in which business is conducted. New entrants have to be able to meet general standards of deadlines, delivery volumes, presentational standards and operational norms; or else they must be able to make their offering in distinctive ways which transcend the existing approach. Again, in sectors where there is a high degree of general operational familiarity, this barrier is high.

■ Legislation

Different sectors have their own legal constraints as well as general duties (such as those concerning employment, trading and financial practices). For example, those producing furniture, toys and clothes have to meet legal minimum standards of fire resistance. The distributors of these must also address this, and purchasers and buyers of these goods from manufacturers and wholesalers must satisfy themselves that the required standards have been met. It may be necessary to gain licences, or professional and personal qualifications in order to be able to operate in these sectors and activities.

All sectors have more general constraints placed upon them in regard to health and safety, and accident and disaster prevention. In some cases this is also very highly specialised and technologically driven. In these cases, this barrier has to be overcome in order to be able to operate.

■ Switching costs

Switching is the term given to the ability of an organisation to move or switch from one sphere of operations to another. In general, switching costs are low where the organisation in question has a generic or multi-purpose technology, where the staff are flexible or multi-skilled, or where no specialist attributes are required to make the proposed move, or where the existing product range can be repackaged or re-presented to gain entry.

Switching costs are high where the reverse of these elements is true. They are also higher where other entry barriers are present. Strategically the cost of switching will be balanced with other elements present. These include the need or desire to gain a foothold in the sector targeted, the state of the existing sector, the opportunities and consequences present, spare capacity, and the volatility or stability of both the present and proposed range of operations.

■ The ability to differentiate

In many sectors – cars, foodstuffs, clothing – other entry barriers are relatively low; nevertheless, a foothold in the sector may not be gained if a perception of distinction or uniqueness cannot first be generated. In these sectors differentiation is not just an entry barrier, but also a fixed cost: a consequence of operating in the sphere.

■ Market size

An assessment must be made of the current size and state of the market (whether in growth, steady state, maturity or decline). This is then followed by an assessment of whether the new entrant is to gain business at the expense of existing players in the field, or whether it is to expand the total size of the market (see Box 5.4).

BOX 5.4 Market Size

Gaining Business from Existing Players

An example of this is the threat felt by major grocery supermarket chains by the entry of cut-price operators – Netto, Costco, Aldi – into the field. The market is felt to be well extended, with little prospect of large volume growth. The activities of cut-price operators are therefore set up to take market share from the major players.

Expanding the Total Market

An example of this is the operational projection of the Channel Tunnel. The cross-Channel traffic volume between south-east England and north-west Europe has grown by between 10 and 20 per cent per annum over the period 1982–95 and is projected to continue to grow at this rate until 1999. Eurotunnel based its operational capacity, carriage projections and volumes on the view that this would continue to happen (despite recession). There was thus the conviction that the trading relationship between the UK and mainland Europe would continue to strengthen, and that the Channel Tunnel traffic would be picked up from this expanded capacity.

■ Exit barriers

Exit barriers occur when considering withdrawal from a niche, sector or sphere of activity. These are as follows.

■ Costs

There are costs and charges to be incurred as the result of ceasing operations and activities. Consideration is given here to the extent to which manufacturing plant and other operational capital goods still have life left in them, and the cost of forgoing this and the income that the sales of the resulting goods would generate. There may be redundancy, redeployment and retraining costs to be incurred as the result of withdrawal. Any other fixed charges have also to be considered.

In some circumstances, therefore, organisations find it more beneficial to continue operating at a loss than to withdraw altogether. This is clearly viable if the loss of market size, downturn or retrenchment is temporary and if a subsequent reversion to previous levels of prosperity is envisaged or indicated. It may also be necessary to consider or reconsider the contribution of the range of offerings in question. Withdrawal from one sector may lead to losses in others (caused, for example, by a more general loss of confidence); withdrawal of one product may lead to loss confidence in the rest of the range.

■ Confidence

This follows on directly from the previous point. Where a serious and general loss of confidence would occur by withdrawal, this exit barrier is clearly very high. Organisations therefore weigh up the effects of withdrawal from one product, service or offering range in terms of the general effect on the rest of their operations. It may be essential to maintain the full portfolio in the interest of this, even though certain elements are effectively a drain on it.

■ Reputation

Also related to this is the question of the organisation's general reputation. Any organisation ceasing operations and activities in one sector needs to do so without losing its general reputation. Again, the barrier is high where this is likely to occur. If it is nevertheless essential to withdraw for commercial reasons, intensive marketing activity is likely to be necessary to boost the remaining portfolio or product range. Conversely, it may be possible to present the divestment or withdrawal from the standpoint of refocusing, retrenchment, or concentrating on core business.

■ Familiarity

This is again related to confidence and reputation. Organisations may risk losing their general image of familiarity if they withdraw from some of the activities that have helped to build up that familiarity. Again, concentration elsewhere may require intensive marketing activity to refocus the customers and clients, and replace the previous familiarity and image with a new equivalent. It may also be that the organisation wishes to divest itself of its old familiarity; although in that case, it will need to have a new image to replace the old rather than leave a void.

■ Destabilisation

The organisation may need to consider the wider effects of its actions on the sector in which it operates. Where destabilisation is likely, this may lead either to merger or take-over with the consequent loss of identity to competitors.

In cases where a national presence in the sector was deemed essential, this led to nationalisation: the taking-over of the particular industry by the government of the country in question (for example, in the UK where the coal and steel sectors were taken into government ownership in the 1940s and 1950s).

Withdrawal of one player may lead to undercapacity in the sector, and a cost and price restructuring of it.

In any of these cases, both the withdrawing organisation and the sector concerned need to appraise the situation and be aware of the consequences of any such action. Again, in cases such as those indicated this exit barrier may be very high.

■ Domino effects

This problem arises where one course of action undertaken by one firm sets in train a whole range of other actions. Again, both organisation and the sector at large should be aware of the circumstances in which this might happen.

Domino effects in this context are caused by the withdrawal of a base product, element or service, which in turn causes other activities to be stopped. Thus the sudden unavailability of aviation fuel affects the whole of the air travel and airforce sectors. The sudden unavailability of hotel rooms on the Mediterranean coast affects the package tour industry of northern Europe. Downturns in production and the resultant unavailability of steel affects all manufacturing and engineering. Shortages of petrol affect transport, distribution and the personal motoring sectors. In all these cases the effects of one is to reduce the capacity of others to do business. This form of exit barrier can also therefore be very high.

■ Other wastage and losses

Most withdrawals are likely to lead to some wastage, scrap or decommissioning. This becomes a problem if it creates difficulties related to disposal. Again, there may be destabilising effects on the sector in question, related to the sudden availability of cheap second-hand production technology that still has a useful life, for instance. Extreme examples of this may be found in steel, coal, chemicals and nuclear sectors.

In each case where withdrawal is contemplated a decommissioning process is invoked. In all these cases there is the need to dispose of the toxic waste and to detoxify the operating plant. In each case, also, there are special considerations. Steelworks require dismantling and disposal. Mines require sealing and making safe both in general terms and to minimise the effects of subsidence. The chemical and nuclear industries both require the isolation and removal of the lethal and toxic elements until they can properly be made safe. In the case of some chemicals and nuclear industries, this requires the ability to isolate particular radioactive elements for thousands of years.

■ Secrets

Withdrawal from a sector may bring a range of people with specialist and expert knowledge on to the labour market. They may also come away from their current organisation with customer lists and preferences, charging policies, or other marketing secrets that would be of great value to the remaining operators. This has to be regarded as an exit barrier again from the point of view that the pressure or openness of such privileged information may be destabilising for the rest of the sector.

Excess and spare capacity

Excess and spare capacity is an exit barrier dependent upon the ability or otherwise to switch into other sectors. Part of this has to be seen in absolute cost and efficiency terms: for example, where sufficient production can be achieved in less than full speed of production. It must also be considered from the point of view of the sector concerned, and in relationship to the actual production technology and the other uses to which it could be put, and markets that it could serve. The final element is in relation to the other players in the sector: for example, if it is a slack sector, others may withdraw first, leaving the market in a better state for those who remain.

Risk

The concept of risk in strategy is the relationship between the path chosen, the obstacles to be encountered and the rewards that are to be achieved.

The distinction should immediately be drawn between risk and uncertainty. In simple terms risk may be measured and evaluated; uncertainty is the outcome of unplanned and unstructured activities. Risk may be insured against, uncertainty may not.

Extent of risk

The lower the level of risk the greater the degree of certainty; the higher the level of risk the greater the degree of uncertainty. The measurement of the extent of risk is the recognition, combination and evaluation of all those elements present in a situation and inherent in the proposed courses of action. Judgement is then based upon the net effect of this.

Analysis of risk

The components of this are as follows.

1. Market and sectoral trends. This is whether the sectors in question are growing or declining, either in size or prosperity and whether this is likely to continue. It also involves assessing factors affecting this at present which are likely to affect it in the future, and also those which could possibly or remotely affect it sometime in the future.

2. Substitutes and alternatives, and the substitution processes that are present in the sector. This includes what else people could do as alternatives to their current set of activities; those offerings that they might otherwise choose to buy; and the range and choice of alternative offerings that are available.
3. Social, political, legal and economic issues. This includes ethical and environmental considerations, and the question of doing something (or not) because it is acceptable (or not).
4. Operational aspects. Levels of resources, staffing, skills and capabilities (both available and required), and projections and prognoses for these for the future.
5. The constitution of the organisation: its directorate, executive management and the style and attitude and the extent to which these are stable, or changing, or open to reform, change or take-over.
6. Identification of the critical requirements of the success of the strategies and related operations, the desired and essential outcomes, the hard elements of profits, turnover, sales and activity volumes; and the soft elements of reputation, ethics and moral position.
7. A full consideration of the questions 'What can possibly go wrong?', 'What is the single most important factor for success?', and 'Where do the critical barriers or incidents along the pathway to this success lie?'
8. A projection and extrapolation process that addresses the identification of the best, medium and worst outcomes; an analysis of any critical path or critical incidents; the ability to extricate oneself from a situation and the consequences of this; the extent to which the direction taken is linear, and the entry and exit barriers to it; assessment of the full range of costs and benefits of the proposed direction.
9. Factors outside the control of the organisation and its managers.
10. Behavioural and perceptual issues and factors.
11. A crisis or early warning system, the development of strategic, operational and managerial antennae.

Quantitative, statistical and mathematical approaches are available to be used to project likely results and possible outcomes. These include:

- accounts, profit and loss modelling to assess commercial and cost viabilities;
- extrapolation, forecasting and projection techniques, (this also includes statistical modelling to assess profitability and likelihood; the critical path of a given project, balances and variables in relation to quantity, quality and time; and space and resource utilisation);
- the inclusion of given variables to project changes in circumstances and outcomes;
- required, projected and expected deadlines and assessment of the consequences of success or failure in meeting these.

This must then be placed in a situational context that includes:

- ways of working;
- the positioning of power, authority and influence;

- key characters and groups, *realpolitik*, over-mighty subjects and overmighty and influential stakeholders, pressure groups and lobbies;
- local factors and institutional aspects;
- strengths, weaknesses, opportunities and threats;
- aspects of difficulty, value, frequency, importance and presentation that are the components of critical incidents;
- the decision-making process, scalar chain and channels of communication;
- the culture, values, ethics, attitudes and beliefs of the organisation.

The end result is that an accurate and informed assessment of the risks in any activity is produced in advance. It does not mean that risks are not taken, but rather that an informed judgement of what these are has been made in advance. The purpose of doing this is to ensure that a truer range of the outcomes can be projected. If the activities indicated are undertaken thoroughly it also ensures avoidance of group-think and bunker mentalities. Finally, again, the assessment of risk can be used as part of the processes of strategy development, monitoring, evaluation and review. From the point of view of success or failure, an understanding of the nature of the risk undertaken and the way in which it was assessed and evaluated is essential.

The model is therefore for an assessment of risk and not for risk-free activities. It is a basis for informing strategic and managerial judgement. It should indicate those things that cannot possibly be done (for example, where there are absolute timescales) and absolute blockages on production paths and outputs (for example, in communications and technology). Risk analysis also indicates behavioural and perceptual propensities (both positive and negative), thus indicating where efforts in these regards on the part of the organisation need to be made. It is, to summarise, a process that has to be applied to all aspects of activities: the organisation and its capabilities, the markets served and their properties, the wider environment and the community and the interactions between each.

■ Segmentation

A segment is part of the business sphere, environment, community, fields of activities and operations which is both large enough and accessible and distinctive enough for an organisation to consider for the purpose of engaging in a range of profitable, successful and/or effective activities. The distinction is made here between profitable and effective in this context because of the particular concerns of the targeting of public services and not-for-profit sector activities. Whichever the context, the purpose is to define and understand the nature of that part of the market which is to be served, and to understand the wants and needs of those within it, their hopes and aspirations and the extent to which the offerings proposed by the organisation in question can satisfy these.

Segmentation is based on the following elements. The boundaries between each are not clear and sometimes more than one of these elements (or indeed all of them) may be used to define the segment.

■ Social

Social segmentation in the UK is as follows.

A	Aristocrats, upper middle class, higher managerial, administrative and professional.
B	Middle class, intermediate managerial and administrative, professional, technical; anyone holding official or professional positions in organisations.
C1	Lower management, clerical, white collar.
C2	Skilled manual workers such as electricians, builders, engineers: those with a trade, or technical, or technological training.
D	Semi-skilled and unskilled manual workers.
E	Those without job-related incomes: the unemployed and those on benefits and pensions of one sort or another; casual workers; the underclass.

This listing is based on the occupation of the head of household (who, in turn, was normally taken to be the male in the situation of a married couple). It is regarded as a useful and convenient, rather than an entirely valid basis for segmentation. It is not straightforward to assess segments on this basis alone.

■ Demographic

Simple demographic measures of the population are age; gender; location; and density and distribution of the population. It is possible to segment certain markets on this basis alone (the emphasis on Coca Cola sales to young people, for example), or the need to be able to sell toys to women since mothers buy them for use by their children). It is also possible to assess and decide what other needs they have. This enables the decision to be taken to make other offerings to a particular sector. Thus the Coca Cola drinker, for example, may also want distinctive or designer clothes. The success of the toys with their children may induce mothers to buy them clothes or crockery with the same motif, or comics telling stories about the toy characters.

This can then be further developed. If brand loyalty occurs as a result of these operations it may be profitable to extend the brand range. If organisation or company loyalty is developed the customer is likely to be sympathetic to other offerings that the organisation makes outside the particular sectors (for example, if the toy seller also offers garden furniture or plastic crockery under the same brand name). In the first place, the organisation develops its importance in the given segment; and this is followed by developing its expertise and profitability in a range of sectors and with a range of offerings.

BOX 5.5 Population Sectors and Segments

Summary and Elements

Sectors consist of one or more of the following:

- social: society groupings by income, age, status and location;
- generalised: for example, travellers, food shoppers;
- specialised: for example, first-class travellers;
- seasonal factors: influences on buyer behaviour (for example, ice cream in the summer; soup in the winter);
- characteristics and appearance: especially glamour, happiness, prosperity, fashion;
- fashionable, transient, faddish: short run, superficial;
- national, international, cosmopolitan, global;
- supply driven: for example, oil, public transport, foodstuffs (again);
- demand driven: for example, package holidays;
- technology driven: for example, components; specific sectors, especially information;
- means of purchase: cash, credit, hire purchase, deferred payment, credit cards, charge cards, loan, mortgage;
- means of payment preferred/desired/available to consumer: as above.

BOX 5.6 A Note on the Family

The Family

In the West, much segmentation continues to be based around generic concepts of the family, whatever the social reality may be. It is a very strong image and transcends a range of social situations, even where this archetype is not truly the norm. It is used as an image by all those operating in the consumer goods, car, holiday, sports and leisure sectors. Moreover, most organisations have fought shy of countering these images with the presentation of other family unit types (the single-parent family or step family, for example).

Ethnic Groups

The UK and USA both have significant ethnic group populations. In some cases they generate, or are perceived to generate, their own distinctive market sectors; an example is the branding of some facial cosmetics for women. In others there are important general issues to be faced; government marketing and presentations include images drawn from all sectors of the population in the pursuit of presentation of a unified and comfortable world.

Location

The segmentation process also concentrates on those in particular locations. This covers the entire spectrum from highly distinctive localities (the segment served by small shops and localised builders for example), towns, districts, regions, catchment areas, countries and continents.

■ Economic segmentation

This is the ability to group the population according to the amount of income of its members. This is then developed: patterns of spending are assessed. The amounts of disposable income that people have are calculated, together with what they spend it on, when they spend it, where they spend it and what the driving forces behind this spending are. Means of spending are assessed: the propensities to use cash, cheque books, credit cards, hire purchase, deferred payments, mortgages and the making of other long-term commitments. Major commitments that the segment has or is likely to have are assessed and deducted from the disposable income. Spending patterns are then prioritised. The end result of this is the relative ability to assess the amount of income the person has to spend in general and on each given product or service, the ways in which they are likely to spend, the frequency of this and where this falls in their schedule of priorities.

It should also be noted that economic segmentation can and does change especially as the result of outside variables. For example, rises in interest rates mean that those with mortgages to repay have greatly reduced disposable income, and this in turn leads to loss of sales, markets and, in many cases, livelihoods in other sectors. It also leads to stagnation in the property market, with people no longer able to afford to move into it; and those already in it are unable to afford to move on.

■ Segmentation by buying patterns

Buying patterns reflect the nature, intensity and frequency with which purchases are made by customers and consumers. It is important to distinguish the two. Most supermarket purchases are made by women, yet a high proportion of the purchases will be clearly consumed by men, boys and girls. In such cases, the products purchased have clearly therefore to appeal to both buyer and consumer.

The intensity of the buying relates to the volume and quality purchased at any one time. The frequency is the number of times that this 'any one time' occurs.

The question of location must also be addressed. This is the propensity to use different types of retail and distribution outlets in general and for specific items, and the frequency with which they are used.

Brand organisation and store loyalty have also to be considered. The first is related to the product itself (for example, where the customer buys Coca Cola rather than a cheaper substitute). The second is where the customer, say, always buys Ford cars, having started off with an old second-hand Escort as a teenager, he moves on to an XR2 in his early twenties; a second hand Fiesta Ghia in late twenties; an Escort or Orion when with a young and growing family; a Mondeo or Sierra with a large family, and so on. The third is the extent to which the customer can be persuaded to use the store for several purchases; in supermarket and department stores this is one-stop shopping.

■ Personality

Successful personality segmentation is achieved when strong positive personality types are presented with which customers can identify and which reflect their own patterns of behaviour (or a positive and comfortable version of it). Organisations therefore set out to try to create a personality or personality types for their offerings, which in turn reflect this.

Organisations may additionally use famous personalities as part of this process. When this is successful the customer and consumer therefore buy into the lifestyle of the top person in question.

The problem with both is being able to prove the effects of the association. The customers clearly buy products and their associations with which they are comfortable and confident. There is the question of the extent to which the brand personality (and any superstar involved) is the focus for this rather than a smaller element of it.

The presentation of personality is faddish and transient. It has currency only until it is superseded. Too great an emphasis on this means of segmentation may lead to an instant loss of market if the product personality is suddenly disgraced or rendered obsolete by its successor that has sudden appeal. In the particular case of the use of superstars there is an even greater risk. Products become passé when the next star comes along and endorses another offering. They may become untouchable if the celebrity in question is allegedly involved in immoral or scandalous conduct (see Box 5.7).

■ Quality

This is the identification of the extent to which quality is a concern. In some sectors there is a clear economic advantage for those able to satisfy demand (that is, where customers are prepared to pay almost any price provided that the

BOX 5.7 Personality: Cola Wars

During the period of the late 1980s and 1990s the Cola War raged between Pepsi and Coca Cola. It consisted of a range of creative, controversial marketing campaigns. These were conducted in a variety of ways. The overall purpose was for each to gain market share at the expense of the other; to regain market share from the peripheral offerings (department store and supermarket brands); to regain market share from alternative offerings (bottled water, Idris, Lilt, Seven-Up); and to transform the product from a high image soft drink into an essential feature in the life of the Western world.

The climax of the campaigns came when each picked a celebrity as the brand focus.

Coca Cola chose Madonna, who was known as a colourful and controversial character. In the period following this association she became involved in media stories relating both to her private life and the conduct of herself and her retinue during tours.

Pepsi chose Michael Jackson, a character strongly identified with the young child and teenage sectors. He was perceived to be a gentle and wholesome character. He also subsequently became involved in media stories relating to his private life and conduct.

The retention of these stars cost each company hundreds of millions of dollars. Neither the positive association and the effects on profits at the outset, nor the subsequent negative and any adverse effects on business have been published or demonstrated, and both brands are still clearly extremely strong.

quality is supreme). Otherwise, the ability to pay high prices is not universal and, as we have seen elsewhere there is normally a general price/quality trade-off balance to be struck.

Away from the extreme there are normally high-quality and good-quality segments as well as other general variations. These are often associated with other elements, such as lifestyle and status.

□ *Lifestyle*

Segmentation by lifestyle is conducted either by product strategy or by adoption. Lifestyle product strategy is the means whereby persons who live (or aspire to live) in a particular way are offered given clusters of products. They then buy from among these clusters in order to identify themselves with the given lifestyle.

Conversely, they may adopt the attitudes, values, beliefs, opinions and prejudices (or those that are perceived, expected or believed to be held) of those who already lead this lifestyle. This is of critical importance in the personal appearance and clothing sectors where fashion and fads are endemic. It is also important in the sectors where a fashion element has been introduced (such as with furniture, cars and electrical goods).

□ *Activities, interests and pursuits*

This is a derivation of the lifestyle approach to segmentation, but instead of concentrating on fashions, fads and opinions, the emphasis is on the nature of activities and pursuits in the sector. Segmentation is therefore defined in terms such as 'the ski set', 'the camping set' and 'the air travel sector'. Association is with these pursuits.

This segmentation has also been extended into job holding and working patterns. Segments exist and have been generated on this basis for such diverse offerings as microwave ovens, cosmetics, hairstyles, mobile telephones, ready meals and instant coffee.

□ *Status*

In this case segmentation is on the basis of the position of persons in society. Again this is broken down into two aspects; that of the actual position held in society; and that of the aspired or desired position in society.

■ Summary

Segmentation is not a science. There is no absolute or entirely accurate means of segmenting the population. Each means of segmentation tends to overlap with others and each segment invariably exhibits other qualities and attributes. It is however, a useful means of assessing the basis on which offerings are to be made and of forming judgements about the likely volume, buying power, durability and profitability of activities.

BOX 5.8 The Traditional Life Cycle

This is one way of looking at the basis on which segmentation is conducted. It consists of identifying each stage of the development of human life and the market opportunities that are related to them. The stages are as follows.

Childhood: This includes birth and infancy; the progress of the child to becoming a toddler; her arrival as a child at nursery, play group, infants, junior and secondary school age; her development as a consumer of food, drink, clothing, electrical goods, toys and books; her development of hobbies, interests, sports, pastimes; her entry into organisations and clubs such as the Brownies and Guides.

Adolescence:	This includes progress through the secondary school years to college, university, professional, skills, training and qualification; it includes the development of a child into young man; it includes the broadening of his development as a consumer and customer also and the recognition of fashions and fads and particular demands that go with this.
Young adulthood:	This includes progress through college and university, and the completion of professional and skilled training. It includes the establishment of the individual both at home and in her role as an independent consumer. It includes the first and subsequent steps in work, occupation and career paths and the earning of an independent disposable income. In all of these matters it generates opportunities and propensities to consume. Young men and young women both complete the transition to adulthood. For each there are distinctive social, occupational, recreational and leisure opportunities and pastimes.
Marriage:	This includes the progress through the period of betrothal or engagement, the marriage itself, marriage with no children, pregnancy, marriage with babies. The life cycle is then reviewed from the point of view of the parent: marriage with young children, older children, teenagers, adolescents and young adults. There is then the phase of marriage without children at home, and the development of relations between parents and children as independent householders.
Ageing and old age:	This is progress into grandparenthood, retirement, bereavement and dependency.

Clearly this is an archetype, the general version only of the progress of development of the human being. It presents a stereotype which used to be average and predictable. It is now less so. Clearly great changes have taken place and continue to do so in actual patterns of living. The purpose, however, is to recognise that there are distinctive life phases, and that each generates its own segments, niches and demands for products and services. It also draws a distinction (where these exist) between the customer, who is the person who pays for the offering, and the consumer, who is the person who actually uses it.

■ Nature of offerings

The excellence of a product or service, its own technical merits, are not enough; excellence and those merits must be translated into benefits for the customer, consumer or client.

■ Confidence

> 'I don't know you. I don't know your company. I don't know your products, their properties or qualities. Now what was it you wanted to sell me?'

For all activities, the confidence threshold has to be overcome. This means presenting the benefits of the offering from the point of view of the customer.

□ *'Consumer pull–product push'*

Many consumers do not actually clamour for products but once presented with them will enthusiastically accept them. The Walkman for example was originally developed from the extreme product push end but is now sold at the extreme consumer pull.

□ *Illusion and association*

Buildings are the ultimate reality in these terms, yet they may gain a reputation, positive or negative, based on the analysis of commentators, and thus be subject to the balance between reality and benefits. At the other end of the spectrum, tobacco products sell purely on the basis of the lifestyle and illusions that the customer is supposedly adopting or identifying with by buying the product. If a smoker subsequently develops heart or lung disease attributable to the cigarettes, he is then faced with the reality of that illusion (if that is the correct way of putting it).

BOX 5.9 Reality and Illusion

Useful examples of both the extremes – building and tobacco – referred to in the text may be given to illustrate the point.

The extension to the British Museum in London was designed by Sir Basil Spence and built in the late 1970s and early 1980s to a high standard and quality of both design and function. It lost much of its general credence not on the basis of operational or visual criteria, but on the criticism of the Prince of Wales. He described it as 'a monstrous carbuncle on the face of a much loved friend'. Its reputation is based on this analysis. The building therefore in turn suffers from this illusion. This is reflected in the shift in reputation of the organisation concerned.

The tobacco industry is not allowed to glamorise its products overtly. They must not be advertised in ways that give any impression that sporting, athletic or sexual prowess might accrue from their usage. This does not prevent Malboro from being the major sponsor of the Formula One Grand Prix circuit in which it gains extensive global television coverage; nor does this prevent Benson & Hedges from being the major sponsors of cricket in the UK and Australia.

■ Integrity

Offerings must have their own basic integrity. This is very difficult to define in absolute terms, and again it varies between sectors. It is the combination of quality, location, price, appearance, utility, presentation and support service, both of the offering in question and of those who offer it for sale or consumption.

■ Substance

The offering must fulfil the purpose for which it is designed, and meet the expectations of the customers. Otherwise, neither repeat business nor positive reputation is generated. Very few organisations indeed exist on the basis of one successful sale of one bad item.

Anything offered must therefore be as durable as required, for as long as required – whether hours or years – to fulfil its useful life.

■ The price quality value volume time mix

This is discussed in detail elsewhere in Chapter 5. At this stage it is useful to drive home the general point that there is an expectation of the presence of each of these elements in all offerings. Where quality is absolute there is still a price ceiling above which consumers will not buy but will rather look for a substitute. At the other extreme (where the price is low) there is still nevertheless a basic expectation of quality. Similarly, the offering may only have value to customers if it is easily and universally accessible (for example, groceries); or if it is only accessible at one exclusive place (for example, Marks & Spencer or Harrods).

■ Reputation

The components of this are familiarity, confidence, consistency, identity and impressions. These are reflected in the nature and type of perceptions, respect, esteem and value in which organisations and offerings are held.

A good reputation has to be earned. The only way to do this is to become a sound provider of offerings that meet the needs of the customer base. The building blocks of the reputation are both real (the actual performance of the organisation and its products and services), and behavioural (the marketing activities, brands and images that are generated in support of the reality and alongside it).

It is easier and quicker to lose a good reputation than to gain one. Part of the design and development of strategy must tackle this. As well as reputation building, organisations also invariably have public relations machinery for the handling of crises.

■ Core business

The core business is the organisation's cornerstone: that which is critical or central to the organisation's existence, performance, profitability and well being.

It will be one of the following:

1. The major source of organisation reputation: the one core product (or, if a product range, the key range) upon which the reputation is founded. In the case of Hoover, for example, this is the domestic floor cleaner. In the case of Coca Cola, it is 'the real thing'. In the case of McDonald's, it is the burgers.
2. The major source of organisation income: the one product (or narrow range of products) that brings in high levels of income or upon which the organisation is dependent for survival and continuity. This may or may not be the same as the source of reputation. In the examples given above, the major source of organisation income is the same. For car companies however, sales of service arrangements, extended warranties, finance plans, used cars and components often have a higher mark-up and trade volume than the sole sale of new products. For supermarkets, the sale of own-brand goods carries higher returns than those on branded goods, yet the customer is often attracted in the first place by the availability of the branded goods. Customers may also choose to go elsewhere if the full variety is not stocked, even if they always in fact buy the own brand.
3. The dominant product: this is easy to recognise in single or dominant product-type organisations (such as Guinness, Coca Cola and Hoover). Elsewhere this may be harder to identify: the essence is to be able to identify the chief or overwhelming source of organisation business. For a travel agent this may be package tours, plane tickets or car hire. For high-fashion clothing outlets this may be the 'by appointment to Her Majesty the Queen', or the fact that the clothes are worn by a particular person (for example, film and sports stars).

The core business may also be seen from the point of view of capital, technological or skills usage. This is especially true of small- to medium-sized batch production organisations and also consultancy and professional services activities, where the core product is likely to be speed and effectiveness of response, attitude to deadlines, and customer and client satisfaction.

It is also prevalent in those occupations where there is access to a range of information that may be presented in a variety of ways, to a range of different sectors.

The core customer

This is where the survival and prosperity of business depends upon the continued ability to satisfy the key or dominant customers, or customer bases, of the organisation. This occurs where whole product runs are bought up by a single customer (often, for example, in the food, clothing and component sectors). It also follows that the survival of the supplying organisation is inextricably linked to the continued prosperity of the organisation that is being supplied. It also occurs in relation to general groups: the price and sales of package tours and groceries are dependent upon levels of disposable income and the propensity to spend of these more generic customer bases.

Core image

This is where the organisation is dependent upon a dominant or overwhelming image that requires it to keep up the product around which the image is built. The core image is generally built around confidence, longevity and durability.

Peripheral business

Peripheral businesses are the other areas in which it is profitable or otherwise suitable for the organisation to be involved. This occurs normally for one of the following reasons.

1. Spare production, operational and output capacity, often based on the premise that it is more cost-effective to be producing for a limited return than not producing at all.
2. The relationship of the peripheral offering to the core. It is easy for a baker to make rolls with the end of the dough or cakes as an offering variety, even though the core business is bread.
3. The activities of competitors and the need to supply a range of benefits equivalent to those offered by the competitors. Failure to do this may risk losing market share to them.
4. The Packard effect: where the customer is attracted by the luxury peripheral product but actually buys from the core range. If the peripheral product were not kept on the initial means of attracting the customers to the core would be lost.
5. The 80/20 rule. The 80/20 rule is founded on the legend that '80 per cent of business is generated by 20 per cent of the offerings, and 80 per cent of the profit is generated by a given 20 per cent of sales.'

The wider context of this should now be considered. Regular customers make occasional purchases from the minority range. If this is withdrawn, the dissatisfaction engendered may be sufficiently great to lead them to take their entire business elsewhere. The minority range may also be the most attractive or photogenic part of the whole portfolio, as witness the examples of Concorde and the sports car (and other examples of the Packard effect). There is also the necessity to preserve the competitive position, especially if part of this is based on the offering of variety and choice. Even if customers always buy the majority offering, the removal of the ability to choose may lead itself to dissatisfaction.

One way of looking at this is to see effective product portfolios as consisting of:

- products to advertise;
- products to sell;
- products to make money.

BOX 5.10 P&O

P&O, the ferry operator, advertises itself as *offering* a cruising and leisurely experience. It *sells* meals and refreshments as part of the attraction to the cruising and leisurely experience. Above all it *makes its money* on duty-free sales.

BOX 5.11 Profit Impact of Market Studies (PIMS)

The PIMS strategies began at the US General Electric Company in 1960. They are based on a database of thousands of businesses, both companies and single and strategic business units from within sophisticated organisations.

The main and most enduring result of the studies is the positive relationship between high perceived market quality and excellent (in sectoral terms) returns on investment. The main criticism of the studies is the weighting previously put on market share and leadership, and the dominance that is extrapolated from these results.

These should be seen as a position from which to optimise corporate profits and competitive advantages for these organisations in this position, rather than necessarily being a signal to others to try to compete for this position of market dominance or else withdraw. The sector most dominated in this way was found to be fast moving consumer goods. The studies underlined the need to combine being an effective niche player with some other source of competitive advantage if the position of first or second in the market could not be achieved.

Other sources of market leadership can be:

- dominant local supplier;
- opening hours;
- convenience;
- quality;
- accessibility;
- reliable customer base.

BOX 5.12 The Range of Products, Services and Offerings

The terms product, service and offering are more or less interchangeable in the general context of describing, developing and analysing strategic concepts. Indeed, in practice, the term 'product' is often used by service organisations to describe and define their outputs; the same term is also used by those producing items for the service sectors – especially retail – and in the food and drink sector (Coca Cola, for example, is a product to the licensee who produces it, to the company that distributes it, to the outlet that sells it to the public and to the marketing activities that are generated in support of it). 'Offering' is a more precise academic term, but it has less universal usage and currency. The following sectors may be distinguished.

1. Primary production: mining, quarrying, oil, agriculture, forestry and fishing.
2. Primary processes: oil refining, chemicals, plastics, steel and other metals, concrete, cement and glass manufacture.
3. Energy production and distribution, especially gas and electricity.
4. Secondary processes: heavy manufacturing, engineering, civil engineering, major construction projects and works.
5. Other building and construction.
6. Finance, stockbroking, banking and insurance.
7. Retail distribution and wholesaling, including catalogue and mail order.
8. Mass global and local communications: media, news, information, publishing, television and radio.
9. Cars.
10. Travel, tourism and transport.
11. Fast moving consumer goods: including food sales, leisure products, audio and video cassettes and compact discs, clothing including the fashion sectors.
12. Consumer goods: domestic and household products, white goods (cookers, fridges, freezers, dishwashers, washing machines), domestic television and video personal entertainment.
13. Children's products, including toys and clothes.
14. Industrial supplies: capital goods, manufacturing plants, refinery and process technology.

15. Drugs and pharmaceuticals: both production and research.
16. Public services, both central and local government, European Union, United Nations. This also includes major public organisations such as the National Health Service. It also includes statutory instruments.
17. Health care.
18. Commercial services, including the range of consultancy and personal marketable expertise. This also includes professional sports and entertainers.
19. Leisure, including the provision and usage of sport and leisure centres and amenities.
20. Clothing.
21. Food and drink, restaurants, cafés and bars.
22. Furniture and household products.

This list is neither distinctive nor fully exhaustive. Clearly there are areas of overlap on the one hand, and particular areas that do not fit neatly into any of the sectors indicated on the other. It is, however, a useful indication of the nature and scope of the products, services and offerings. Overall also, the contention is that the principles of effective strategy are to be adopted in context across the board.

Conclusion

The value of conducting these activities lies in the knowledge and understanding of the opportunities and consequences of seeking to operate in particular sectors. If the activities and processes are fully realised, then the outcomes will be as outlined below.

1. Knowledge and understanding of the consumption habits and expectations of the sectors and segments targeted; an understanding of their priorities and aspirations; an understanding of what the concepts of value and confidence mean to them. All of this provides part of the basis on which effective work must be conducted. It is likely to indicate areas of dissatisfaction and lack of confidence within the current range of offerings, and means by which these may be improved.
2. Understanding of the range and nature of hurdles that have to be cleared before successful activities can be contemplated. If the result of some of the environmental analysis is that there is indeed a commercial opportunity present, then the entry barriers must be cleared if this is to become a reality.
3. Understanding of the full consequences of needing to escape or withdraw from a sector. This may have knock-on effects for the sector as reduced supply generally leads to increased prices with effects in turn for the particular customers and

consumers; or for the organisation withdrawing (withdrawal from one set of activities may cause questions to be raised about the confidence and stability of its remaining portfolio).

4. The ability to measure risk in given situations. Any activity has risks attached. The greater the knowledge, forethought and analysis generated at the outset and during the development of particular activities, the greater the chance of an accurate assessment of whether or not the initiative in question is truly worth undertaking.

These strategic processes and activities therefore provide a further basis for managerial and directoral analysis, and evaluation of proposed directions and initiatives. The result of engaging in these activities should be the ability to understand the necessities inherent in operating in a given sector, the obligations and expectations placed on those who do, and the reasons why organisations in it succeed and fail.

■ Work assignments and discussion questions

1. (a) What entry barriers are apparent for companies considering buying up parts of the British Rail range of activities as part of that organisation's privatisation?
   (b) What exit barriers must the government overcome in its pursuit of this policy?
2. Assess the nature and extent of risk incurred by the merger of the Halifax and Leeds building societies, and their change of status to bank/plc.
3. Which market segments are chiefly served by:-
   (a) Nissan Micra;
   (b) Nissan Prairie;
   (c) Nissan Primera?

   Be as precise as possible.

   What are the implications of this for the company in maintaining its competitive position; its pricing policy; and in new product development?
4. Why are some sectors believed to be relatively inaccessible to new operators? Why was The Body Shop successful in establishing a cosmetics retail chain, but initially unsuccessful in persuading department stores to purchase its products for sale as part of a wider range of offerings?

CHAPTER 6

Ethics and Standards

Introduction

All industrial, commercial and public services are concerned with absolute standards of conduct and activity. An ethical or moral stance in economic fields is not soft or unprofitable. It is the result of a wider approach and one that considers the whole of the business sphere and those who depend upon it. It is the result also of a fully considered view of the relationship between the organisation and its environment and of all points of contact and interaction between them. It is the basis on which the particular relationships between organisation, staff, customers and the communities are built. Ethical issues permeate each aspect of organisation conduct.

The ethical position of an organisation has therefore to be seen as the way in which it discharges its obligations to its stakeholders having taken the broadest possible view of what those obligations are. The boundaries of this are detailed in Box 6.1.

BOX 6.1 Obligations to Stakeholders

These obligations may be summarised as follows.

Staff:	The provision of steady, regular, adequate and increasing wages; access to organisation information; openness in dealings with the staff; clarity of communication means and systems; commitment to the quality of working life; regard to any local religious or special traditions and considerations; regular and continuous training and development; regular and continuous work and employment.
Customers and clients:	The provision of offerings in the volume and quality required at an acceptable price level; assumption of responsibilities for faults and problems; meeting complaints, inquiries and requests for information; sensitivity, empathy and understanding; setting standards in marketing, advertising and public relations.
The community:	The provision of steady levels of work for its members; disclosure of information on questions of public health, pollution, toxicity in regard to work practices and activities;

	the maintenance of a good and positive reputation; the question of access to schools, students and other local organisations; commitment to the quality of life; regard for any local religious or special traditions and customs.
Backers:	The provision of adequate, steady and (ideally) increasing rates of return on investment; disclosure of information; the maintenance of confidence; the maintenance of quality and positive images and reputation.
Suppliers and distributors:	Obligations to continue in business; the effects of the organisation's activities and prosperity on these; and any special obligations in regard to these.
The environment:	Obligations in regard to pollution, waste, and effluent disposal; replacing and repairing any damage caused; the search for constant improvements in this area.
The nature of the sector concerned:	All sectors have areas where the question of specific ethics is raised. However, this is clearly more extreme in, for example, the fields of defence, chemicals, medical research, drugs, tobacco, alcohol and pharmaceuticals.

Much of this is unquantifiable. Much also means different things to different organisations. However the matters of principle should always be clear. Moreover, it indicates clearly the nature of these obligations placed on organisations and those who direct and manage them.

The idea is not new. Organisations have taken strong moral and ethical stances through the post-industrial revolution period, and this approach has covered all aspects of business activities.

The UK chocolate company, Cadbury, built a model village for its employees on the outskirts of Birmingham at Bourneville. Those who worked for the company were required to live in the village. Schooling was provided for the children of the employees. Shops were provided and stocked with produce that enabled a healthy lifestyle to be enjoyed and to ensure that the worker was permanently ready to do work. Alms houses were provided for the elderly. The purpose was to provide a stable and healthy work force that would produce good products for the company. The Cadbury family took the view that this was the best way to ensure long-term profitability and viability for the company. They thus invested in the physical, educational, environmental and spiritual welfare of their staff. The returns on this investment were assessed in terms of stability, retention, obligation and capabilities. Above all, the returns were measured in profits, both immediate and continuing. Other organisations followed suit, building both factories and housing on the edges of big cities rather than in the centres (for example, the other UK chocolate companies: (Terry's, Rowntree, MacIntosh).

Models and frameworks

Models for the establishment of what is ethical are essential if a useful discussion is to be held. Adams, Carruthers and Hamil (1991), in a major survey of organisations working in the UK, proposed the following parameters:

- disclosure of information, in terms of volume and quality and to all stakeholders;
- employment issues, pay, benefits and conditions, industrial democracy, equality of opportunity, information and participation;
- community involvement and relations with the environment;
- relations with other countries including those with oppressive regimes; and including also the emerging countries of the Third World, and the relationship of mutual dependence and interdependence that the company has established with them.
- political involvement and donations to political parties, candidates, and other vested interests and pressure groups;
- the nature of products and services, with particular emphasis on tobacco, alcohol, drugs, and military sales;
- marketing policies and attitudes to consumers, customers and client groups, with particular reference again to emerging markets.
- a general respect for people and life.

Christensen *et al.* (1987, 1993) described the company and its responsibilities to society and outlined the following matters for consideration:

- the moral components of corporate strategy and categories of concern, which they identify under the generic headings of 'the world', 'the nation', 'the local community', 'industry' and 'the company';
- the range of concerns that ought to be considered by organisations;
- a choice of strategic alternatives for social action and its relationship with business and organisation objectives.

Johnson and Scholes (1993) identify a conception of business ethics at three levels: the macro (or global); the corporate (or organisational); and the individual, which includes the role of managers in the organisation for the setting and maintenance of standards in both work practice and operations. Inside this outline are internal and external aspects.

The internal relate mainly to concern for employees: their welfare, working conditions, design and configuration of jobs. *The external* relate to 'green' issues and concern for the products themselves; marketing activities; the nature of the market supplied; relationships with suppliers; employment policies and sources of staff; and community activities and the doing of good works.

This approach may also be reversed in order to identify all those factors that limit or modify (or indeed, enhance) what is at first envisaged. This is summarised and illustrated in Figure 6.1. It identifies different aspects through which this occurs as follows:

- the 'public': public interest, public lobbies and pressure groups;
- specific interests: socio-political groups and lobbies, and other vested interests.

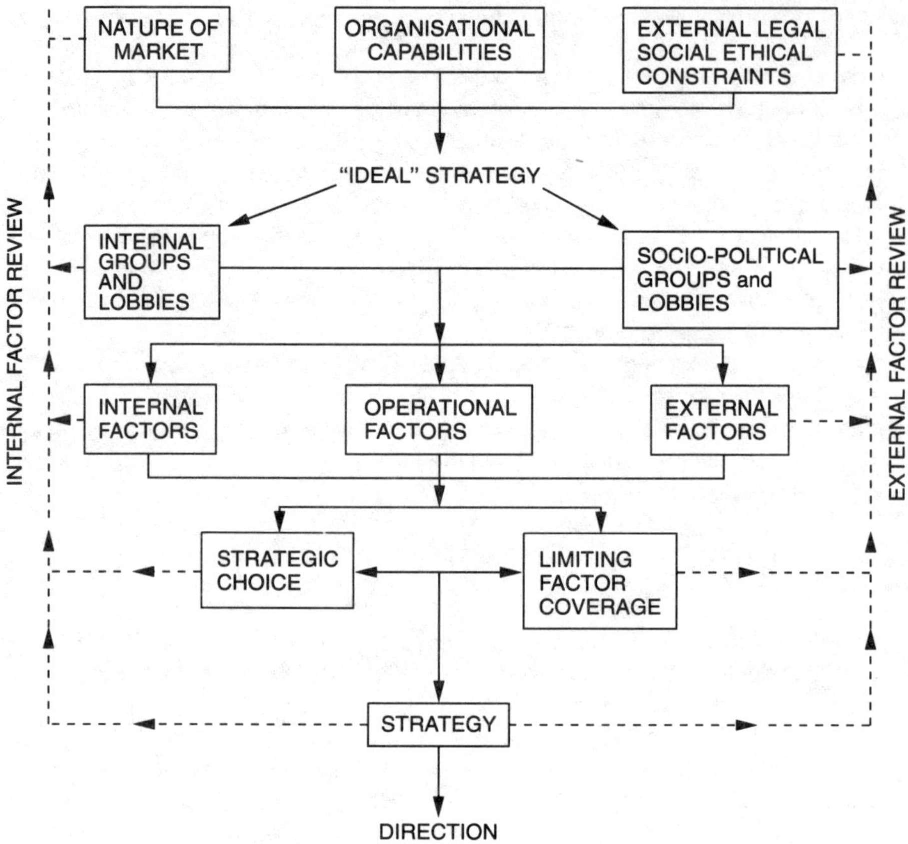

Figure 6.1 The effects of social and ethical pressures on strategy determination

Factors

These include:

- internal factors, or the capabilities of the organisation to take on what is now proposed;
- operational factors, or the capabilities of the technology, production and process methods;
- external factors: social or community pressures, or pressures from other interested parties such as recognised trade unions and employers' federations.

The result of this is that the choice of strategy is heavily influenced by what is summarised as *limiting factor coverage*: the combination of the public interest, other pressures and their interaction.

The whole process is subject to constant review. The end result is ideally an organisation strategy that is both effective and acceptable. At the very least an understanding of this should indicate where social and ethical resistance are likely to lie. It then becomes a matter of organisation choice as to whether these are to be overcome or whether it is unacceptable to proceed.

Sternberg (1995) identified a model of business ethics called 'just business'. In this, the highest moral duty of a business is to remain in existence (that is, effective and profitable) over the long term, providing continuity of service to customers, continuity of employment to staff, and continuity and confidence in the community. Three distinctive strands are identified: maximising long-term owner value; distributive justice (the sharing-out of rewards and benefits to staff according to the value of their contribution); and ordinary common decency.

Sternberg's argument is based on the premise that ethical concerns are to be found in every aspect of business, commercial and public service activities. There is a direct relationship between clarity of purpose and integrity of purpose: to be fully effective, staff must be happy and confident, as well as clear about what they are being asked to do; customers must be happy that they are purchasing good-quality products from an honest company; the community must be happy that it is supporting a principled and sound organisation.

BOX 6.2 Ethics and Language

Consider the following statements.

> Adam appears to be suffering either from dyslexia, or deafness, or neglect. It is essential that further tests are carried out on him as a matter of great urgency. A meeting should be convened between the education psychologist, social services and the education welfare office with a view to producing a report so that his case may be considered further.

> Adam appears to be suffering either from dyslexia, or deafness, or neglect. He must be tested for these by Friday. His case is then to be discussed the following Tuesday. He will then receive the correct remedial treatment forthwith.

Which statement gives a greater commitment to service? Which shows a greater responsibility to the client? Which approach will be of greatest benefit and value to the client?

Ethics and language

The use of direct and positive language means that everybody knows where they stand and what to expect from the organisation. The use of obscure, complicated and indirect language means that the converse is true. The message that is actually given out is that the organisation is either unclear as to its purpose or is hedging its bets, and may not be able to deliver. This is compounded where the organisation uses negative language.

Worst of all is where organisations use phrases such as 'We will monitor the situation' or 'We are watching events closely.' This translates as: 'We will sway with the wind' or 'We will only do something for you if we find it to be in our interests to do so.'

This extends to all activities and to dealings with customers and the community, and in relation to the organisation's own staff. In all cases, the simpler the language used, the greater the understanding of the organisation's obligations and commitments, and the greater the general regard in which it is held.

There are some common strands and some clear inferences and conclusions may be drawn. Overall, however, there is no complete approach to business ethics. The terms are qualitative and require definition; and such definitions require individual attention. They are not absolute, but rather place the emphasis on both organisations and their managers to set and maintain standards. It further requires the recognition of responsibility on the part of organisations and their managers to each of the groups and interests with which they come into contact: the staff, customers, clients, suppliers, markets and communities.

It also requires an accurate assessment to be made of the relationship with each of these groups, so that if what is actually done is opportunistic or expedient, the organisation recognises this and assesses in advance that there are consequences attached to it.

It also becomes apparent that there are gaps in the approach. Organisations themselves must recognise what these standards are and how to set and apply them. This is especially true where they may be economically dominant, or able to operate in ways unrestricted or unfettered by legal constraints, or where the location requires the economic activity above all other considerations (at least in the short to medium term). It follows from this that organisations must assess and evaluate the opportunity costs of activities; whether to take the economic rewards at the expense of all else, or whether to establish a more 'enlightened' approach in which the levels of return are reduced, but in which the purpose is to create a more longstanding, more considered, and socially fruitful relationship between organisation and community.

Again, there are problems with definitions. 'Enlightenment' is a value judgement placed by one vested interest on the standards adopted in principle and practice by another. Something that is socially fruitful or mutually beneficial must be seen in the terms of those who are to benefit; and where, for example, there is an overwhelming imperative to short-term economic growth, a more considered or 'ethical' approach may actually work against this. The organisation may establish itself in a socially or politically volatile part of the world; and may lose resources and capacities that affect other parts of its operations in any subsequent upheaval or revolution in that particular location.

What is certain to emerge, therefore, is a model which is flawed. It lacks precision and is open to subjective interpretation and evaluation. Within these limitations the following concepts are proposed for the consideration of this part of the strategy process and development:

- model employer;
- corporate citizenship.

The model employer

Consideration of this involves setting standards of behaviour and practice towards the employees or organisations on the part of its directors and top managers. A good early example of this is the Cadbury Company (see above). Operating in the West Midlands in the nineteenth century, the approach taken was contrary to the prevailing wisdom of the times which overwhelmingly regarded the work force purely as the means to an end: the output of the day.

The concept of the model employer has subsequently been developed in a variety of ways.

Professionalism, and the related concept of professionalisation of certain occupations has engendered a pride, commitment and continuity of activity among those carrying out these activities. This is especially true among the so-called public professions of teacher, doctor, nurse, social worker, police officer, fire officer and the support activities that go with these occupations, where a great commitment to service has been engendered among those working in the sectors, in return for incremental salaries, continuous professional education, training and development, promotion and mobility prospects, and a direct say, input and responsibility for the actual service delivery. At its height what was thus engendered was a quite extraordinary level of commitment both to the service itself and its recipients and client groups.

Paternalism and conformity, whereby standards of workplace activity, management style and ways of working are clearly established by the employer. Anyone who comes to work for the employer is required to adopt these standards as a precondition of employment. Such employers are not 'all things to all people'. They rather require measures of conformity. This approach is adopted by Japanese companies in the establishment of divisions and operations in the West. It is also to be found in such organisations as IBM, McDonald's, British Airways, Marks & Spencer, Virgin and The Body Shop.

In such organisations employees are required to practise their trade in accordance with the standards and guidelines laid down by the organisation, rather than defining their own scope of operations. For those coming into the company and bringing with them a high degree of education, training or expertise, it is usual to go through an extensive induction, settling-in and orientation programme. The result of this is that ideally a strong organisation perspective, orientation and identity is married up with the expertise brought in; this expertise is then delivered to customers and clients in the ways required by the organisation. This is effectively a variation on the traditional unitary perspective familiar to students of human resource management and industrial relations, which requires the adoption of organisational values and attitudes in the pursuit of one's occupation within it.

In order for this to be successful, the attitudes, values and beliefs of the organisation have to be capable of being received and adopted by those coming to work for it. Whatever these are, a mutuality of interest must be established. The organisation, for its part, must not lose sight of why people come to work for it. As stated elsewhere, general matters relating to confidence and continuity must be clearly indicated. There is also increasingly a prevailing wisdom that an overt statement of profitability (or, in public service terms, effectiveness) is required. There is therefore communicated a clarity of purpose on the part of the organisation to which everyone can aspire and which everyone can recognise.

Participation. Model employers give a clear lead, direction, clarity of vision and purpose to an organisation. However, this must be reconciled with the need for employees to belong, to identify and gain involvement with the organisation itself. The greatest contribution here is through the volume and quality of information made available to employees. This has to be supported by the quality, value and effectiveness of the channels of communication adopted, the extent to which the organisation truly involves its staff in the implementation of decisions and the reasons why they have been taken. This is also true in conveying the reasons, structure and style of the day-to-day operations of the organisation. The overall purpose must be to engage a full and healthy awareness of the position of the organisation in its markets and activities, and an engagement of the commitment of the employees to its continuous improvement. Particular regard will be paid to the levels of grievance and dispute and the grapevine and its operations. Particular attention will be paid also to the use of formal alternative channels, especially where trade unions are recognised, and the nature of the material that is being put through there. Any organisation aspiring to be a model employer will take account of all this. It must further be treated as a process and not an adjunct. As with all other activities, communication at its best is a positive and dynamic process, and one that it is capable of constant improvement.

BOX 6.3 'Fly It? They Own It'

In the hours following the news that United Airlines employees had bought a controlling share of 55% of their own company, solidarity was breaking out everywhere. Outside headquarters near Chicago's O'Hare Airport, senior United Airline executives were grilling burgers on portable barbecues for mechanics and pilots, while many at the gathering had buttons that read 'Ask me, I'm the owner'. The new Chairman, Gerald Greenwald, was flying from New York to Chicago and then on to Los Angeles and Denver to introduce himself to his new employees.

Now that they are in charge the 54,000 new owners of the world's largest airline must earn their keep and pay their bills. There is a tough new challenge from the king of cut price airlines, Southwest, coming just when United's profits are starting to rebound after three years of heavy losses. Until the arrival of Greenwald, everybody assumed that redundancies and lay-offs would be necessary to put United back on track. The previous Chairman, Stephen Wolf, was certain of this – he had strengthened the airline considerably during his six years at the helm, expended the worldwide route system, including that between Chicago and Tokyo (the airline's most profitable) and had cut costs by $1 billion ($1 thousand million) annually over the previous three years. It was Wolf's determination to have further redundancies which brought about the employees' bid to buy the controlling share. Under the buy-out terms, Wolf departed, Greenwald was appointed and employee will select 3 of the 12 United Airlines Directors. In exchange, the employees will put up $5 billion in wage and benefit concessions over 5 years in order to reduce the airlines labour costs by 14%.

As the new crew takes over, it is facing a ferocious fare battle with Southwest. United has launched its own cut price service called United Shuttle. It would be a low cost subsidiary carrier that would compete with Southwest on many of its short haul routes in the Western United States. This particular competition has helped to concentrate the minds of the staff as they look forward to a new era at United Airlines.

Unfortunately, it has taken 7 years for United to get to this point. Since 1987, its employees have fought bitterly with management and one another over terms and conditions of employment. They have also fought among themselves over terms that could be provided as part of a buy out. Buying a chunk of the financially pressed company meant giving up substantial pay and benefits.

As the employees viewed it, the airline lost money: from 1991 to the end of 1993, United lost a total of $1.3 billion. That performance was characteristic of an industry whose 9 major airlines collectively lost more than $12 billion as they engaged in ruinous price wars and spent money to expand into each other's markets. Now after a year of encouraging traffic growth, the top airlines are expected all to take profits in 1994. United is expecting a 1994 profit of $100 million.

Moreover, as part of the take-over, United's employees got a boss that they seem to like. Wolf, the previous Chairman, had not endeared himself to his workers – United flight attendants claim that on one 12–hour flight to Asia he said not a word to the cabin crew. Greenwald is expected to help build the *esprit de corps* that the company will need in the months ahead. A Chicago investment advisor close to the deal said, 'There are going to be a lot of extra hours, and some people are going to see $160 a month less in their pay cheques. I wonder if they understand what they've really done'.

Source: Janice Castro, *Time Magazine*, 25 July 1994.

□ *The workforce as genuine stakeholder*

The elevation of the work force to the status of 'stakeholder' should also be considered. There is an increasing realisation that the adoption of the view of 'one work force', rather than the establishment of and maintenance of divides between staff categories, is of benefit both behaviourally and operationally. In the former case there is the removal of the need for extensive and formalised procedures, except in cases where there has arisen a genuine misunderstanding. In the latter, resources are concentrated on the organisation's activities rather than on matters of status, hierarchy or functional divide. In such situations there is often created a works council or works forum, in which employment and staffing matters and concerns are addressed. This is again conducted from the standpoint that organisational effectiveness, profitability and continuity are of paramount importance, and in no case should it ever become a duplication of any collective bargaining or similar activity. Indeed, many organisations find this to be a much more effective way of conducting human resource and staff relations than formalised systems of collective bargaining.

□ *Pay and reward*

A view also exists of the position of pay and reward in the generation of loyalty, identity, commitment and high performance.

Especially, there is a strong view that leads towards both the giving of share equity in the organisation as part of the reward package, and the encouragement of employees in all aspects and operations to take up equity options. The excellence studies of Peters and others found a strong positive correlation between equity ownership, profitability and continuity (for example in the US steel and textile sectors). In the UK, the privatisation of activities through management and staff buy-outs has greatly encouraged the take-up of equity (for example as with the National Freight Corporation, and Medway Ports Authority). Also, in the UK the franchise auction for regional independent and commercial television stations led to managers and directors of the London Weekend Television Company buying equity in the company in advance of the success of the bid: the level of commitment and interest in the success of the bid was thus assured. In all cases what is and has been generated is both a financial advantage and a positive behavioural commitment and identity with the organisation and its success.

□ *The workplace.*

The workplace of the model employer is designed to ensure that 'utility is the criterion of style'. The location and environment in which activities are to take place will be comfortable, adequate and well equipped. Plant, machinery and technology has to be suitable for the purposes required. All operations are supported by health, recreation, rest and eating areas that are also of a good standard for those using them and which reinforce the messages of positive identity supposedly being generated. The same facilities will be available to anyone and everyone who works in the organisation. The same criteria will be applied to anyone who requires new plant or equipment; these criteria are based on answers to questions relating to improvement in products or service, quality and output.

BOX 6.4 Trappings

Model employers do not waste organisational resources on 'the trappings of success'. Organisations the world over are moving away from this approach to business. The lessons to be drawn from it, however, are very useful. There is a general point relating to the changing nature of the business sphere and the effect of perceptions and expectations on it. Such trappings can, are and were viewed from one of two standpoints. The first was that having and living and working in such luxury reflected the supreme excellence of the organisation. The other was that it was ostentation and self-aggrandisement, and ought to be discouraged. In the past 30 years there has been a steady transition from the former to the latter (although plenty of examples remain of the former). A trawl of the companies in the excellence studies reveals, however, that many of the organisations that made the transition had to make it as part of a radical change (that is, towards the latter). The organisations with the greatest continuity and high profits never engaged in such ostentation and indulgence in the first place.

□ *Employee development*

The capabilities, qualities and attributes of the employee are to be developed as part of the process of continuous development and improvement.

It is the organisation's responsibility to see that this is done, and where necessary to strongly urge and encourage it to take place. Attention should be paid to the development of the whole person, rather than taking merely a narrow view of their operational capacities and requirements; this approach will not only have an impact in any case on their operational capabilities, but also reinforce the positive attitudes and behaviour to maintain the position of being a truly model employer. It is therefore necessary to undertake something that addresses the issues of personal, professional and organisation development as well as that related purely to the operations of the individual. The process of development is actually commenced at the job advertisement, recruitment, selection and induction stage; it is subsequently conducted in a variety of means and settings (classes, projects, secondments, multi-skilling activities, and technical training); and also in matters with regard to the development of character and the formation of corporate attitudes and belief; this is in turn conducted at both the workplace and on the job. Some organisations again take this a stage further and organise, encourage and pay for any training at all, provided that what is done does not actually interfere with the employee's ability to do the job.

□ *Behaviour and demeanour*

Organisations in the West are increasingly assuming responsibility for the standards of behaviour and demeanour required of their employees. This occurs at many levels. At its most basic, organisations ban smoking at the workplace because it is bad for employees, and creates a disadvantageous environment for non-smoking employees (and of course because organisations are likely to face insurance problems and damages claims either for the staff contracting smoke-related diseases, or from customers and clients perceiving that the products and outputs may be contaminated). This is taken a stage further by Ford, for example, which bans all smoking in all company cars.

Organisations also insist that their staff do not have alcoholic drinks on the premises (for example, for boardroom receptions and other public relations functions). They may forbid the staff from drinking alcohol during their lunch hour (however moderately). This is common throughout the banking sector of the City of London.

Organisations may also insist on a dress code or uniform (in the case of the latter, this is normally issued by the organisation). They may also insist that it is worn correctly, especially if it is to be worn in public to travel to and from work.

Organisations may insist on certain standards of behaviour and demeanour in public, imposing severe penalties (even dismissal) when this is transgressed. If an employee becomes involved in a fight during her leisure hours, for example, the organisation may carry out its own inquiry into this, and disciplinary action or even dismissal may result if the organisation feels that the employee was to blame for the incident. They may also take a view that the employee was prevented or disabled from doing their job (for example, as a result of injuries sustained in a fight). The employee may also be disciplined or dismissed for bringing bad publicity on to the organisation.

A balance has clearly to be struck between setting standards and intrusion into private lives and activities. However, organisations are increasingly recognising that an assumption of responsibility for general standards of behaviour and demeanour is part of their overall obligation to their employees.

□ *Employee maintenance*

The model employer takes absolute care of the staff. This involves the design and construction of places of work that are comfortable, efficient, suitable and effective for the purposes required. This in turn contributes to the elimination of accidents, injuries, strains and stresses. The treatment and rehabilitation of those who do get injured or ill is an organisational obligation in response to afflictions gained at the workplace: and often this is extended to all afflictions, injuries and illnesses. Many employers take a broader view of this still, and provide active assistance, guidance, counselling, and rehabilitation for members of staff who smoke or who have drug, substance and alcohol dependency problems.

It follows from this that good organisations take an active interest in the levels, rates and types of sickness incurred by those who work for them. This need not be punitive or intrusive. If the organisation is truly a model employer, the invariable requirement is to convince people to go home because they are ill, rather than to get them to come to work when they are not.

Organisations will therefore design workstations and work practices with a view to avoiding these problems as far as possible. When they do occur the objective is to obtain for employees the best possible treatment as soon as possible, with a view to getting them back to work quickly and fully recovered. Occupational health, medical, physiotherapy, counselling and guidance facilities laid on by the organisation will all be geared up to this.

Other initiatives are being taken in the area of employee maintenance. The standpoint adopted is that the employee is at her best if she is as free as possible from strain or worry. There is an onus on the employer to make a contribution here as the employee is investing amounts of time, skill and effort in it. Matters worth mentioning here include: financial and debt counselling; marriage and family guidance counselling and therapy; extensive relocation guidance (where required by the organisation); retraining and re-skilling; and matters relating to job and occupation design and redesign should also be mentioned here.

□ *Equality and fairness*

Genuine equality and fairness of treatment and opportunity is given to all employees based on occupational capability and potential.

In the pursuit of such a simple concept, great arrays of codes of practice and conduct, legal considerations and definitions have sprung up all over the business sphere. Organisations and their managers discriminate and differentiate between members of staff, and potential members of staff, on grounds of age, sex/gender, skin colour, ethnic origin, race, religion, disability, membership of clubs, societies or unions, and marital status; anything, in fact, rather than capability and capacity to do the job. If any of these issues is genuinely an exclusion to employment (or a genuine occupational qualification) then the organisation should be prepared to say so. If not, to use them as criteria for selection, promotion or exclusion, is simply a clear indication that the managers concerned are not doing their jobs properly.

It follows from this that equality and fairness of opportunity, treatment and general approach to staff is a corporate state of mind, a corporate attitude, and one that is to be fostered and engendered among all those who work in the organisation. If this is successfully achieved, it pervades the whole organisation and all those working in it.

There are sound reasons for taking this approach. Staff respond better if they know that they are to be treated fairly and equally, if there is truly an equality of opportunity and access available to them. Staff respond better also if they know that they are important and valued in their own sphere, and in their own occupation and output, regardless of the actual job that they do. Japanese companies are particularly strong here. The standpoint that is found throughout them may be summarised as 'without cleaners, the premises will not be clean'. Everyone is hired because in their own sphere they are experts.

Related to this is the question of status. If status differentials are used or employed in the organisation this must not be at the expense of fairness and equality. Ideally, status is measured in terms of outputs only, and where such differentials are required or in use again this should be related to performance rather than rank.

BOX 6.5 Equality of Opportunity in the UK and EC

In the UK and EC it is unlawful to discriminate for purposes of employment, promotion or dismissal on the basis of:

- sex and gender;
- race and ethnic origin;
- membership of a trade union *or* refusal to join a trade union;
- spent convictions, unless they relate directly to the nature of work that the individual is to take up;
- physical disability, such as blindness/visual impairment; deafness/hearing impairment; wheelchair confinement.

Notes

UK and EC law is still being developed in these areas. Current initiatives include the inclusion of marital status and pregnancy as grounds of sex/gender discrimination. Initiatives are also proposed to make it unlawful to discriminate on grounds of age or location.

'Best practice' is a concept of UK human resource practices that seeks to promote and develop the required attitudes and approaches in regard to equality of opportunity. National, public and expert bodies such as the Advisory, Conciliation and Arbitration Service, the Institute of Personnel and Development and Health and Safety Executive issue codes of practice and conduct designed to ensure that organisations take positive steps in this area, and therefore indeed regard the staff as a genuine human resource, and not simply as population tranches. Such bodies offer training, development and attitude formation activities as part of their services. It is underpinned by recourse to the law, both through the courts and also systems of tribunals and arbitration.

The effect has been to raise awareness of what equality is, and to take positive steps in the changing of organisation and managerial attitudes and behaviour. However, genuinely changing attitudes, values, beliefs and prejudices in ways that are designed to last is a much longer and harder task.

BOX 6.6 Wendy

Tom Peters was invited to address the Wendy Company annual staff gathering. In his opening remarks, David Taylor, the Chairman of Wendy, said, 'These are the best 1500 people in America, Tom. You do your best for them.'

Source: Peters and Austin (1984).

The outcome of the whole approach of being a model employer is that universal standards are set and effectively agreed and adopted by all those who work in the organisation. Anyone who does not either aspire to these, or conform to them, leaves or is not engaged in the first place. Any deviation from these is easily recognised and can therefore be dealt with before a real problem or bone of contention ensues.

BOX 6.7 Caveats to the Model Employer Approach

There are some problems with the approach. The main features are as follows.

Coercion

As a last resort the approach is prescriptive and coercive. If the boundaries of activity are not accurately drawn, and if the company line is too restrictive, then both business activities and organisation and individual behaviour are stifled.

Furthermore, organisations may become too intrusive in the private lives of those who work for them.

Introspection

The organisation and its staff may become inward looking. This may take the form of an endless round of self-congratulation. At its worst this generates a bunker mentality in which a version of the world is drawn up within the organisation and this is the world that the organisation responds to; it is the negation of operational and environmental reality. In either case the organisation effectively puts up blocks and barriers to outside influences, regarding them with suspicion as intrusive. Again, at its worst it simply denies the reality of the world in which it operates.

An End in Itself

The reality of being 'a model employer' is seen as a goal rather than as a process. Standards are allowed to stagnate, rust, or even decline. The reality of being a model employer falls from pre-eminence, as does its importance to both the organisation itself and its directorate and senior managers.

□ *Shared values*

This concept was first widely articulated in the excellence studies. It is one of the 7 Ss in the McKinsey model of organisations.

In order for people to work effectively and productively in an organisation they must have common reasons for being there. Williams, Dobson, and Walters (1987) identify four levels of this as follows.

1. Alienated involvement, where those present reject the organisation's values and where they possess a negative attitude but go along with the work of the organisation either out of habit or because a lack of choice or alternatives is perceived (or real).
2. Compliant involvement, where those present identify with the organisation on a cooperative basis, and where there is a clearly defined wage–work bargain. Membership is valued to this extent.
3. Calculative involvement, where there is a more far-sighted attitude on the part of those present towards the organisation. There is recognised a coincidence of interest, effort, and commitment, but where this is still regarded, basically as the means to the end of ensuring the rewards of those present. They will leave for better offers (in whatever terms that is meaningful to them).
4. Moral involvement, which represents a positive and intense orientation and identity with the organisation and all its works and institutions. Those present internalise the

goals and objectives of the organisation and its functions; and the values that it espouses. Those involved give spontaneous, cooperative and dedicated behaviour in their service, and in the pursuit of the organisation's continuing success.

This may be compared with the Affluent Worker studies of the mid-1960s. Here, the involvement was limited to a mixture of alienation and compliance. It was alienative in that those present had no identity with any part of the organisation except their own particular workstation, area, and (to an extent) group; they saw the work purely as a means to the end of having a standard of living outside the workplace, together with the ability to purchase necessities, wants and trappings. It was compliant in that the wage–work bargain was clearly understood on the part of all concerned: organisations, managers and work force. At the time, also, part of the bargain was an agreement that wages would go up and up. The reason for carrying on working was to improve the standard of living and quality of life, as well as the ability to continue to purchase the essentials, and increasingly the desirables.

BOX 6.8 Clean Up

Organisations purchasing sites that have previously been used for industrial or commercial services have to face the costs of restoring these. They may also become accountable for any toxic materials and other pollutants that may have been left there by previous site occupants. They may additionally face the costs of defending actions brought against them by staff, customers or the wider community arising from this pollution or contamination. This is likely to occur whether or not they were the originators of it.

This is worthy of note here for two reasons. The first is to explain the reality of supposed prime commercial and industrial sites that are being left derelict and undeveloped in the traditional and historic centres of these activities. The second is to illustrate from a different point of view the true cost of industrial and commercial activities and their consequences. In a report published in November 1993 concerning such sites in the UK, the UK government put the cost of cleaning up such sites at approximately £40 billion. The problem is prevalent throughout the Western industrialised world. Additionally, there are specific concerns regarding these matters in relation to the former Communist Bloc; of particular concern to the EC is a large bill for this in the former East Germany. It is also becoming apparent there are serious industrial pollution problems across the entire former USSR, especially in northern Russia and Siberia.

Throughout the Excellence studies (of Peters and Waterman, Peters and Austin, Peters himself, and also those of Goldsmith and Clutterbuck, Lessem, and Kanter) there runs a thread that says that this is not enough, either in the delivery of profitable business or in the pursuit of excellent public services. The drive must be towards what Williams, Dobson and Walters called moral involvement: all those who work in the organisation must be both valued by it and identify with it. This can only be achieved if it is first possible to instil in those concerned a sense of pride and identity with the organisation; a commitment to its purposes (whatever they may be); and a positive response to the ways in which the organisation carries itself, internally and externally.

Japanese organisations have this as a cornerstone. Whoever the person is, whatever part they play in the organisation, the message that is instilled in staff during induction, and reinforced throughout the period of employment (which is traditionally for life), is: 'You are important. We need your contribution. We have no spare staff, no slack to be taken up. We want you on our payroll to work for us. In return for this we will pay you well, look after you well, and make you prosperous.'

In order to be able to do this successfully, it is reasoned, organisations must generate not only effective, pleasant and suitable working conditions and practices, but also the 'moral' commitment referred to: that is, a combination of pride and positive attitudes in the organisation itself. All staff are to adopt these.

The generation of shared values among the staff is an organisation and managerial imperative, a positive set of activities to be designed and undertaken. Left to themselves, staff will evolve their own set of shared values suitable (if that is the right word) to each working group. Identity and commitment is thus moved away from an organisation focus to a work group focus. In such cases conflict inevitably ensues. In such cases also behaviour reflects perceptions rather than requirements: that is, the staff will behave as they think the organisation wants them to behave, or as (they reason) the managers and directors of the organisation would themselves behave in similar circumstances. To avoid this, therefore, organisations must actively set their own agenda, so that any alternative patterns of behaviour are restricted to being within clearly defined boundaries, limits and norms. Such values must, finally, be such that everyone involved can aspire to them, and identify with them. They will therefore reflect the combination of economic security and prosperity, with positive values of the society and community, and an organisational commitment to the staff. Shared values are not therefore an adjunct to business or strategy, but ingrained in it, a prerequisite to its successful outcome.

BOX 6.9 Shared Values

There are extremities that should be recognised. The first of these is where the member of staff is also, or has been, a customer or client of the organisation in question. This is likely to be true of national and local government and the public, health and transport services. In such cases, the client who becomes the member of staff will behave in ways that reflect how they in turn have been treated, if the attitudes required by the organisation are not positively formed when they first start work.

It is also necessary to consider the case of the professionals: persons who have particular expertise, capabilities or qualities to bring to an organisation, and that give them a distinctive identity. In such cases, if no organisation identity is generated, the person will revert to her professional identity and away from the organisation that is paying her and using her expertise.

■ Corporate citizenship

The concept of corporate citizenship relates to the set of standards and values transmitted to the community and environment by an organisation. It is present by accident or design: a set of values is in any case transmitted to the community, whether the organisation takes any active responsibility or part in it.

A consideration of this is essential on the part of all organisations. While it is true that in certain parts of the world organisations may dominate rather than truly interact with their environment and community, the model or responsible undertaking will in any case take a responsible view of this. It remains true that there may be expedience, short-term or even medium-term advantages to be gained from a dominant approach; in the long term, the organisation is nearly always required to re-orientate.

BOX 6.10 Corporate Citizenship

A useful if stark illustration of the problems that are eventually to be encountered may be drawn from examples arising from the emergence of the Eastern European countries from the collapse of the USSR.

The Chernobyl nuclear disaster that happened near Kiev, Ukraine, under the former USSR regime, is an excellent example of the expedient approach. Essentially it was a crude and primitive system of nuclear electricity generation, inherently inefficient and unsafe, but cheap to use as long as the generators were kept going and no breakdowns took place. Following the fire, the fall-out, social problems, health problems, land reclamation, and the search for alternative sources of energy (in a nation that suffered the collapse and bankruptcy of the ruling regime) must all be measured against the cheapness of the electricity generated by the station during its working life.

There are ecological disasters taking place in the Caspian Sea which is bordered by the former Soviet countries of Russia, Kazakhstan, Azerbaijan and Turkmenistan; and also the Aral Sea, bordered by Kazakhstan and Uzbekistan. Organisations and communities have been using the inland sea and its tributary rivers as waste, sewage and effluent disposal outlets, and the result is that the sea is silting and drying up.

Massive investment has been required by Western companies entering into Eastern Europe in order to open it up commercially. This investment has taken the form first of cleaning up the effluent and pollution. It has also been necessary to make heavy capital investment in plant and machinery in order to modernise production techniques, and to bring production standards up to those required in the West.

Under the Communist regimes the reward for the previous approach was full, or near full, employment combined with a shortage of consumer goods and a closed market, insulated from true competition and considerations of quality, desirability, or reliability. In each case, a narrow and expedient view was taken of the matters in question by those responsible for their direction. In each case, there have been truly horrendous consequences of the nature referred to above.

The optimum position, therefore, is for an organisation to assume a level of responsibility, and to set its own agenda. Corporate citizenship emerges first and foremost in the relations with the community or country within which it is located. This is especially true where people are both customers and employees of the organisation. In such cases, there is pressure on the organisation to be a model (or at least a good) employer, and to take any wider ethical and environmental stances that reflect the habits, customs and expectations of the community, as well as being a supplier of quality goods and services to those who use them.

BOX 6.11 Corporate Citizenship (2): Disasters

If it is decided that the expedient view is to be taken, worst case scenario projections are nearly always not as bad as the reality of the disasters that do occur. The fire at Kings Cross Underground Station in London in 1986 caused 30 deaths and hundreds of injuries. The cause of this was traced to a lighted cigarette thrown on to a pile of rubbish that had gathered under a wooden escalator.

The crash of the Pan-Am flight at Lockerbie, Scotland, in 1985 was directly attributable to the ability of a terrorist group to get the bomb on to the plane at the airport at Frankfurt, Germany. In these cases, the problems were both foreseeable and avoidable. Effectively decisions were taken that these were risks worth running. In each case also, the lack of standards at the outset led directly to huge levels of damages, legal fees, organisation time and resources, inquiries and inquests, and repair activities that could have been avoided if the correct standards had been established at the required operational level in the first place.

Organisations also have a role as resources to be used by the community, including the opening of organisation premises to the public for exhibitions, visits and educational activities, such as creating links with schools and colleges. Organisations are also normally a focus of general interest to their community. Organisations may be asked to sponsor particular local events, to put up money or other resources in return for good publicity and maintaining their standing and reputation. They may further simply be asked to make donations to charities or local groups.

In each case there is a reciprocal and mutual interest. Those visiting the place will not wish to do so if it is, or is perceived to be, a bad employer, producer, server, or organisation in general. Neither do organisations wish to give any of these negative impressions. Indeed they invariably go to great lengths to avoid them and to create opposite and favourable impressions; and so everyone benefits.

This is how organisations take their place in the community. The ultimate corporate responsibility is clearly to maintain itself as a relatively permanent, stable and profitable undertaking, in order to preserve a continuity of confidence and quality, regularity and volume of products and services to its customers and clients. It also includes permanent and continuity of employment for the staff. Communities have expectations of this. Organisations also have an obligations to their community and environment as a generator of economic activity, and also as a contributor to both general economic and social confidence in their area. Their capacity for this depends on this broad global perspective. It is true that within this perspective a pragmatic and realistic view must be taken. However, this is never an excuse for an approach that is shoddy, dishonest or short term.

It must be recognised that different views of organisations and their activities are held by different stakeholders. An organisation, for example, may bring jobs to an area (and create many more indirectly by giving spending power to its own work force). This may have to be balanced against the nature of the work itself (for example, if it is dirty or dangerous); the nature of the products and outputs (for example, if they are dirty or dangerous, or marginalised in some other way); any ethical considerations (for example, if the company is in the armaments industry); and the effects of any by-products, waste or effluent, especially if it is toxic or otherwise damaging. Also, while communities generally welcome non-contentious industries as well as hospitals and schools, the organisations concerned may have difficulty staffing them themselves, or offering the full range of services without bringing in outside expertise.

BOX 6.12 Redlining

This is the term used to describe the decision not to operate in a particular community or locality. This is usually because the area in question has a bad social reputation. It may also have or be deemed to have insufficient commercial prospects to make it a truly viable and profitable area in which to operate.

For example, banks and consumer goods companies have withdrawn operations from some inner-city areas and other places of social deprivation. This is especially true of the cities of the UK and USA, and may also be found to hold in France, Spain, Italy and East Germany.

It has been done because the costs of continuing to operate in the locality are not viable in relation to the business returns gained. In socially deprived areas there are additional problems of security to be addressed.

A variation on the process is also used by some consumer goods organisations, supermarkets and department stores. When sales of a given item drop below particular levels in the outlet in question, it is automatically removed from the range of products stocked.

The reduction of costs or risk achieved by the decision to withdraw has to be balanced against wider considerations of loss of reputation, loss of universal presence and the narrowing of the portfolio range. The process thus gives an additional aspect to any measurement of organisation performance in terms of turnover, earnings or profits per outlet and the context for the further debate and analysis of this in given circumstances. Redlining has also to be seen in the context that withdrawal may simply allow the consolidation of position by competitors in the field. There may also be a loss of social reputation.

BOX 6.13 Respect and Regard

A divisional manager of a large financial services organisation operating in the south-east of England in the 1990s hotly disputed the validity of concepts of respect and regard in relation to managerial practice. Its sole purpose, he declared, was to meet his targets (to make margin, in the jargon of the organisation). The way in which this was to be achieved was through instilling fear into the staff who worked for him. They were all, he went on to say, scared stiff of him. They knew that he would discipline or dismiss them if any question arose over the level or quality of their performance. He stated that he would compound this by having days and weeks in which he would make a point of picking on individuals, for no better reason than to keep them on their toes. In support of this approach, he went on to declare proudly, his margins were the highest in the organisation.

The point came to light during an attitude survey conducted through the organisation (and including his department) by a firm of management consultants. Pursuing the points made further, and following up the hypothesis of the manager in question, additional discoveries were made.

1. Absenteeism in this department was the highest in the organisation (at 14 per cent) and seven times the organisation average of 2 per cent.
2. Attendance levels rose when the rest of the staff knew that he was going to be away. Checking the staff time sheets against the manager's diary movements revealed that self-certificated absence was negligible on those dates when he was booked out of the office. This could be traced back over the previous two years (1990 and 1991).
3. The department was regarded by everybody else in the organisation as a place to be avoided. On the three occasions in one year (1991) when promotions became available, the positions were filled by taking an external candidate. Neither the staff working in the department, nor potential transferees from elsewhere within the organisation, applied for the particular posts.

Further pursuit of this point and this manager's hypothesis led to an analysis of the results achieved by the department. This in turn demonstrated that the margins in question were being made in spite of this manager and not because of him. It also revealed that while the margin volumes were indeed quite substantial, in percentage terms they were extremely poor in relation to those achieved by the same activities elsewhere in the financial services sector.

This was attributed by the consultancy firm overwhelmingly to the lack of respect and regard shown by the manager to his staff. The atmosphere generated by his unique approach had contrived to destabilise the department so thoroughly that there was little chance of any effective work being carried out. The margins that were being achieved were seen to be inherent in the given nature of the activities.

A more general point should be made here. The nature and style of communications between organisations and their staff, by managers in relation to subordinates, by head offices in relation to their subsidiaries and divisions reflects the true nature of respect and regard in which they are held.

They reflect also the extent to which a general clarity of purpose is present. The converse of this represents the extent to which this has been lost in the pursuit of internal organisation advantage, place in the pecking order, *realpolitik* and over-mightiness.

The giving out of duplicitous messages, hidden meanings, secondary agenda and other forms of the *realpolitik* that is present in general carry a form of lack of respect and regard. The general staff response and the nature of the organisational *realpolitik* takes its lead from this and subsequently draws its life and energy from it also.

Footnote

The usual argument against openness and straightforwardness of communication concerns the giving out of trade, commercial and operational secrets. There is, however, no actual correlation between the two: all organisations that treat their staff with respect also have trade secrets and there is no evidence to suggest that those that do treat their staff with greater openness (for example, Marks & Spencer, The Body Shop, the Virgin Group) suffer as the result of loss of trading confidentiality and the advantage that accrues from this.

The other usual argument that is offered against this normally takes the form that this is tantamount to 'having the monkeys run the zoo'. There is no more eloquent statement made by organisations about their staff.

BOX 6.14 Organisations and Ethics: A Summary

1. Absolute standards of honesty, integrity and probity in behaviour and dealings with staff, customers and the community.
2. Commitment to all aspects and effects of the business, including the disposal of waste and effluent created by the processes.
3. Recognition of the concept of corporate responsibility in the widest sense, with obligations to the community as well as customers and staff.
4. Adoption of absolute standards of product and service integrity and delivery.
5. Adoption of particular positions concerning exploitation, dealings with disadvantaged groups, dealings with public interest groups and lobbies, dealings with trade unions and other forms of staff representation.
6. Recognition of the concepts of 'right' and 'wrong'.
7. Recognition of the all-pervasive nature of ethics and ethical considerations.
8. Recognition of the relationship between integrity and honesty of business, commercial and public activities and their effectiveness.

■ Conclusions

It is apparent that there are right and wrong ways of doing things, of dealing with staff, customers and the community. It is apparent also that the onus is placed firmly on organisations (and therefore their top managers) to establish what they mean by right and wrong. This then becomes the basis on which judgements of their general probity are made by the rest of the world.

Organisations that enjoy high levels of regard and respect always do so because their conduct stands up to social and ethical scrutiny as well as commercial viability. It is, indeed, very difficult to find examples where commercial success has been achieved without regard to social factors or public colloquy except in the very short term. In the longer term organisations have to operate in, and be acceptable to, their staff, customers and communities. For this to occur a mutual, continuing, positive regard is necessary. This is always damaged and often destroyed when the general integrity of the given organisation is called into question (for example, after an accident or disaster: see Box 6.11).

Organisations must therefore have full knowledge and understanding of what is acceptable, both globally and locally. This extends to all spheres of business operation. Marketing initiatives strike a balance between being positive and exciting, while at the same stopping well short of making claims for the product that are simply not true, or presenting something in ways unacceptable to sectors of the community. Successful staff management is based on mutual respect and trust as well as effective work organisation. The management of change is always more successful where those involved understand why they are changing and can trust the organisation to lead them successfully and effectively in the required direction and then deliver the desired results. The production of shoddy or inadequate goods is only feasible until another organisation comes along with improved adequate and satisfactory products to put in their place.

There is also a correlation between the taking of a strong moral and ethical stance and long-term profitability. Examples of this can be drawn from all over the world. Japanese car and electrical goods companies all set high standards of probity and integrity, and through their published documentation place the onus on their managers to deliver. The Body Shop has made a strong and highly profitable feature of its concern for the environment and the standards that it has set in its dealings with the Third World. McDonald's have set absolute standards of quality, cleanliness, value and service across every operation everywhere in the world. The conclusion is therefore that the building of a successful and long-term respect and reputation can only be achieved if attention is paid to the ethical aspects: that all people, given any sort of choice at all, will gravitate towards organisations that are honest, truthful and trustworthy; and that they will gravitate away from those that are not. The strongest argument, therefore, for a distinctive ethical stance and the setting by organisations of high absolute standards is that it is profitable and effective.

■ Work assignments and discussion questions

1. What special problems are faced by those who work in the tobacco industry? How are these overcome? In what ways do these differ with respect to those of the armaments industry, and to those responsible for commissioning vivisection experiments and research?

2. (a) Discuss the view that effective pollution control is impossible given the demands of a competitive market economy.
   (b) In this context, outline the actions that are both effective and cost-effective to address this issue.
3. Devise a code of absolute moral and ethical standards for the organisation within which you work or study. What would be the costs, benefits and problems with its implementation?
4. What are the main social responsibilities of an organisation to its community? Taking the main employers from your area as examples, evaluate the extent to which they accept and discharge these.

CHAPTER 7

Behavioural Influences on Strategy

Introduction

Product and organisation excellence are not enough to guarantee commercial success. People must feel good and confident about working in the particular organisation and on its products and services. Others must also feel good about using and consuming these products and services as customers. This is true even where the organisation in question is the major source for the area as, for example, with Boeing at Seattle, and Ford Chrysler and General Motors at Detroit, where great cities have been built around major industries. Elsewhere, communities have grown up around smaller pockets of activity, as witness the coal mining industry. The establishment of activities in hitherto undeveloped regions has brought fresh prosperity to these places. In each case the particular community must feel good about playing host and supplying it with staff and customers. Organisations must bring a general positive aura, reputation, confidence and integrity, whatever its business and activities.

Those who are to have commercial dealings with it must also have this confidence. Except where a true monopoly exists consumers, clients and customers have choice. General confidence is important; it is also necessary to understand the elements of choice, the behaviour of people as they choose and the influences and persuaders that are brought to bear.

Beyond this, there are cases where people in any case go elsewhere. For example, Tesco and Sainsbury's are the two largest operators in the UK food supermarket sector. They have strong reputations and high levels of public confidence. Yet each has 15 per cent of the total market only; this represents the fact that 7 out of 10 grocery products are bought elsewhere. It is therefore necessary to consider these matters that contribute to confidence and reputation. These are summarised in Box 7.1.

Negativity

The biggest behavioural and psychological barrier to break is negativity. Any negative connotation of an organisation or offering reduces its effectiveness, marketability, saleability and therefore profitability. Any product or service over which there has been trouble or complaint, or any history of unreliability,

BOX 7.1 Behavioural Aspects and Influences on Strategy

1. Product confidence and reputation: the combination of performance, utility, appearance and perception that gives particular offerings their standing.
2. Organisation confidence and reputation: the combination of performance activity and interaction with the environment that gives particular organisations their standing.
3. Products and organisation image: the combination of promotional, marketing and public relations activities with performance elements.
4. Internal reputation and colloquy: staff groups, shareholders.
5. Value chain reputation: suppliers, distributors, competitors and substitute sectors.
6. External reputation and colloquy: community, environment, lobbies and pressure groups.
7. The effects and influence of overmighty departments, divisions, groups and individuals (see Chapter 1).

These have to be considered from both negative and positive standpoints.

must have confidence in it restored by the sector or niche. It is not enough that the producers of the product know that the corner has been turned, and that it does now actually work well all of the time; the market itself has to be convinced of this. In extreme cases it is necessary to repackage, re-present or even redesign and rename the item in question. In other cases extensive marketing and promotional activity may be required. Where there are teething troubles for a new product or service, or where an organisation is going into a new sector for the first time, it is often necessary to support this with public relations resources and activities.

Serious problems are extremely costly and organisations go to a great deal of trouble to avoid them. However, when they do occur, there is a derived public relations advantage in getting the matter sorted out as quickly as possible.

BOX 7.2 Perrier

The Perrier company bottles mineral water in the South of France. During 1993 it became apparent that the product – naturally carbonated spring water – had been extensively contaminated during the bottling and purification processes. Perrier recalled millions of bottles and paid out compensation to wholesalers, retailers and the public. The bottling plant was closed, cleaned, purified and inspected, and the whole process was carried out with maximum publicity, and incorporated into the wider public relations response to the contamination. A public relations feature was also made of the final inspection and the clean bill of health granted at the end of it. There was a risk attached to adopting this form of strategy in response to the problem. However, by doing so the company managed to maintain its general level of public awareness and turn the bad publicity to some advantage.

This may be contrasted with the experience of customers of Hoover UK Ltd during the period October to December 1992. As part of the pre-Christmas promotion of products and to generate interest and sales, Hoover offered free airline flights to those who bought their appliances.

The company realised at an early stage that this was a serious strategic blunder. However, instead of withdrawing the offer as gracefully as possible, staff were employed to try and make it as difficult as possible for those people who were entitled to their free flights to take them up. The matter came to a head for a variety of reasons. One marketing president was quoted as saying that 'Anyone who thought that this was a serious offer must have been stupid.' One national newspaper picked up the story of trying to put people off their flight entitlements, and found that the company was seeking to reinterpret the rules of the offer to get it out of this mess. Finally, a national consumer television programme ran the story, carrying interviews with those who had been hired to talk people out of their flight entitlement.

The organisation eventually rescued the situation. It established a public relations troubleshooter function at its head office in south Wales to deal with the complaints. It sought to provide redress to those who had been talked out of their offer, and to ensure that they did indeed get their free flight. It undertook to honour all commitments to fly that had been issued. It finally engaged in the positive public relations activity with which Perrier had started. The issues rumbled on into the summer of 1995.

In each case the company was faced with a negative connotation to itself and its products. The two examples are a useful and effective comparison and contrast of the different approaches that may be taken, and their outcomes.

As a consequence of this, positive forms have to be found for negative features and characteristics. People do not wish to be associated with 'cheapness' because there are connotations of low quality, and also reminders (possibly very precise) that the consumers in question have not got much disposable income. Alternative connotations have therefore to be found. The most universal positive and enduring phrase is that of good value. Others that are included in this alternative positive approach include seasonal, faddish and fashionable: that is, something with a limited useful life. Neither is the concept of cheapness or cheapening confined to the bottom of the price scale. Those who purchase expensive or exclusive goods may be seriously dissatisfied if the producer brings the price down and thus cheapens them, reducing their exclusivity, and opening them up to those with whom the original clientele did not wish to be associated.

People also do not wish to be associated with tackiness of advertising, lack of or loss of ambience in the retail outlet or other means of distribution, and neither do they wish to purchase goods that are poorly packaged or presented (or are deemed to be so). Organisations operating in niches where advertising and promotion are basic, or from wholesale, warehouse or other good value outlets, must create alternative features, so that the benefits of going to the establishment on the part of the customer clearly outweigh the negatives. Successful approaches to this have included emphasis on access and the ability to park the car, and also forms of exclusivity (Costco, for example, require all potential customers to enrol as members – the equivalent of joining a club).

BOX 7.3 Negativity and Control

Some sectors have negatives associated with them over which they have no control. Trains are late, seas are rough, the air is turbulent, roads have roadworks, cars break down. Those operating in each of these sectors find benefits to emphasise as a means of counteracting the negative. British Rail has had great success in the past with its 'Let the train take the strain' campaigns, and more recently with the sale of tickets to London that are integrated with London regional transport. Shipping and air transport design is now sufficiently far advanced to cope with all but the worst weather; and the companies have a great variety of benefits on which to concentrate. Cars are sold on power, range, appeal and comfort, as we have seen elsewhere (the comfort is a direct benefit in the situation illustrated).

There are always general sectoral negatives that must be either accommodated or countered. If an organisation is the slowest deliverer in its sector it must find other virtues on which to draw. If an organisation is the fastest deliverer in the sector, it will invariably use this as a major source of competitive advantage.

It is therefore essential to recognise where the negatives lie, and to take effective steps to overcome them.

BOX 7.4 Negatives

As indicated in the main text there are general matters relating to all business activities that must be addressed. These are both sector-generic, and customer- or consumer-generic.

There are specific issues that require addressing from time to time also. These are as follows.

1. Loss of confidence: in the organisation, its products/services, its staff (especially its Chief Executive and senior staff), its stability, its future, its quality and reliability.
2. Loss of reputation: of the products and services in question, of the staff (again, especially the Chief Executive and the senior staff), of the organisation ownership.
3. Loss of performance: both overall and by individual division, department and offering. This includes performance aspects of quality, volume and reliability, and the ability also to meet deadlines. Loss of performance in this regard also includes financial aspects.
4. Obsolescence of offerings, marketing, presentation and public relations, both in performance and behavioural terms.
5. Bad and negative news media stories, whether warranted or not.
6. Long-term gradual decline, often based on long-term negative workplace relations, lack of investment, or lack of strategic stability. Again, the decline may relate to a whole organisation and offering range, or individual departments, divisions and functions.

These have to be considered in reverse if one organisation is taking over another which exhibits any or all of the negatives indicated. The critical part of the strategy for revamping the organisation being taken over must therefore address these if any measure of success is to be achieved.

■ Positivity

The converse of the negative is clearly the positive. It has the function of countering the negative, of representing both elements of an offering and the circumstances surrounding it which have negative connotations and influences. It is useful only to the extent illustrated. Beyond this it is essential to go on and create positive feelings, images and impressions about the offering for its own sake. It must become positively attractive.

Again, there are pitfalls that must be understood. Whatever is presented must be attainable and achievable in the eyes of the buyer, customer, client or consumer. It must represent a view of their world, not some Utopia or Shangri-La which is plainly beyond their range or scope. Images of glamour, luxury, status, style, sex appeal and sophistication must also therefore be presented in relation to the real world of the consumer group in question. If this is not present, or if the levels presented are too high or unattainable for some other reason, the offering in question is rejected. As we have seen, the car company uses its glamorous brand to attract people into the showroom to buy the workaday variety. They do not buy the glamorous brand itself, and if this was the only offering, they would pass it by. Holiday promotions include pictures of 'normal' families; people used in the pictures look happy and they are 'everyday persons'. Indeed, the use of film stars, television, music and show business personalities has to be very carefully considered. For the same reasons – of unattainability and unachievability in the wrong places – the usage of these personages has negative effects on the products and services in question. For success and effectiveness, they must be introduced into the world of the consumer.

■ Happiness

The use of laughter and smiling happy faces pervades the creation of all positive images and associations. The use is universal, to be found in life assurance and health-care promotions as well as those for consumer goods and services. The only variation on this is where pantomime-type baddies and caricatures are used for a contrasting effect. Again, however, the usage has to be very carefully assessed, as even such an obvious and overt caricature may nevertheless give off negative impressions.

■ Sunshine

The other universal image is sunshine and the associated brightness and warmth that goes with it. Again, the only exception is for a contrasting effect. American Express ran one commercial set in the rain, where the card user, a man, was portrayed as a rugged, tough and caring individual helping a woman change her car wheel in the bad weather. Otherwise, bad weather is used only to emphasise contrasting messages, such as warmth and comfort. It is also worth pointing out that ski holiday brochures, while making sure that they have plenty of snow in the pictures, always ensure that there is sunshine.

■ Language

The language that is used must also be entirely positive. This extends to the avoidance, as far as possible, of words such as 'but', 'not', 'no' (and their compounds of 'do not', 'cannot', 'will not', 'must not', and so on). This extends throughout all contexts. Whether the message being put across is negative or not, the use of negative words ensures that part of it is perceived as negative, and the receiver therefore has a high tendency to reject it. One of the caveats attached to negative or critical advertising – which is where part of the message is the unfavourable comparison of competitors' offerings with those of the organisation in question – is in the reading of the negative words in the advertisements themselves. Again, unless carefully handled, the negative message rebounds on to the advertiser and not on to the products of the competitors.

Size

Both the concept and use of size is important in this context. Images used will be as expansive as possible in the context. As well as being fast, cars travel long distances. Supermarkets have shelves stretching away into the distance, and they are all fully packed. Restaurants have plenty of room and plenty of tables (and thus which emphasise perceptions of success, also an important positive image). Airlines serve the whole world (British Airways even produced one advertising campaign from, as it were, elsewhere in the universe, and a final shot in many of their advertisement is a picture of the earth as a globe with the British Airways route network spreading out over it).

Prosperity and plenty

This is where shelves, tables, airliners, and even town centres are full (in the case of people, not too full: the desired image is one of bustle, prosperity and success, not overcrowding). In the particular context this reinforces the desired associations with success, prosperity, fulfilment, and also choice and happiness (both of which are very strong and positive images themselves).

BOX 7.5 Milton Keynes

The City of Milton Keynes devised and ran a marketing campaign in the late 1980s and early 1990s in which it promoted itself as *the* place to live and work. The images used were extremely powerful and covered all of the positive aspects indicated. Those included were:

- peace and tranquillity (of the dawn and of the countryside);
- safety and security, both of housing and of the roads, and reinforced by pictures of children riding their bicycles;
- gatherings of people for holidays and festivals and to watch a balloon race;
- pictures of shopping and work areas giving the impression of stability and prosperity, and also of modernity and comfort;
- access, the wideness of the roads and the Intercity rail link;
- the position of the city at the centre of the UK with easy access to London and everywhere else;

- the use of sunshine in all the pictures to reinforce each of the positive messages indicated.

The end result was and remains an extremely powerful and successful campaign, both in the general promotion of the city, and in the specific regard of attracting business, commercial and domestic interest.

Motivation

The motivation of buyers, customers, consumers and clients is clearly fundamental to the purchasing behaviour. It follows from this that any understanding of the motives of those in their sector or segment that can be achieved by organisations is going to contribute to competitive advantage. In general, motivation arises from needs and wants on the part of the consumer that occur and are important at different times of the hour, day, week, month, season, period, year or lifetime, and a general understanding of where the offering in question lies in regard to this is fundamental to business success. Consumers prioritise their demands, into 'needs' and 'wants': food, drink and shelter are essential, a car is desirable, a holiday would be nice. They also prioritise even the essential needs: food is essential; biscuits are cheap; steak is expensive; caviare is extremely expensive and not very filling.

Expectations

Strategists should also understand the importance of considering motivation in terms of expectation, fulfilment and reward. People make purchases with certain expectations in mind. They expect particular benefits to accrue from the acquisition, ownership, use and consumption of the product or service in question. Levels of expectation are set by a variety of needs. There is the price paid and, in general, the higher this is, the greater the expectation. There are also always value and quality considerations.

Additionally, there are impressions, associations and images created by the marketing activities that surround the product or service in question. Packard cites 1950s perfume adverts which had an overt message to women users: 'Wear this perfume and get the man of your dreams.' When the man of their dreams failed to materialise, the women rejected the perfume itself. More recently, top UK football clubs have brought out ranges of leisure-wear to complement their sports goods offerings. Many supporters of the clubs would not buy the sports goods because they had no actual use for them (that is, they did not play football, but only watched it). They also might, by putting the football shirt on, be faced with or reminded of their lack of prowess at the sport itself, or their own physical or behavioural shortcomings that contributed to this (their weight, or the fact that they smoke or drank, for example). However, distinctive leisure-wear both fulfilled the expectation and association, and in ways neither threatening nor otherwise confrontational.

If something is offered on the basis of status, prestige or esteem, then these elements must be conveyed by ownership, use or consumption of the product in question. The top-of-the-range car, executive home, or exclusive holiday must be exactly this, if the expectations are to be fulfilled. If these are not delivered dissatisfaction will ensue. The holiday may have been truly wonderful, but it was not exclusive. The car may be fast, reliable and economical but again it is not exclusive.

Each organisation will therefore take steps to understand the motivations, needs, wants and expectations of the client groups that it serves and wishes to serve, as part of the strategy process.

■ Attitudes and behaviour

The fact that people have positive or favourable attitudes towards companies and their offerings does not mean that they will buy from them or use them. Attitudes (the positive and favourable) and behaviour (the act of buying) are therefore different and distinctive. For approaches to the question of attitude to have any value, it is the attitude to the purchase ownership and usage of the item that requires consideration, not the attitude to the item itself. Otherwise the strategist must address the behaviour of the consumers or consumer group, their propensity to consume, the level of priority accorded the offerings in question, and other leaders and triggers that cause them to choose between items and to choose between brands.

It is also true that where people have a negative attitude towards companies (for example, because of the organisation's involvement in an accident or disaster, or because of the nationality of the parent company), this does not mean that they will not buy its products. Many consumers buy Japanese goods, in spite of prejudices against Japan, because the products are of excellent quality. French and German car sales are dominated by the indigenous brands (Renault, Peugeot, Citroen, Volkswagen) in spite of the varying and uneven regard in which the organisations themselves are held in these countries. Consumers carry out the bulk of their shopping at out of town supermarkets, superstores and do-it-yourself emporia, in spite of the fact that they have more favourable attitudes towards the smaller town-centre shops where service is personalised. The larger stores have therefore addressed the behavioural rather than attitudinal issues. It is convenient to carry out a high proportion of purchases in one single visit, and in addition car parking is likely to be easier.

This is compounded by the comfort that arises in an organisation when its products receive favourable responses in attitude terms: the question '*Would* you buy/consume/use our product?' is always more comfortable than the question '*Will* you buy/consume/use our product; and if so how often, when, where, why (etc.)?' However, a general attitude to the product or service in question is of little value other than a passing comfort. It is the attitudes generated by commercial success that reflect reliability, quality and value that are important.

■ Group influences

These are present in all patterns of consumption and have implications for esteem, regard, respect, status and acceptance in different situations. People belong to a variety of groups which can be permanent, temporary, *ad hoc*, and transient.

The family is perceived to be a special and relatively permanent group. This has additionally a variety of complexities, such as the extended family and the in-laws, for example; and it also changes its emphasis during phases of life, from childhood, to adolescence, to adulthood, to maturity and to old age. Clearly, an understanding of this is essential in the successful and effective devising of consumer goods orientated strategies. For example, the consumer or user of a toy is the child. However, its appeal has to be sufficiently positive in general to persuade the adult to buy it for the child.

Similarly, sellers of male and female clothing must consider the opposite gender. Men are likely to be put off if the women in their life do not like their clothing for any reason, and vice versa; and the reason for dislike may be ethical, associational or related to a bad past experience, as well as concerned with price, appearance, quality and value.

Other groups to which people belong also influence their patterns of consumption. Social, sports, leisure and work groups all establish norms and patterns of behaviour which include consumption. There are also groups to which people aspire – higher status groups, lifestyle groups, peer groups, exclusive groups and hero identification – which influence patterns of consumption and behaviour.

Related to this are notions of fashion and opinion leadership. This is deemed important from the point of view of influencing the groups: the onus is placed on supplying organisations who identify and influence the most important members of the group, in the knowledge that other members would tend to follow. It is also important from the point of view of 'fashion leadership': the ability to persuade film, sports and music stars to use or wear a particular item or brand, eat in particular restaurants, or travel in particular cars or with particular companies.

It is essential to recognise and be able to influence positively patterns of group think, conformity and other influences that are always present. In more general terms, a similar approach is required when establishing the needs, wants, characteristics and aspirations of sectors, segments and niches.

■ Perception

The basis for the study of perception is that all the senses of each individual are constantly assailed with far too much information to interpret all of them accurately all of the time. People, therefore, recognise and receive certain cues and signals and interpret the gaps between them. This extends to what is seen, felt, tasted, touched, smelt; and also to what is thought, believed and valued; and also as the trigger for actions and behaviour. The keys to a good understanding of this are as follows.

■ Stereotyping

This is the ascribing of a range of characteristics to people, items, places and services on the basis of a known single or small group of characteristics. For example, professors are absent-minded (and, conversely, if asked the question 'Who is absent-minded?' the answer is likely to come back 'A professor'). Japanese electrical goods are reliable. Spain is hot and full of British and German holiday-makers. National Health Service hospitals are places where the sick and injured have to wait a long time for bad service. None of these statements is necessarily true, yet each has the feeling or perception of truth because of the stereotyping process which is based upon anecdotal evidence that has received a wide coverage.

■ Halo effects

This is where the product, person, place or service exhibits one extreme characteristic and everything else is perceived from it. It happens all the time in interpersonal relations: a firm handshake must mean that the person is strong; a strident voice must mean that the person knows what he is doing; and so on. It also happens with places, service and products in the same way. For example, as Spain 'is full of British and German holiday-makers' those who believe this will notice these groups of people to the exclusion of all others. People notice and remember the bad ways in which they were treated at National Health Service hospitals to the exclusion of the good. People remember the good Japanese products and put any bad ones down to abberation or exception.

■ Self-fulfilling prophecy

Following on from stereotyping and halo effects, there is the great tendency for people, products, places and situations to conform to pre-expectations and preconceptions. People who are thought to be clever, brave, powerful or influential are treated as if they were so, and thus become so (and more so). The unreliable product becomes treated as such because of this preconception and reputation, and any failure of performance on its part will reinforce this; eventually the users of it will (perceive themselves to) have had enough of it, and change it for a substitute. People use a restaurant because the service is good; they consequently become known by the staff, and so tend to get good service (if there are any lapses in this, it is put down to a break between courses, they are busy, or new staff who do not know them).

British Rail attract complaints about UK railway services to such an extent that examples of poor service are actively sought out. This has led to a collapse both of public confidence and staff morale. This is in spite of the many examples of good and high service with which the organisation is endowed.

The self-fulfilling prophecy must be considered from the opposite point of view also. It is easier for people to live up or down to the expectations that others have of them (especially in work, political or social positions) than it is to change the expectations, especially in the short to medium term. Places that have built success and prosperity on a particular reputation will tend to ensure that the reality behind it is maintained. If something is perceived to be reliable, then it had better actually be reliable.

■ Adaptation

This is important in this context for a slightly different reason. Initially it requires a recognition that a person's view of the world and what is important in it is constantly, and often suddenly, changing. For example, the person who is cycling home from work early because of his daughter's birthday, and suddenly realises that he has not bought her a present, has the overwhelming need for a toy shop or sweet shop. He makes his purchase and returns to his bicycle only to find that he now has a puncture. He therefore has a need for a new tyre or puncture repair kit. He also has a need for a telephone, to let his family know that he will be late (or possibly to try to get someone to come out and fetch him and the bicycle). This in turn causes disappointment and anger because he will be late. He therefore returns to the shop to buy a box of chocolates for the others to try and make up for this. He finally gets home and needs a hot bath and a cup of tea . . . and so on.

The converse of this is when organisations have to be able to offer acceptable alternatives for products and services that they no longer maintain. The person who goes to the shop and asks for product *x* only to be told that it is no longer stocked always experiences an initial frustration and disappointment. Dependent upon the nature of the rejection and the current importance of the product in question to the customer at the time, the shop may lose all of that person's business for all time. Behaviourally, therefore, there is the necessity to be able to respond with a rider to the effect that there is now a good, ideally better, alternative available. This is a strong behavioural reason to explain why organisations maintain the extremities of their product range.

■ The behavioural needs of customer and consumers

The behavioural needs of customers and consumers may be summarised as follows.

Emotional security, comfort and confidence This can be related to bulk purchases of food in the freezer sector, safety features in cars, and domestic security systems. The comfort, confidence and security needs of the customer in question are satisfied in turn because there is 'plenty in the house'; 'we are safe in the house'; and 'we are safe in the car'. This is a clear response to the basic needs identified by Maslow of security, survival and stability. It is also a particular response to the domestic crimes of burglary, and the carnage on the roads of Western civilisation.

Reinsurance of worth Purchases must make customers feel good. They have to satisfy themselves both in their own eyes, and in those of their circles of friends, acquaintances and colleagues. Successful products and services therefore exude reinforcements of these. It is also essential that where the product is for menial or domestic use, it must be presented in such a way as to give the users feelings of self-respect and self-worth. Packard (1957) quotes research carried out in the 1950s by the soap powder and detergent sectors; this research found that unsuccessful marketing of the products was directly related to those campaigns where no self-worth on the part of the user was evident.

It is also essential in the purchase of major items. Domestic appliances and cars are required to have a long, useful life. They are also required to have a long 'behavioural' value. Styling and presentation of these has to reflect this. Those bringing new products on to the market must ensure that this is done alongside maintaining a current and residual value for the existing products otherwise customers may respond unfavourably to the organisation. They have been left with a product that is operationally excellent but behaviourally obsolete, and there are clear implications for overall levels of customer satisfaction to be considered.

Ego gratification Anything that is sold successfully must include a measure of products/service/offerings/customer in harmony. Part of the initial resistance to television dinners, instant mixes, cook-in sauces, and instant coffee was related to the fact of their convenience: the host, cook, wife, mother, husband, father or friend who was producing them effectively had no input to them. They were created by the company and the person serving them up simply acted as the middle person. Approaches based on lifestyle, convenience, luxury, sex and opulence, as well as involvement and satisfaction, had to be generated for these in the same way as for other product and service ranges.

Packard quotes two further examples. Earthmoving equipment which met resistance, because the machine (rather than the driver) was perceived to do the work, had to be represented with the driver at the centre of the promotion. The other example was the success of vanity publishing, which promised (and continues to promise) immortality rather than riches, and which remains a huge industry.

Creativity

A variation of the ego need is creativity. For example, cake mixes that required the addition of eggs were found to be more successful than those that simply required the addition of water. The perception was that there was a greater input on the part of the user or consumer, while at the same time maintaining the benefits of convenience. The requirements to make a positive addition or contribution ensured a measure of involvement so that the very least that occurred was a perception of a partnership between the manufacturer and the consumer.

It is also worth drawing attention at this stage to the opposite side of this coin: the extreme value and identity that people place on something that they have themselves created. It is very difficult to tell somebody that what they have produced is of no value (whether in a commercial or domestic situation). Nevertheless in organisation terms, if the item in question has no value then ways have to be found of letting the individual who produced it know this which both satisfy the organisation's requirements not to have useless or worthless products, and at the same time reassure the individual of her general worth and value to the organisation. There are thousands of ex-organisations that have followed the brainchild, creation or invention of their originator into oblivion.

Love objects

This aspect may be summarised as cuddly toy, dear little child or sweet/cute little animal. Andrex, the major suppliers of toilet tissue to the UK retail sector, has used labrador puppies as the central feature of its commercials throughout the 1970s, 1980s and 1990s. The images are so strong that the company now includes the slogan 'A puppy is for life, not just for Christmas' at the end of all its presentations during the period of November, December and January of each year.

Children are used extensively in television commercials in the pursuit of engendering this sense of love and warmth. This usage extends to washing powder, washing-up liquid, grocery shopping, fast food, cars, car parts, petrol, holidays, central heating and double glazing. The image of the child in each case is extremely powerful and central to its success.

Power

The power of the product or offering is reflected in the user of it. This is manifest in a variety of ways. There is a power = strength = security aspect to be considered (as in the presentation of health care, for example). Nearly all automobile advertising and marketing is on the basis of power, performance and speed. Many newspaper and magazine advertisements and public relations material for cars contains the phrase '0 to 60 miles per hour in x seconds'. Where the product range includes offerings at the 'least powerful' end of the range, these are often not used in the marketing strategy at all; or, where they are used, a small engine is described as lively or nippy.

The power and strength elements are integral to the successful promotion of cigarettes. The central images generated all reflect this: Formula One motor racing cars (Malboro); power boats (John Player, Camel, Malboro); personal strength and fortitude (the Malboro cowboy); athletic power and strength (Benson & Hedges cricket sponsorship).

Power is also a progressive theme. One's first car (a three- or five-door small saloon, for example) has a certain amount. The second has more (a four-door large saloon). The third is in the executive range (for example, Volvo, Saab or BMW).

Power has been used in peripheral ways to reinforce messages in other spheres. British Gas ran commercials entitled 'Being in control'. In these celebrities were placed in different situations to illustrate the virtues of using gas as a domestic power source. The punchline was always the same: 'Don't you just love being in control?' The celebrity would then raise his or her thumb, and the gas would appear to come out of the end of it. It was (and remains) a very effective presentation of control and influence.

Traditions and roots

This is the use of 'a sense of the past' to create positive and comfortable images. Food promotions use phrases such as 'Just as good as mother used to make.' Morgan cars retain their traditional design as the distinctive selling feature and mark of exclusivity. Also in the car sector Rolls-Royce maintain the traditions of fittings and furnishings and reliability on which their original reputation was built.

Other aspects of this also bear illustration in this context. Bailey's Irish Cream, the after-dinner liqueur, was invented and created on this basis in the 1970s. Its traditional image with a rustic-looking label and distinctive brown bottle is the key to its commercial success.

Elsewhere politicians exploit perceptions and visions of golden ages with calls for 'returns to traditional values' and 'back to basics', because there is a very strong association with historic success, order, stability and prosperity (see Box 7.6).

Traditions and roots are also the key to nostalgia booms, period revivals and fashion recycling.

BOX 7.6 Back to Basics

The inventor of the 'back to basics' slogan was John Major, UK Prime Minister, in the early 1990s. He first used the slogan in the autumn of 1993. At almost the same time he had been heavily critical of dissidents and factions in his party whom he accused of harping back to 'a golden age that never was', the UK consumer boom of the mid-1980s.

Immortality

Reference has been made to this above in the Vanity publishing example under the ego gratification heading. It is also important to consider it from other points of view.

Stability, order and control are all associated with longevity and are important in the presentation of long-term offerings such as bought housing, life assurance, other insurances, loans and other financial products. Those that are successful are presented alongside images of steadiness, increased prosperity and value and also alongside a stable, happy and successful domestic situation. Even in days of high levels of divorce and the consequent traumas of family break-up, these remain powerful and positive images. By association, reassurance of worth and value and emotional stability are all so very positive.

Conclusion

This constitutes an outline of the main elements of the behavioural and perceptual impacts on strategy. The mixture of these will vary between sectors. They will vary between organisations operating in the same sector, and there is no reason why a variety of approaches should not be applied with equal effectiveness within a sector. A variety of cues, levels and triggers motivate and induce buying within the customer group, and it is likely to be beyond the means of one organisation to strike them all successfully.

It is also likely that consumers will view the organisations and their products in a positive and comfortable way if they have strong images and attractions, rather than a diversity. Organisations will therefore tend to follow those cues and levers that have been successful in the past, and that are successful at present. If they do propose to make radical changes, they must be aware of the risks of this: the Abbey National plc, a UK bank, lost impact, confidence and, above all, market when they attempted to change their marketing cornerstone from 'The Abbey Habit' to 'Abbey (that is, happy) Endings'. The Abbey Endings campaign was stopped and the organisation retrieved the situation with a revamp of the previous slogan as 'The Habit of a Lifetime'. 'Endings' is highly negative, and certain to fail the immortality and ego gratification tests indicated above.

As well as choice, an understanding of the behavioural elements is the key to generating confidence: in the organisation, its products and services, the level and quality of service that is on offer, and the ability of the organisation to continue to be of service into the future. The converse is extremely destructive and potentially fatal to the organisation: if there is no confidence in the organisation or its products, it does not matter how good they actually are since they will not be bought or used. Engendering and maintaining confidence is therefore a combination of the behavioural processes indicated above to ensure that both organisation and offerings are presented in ways and with benefits and usages that appeal to the sector or segment in question.

The final element of this is to recognise that people do not act rationally. They may buy something and then rationalise why they bought it (especially if they are not sure they made the right choice or if their peers have chosen something else). They may buy something for one purpose, and find that the item does not fulfil this purpose (though it may be found to have others). They may and do buy on whims and fancies. Research conducted by UK supermarkets shows that 86 per cent of those entering their doors make more purchases than they intended when they came in. They may buy something because others within their ambit bought it and then cast around for uses for it.

This applies to industrial and commercial buying also. For example, many organisations have bought off-the-shelf office information and software systems on the recommendation of others in their sector and have subsequently found that they do not precisely fit the bill required. In such cases, even with this form of buying, there is a strong pressure to conform. The individual in question does not want to be a part of the only organisation, and above all the only office manager, without the particular system to his name.

The main lesson to be learned and emphasised is therefore an understanding of the range of behavioural considerations, and the realm of uncertainty that exists within them. It is important to recognise the critical elements of choice and confidence, and the ways in which these are made and generated. It is, finally, essential to reiterate the point that not only must the offerings be good, but customers must perceive this to be so, and also believe in the qualities and benefits that they bring with them. That, above all, is why attention to this aspect is so critical for all those responsible for organisation strategies.

■ Work assignments and discussion questions

1. Why is The Body Shop held in such high esteem? What are the lessons to be learned by other organisations from this?
2. What actions should Hoover have taken in response to the air tickets problem? Why did the matter become a serious problem in the first place?
3. Compare and contrast the perceptions held about Sainsbury's and Marks & Spencer. What actions should be taken by Sainsbury's if they wish to change their levels of expectations to those of Marks & Spencer?
4. Identify the keys to loss of confidence, and the actions that should be taken by organisations to ensure that this does not happen.

CHAPTER 8

Sectoral Strategies

Introduction

While basic principles of strategy formulation and development are universal, they must be applied in particular ways in different sectors. The purpose of this chapter is to identify the aspects of different sectors that affect and influence the strategies adopted. Three sectors are distinguished:

- manufacturing, using the classical model of scales of production, of unit, batch, mass and flow;
- commercial services, including retail, distribution, banking and leisure;
- public services, and the limitations placed on these by the special factors and circumstances included in the facts of political life.

There are also notes on capital and infrastructure projects, and on the activities of the voluntary/not-for-profit sectors.

Manufacturing and production strategies

At the core of any manufacturing organisation is the strategy that determines the nature, volume, quality and regularity of the product or product range. There are elements of successful manufacturing strategies that are universal; and also elements that are specific to particular sectors and to the scale of production adopted.

Classically four archetype manufacturing standpoints are identified:

- unit production;
- batch production;
- mass production;
- flow production.

Organisations may operate in one or more of these ways or in all of them.

Unit production

Unit production is normally highly specialised and highly customer-focused. Unit producers manufacture their items in response to specific or near-specific orders. Unit output is usually for highly specific and clearly defined market niches. In some cases the quality and exclusivity of the offering overrides any consideration of timescale, deadline or price. In others there will be a price, deadline and quality balance to be struck. The relationship between manufacturer and client is likely to be close so that customers receive satisfaction and a full understanding of their requirements is achieved.

There are vagaries of operating in this way. A balance of quality and exclusivity is essential, as is the ability to charge an economic rent for the output. The production technology of unit manufacturing is a combination of high levels of personal, technical and often artistic skill with generic, flexible and high-quality equipment.

Customers of unit producers have strong and distinctive requirements. In the commissioning and/or purchasing of an exclusive item, exclusivity is sought.

Successful unit production requires complete adaptability and flexibility of technology, staff, approach and attitudes, and work methods and patterns. This is likely to include the ability to call upon specialists as and when required.

BOX 8.1 Unit Manufacturing: Examples and Illustrations

1. Portraits, paintings, sculptures: normally commissioned both for public and private display. The imperative for the producer is in ensuring that the finished work mirrors the expectations of the commissioner (especially in regard to portrait paintings and sculptures). Variations on this theme include company logos, ensigns and promotional furniture (such as is to be found outside large hotels and company head offices). Also included is distinctive pottery, ceramics, glassware and woodwork.
2. Rolls-Royce cars: built to a standard model range but the fixtures and fittings are individual and order-responsive. There is sometimes a deadline to be met: seldom a budget.
3. UPVC double glazing: uses a generic production process and design range but each has to be tailored to the precise requirements of the premises in question. This also applies to house extensions, conservatories and other aspects of the home improvement sector.
4. Design activities from which exclusive products are to be manufactured. Included in this are the construction of exclusive homes, corporate headquarters and landscaping. A variation on this is to be found in the refurbishment of old and/or historic buildings.
5. The design and construction of specific amenities, such as sport and leisure centres and waste disposal units.
6. Skilled activities (such as carpentry): the carpenter could, for example, be making window frames for a building one week, and dolls' houses for a toy shop chain the next.

BOX 8.2 The Unit/Batch Grey Area

This is where a batch of basic items is produced without the exclusive fitting-out referred to in the Rolls-Royce example.

In the car sector an example of this is the Morgan Company. Morgan is a distinctive and unique product constructed mainly by hand (though using standardised manufactured elements). The cars are not produced specifically to order, though each one is sold to order. The end result is effectively the production of cars to order, however; the means to this end is different.

This is also to be found in parts of the do-it-yourself and small domestic building sectors, in which the general nature of the product (bricks, cladding, fencing, outbuildings, summer houses and sheds) is balanced with the needs of both the given property and the perceptions and requirements of its owner.

This could also be said to apply to the kitchen, bathroom and bedroom furniture sector. This is batch produced, but has then once again to be fitted on an individual basis.

■ Batch production

Batch manufacturing is the name given to the production of small to medium-sized volumes or batches of items. Effective batch production is achieved through a combination of the following:

- high-quality, up-to-date and flexible technology which can easily be reconfigured or rejigged to meet particular demands;
- flexible multi-skilled regular work force, working to both standard and flexible patterns of work;
- flexibility and dynamism in response to orders, balanced with a regular customer base;
- a distinctive, well-recognised and well-received range of offerings that is nevertheless capable of variation, modification and change, often at short notice;
- a distinctive, well-recognised and well-received way of working, suitable both to the given production efforts and the demands and expectations of the customer base;
- a distinctive price, value, quality and deadline mixture which is well understood, and which can be varied when required.

Batch production is a combination of high output and short (or shortish) production runs. It requires a combination of the ability to respond to orders with the capacity to anticipate likely demand for the products. Batch production activity is therefore concerned with both dealing with orders and producing stocks ready for sale as the orders come in.

Effective batch manufacturing strategies are founded in a full understanding of the capacities of the technology that is used and the staff using it, together with the imagination and creativity to envisage the full range of outputs that it could produce, and to which this expertise could be turned.

Continuous investment in production technology and the ability to maximise its use is therefore critical to the continued success of batch manufacturers. Competitive advantage and organisational reputation is gained through speed of production and response; quality and reliability.

BOX 8.3 Batch Production: Examples and Illustrations

Batch production activities and strategies are effectively used in the following sectors.

1. Component supply: the production of items to be sold on to other organisations, for use in their own manufacturing processes. The output is simple and produced in high volume. The production technology used can be easily re-jigged to produce the same item to varying dimensions, tolerances, quality and durability in accordance with the specific requirements of particular orders.
2. Foodstuffs: the production of meat and dairy products; the production of tinned, dried and other homogenised items; the production of instant consumables, such as bread, cakes and biscuits.
3. Drugs: the production of proprietary branded items such as aspirin and paracetamol (and the brand name equivalents such as Panadol, Phensic and Anadin) for retail sale.
4. Furniture: especially kitchen, bathroom and bedroom furniture. In this case the output is often differentiated by appearance and design. The manufacturer must therefore have the capability of responding to this, and perhaps also of creating new distinctive and positive designs. (See also Box 8.2 above.)
5. Some fabric production, especially that which is relatively distinctive or differentiated in some way (for example, Laura Ashley patterns and designs).

■ Mass production and manufacturing

Mass production and manufacturing takes place in order to satisfy mass, even global, markets and their demands for consumer goods and the components. Effective mass manufacturing is dependent upon heavy and continuing levels of capital investment in the production technology used, and in the capacities of the staff involved to operate it effectively. The main differences between this and the production of batches are the sheer scale of activities and the steadier and more stable nature of the outputs. Thus, for example, while a batch production run may result in a batch output in hours or days, the mass producer's aim is likely to be the continuity of production over a period of weeks, months or even years. In car and consumer durable production the main reason for changing the nature of the item is design improvement. Only then, therefore, are the production activities altered.

Mass production activities are driven by maximisation of production technology, economies of scale and the universality of the product, design, appearance, quality and performance.

In mass production, competitive advantage is only to be sustained in long production runs. Products are supplied on the basis that there is a continuing general demand for them. While there is a general relationship between orders placed and output, mass production is not order-specific or directly order-responsive.

Opportunities and causes for concern are indicated by general trends in product consumption, whether upward or downward. The mass producer works to satisfy markets often months, sometimes years, in advance.

BOX 8.4 Scientific Management

The concept of mass and universalised production and the invention of the production line arose from the researches of F. W. Taylor and the scientific management school of the early twentieth century. It effectively meant that each person on the production line became a cog in the production process. Each would carry out a single activity. The item would then pass on to the next person to carry out their single activity; and so on. The attraction was (and remains) that by concentrating on a single activity in this way the operatives are likely to become very good at what they do. The standardised output was (and is) therefore possible.

Much of the human endeavour involved in this has been replaced by production technology: that is, machines do the work. The benefits can be seen in terms of increased quality and exactitude of the production.

The benefits are also to be found in the vastly improved quality of working life. The boredom, frustration and alienation that were to be found on mass human production lines are well documented (for example, in the affluent worker studies of J. H. Goldthorpe *et al.* in the 1960s). They were a major cause of strikes and disputes and a major general barrier between the staff and their organisation.

Empirical research such as the Hawthorne experiments of the 1930s, and again the Affluent Worker studies, together with the experience of specific organisations (such as Volvo in the late 1960s and early 1970s) has led to some understanding of these problems and some willingness to address them. There is also increasing evidence that work that is undemanding mentally has a negative effect on both physical and mental health.

It is therefore necessary to be concerned with identifying and assessing future trends in the sectors and markets served, those which could potentially be served, and the means by which they are served. Lead times and investment levels, together with elements relating to the commissioning, design, development and ordering of installation of new product technology, are all integral to mass manufacturing success, and should all therefore be considered as part of the mass production strategy.

BOX 8.5 Mass Production: Examples and Illustration

1. **Car manufacture.** Comparisons may be made between different parts of the world. The best price, quality and value mix is produced by Nissan and Toyota, the Japanese companies. The largest volumes of cars are produced by Ford, General Motors and Chrysler. The only indigenous mass manufacturer in the UK, the Rover Group, has spent years trying to restore its reputation after a long period of decline in the 1960s, 1970s and 1980s. In pursuit of this it has engaged in partnership with Honda, the Japanese company; in 1994 it became a wholly owned subsidiary of the German BMW Group. Part of this decline was due to the reality of poor production technology and expertise and this is also apparent in the output of the car companies of Eastern Europe; the Skoda company of Czechoslovakia is addressing this problem by entering into partnership with Volkswagen.
2. **Electrical, electronic and white goods:** consumer durables are more or less universally required and demanded. The most recent standards of manufacturing production and quality have been set by Sony, Sanyo and Matsushita. Other producers – Zanussi, Tricity, Bendix, Hoover, Maytag – have had to transform both technology and activities in order to remain competitive.
3. Some **clothing**, principally that which is sold on through hypermarkets, supermarkets and department stores, and including above all universalised items such as socks, stockings, tights, vests and underpants.
4. **Building materials:** bricks, breeze blocks, wooden and plastic planking (for cladding, fixtures and fittings), concrete and plaster products.

■ Flow production

Flow production takes place in response to universal and continuous demand for a unique (or nearly unique) product or commodity. The technology used is extremely capital-intensive, designed and installed for the precise stated purpose. It is not normally flexible or transferable. The process used is normally continuous; there are huge costs incurred in switching it off and restarting it.

The competitive advantage of involvement in flow manufacturing and the sectors that lend themselves to it stem from the very nature of the products: oil and petrol, chemicals, steel, glass and plastic. Operating in these sectors depends on the continued ability to command and maintain sufficiently high levels of capital for investment in this scale of technology. The level of capital required is a high barrier to entry. Other barriers also exist in the form of, and access to, technology and expertise. The ability to transform and replace existing technology is also dependent upon the command of high levels of capital.

However, the variable costs incurred in operating are low as a percentage of total cost. The processes indicated all simply transform raw materials into commodities with a universal demand. The absolute charge necessary for a litre of petrol at the refinery gate or glass bottle at the factory gate in order to cover variable costs is negligible. The ability to charge commercial and economic rents for these commodities is dependent on the sheer volume of demand, and this ensures high and continuing levels of returns on total capital employed.

BOX 8.6 Flow Production: Example and Illustration

1. Chemical manufacturing and oil refining processes, which depend upon the continuous operation of the process technology used.
2. The production of plastics, including plastic extrusion after which the product is sold on for processing; and also the production of plastic products with a universal use, such as bottles and containers for food and drink packaging and storage.
3. Some fabric production, especially for industrial, commercial and domestic furnishings.
4. Paper and paper products, again for both industrial processes and consumer goods; and again for usage as both primary products and packaging.
5. The production of other basic primary requirements, especially steel and glass. These products have universal applications in a great variety of sectors, both as raw materials themselves and as complementary items (especially as packaging, storage and distribution) for ranges of foodstuffs and drinks.

BOX 8.7 'Our Cars Don't Work'

Peters, in his 1986 address to the Royal Society of Arts in London, succinctly stated the reason for the advance of the Japanese car industry as follows: 'It's real simple. American cars don't work.' He then went on to identify the lack of investment in staff and technology endemic throughout the Western car industry on the one hand, and the vast levels of investment in both by Japanese companies (especially Nissan and Toyota) in their setting-up of operations in the West in support of this.

Supply and demand

The supply and demand balance has to be assessed because it creates stresses and strains, especially where the emphasis is on responsiveness. There are also matters of concern relating to the length of time that finished goods remain on the shelf awaiting purchase and order.

In flow processes, where the emphasis is almost entirely on the supply side it is necessary to open up product storage facilities during periods of low demand. If such periods persist, this may lead to stockpiling and in some cases to product-dumping activities by the organisation concerned.

BOX 8.8 Dependence and Dominance

Command of sources of supply

In general, it is perceived to be desirable to establish a multiplicity of supplies of essential raw materials and components. Each of these is ideally also interchangeable, so they have to be identical or near-identical in terms of access, volumes, quality, cost, service arrangements and stability, regularity and frequency of deliveries.

It may be possible to establish a sequential relationship with the supplier sector such that products will be taken from one company and that alternatives will only be sought as and when the company in question defaults.

Command of sources of demand

Organisations are vulnerable to dominant customers. It is superficially attractive to have the regular and steady ability to sell the entire product run (or a great majority of it) to one customer. This has to be balanced by a realistic appraisal of the true nature of the commercial relationship and the extent to which this is in truth dominated by the client organisation. Organisations that pursue this relationship find themselves vulnerable to unilateral price-cutting activities or delays in bill payments. They may be faced with a sudden decision of the client organisation to purchase elsewhere.

True advantage is only to be found if a position of responsibility or enlightenment is adopted alongside the purely commercial. This is, however, only to be sustained if the relationship is preserved ultimately as one of mutual benefit. The client organisation does not actually want the supplying organisation to collapse or the sector to be destabilised.

Other positions of dominance occur in the following circumstances:

- command of capital resources;
- command of key, raw and primary resources;
- command of particular technology and of the skills and qualities needed to operate it effectively (this also includes research and development elements);
- command of market share, which is achieved through the command of means of distribution outlets, access to customers, reputation and confidence among customers. Again, if continued market share is dependent upon the last to a greater extent, a longer-term and enlightened view of responsibilities in this area must also be taken.

Short-term advantage is gained by exerting pressure on those organisations dominated by the relationship, in price-cutting and cost-cutting activities, delays in the payment of bills and the settling of accounts, and also (from the supply side) delays in deliveries. A pragmatic view should be taken of this. Short-term advantage may indeed be gained; overwhelmingly, however, pursuit of strategy depends upon steadiness of business activities. The dominant relationship is best used in the enforcement and ensuring of quality, volume and delivery targets rather than the pursuit of short-term cost or other expediency advantage.

Production environment

There is overwhelming evidence (see Warr, Mayo, Peters) that the quality of working environment has a direct impact on the quality of work and the motivation of the staff. The necessity is therefore (in whatever situation) to make the work environment as comfortable as possible within any operational constraints. In extreme cases – such as those of extreme noise, dirt or temperature – there are legal minima to be observed in the provision of protection and clothing and in the length of time to be spent on activities in any given situation.

Above and beyond these minimum requirements there is an increasing perception of the business value and profitability and effectiveness of performance that can be gained through adherence to thc golden rule of Mary Kay Ash: 'Do unto others as you would have them do unto you.' This is in turn reinforced by current notions of egalitarianism and the setting of distinctive, high and precise standards of operation, and behaviour at work. It is impossible to do this in an inherently bad working environment.

Service strategies

It is necessary to consider the different service sectors as entities with separate and distinctive identities. This is in spite of the fact that many outputs of the service sectors are clearly highly tangible. Retail, for example, is classified as a service activity, yet the items purchased from outlets are clearly highly tangible. Travel, tourism, sports and leisure pursuits, health care and the outputs of bars, cafés and restaurants all offer a product service mix in fact.

The general concept of service is developed most sharply and distinctively in Western Europe, Australia, New Zealand and, above all, North America. The hub of this is intangible: the expectation and satisfaction of the customer. Where this occurs, a mutually satisfactory business relationship is established. Otherwise, the customer may seek redress; if this is not forthcoming, the customer seeks better service elsewhere. If satisfaction is continually not afforded, the customer will in any case seek alternatives. If expectations are consistently exceeded, this eventually becomes the normal level of satisfaction, and to fall back to levels of what was previously quite adequate will then be perceived as a decline.

The product service mix is also important. The purchase of a new car normally carries a commitment to maintenance, service and repair on the part of the manufacturer through a recognised and approved outlet. The purchase of a sandwich has clear service implications in relation to the freshness of the product. The purchase of a public transport ticket carries with it implications for the timing, speed and quality of that service.

BOX 8.9 My Little Pony

My Little Pony is the trade name of a range of toys targeted in the UK at girls up to the age of about 11. They are bought for the girls by mothers, aunts, grandmothers and older sisters, and the friends of each of these groups.

The outlets through which these toys are distributed are urban and suburban toy shops and department stores. The targeting of these toys is at urban and suburban girls and the relatives indicated above. They are bought with cash (rather than credit or other deferred payment). The purchasers are regular and frequent visitors to the shops and stores indicated.

To be an effective operator in this field therefore requires the offering of a wide range of core products, clearly differentiated (through colour, appearance and name, for example); and a complementary range of peripheral products (such as books, comics, accessories, stories, videos, clothing). These are all offered within the cash price ranges indicated. The range of products is constantly being added to. The displays are very visual. The message to both client and consumer is that the products are continuously being brought on to the market, that they are collectable and usable. On the buying front, if an item is not bought this week, it can be bought next week on the next visit. On the consumption front the product is always fresh and new, complementing the existing range and providing a steady and constant source of increased satisfaction to the consumer group.

Hasbro are the manufacturers of the range. The products and product mixes are designed to ensure that each My Little Pony customer is worth between £60 and £100 per annum to the organisation. In the light of the nature of the offering indicated – cash and urban/suburban – this has to be a continuous process and not dependent upon once-only sales.

BOX 8.10 Meeting and Exceeding Expectations

A useful illustration of this is that of the medium- to high-quality restaurant that includes wine with the meal and coffee afterwards in the purchase price. This is an attraction (provided that the food and ambience are good also). Expectations would tend to be exceeded by the ability to have as much wine and coffee as desired. Dissatisfaction would tend to arise if subsequently this was to be limited to one glass of wine and one cup of coffee. This would be exacerbated if the free wine and coffee was withdrawn altogether, even if the price of the meal remained unchanged.

■ Commercial service strategies

These are dependent upon the following factors.

1. The nature of service itself.
2. The nature of the benefits, expectations and satisfaction required by the customer.
3. The nature of the relationship between the service organisation and its customers. This includes the frequency or regularity of visits by the customer, the length of each visit, the nature of the transactions entered into, and the nature of the personal and profitable elements of the relationships that are to be developed.
4. The mode of service delivery.
5. The nature of service demanded and supplied. This includes seasonal and weekend factors, and the ways in which demand for the service may be varied up and down. This is heavily affected, above all, by levels of unemployment (in local

	Service Nature People services:	Goods and possessions services:
Tangible:	• health care • passenger transportation • beauty salons • exercise clinics • restaurants	• freight transportation • industrial equipment • repair and maintenance • laundry and dry cleaning • landscaping
Intangible:	• education • broadcasting • information services • theatres • museums	• banking • legal services • accounting • securities • insurance

The components of service

- Frequency of delivery
- Time from order to delivery
- Reliability of delivery
- Emergency deliveries when required
- Stock availability and continuity of supply
- Orders filled completely
- Advice on non-availability
- Convenience of placing order
- Acknowledgement of order
- Accuracy of invoices
- Quality of sales presentation
- Regular calls by sales representatives
- Manufacture monitoring of retail stock levels
- Credit terms offered, other financial arrangements
- Dates of payment
- Dates of service delivery
- After sales and service support
- Replacements/alternatives
- Customer query handling
- Quality of outer packaging
- Easy-to-read packaging, brochures, literature
- In-store handling and display
- New product/package development
- Reviews product range regularly
- Coordination between production, distribution and marketing
- Meeting expectations
- Constant improvement
- Politeness
- Honesty
- Trust
- Confidence

Figure 8.1 Features of customer service

terms, the higher this goes the greater the decline in demand for all commercial services). It may also be affected by the availability of a substitute; conversely, demand for one service is likely to rise if a substitute closes down or becomes unavailable.

6. The extent to which the service is standardised, universally and equally offered or tailored and customised to the requirements of individual consumers or consumer groups.
7. The technology and equipment required to produce the service. In the restaurant example this is the equipment necessary to store, prepare, cook and serve the food. In the travel agency sector this is the equipment necessary to gain access to the databases of tour operators, package companies and transport services and to make quick and effective bookings. In the personal finance sector it is the technology that enables instant withdrawals and credit to be made (the debit/switchcard system, cashpoints and front of branch database technology).
8. Information requirements, both in the presentation of the services on offer and to illustrate the benefits and satisfaction to be gained on the part of customers. For example, the travel agency books the holiday – the service – on the basis of the brochure presentation, which shows the benefits and potential satisfaction to the customer. The bank offers free and accessible banking to its customers – the service – and also its invulnerability and confidence.
9. The general cost, price, quality, volume and volume mix. For example, if all banks offer free personal banking to individual customers, any bank that then decides that it will make charges must have a range of benefits to offer which outweigh and override this particular benefit.
10. Quality, maintenance and control. This is often extremely difficult to define. On the one hand, the service is being instigated or delivered by a human (and therefore an imperfect being whose performance will vary); on the other, it is being delivered to human beings whose expectations vary. The best organisations get over this to a great extent at least by instilling particular attitudes, values, beliefs and modes of service delivery that are successful, effective and profitable.

BOX 8.11 Benefits, Expectations and Satisfaction – Example: The Restaurant Sector

In this sector different establishments exist to fulfil different benefit ranges and mixes as follows.

1. Status and exclusivity: a place to be seen in (for example, Quaglino's).
2. Value, which may be seen from various points of view. Someone taking a guest or guests to a highly expensive place reflects the value, importance and esteem in which they hold those guests. Value may also be offered on the basis of value for money and the price-quality mix. Some establishments may

themselves place added value on regular customers in the offering of extra benefits in return for this regularity of patronage.

3. Uniformity: the attraction of restaurant chains such as Pizza House, Berni, Steak House (and also McDonald's and Burger King).
4. Speed of service: this is the attraction at the one extreme of McDonald's and Burger King. At the other the customer may wish to spread the meal out over several hours. Conversely, it may be the nature of the restaurant that it is spread out over several hours.
5. The style and type of food, the volume, quality and location mix. For example, there is a preponderance of fish and chip restaurants in English seaside towns. Fast food chains tend to be concentrated in the centre of towns and cities.
6. Presentation and appearance of the restaurant itself. This is important for confidence and comfort; the presentation and appearance of the food; and perceptions of freshness and wholesomeness.
7. There are also particular visual aspects. In *nouvelle cuisine*, for example, part of the attraction is the design, presentation and colour complementing of the food itself. Elsewhere there is the visual impact of large plates completely filled. Elsewhere again, buffet arrangements give the impression of large and varied offering ranges.
8. Price: the price range on offer and the means by which it is gathered (cash, cheque, credit card and charge card).
9. Personal elements such as recognition and esteem. This is perceived to be a critical reason why people regularly patronise a given restaurant.

BOX 8.12 Substitution in the Service Sector

In general terms the following are all substitutes for each other. That is, the customer will make choices between each, choosing one rather than the others according to particular circumstances and situations.

1. Restaurant, bar, café, cinema, television dinner, sports activities, watching a sporting fixture, day trip or excursion, concert, theatre, museum and galleries. The substitution process is compounded by matters to do with personal mobility and the range and mix of each of these (and other equivalents) in both the immediate and wider locality.
2. In given circumstances, there is also a substitution process between the purchase of a package holiday, the purchase of a new car, the making of mortgage payments and other domestic financial commitments.

BOX 8.13 Staff Training and Development in the Service Sectors

The best organisations in these sectors include staff training and development as a key feature of their strategy. The emphasis is not so much on job training, which is often simple and straightforward, but rather on customer focus. This involves instilling a full understanding of the nature of being a customer of the organisation and concentrates on empathy, interest and concern. It is reinforced by attention to the behavioural aspects that underline this – listening, eye contact and attention – and underpinned by speed of response and service (and therefore satisfaction). Finally, those entering these sectors at whatever level are increasingly required to undertake some form of business training.

Storage and preservation

Some services cannot be stored at all; for example, travel tickets can only be sold up to the point of departure of the train, plane or boat. Theatre, concert and cinema tickets are also sold for particular performances: customers do not buy tickets and then turn up to see what is being put on. Package holidays have a longer shelf-life equivalent: summer packages are sold from the previous December onwards, and winter packages from September onwards; in both cases there are early booking advantages (to give business an initial boost) and last-minute offers (at the point at which the package sale would otherwise be lost). Restaurant services are subject to the perishability or durability of the food and drink stocks.

Some financial services are relatively durable and universal: for instance, bank branches and insurance companies do not normally limit the number of accounts or clients that they take on. However, the nature of some of the services offered and the implications for the customers may change out of all recognition due to variations in charge and fee levels, interest rates and dependency on cash points rather than over-the-counter provision.

Inseparability is the term used to describe the fact that a critical part of the service takes place at the point of transaction between producer and customer. Both are therefore involved in the service production: the producer in the demonstration of the range of offerings and permutations that are available, and the customer in the articulation of the precise requirement. Customer satisfaction and profitable and effective business occurs where there is a sufficient measure of overlap between the two.

The environment in which the service is offered is also important. There are two major reasons for this: that staff have to work in it, and the customer has to come into it. There are also aspects specific to the nature of the particular service to be addressed. Kwik-Fit, the UK car tyre and exhaust replacement service company, offers hot and cold drinks and newspapers in a waiting room area (akin to that of a doctor or dentist) while the work is carried out. Boots offers chairs for immobile and disabled people to sit and wait while their prescriptions are being made up. Banks and post office counter services now ask customers to wait in a single queue (rather than one at each desk) so that people are served strictly on a first-come-first-served basis. This is perceived by all to be much better than suffering the vagaries of the queue in which one happened to find oneself.

Where the service is not conducted on a face-to-face basis (as, for example, with telephone or mail-order arrangements), the total environment of the service provider has to be substituted by the quality of the telephone transaction and thus created by it to a degree sufficient to ensure both immediate satisfaction and repeat business.

BOX 8.14 Attitudes, Values and Beliefs in the Service Sectors

Example: Banking

Randall (1992) cites the UK banking sector in support of this. He acknowledges the extent to which the face of personal banking has changed. However, he queries the extent to which the sector has truly transformed the attitudes which he acknowledges have deep and ancient roots. He quotes that 'they have had to respond to new competitors by offering interest on current accounts and they are finally using new technology' in the pursuit of greater customer satisfaction.

Further examples of this may be given. There are invariably time delays between a request to see someone in authority and actually getting to see them. There are charges levied on accounts without full warning or explanation. In particular, charge levels were targeted at existing and solvent customers with a view to recouping the extensive bad debts incurred by the banks during the period 1990–92.

Body Shop

This may be contrasted with the attitudes, values and beliefs exhibited by The Body Shop organisation in 1992 in the south-east of England. The local Body Shop franchisee was dismissed by the company following an inquiry into allegations by the franchise staff that they were being forced by the franchisee into the adoption of extreme religious activities and articles of faith. This left the region without access to Body Shop products.

The organisation undertook to satisfy customers on an individual basis. Those who wanted Body Shop products simply telephoned an order line at headquarters with their request. The company undertook to have the delivery made within 24 hours. If the request was urgent (for any reason at all) the order was instantly dispatched to the customer's address by courier.

New products, research and development

New products, innovations and developments are continually required by all organisations because of the competitive nature of business, the drive for advantages and the resultant increased expectations and demands of consumers. All organisations therefore do this in some shape or form. Public social security and health services are developed to meet the changing needs of the population, the changes in the population mix and in response to economic factors and circumstances. Education services must constantly be developed and updated through technological advance, the ever-changing history and geography of the world, scientific advances and changes in the general state of understanding and enlightenment. It consists of the following.

1. The invention of something that is radically new or different. This does not happen truly very often. Recent inventions (that is, since the Second World War) include the television, computer and space satellite.
2. The application of new technology to existing production processes causing cost and quality improvements and therefore price and value advantages to the customer.
3. The re-presentation of existing products in new forms and to new sectors. Much of this is carried out by some process or other of differentiation, and includes repackaging, redesign, new advertising and promotion campaigns, and new names for existing products.

BOX 8.15 Product Range Extensions

Electrical white goods and car companies regularly do this. Car companies, for example, bring out limited editions at the value end, high power and high comfort versions at the most expensive and exclusive end, and high performance models at different intervals of the whole product range. If this is carried out correctly it opens up new segments without compromising the purchases of the existing range of customers.

A similar range of activities also occurs in these sectors every year or two. Customers require a combination of familiarity and comfort with marginal improvement, both in product specification and value for money. New models are brought on-stream. This is carried out regularly enough to ensure the attraction of those coming into the sectors for the first time (for example, new car owners, new home owners) and to provide generally improved products, but without upsetting the current client base which inevitably has expectations of both operational and behavioural longevity.

Products new to the market sectors or niches are introduced following market research, buying patterns and habits, purchasing power, and current levels and density of activity. The organisation brings its existing levels of corporate image and expectation together with the amount of precise and targeted interest it has managed to generate by virtue of the proposed new activities.

BOX 8.16 Wellingtons

Wellington boots are a peculiarly British institution made out of black plastic or rubber. They are impermeable and keep the feet dry in wet weather. They are more or less universal in their usage in this context by persons of all sectors of the population.

Versions have, however, been sold extremely profitably to particular niches. Coloured versions have been produced for children. Reinforced and toe capped versions have been produced as safety as well as dry wear for the construction, quarrying, engineering, farming and fishing sectors. A green version has been produced and marketed most effectively to a niche that is defined by country pursuit, opulence and lifestyle. Indeed, this niche has been described as the 'dogs and green wellingtons set' by both news media and marketing organisations. It has been presented as such by the clothing catalogues of the Racing Green and Barbour companies.

Products new to the company

This is where the company adopts or introduces a distinctly new product to its range. Supermarkets and department stores go into (and come out of) fashion ranges, furniture, furnishings, books and magazines.

BOX 8.17 New Products: Tesco

Tesco once offered a large home-based range that included a wide selection of household, domestic, kitchen, living room, bedroom and garden furniture. This is now limited to kitchen utensils and household furniture in larger stores only.

The company's venture into book, magazine and newspaper sales has been extremely successful. In particular the offering of daily national newspapers is an incentive on the part of the consumer to go to the shop every day (and therefore inevitably to purchase other things at the same time).

BOX 8.18 Product Range Development: Barbie

The product range development of the Barbie doll is carried out along the following lines.

The humanity and personality of Barbie herself. She has had a life created around her with activities, interests, leisure pursuits, sisters, a boyfriend, other friends, a home, holidays, cars and travel. She has the illusion and appearance of glamour, sophistication and opulence (without distancing herself too far from the lives of those who actually buy her).

The Barbie doll is central and universal. She has remained largely unaltered over the 35 years of her life. The dolls have long blonde hair, and are distinctively shaped. Differentiated models are brought out in addition (for example, with extra long hair, glittering hair, hair which changes colour when washed, curly hair, straight hair; one of the competitors, Sindy, in 1994 introduced a version with short hair, which represented a radical move in the market and a first in the 35 years of its existence).

The fashion range mirrors the life that Barbie leads. Distinctive outfits are produced for each activity and pursuit range. This covers the whole gamut; from ball gowns (and tuxedo for her boyfriend) to leisure and beach wear for different locations around the world. These are a combination of the well tried and familiar (such as normal swim wear for the beach); the far away and exotic (such as Bali); and the 'truly magic' (e.g. Aladdin, Mermaid).

The fashion range is constantly being developed. It mirrors the offerings of clothing houses and department stores to real people: swim wear is offered after Christmas, winter wear in the summer and autumn. The imperative is to produce new differentiated products each season. As this happens the previous season's items are allowed to fall off the end of the range and are no longer offered (again, this mirrors the real world of those who buy her).

The quality of the product range must remain fashionable and desirable, positive, glamorous and wholesome. It has to remain attractive both to those who buy the dolls and their accessories (parents and especially mothers) as well as to the users (girls aged between 3 and 16).

The product range output continues to be sold on overwhelmingly a **cash sales basis.** The client/customer base continues to be urban and suburban girls aged 3 to 16 and their mothers, older sisters and other female relatives. The imperative, therefore, is to continue to be able to develop and offer a differentiated new product range of between 10 and 20 items each season in order to keep up the level of interest and identity to develop the life, humanity and personality that is a part of this and which feeds it, and to prevent the child looking elsewhere for this level of interest.

There is in the UK a Barbie help line. This was created by the Mattel UK company's public relations department. Its purpose was to provide an exclusive service to the thousands of small girls that used to phone the marketing and public relations departments to try to speak to Barbie or to find out news about her activities and new product ranges and proposals for these.

The creation of the **exclusive service** means that everyone is happy, especially the clients. It also frees up the company's creative and marketing functions to engage in the pursuit of maintaining the client's happiness. Above all, there is a substantial element of excellent public relations to be gained from this; as well as this, it is a prime source of market research information and assessment and evaluation of the motivation of the clientele.

Commercially the sector is known in the UK as the 11.5 inch doll market. There are ranges of differentiated offerings both for the dolls (the sector includes Sindy, Disney and film and television characters), and their clothing (offered also by the makers of Sindy and the other dolls and also by distinctive doll's fashion houses, such as Pastiche). The clothes, accessories, outfits and trappings are interchangeable and interusable between each of the sectors.

In the 35 years of her existence, Barbie has generated $770 million worldwide for her owners, the Mattel Corporation. In the UK, in the spring of 1996, the average price of a doll with clothes is £4.99.

Most new products do not get to the start of commercial production. Commitment to new product development in spite of this is essential. Lessons and information are drawn from the whole process so that successful innovation takes place eventually.

BOX 8.19 New Products: Sony

The Sony organisation produces 15 new products per day. Nearly all fail to get further than the drawing board, prototype, initial product and market testing stages. The organisation pursues this because at this level of output there are certain to be regular exceptions to the rule which could turn into successes. Sony is synonymous with the Walkman and the resultant creation of the billion-dollar personal entertainment sector. However, the company has created, pioneered, improved and refined a great range of other products. These include miniature televisions, camcorders, personal telephones, both audio and video micro-cassettes, wide-screen televisions for both domestic and commercial usage. It has also adopted the branding/differentiation approach with the introduction of the Aiwa marque. The result is a steady stream of new improved and distinctive products on to a major global market and market segments. This will only be achieved by continued commitment to the principles of new product development and investment in invention, research, design, development and testing.

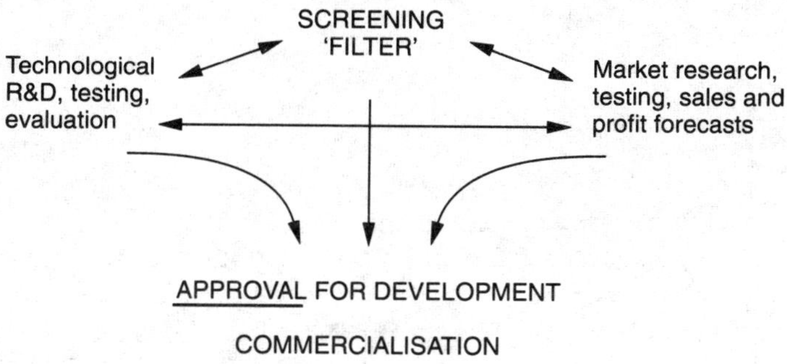

Figure 8.2 Input of new product ideas

Source: Buell (1985).

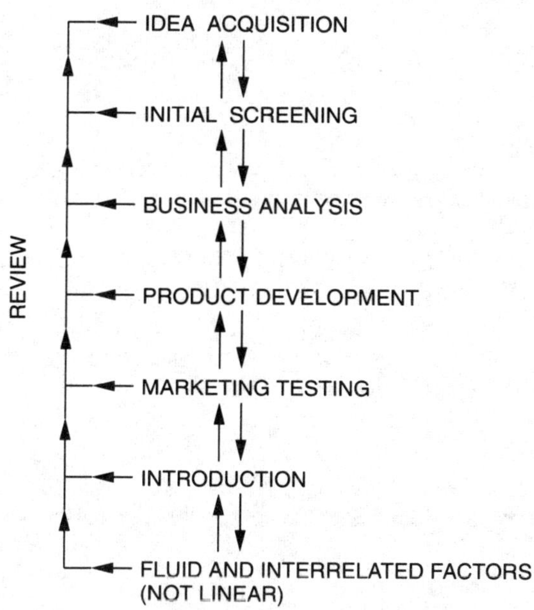

Figure 8.3 New product development: six-step model

Source: Cohen (1988).

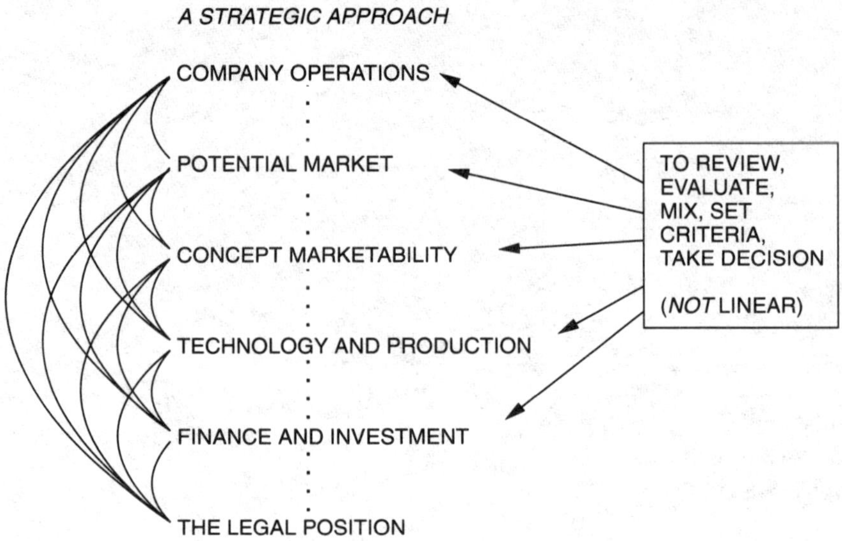

Figure 8.4 Screening and development model

Source: Cohen (1988).

■ Success and failure

Organisations clearly strive for as high a success rate as possible in the bringing on of new products.

The Sony example illustrates the prerequisites for success in the development of new products. Success is never guaranteed. A long-term and committed view of the process is essential. A new product cannot be invented, tested and produced commercially overnight (even if success for it were actually guaranteed). Problems and pitfalls, and the nightmare/worst-case scenario must be addressed at all stages: the development of the product, its operational capacities and market take-up. Organisations need to learn from failures and analyse the knowledge and experience gained.

The failure of new products is exacerbated by the following.

□ *Short-termism*

This is the anticipation and expectation of instant or near-instant results. When this is not achieved the organisation questions its whole commitment to the research, development and new product processes undertaken, rather than the timescale.

□ *Resourcing*

Failure of new product strategies and activities is accelerated through resource lack or starvation. In some sectors there is an expedient short-term cash flow advantage to be gained by cutting research and development budgets. The inevitable result of this is a reduction in the quality and effectiveness of the total research and development effort.

□ *Product to market*

The ability of the organisation to get its new products on to the market quickly enough is also critical to success. Brilliant inventions have still to be marketed and sold. If an equivalent substitute quickly produced and effectively presented is offered by a competitor, the original organisation is likely to lose market share, and may indeed lose their entire competitive position (as, for example, with IBM in the personal computer market).

□ *Elitism, isolation and group-think*

This is an organisation's concern with itself and its own brilliance and expertise (which may be extremely high) without adequate reference to its markets. In such circumstances neither concepts and ideas nor products are truly market tested. Organisations further confuse prevailing attitudes to them, especially if these are favourable, with the behaviour of buyers. (A general feeling on the part of consumers towards a particular organisation does not mean that they will buy from it; conversely buyers may loathe an organisation but buy its products nevertheless.)

These matters will be compounded by internal organisational politics, in-fighting and jockeying for position. Product champions, think-tanks and other overmighty subjects need triumphs; their internal opponents need them to fail.

These matters are also likely to be compounded by the faddishness of approaches to new products and initiatives. This is extremely prevalent in public policy initiatives, especially in health, social services and education, where such developments (given neither the time nor the resources to work anyway) are superseded at short-term intervals by the next idea. This becomes infinitely worse where the structure and management style (and also the minister and director) are themselves short term and transient.

BOX 8.20 Elements of Successful New Product Development

These include:

- resources
- volume and quality of new ideas;
- the speed and volume with which they are generated;
- the means by which they are screened and assessed and the time that is taken over this process;
- the prevailing attitude of the organisation and its directors, managers and strategists to such new ideas as are generated;
- the relationship between this and more general approaches to constant and continuous improvement;
- the relationship between this and the prevailing cost, price, quality and value mixture under which the organisation is operating and the general effectiveness of this;
- the balance and priority in which the new product is to be held in regard to the rest of the product portfolio;
- the effects of the new products and new product development upon the markets and customer bases which are already served;
- other behavioural and reputational aspects both in regard to the new product and also in regard to the existing range (this includes the meeting of expectations and projections on the part of each of the stakeholder and interest group involved);
- identification of the customer base and its propensity to buy;
- identification of the parameters of the market sector or segments;
- meeting stakeholder expectations.

■ Public service strategies

Public services are provided to support the qualities of life and standards of living that society requires and expects. They reflect the political, social, economic and ethical values and stances of the given society. Societies with strong political ideologies and priorities reflect these in the nature of the services that are provided. (For example, the former USSR concentrated its resources and expertise on defence and military activities, reflecting both its authoritarian and expansionist political drives.)

Conversely, where there is no clear sense of public purpose, this also is reflected in the lack of clarity and direction of the services offered. In extreme cases this is likely to lead to a collapse of services. This is especially acute where there is a lack of direction compounded by conflicting demands for resources overtly based on the need to satisfy and fulfil them all. (When the USSR collapsed, so did all of its instruments of state, leaving a vacuum.)

If the quality of life is to be supported effectively, there is an absolute necessity to give stability, order, clarity of purpose and resources.

There is a large degree of professionalism and professionalisation. The services are run by officials (managers, administrators, officers) and service experts (soldiers, lawyers, doctors, teachers). These are, and are deemed to be, the highest form of experience and expertise in the given field. In return for bringing this expertise there are expectations of rewards, progress, promotion and career paths on the part of the job holders. Influence on the nature, direction and operation of the actual services is exerted by both officials and professions, and their representative and supportive bodies.

There is a degree of public accountability required. Services are normally paid for from revenues raised through taxation or other public charges. Both the volume and quality of expenditure is subject to scrutiny. This is normally carried out by both politicians and officials. Responsibility for overall policy control and direction of services rests with politicians. This is implemented through government departments, public bodies, instruments of state and their experts and officials.

BOX 8.21 UK National Training Policy in the 1980s and 1990s

This is an excellent example of what happens when there is no permanence or stability or continuity of an area of public policy. The outcome over the period is that in the particular case there are sectors of the UK population whose training, qualifications and experience have no currency or substance. Neither is there any continuity in the standards and quality offered over the period. The outcome of such programmes and the value placed on them is therefore subject to individual interpretation.

Initiatives in the field proliferated over the period. The training policy programme names are legion. They include the New Training Initiative (NTI), Unified Vocational Preparation (UVP), Youth Opportunities Programmes (YOPS), Training Opportunities Programmes (TOPS), Youth Training Schemes (YTS), Youth Training (YT), Adult Training Schemes (ATS), and Adult Training (AT), restart, into work and back to work programmes have all been created and have subsequently withered and died. National Vocational Qualifications (NVQs), General National Vocational Qualifications (GNVQs), National Records of Vocational Achievement (NROVA), and Records of Achievement (ROA) have all been created over the given period.

These programmes have been operated under the aegis of a wide variety of organisations. They have been run variously by Industrial Training Boards (ITBs), the Business Education Council (BEC), the Business and Technician Education

Council (BTEC), Information Technology Executives (ITEC), Training and Enterprise Councils (TECs), the Department of Employment, the Department of Trade and Industry, the Manpower Services Commission, the Training Agency, and Employment Agency. The overwhelming result is a general lack of credence, value or confidence placed on any of the products or programmes. The activities have also been dogged by budget cuts, cost centre changes, and matters of political expediency.

The first of these programmes was created by the Manpower Services Commission in 1981, and was entitled 'Work Experience on Employers' Premises'. The acronym used was WEEP.

Political and ethical stances

Those responsible for the direction of public policy usually take distinctive political and ethical stances (their perspective from which the world is viewed).

Sometimes this is very strong. Others gain support from their ability to reflect the more general social aspirations and expectations of the people whom they seek to serve. Others gain general support from longevity, and they become familiar and comfortable. It is almost as if people expect them to be in charge. Others gain their support largely on the basis of differentiation, especially concentration on personalities and media coverage. This occurs where political and ideological distinctions are small.

This is the general political background against which all public policy is carried out. Priorities and emphases derive from the particular stance adopted.

BOX 8.22 Privatisation of Public Services

Privatisation is the term used to describe the transfer of public services and activities, and state-owned and operated (nationalised) industries, utilities, commercial services and transport systems.

The hypothesis is that 'private' management is 'better' than 'public' management, and that the activities will therefore be delivered to higher standards of quality and excellence to the customers. Privatisation brings in cash windfalls to the governments concerned. They also anticipate increased tax revenues as the activities become more profitable and effective in their new ownership. There is also a reduced (or zero) commitment of public funds once privatisation has been completed.

The most common forms of privatisation are:

- the sale of shares, either to a single buyer or on stock markets to the public at large;

- trust or agency status, giving the new body autonomy in choosing its clients, establishing its own level of service provision and charges and setting its own budget (this is normally supported by a government guarantee, either one-off or reviewed regularly);
- market testing, in which services are required to tender and bid for their own work in competition with other interested parties;
- competitive contract tendering, in which services are put out to tender and bids are taken from all interested parties (the contract is normally awarded to the organisation most able to satisfy the price/quality/value/volume/time mix required);
- commercialisation, in which services hitherto provided free at the point of delivery are now to be charged for at the point of delivery.

These activities have taken place all over Western Europe and the ex-Eastern Bloc over the period of the 1980s and 1990s. Some useful examples and illustrations are set out below.

UK	Telecommunications; gas, electricity, water; British Airways; national and local bus services; car ferries; care of the elderly and disabled; refuse collection; education support services; research activities; the delivery of social security benefits; oil refining and exploration.
France	Banks, insurance; chemicals; oil and petrol services; (envisaged) Renault, Peugeot and Citroën car companies, Air France.
Czech Republic	Engineering; chemicals; car and commercial vehicle production (Skoda – managed by the German Volkswagen company).
Sweden	Railways.
Germany	(Especially the former German Democratic Republic): engineering; chemicals; defence; shipbuilding.
Russia	Electricity; shipping; engineering; car production; oil and petrol production and distribution; airlines (Aeroflot); airports.

BOX 8.23 A Note on the Voluntary Sector

This is the sector that fills gaps left in the total provision required by given societies by tradition, accident or design. The coverage of the sector is vast and complex and addresses a range of social, economic and ethical needs; it also provides some essential public services and funding for essential research into illness, sickness and disease. It covers the following.

1. The Red Cross. This maintains a deliberate status of independence through its voluntary standing. Wherever it operates in the world it is therefore not open to charges of partiality by anyone. Consequently, it is able to penetrate the most extreme and deprived areas. It may enter war zones, prison and concentration camps that would normally be barred to anyone else, by virtue of this independence.
2. Other bodies wishing to preserve total independence. Examples of this in the UK are Oxfam and the Royal National Lifeboat Institution.
3. Disease segments. These are those sectors which provide and endow research into heart, lung disorders, cancers, muscular dystrophy or Parkinson's disease, for instance, all of which are major disablers and killers in Western society; there is great pressure to find cures, or palliatives, for all of them.
4. Population segments. These are represented by charities that generate resources, facilities and support for different sectors of the population: the aged, the homeless, the abused, the disadvantaged, orphans, the destitute, the diseased, the starving and the hungry.
5. Rehabilitation. These are charities especially for offenders following their release from prison; drug and alcohol misuse; and for those who have suffered major trauma (for example, those who have been present at disasters).
6. Special events. These are the charities that seek to raise funds, say, with the purpose of sending someone to a specialised location giving them the opportunity to compete in sporting events where funding for them would otherwise be denied. This may also to apply to some scholarship and academic endowments. It has also occurred on a localised basis where, for example, small children with a terminal disease have had funds raised by the community in which they lived to send them on a special holiday before they die.
7. Rare diseases. These are activities whereby funds are raised to enable somebody who has such a complaint to undergo research, testing and treatment; and also to provide the wherewithal (including the staff and expertise) that enables this to be done.
8. Local provision. This is where a charity foundation is set up in memory of an individual or to provide means for that individual (usually disabled or disadvantaged) to lead a normal or more fulfilled life than would otherwise be possible.

Common to all is the fact that they all exist only because of the willingness of people and organisations to make voluntary donations to them. The critical nature of the work is self-evident from the list above. It is also increasingly recognised that the rules of business and public service provision that apply to mainstream, commercial and public sectors also apply in the delivery of effective outputs by the voluntary sector. Great advances have been made in this sphere in all aspects of their activities: above all, in the marketing and promulgation of their cause. In general, each of these activities, organisations and foundations requires the same distinctive clarity of purpose, strategic focus and in-house expertise if it is to be successful. The different parts of the voluntary sector are, after all, competing for the charitable donations and those who can afford to make them and who are willing to do so. This sector has finally to be seen in the context that it to is constantly expanding and becoming ever more sophisticated; that is, greater demands for voluntary donations are being placed upon those sectors of the public that can afford to make them. The consequence is that some charities are succeeding at the expense of others. Pursuit of effective strategies by these organisations is therefore essential as they seek to achieve their own competitive advantage.

Conclusion

The purpose of this chapter has been to illustrate the particular pressures and effects that are brought to bear dependent upon the given nature of activities. These may be summarised as:

- the nature and levels of investment required to sustain them;
- the nature and types of human resource, the skills and qualities required, means of organisation, and approaches and style of management necessary;
- understanding of the nature of the markets in which business is conducted;
- understanding of the processes of prioritisation and substitution that occur in relation to these activities;
- understanding of particular limitations within which activities have to be carried out (this is especially important in the consideration of public services, but each sector has its own constraints);
- understanding of the 'new product' effect: the need to develop any product, service or activity to maintain and enhance competitive advantage without detriment to the existing range of activities;
- recognition of the fact that in no sector is there any prospect of total domination, especially over the medium to longer term; customers and organisations will always seek alternatives where they feel that current business relationships do not serve their continuing interests or may not continue to do so.

The distinctive strategic position (cost leadership, specialisation, differentiation), and the ways in which this is developed (offence and defence, and so on) must therefore be set in a particular context. This reinforces the view that it is impossible to devise or adopt a blueprint for success; instead, these are a set of principles which require distinctive application.

■ Work assignments and discussion questions

1. Why do drug and pharmaceutical production runs tend to be on a batch rather than a mass scale?
2. Conduct a SWOT (or other suitable) analysis for a small company that produces pine tables, chairs, bookshelves and wardrobes to individual order, and that has just been offered the opportunity to mass produce for edge-of-town hardware stores.
3. What are the main problems and issues surrounding health service strategies, and how can the effects of these best be minimised?
4. (a) What are the benefits and threats to a small antique shop of selling its entire stock at a premium price to an overseas dealer?

   (b) The Saga Company sells package holidays to people of 50 and over. What are the benefits and consequences to be considered if the company brings its threshold age down to 40? Or 30?

CHAPTER 9

Strategy Development

Introduction

It is now necessary to consider the main forms by which strategy is developed. These are as follows:

- expansion and growth;
- market domination;
- branding;
- brand leadership;
- consolidation, the preservation and enhancement of the existing range of activities;
- withdrawal, retrenchment and contraction, often related to divesting peripheral activities and strengthening the core;
- diversification, either related or unrelated;
- product improvement;
- integration, along the paths of the five forces of competition;
- new product development;
- mergers, take-overs and acquisitions;
- collaboration and joint ventures;
- project work.

Some basic issues must be addressed. These concern:

- levels of investment and funding;
- the timescale for achievement and completion for the whole of the particular activities along the way;
- the quality of performance of the new form of organisation and the future range of products;
- the new position in the market or markets, and the reactions of existing players to this;
- the availability and accessibility of technology, supplies, services and expertise suitable to the new scale;
- the position of these activities in relation to the organisation's overall strategy and direction;
- the position of these activities in relation to the organisation's history, traditions, image, confidence and well-being.

■ Expansion and growth strategies

These take one or more of the following forms.

1. Expansion and growth of market share. This is related either to expansion of the total market size, or else takes place at the expense of other operators in the sector.
2. Expansion and growth of turnover, volume, income or profit. This may relate to market share also, or to a drive for efficiencies within the organisation, or in the seeking of greater levels and volumes of business with the existing customer base.
3. The achievement of economies of scale; and command of technology and distribution.
4. The command of the means of gaining and maintaining customer and consumer confidence.
5. Expansion into new market areas and niches. This is where the existing product ranges are priced or differentiated in ways designed to appeal to different niches. Additionally, in a highly competitive sector the requirement is to broaden the appeal of the offering in question in relation to those of the other players. Related to this is often the extension and expansion of the offering range (real or differentiated). There are diversification elements in this which will be discussed fully under that heading below.
6. Expansion into new locations, both indigenous and international.
7. Diversification, integration, acquisition, merger, joint ventures and alliances. All of these are discussed fully under their own headings below.

Expansions take place for their own configurations of the rational and irrational. Rationally, organisations expand because they have spare or under utilised resources, finance, staff, production and output technology. Some organisations in some sectors may need to grow in order to remain viable players in a turbulent sector (as with national and global companies in the civil engineering sector). Organisations make acquisitions to seek more and alternative outlets for their products (for example, the purchase by Sony of Columbia). Organisations expand production volumes by using their existing technology more effectively and thus bringing unit costs down (and generating the opportunity therefore to bring the price down also).

The irrational must also be considered. Some organisations have overwhelming pioneering cultures which require constant prospecting and exploration. This, in turn, leads to a constant expansion and extension of the range of activities. Organisations may choose to go down a particular line because it is a high-profile or fashionable area in which to be involved. Organisations may pursue a particular strategy on the whim of the Chief Executive, a bunker mentality, or an overmighty subject or group. Organisations may choose to go into a sector because it is, or is perceived to be, highly profitable (rational enough) but without having any previous experience or expertise in it.

In regard to all the above points, the rational does not of itself lead to success, and neither does the irrational lead to failure. The key to success in expansion is again rational, however. The proposed direction has to be subjected to the same standards and level of scrutiny as any other strategy. Timescales, targets and intermediate markers are established. The extent of investment and resources required for the purpose is the same. The capabilities, capacities and expertise required to be a successful player in the sector are analysed and evaluated. Whatever the source of the proposed expansion, it will succeed only if these elements are applied.

■ Market entry and penetration

This occurs in the following circumstances and conditions, and where new organisations are able to satisfy them. In passing, it should be noted that there are very few sectors that are not open to potential entry (see Box 9.1).

1. Where the overall market is growing, can be made to grow or has growth potential. In this case there is a capacity or potential that existing players may not be able to fill, and they may not be willing to fill it either, preferring to concentrate on keeping their existing customer bases satisfied rather than diluting their efforts in this regard in the pursuit of larger volumes.
2. Where organisations leave the market, again, leaving spare capacity in it.

BOX 9.1 Impenetrable Sectors?

1. Apple Macintosh command a 10 per cent share of the Japanese commercial and domestic personal computer markets. This is due to the excellence of their products and service, and the high regard in which they are held.
2. SNCF, the French National Railway Company, has built an extensive network of high-speed trains (TGV), and generated a national high-speed public transport network. This is set to expand across Germany, Italy, Switzerland and Spain.
3. Virgin Atlantic has generated a series of top-quality air transport routes between the UK, North America and the Far East.
4. The Body Shop is a distinctive retail cosmetics company. Its stores only sell cosmetics (as distinct from other department stores, which sell them as part of a range of offerings).

The one factor common to all of these sectors is that they have each been assessed as impenetrable or unworkable by other operators.

1. No manufacturing organisation believed that it was possible to take 10 per cent of a domestic Japanese sector unless it was itself Japanese.

2. British Rail is waiting to have the need for high-speed rail travel proven (and indeed *all* rail travel proven) before it upgrades and enlarges its network to become part of the European system.
3. Other airlines have engaged in joint ventures, hook-ups and price wars with varying degrees of success. The Virgin example is unique.
4. The concept of a cosmetics-only store was rejected by a variety of UK department store chains before The Body Shop opened. The distinctive packaging, ethical stance, and tribal mentality was also rejected.

3. Where the potential entrant has a real, perceived or differentiated advantage to bring to the sector in question. In real terms this is likely to be a cost-price, value or quality advantage over the existing operator. These were the overwhelming advantages brought to the consumer, electronics and car sectors by Japanese companies coming into Western Europe and North America.

   In perceived or differentiated terms new entrants bring associations, image and lifestyle connotations to the sectors in question. Again, these were the main qualities brought to the take-away food sector by McDonald's and Burger King. They are also the basis on which Coca Cola and Pepsi Cola is sold, and any potential entrants to the soft drinks sector must be able to compete on this, or else find something that supersedes it.
4. Where a niche operator builds up sufficient reputation, resources and capacity to engage in offensive strategies with a view to taking share from the main players involved.
5. Where complacency exists on the part of the existing operators in the market; where there has been a fall-off in the levels of quality or service; where profit-taking exists; where sectoral norms exist; and in all of these cases where there is an opportunity in relation to these. This would tend to indicate sectors where entry barriers were in reality relatively low. The capacity for complacency, fall-off in levels of quality and service, and profit-taking tends to be greatest in sectors where entry barriers are relatively high.
6. Where an organisation is able to bring its reputation from one sphere to another and to gain a foothold in a sector as the result of expanding in another. This may apply where the new sphere is related to previous experience or not. In either case a high level of existing reputation is necessary.

■ Market domination

This occurs where an organisation either finds itself in the position of being the major player in the market (for example, as a result of mergers or take-overs, or withdrawal by competitors from it); or, conversely, the organisation sets out to become the dominant player.

Dominance may occur in a variety of ways. It may come about because of sheer organisation size and the resources that are available to it. The company may be the only multi-national or public company in the entire sector. It may have a particular national, regional, sectoral or local appeal. Dominance may be of a large sector (cosmetics, for example); one that is more clearly defined but still large, such as toothpaste; or more specialist still, such as non-silicon based toothpaste; or highly specialised, such as herbal toothpaste. It may mean command and production or process technology that give enormous cost advantages. It may mean control of the critical sources of supply, or critical retail and distribution outlets. One organisation may be able to offer premium salaries, thus enabling it to attract all the best expertise in the field. The nature of the market in question may have given rise to virtual monopolies, or oligopolies, which have in turn created entry and protection barriers making it very difficult for anyone to enter who does not have ready the capital, equipment, resources, technology, expertise and distribution outlets (oil, banking, energy supply, transport and telecommunications are all examples of this). There are clear advantages to be gained from being in the position of dominant operators. There also particular responsibilities and obligations that are related to market management, stability and influence. It is possible for a major component supplier to favour one assembly company, or to be induced to favour it, at the expense of others in the sector. It is possible to regulate price levels, delivery dates, production runs and the volume of the item in question that it available at any one time. However, these capabilities are not eternal. If the business relationship that is part of the strategic focus is lost, the capabilities may only last until the customer organisation either redesigns its product or finds another source of supply.

BOX 9.2 Market Domination

In some sectors there is no true market domination. In the UK, two major players in the grocery sector are Tesco and Sainsbury's, with 15 per cent of the market each. As such they have great influence on the market but do not dominate it to the extent that de Beer dominate the global diamond sector, or even to the extent that British Airways dominates the British air travel sector. If the dominant organisation fails to keep its market satisfied, the customers will inevitably look elsewhere. By the same token, organisations casting around for opportunities would see such sectors as ripe for entry and exploitation. If the dominant and other players were unable to respond to this they may lose part of their existing share to new, powerful and focused entrants.

Market domination may also lead to additional benefits such as the ability to command resources, technology and expertise.

Brands and branding

The purpose of brand creation is the establishment of identity and uniqueness for a product or service. The following types of brands may be distinguished.

Company Where the company itself is a brand (for example, Marks & Spencer, Sony, Ford, British Airways).

House Where the product range of the company is branded. For example, the Ford house brands are Mondeo, Escort and Fiesta; the Sony house brand is the Walkman; British Airways house brands include Poundstretcher, Club Class and Concorde.

Individual brands This is where the owning company's name often does not appear in the branding process. Offerings are allowed to stand on their own: for example, Persil (owned by Lever); Daz, Radion (Reckitt & Coleman) detergents; Singapore Airlines is owned by the Swire Group; Butterley Brick is owned by the Hanson Group; Jaguar is owned by the Ford Company. The owning organisation has no prominence in relation to these brands.

Generic brands These exist as a form of umbrella for a range of products. To all UK consumers Bird's Eye, Ross and Findus are frozen food brands. The range of each is constantly being varied. It is easy for the companies in question to do this as they have the general strength of the brand on which to base the new product. There is no need therefore to engage in a separate marketing activity as each new offering is made. Further marketing activities conducted on behalf of one of the offerings under the generic brand also promote and reinforce its strength.

Distribution outlets This is the branding of retail establishments such as Currys, the John Lewis Partnership, Tesco and Sainsbury's; wholesaling such as Booker and Arcoll; transport such as Norbert Dentressangle, National Freight Corporation and TNT; mail order such as Kays and Great Universal; and catalogue stores such as Argos.

Universal brands These include Coca Cola and McDonald's which have a global general identity and perception.

Specialist brands These have no meaning or identity outside their own sector but they are of critical value within it. The properties of distinctive branding therefore apply to the manufacture of components and parts for assembly, and to industrial business just as they do to consumer orientation and distribution. For example, the manufacturers of aero engines have to use components of a particular distinctive brand strength.

BOX 9.3 Strong Brands and Brand Names: Examples

The following words (originally commercial brands and marques) have found their way into the language of various parts of the English-speaking world.

More or less universal: Coca Cola and Coke; Pepsi; McDonald's; Concorde; Biro; Martini; Cinzano; Aspirin; Dubonnet; Gillette; Kleenex; Kraft; Lego; Mars; Marlboro; Camel; Pyrex; Rolex; Barbie; Tarmac; Teflon; Valium.

The following have verbs derived from them: Hoover; Xerox; Tippex.

The following were once household words: Bourneville; Brownie; Elastoplast; Cortina; Bryant & May; Fablon; Green Shield; Kalamazoo; Omo; Smash; Thermos.

Distinctively British: Cadbury; Bourneville; Ever Ready; Andrex; Kit-Kat; Wispa; Heinz; Formica; Horlicks; Marmite; Liberty; Selfridge; St Michael; Schweppes; Sindy; Oxo; Bisto.

■ The purpose of branding

The purpose and function of branding is as follows.

□ *The generation and maintenance of a strong identity*

Commercial advantages are gained by supplying large generic markets. Organisations that make dolls' clothes, for example, are able to charge much more for them if they are to be sold on as part of the Sindy or Barbie range. Manufacturers of copper piping are able to charge much more for this if they are able to generate a positive identity and confidence in the construction sector.

□ *Commercial protection and development*

Organisations normally register the name of the brand and also any distinctive slogan, description or slang that has been generated as part of the branding process. Thus, Gillette and 'the best a man can get' are both trademarks. Coca Cola, Coke, Diet Coke, Cherry Coke and Fanta are all registered as trademarks by the Coca Cola Organisation. This also extends to intellectual and creative property: Terry Pratchett, the UK best-selling author, has registered the name Disc World and the characters in his novels so that a range of other products, including figurines, pictures, T-shirts, videos and tapes may be developed.

☐ *Added value*

The brand mark is a part of the differentiation process. It offers distinctive benefits, both operational and behavioural, to customers and consumers. These are the realities of value and quality; and the intangibles of expectation, esteem and identity. For example, this is the element that enables Coca Cola to charge a premium price over supermarkets and other non-distinctive Cola brands. The distinctive Nike, Hi-Tec and Reebok logos all add value (and therefore price premiums) to their trainers and leisure wear.

☐ *Confidence*

The purchase of an item brings with it levels of expectation, satisfaction and performance; and an actual or perceived statement of price quality and value. The repeat purchase of familiar brands should thus be safe consumer activities.

☐ *Loyalty*

The brand is the cornerstone of customer loyalty. Thus the person who always books her holiday through Thomas Cook, always flies Virgin Atlantic or British Airways, or always buys her groceries from Tesco or Marks & Spencer does so because her loyalty has been engaged.

☐ *Product summary*

The brand name effectively acts as a summary of everything that is known, understood and perceived about the given item and its value and benefits. Thus when Coca Cola is mentioned the consumer perceives not only a drink but also the sunny happy images that are associated with it, its even and universal quality, and its lifestyle associations.

The person using Wolf tools not only perceives their usage and dexterity with them, but also the finished job or products, the feeling of satisfaction (and profit) that will go with it, and the positive response of the person for whom the job is being carried out or the product being made.

BOX 9.4 Developing and Building a Brand

The critical factors in building the brand name and identity are as follows.

Quality

This is addressed from the point of view of the customer. It is quite possible to manufacture or produce goods on the part of the supplier to levels of quality that are neither sustainable commercially nor required by the great majority of consumers.

On the other hand, people who drive high-performance cars require after-sales service and a guarantee of spare parts as well as the esteem and kudos that goes with the car itself (and, if this is not forthcoming, the customers will look to a competitor to satisfy this).

Expectations

Whatever is purchased must meet the expectations generated by the properties, promotion and associations of the brand. This is reflected in all processes by which the brand is developed and maintained.

Consistency, time and resources are required to develop standards and levels of expectation. Consistency is also required in some form in the advertising and marketing campaigns generated to support brands.

BOX 9.5 Brand Development

Storylining

This is where the brand is developed through media, public relations and advertising campaigns using the vehicle of a story in which the lives of the characters involved are punctuated by the use of brand in question. This was highly successful in the UK with Nescafé Gold Blend, the instant coffee brand. It has also been used to a lesser extent in the brand development of Cointreau, Oxo gravy and American Express credit cards.

Omission

This is where the brand itself is not actually mentioned. A leading UK exponent of this is the Benson & Hedges Silk Cut brand of cigarettes. Pictures used simply featured pieces of purple silk with cuts in them, and with the mandatory Government health warning at the bottom of the page or poster. In these circumstances, and when successful and effective, the brand becomes sufficiently powerful to generate instant and universal recognition.

The same also applies to distinctive company logos. UK examples of these are the P&O flag; the National Westminster three-piece triangle; the black horse of Lloyds Bank; the Qantas kangaroo; the Coca Cola signature; the McDonald's M. The presence of the logo without additional reference is sufficient identity for the brand.

Where the process of branding is successful the returns are considerable. Brands with a market share of 40 per cent generate three times the return on investment of those with a share of only 10 per cent. The top UK grocery brands generate six times the return on sales of the number two brand. Premium brands earn 20 per cent more than discount brands. Differentiated brands command premium prices rather than having to rely on cost advantage. The best feasible strategy to achieve high brand profitability, reputation and growth is therefore to differentiate (Doyle, 1989; Randall, 1992).

BOX 9.6 Brand Acquisition and Take-over

This occurs where an organisation takes the view that the process of designing and building its own brand from scratch is going to take a long time and be extremely expensive. The process also carries no guarantee of success. It therefore decides to buy a strong brand in the sector required. This approach has been pursued most effectively by Grand Metropolitan, for example, in its acquisition and revamping of the Burger King fast food chain, giving it a global brand name to be used in competition with McDonald's, rather than as a niche in the sector. In its take-over of the US Pillsbury Corporation, Grand Met has also acquired the high-prestige, high-fashion, high-image and above all highly profitable Häagen-Dazs brand. Ford has failed in the past to generate a successful product in the luxury, executive and glamour niches of the car markets and so has acquired Jaguar.

□ *Imitation*

This is where the characteristics of other brands which are seen to be successful are taken on. Thus all airlines have a club or business class (first created in the 1970s by TWA), and this is now being extended to rail and sea travel and car hire. Business facilities, computer terminals, typing pools, fax and quiet work areas were first offered by Hilton hotels and have now been introduced by all the other global chains. Cadburys have brought out their own version of the Irish cream drink of whisky, brown sugar and dairy cream first designed and introduced under the Bailey's name in the 1970s.

□ *Co-offering*

This is where organisations use other brands for their own advantage. Car companies, for example, use particular brands of tyre, spark plugs, seating or in-car entertainment. Clothes manufacturers use proprietary prints, distinctive fastenings and ornaments, and may coordinate these with the offerings of other producers or of the retail outlets in which they are being sold.

Retail and mail order outlets may also expect to gain from the offering of proprietary brands as part of the total portfolio. They may enter into promotion and brand development partnerships with the manufacturers of other offerings. They may also be able to introduce a range of other offerings on the back of one proprietary.

☐ *Enhancement*

This is where one company uses another's brands to add value to its own offerings. A travel agent, for example, may offer the ability to stay in a Hilton Hotel as part of a package, or they may offer Thomas Cook travellers' cheques or Avis care hire at special rates, also as part of the total package.

BOX 9.7 The Brand Name

Currys Dixon, the UK electrical consumer goods retailer, was forced to change the name of its in-store brand from Triumph to Matsui in order to compete with the Japanese goods also sold. This enabled the store to recapture market share and confidence for its own product without damaging sales of the Japanese goods. The in-store products remained the same. The increase in sales was attributed directly to the change of name.

Organisations protect the strength of top brands. Sony, for example, is highly successful in the electrical consumer goods market at the top of the price/quality range. To expand into other sectors it chose to open up a new distinctive brand – Aiwa – for this purpose rather than risk diluting the Sony brand strength.

Instead of bringing out a cheap, good-value or price-advantageous range of cars under its own name, Volkswagen has purchased the Skoda and Seat companies. This has enabled them to extend their range of operations and activities, and also expand the markets and potential of Seat and Skoda, while at the same time preserving the distinctive qualities of the Volkswagen brand.

BOX 9.8 Threat to Brands

These are constant and present in the activities even of the most powerful and well established of brands.

Loss of confidence

The main threat is that of loss of confidence. This can occur at any time. A famous and notorious example of this in recent UK commercial history is that of Ratners, the high-street jewellery and ornament retail chain. In a speech in November 1991 the Company Chairman, Gerald Ratner, delivered a speech in which he effectively stated that the reason that the shops were able to offer their products at such great price advantage in relation to the rest of the sector was that they were rubbish. Faced with the company's own admission of this, the customers simply went elsewhere.

Loss of appeal

This occurs where the benefits and images cease to appeal or become obsolete. This is caused by technological advance and/or changes in expectations. For example, the manual typewriter gave way first to the electronic typewriter; then to the word processor; and then in turn to the home or personal computer which could be used just as easily for producing documents as for data processing and storage. In each case the brand owner – of the typewriter, the word processor, the home computer – has had to change design, image and technology in order to preserve brand strength and therefore market share.

Loss of advantage

In this context this occurs where the costs and price differential and premium attributed to the brand in question become simply too overwhelming to sustain whatever the position and high-quality image may be. Often related to the introduction of price advantage substitutes, this then causes a general change of brand perception by the public.

Adverse performance

This affects brands in various ways. Performance may not live up to expectations. There may be faulty public relations. A strong personality, key executive or employee identified with the brand may become embroiled in scandal. The brand comes to be seen as unwholesome and its users turn elsewhere.

■ Brand leadership

This is where the organisation sets out to have its product or one of the range of its products established as a brand leader in the sector. This is measured from a variety of standpoints. It may be to get the product established in the language of the world. On a truly global basis, examples of this are Coca Cola, Pepsi and McDonald's. Or, again, it may be designed to be the most profitable of a range of generic offerings, or that with the strongest image. A brand leader also helps to sell the rest of the product range.

Brand leadership is often confined to leadership of its own sector, the holding of a high reputation and status. It is also often confined by national boundaries. Nescafe Gold Blend is the leading brand of instant coffee in the UK, for example, but it is virtually unknown elsewhere. Indeed, it has different names in other countries, and therefore the branding is overtly national.

In France the competition for brand leadership in the motor car sector is confined to Peugeot, Citroën and Renault; the multi-national and foreign marques have all had to take their places behind these.

BOX 9.9 Brand Leadership: Soap Operas

Soap operas were originally an American invention. They were created as regular low- to medium-quality real-life situation television series, and designed to fill up the time between advertisements for soap powders, household detergents and other domestic offerings. In the English-speaking and viewing world (UK, North America, Australia, New Zealand and South Africa) they form a substantial slice of the television offerings. Many of the programmes are long established. In the UK especially they are akin to national institutions.

From time to time in each of these countries storylines from the current range of soap operas make the national news. In 1982 the American series *Dallas* drew the highest fiction drama audience ever achieved in the USA (and subsequently also in the UK) with its episode entitled 'Who shot J.R.?' The scenario revolved around an attempt to murder the central character, J.R. Ewing. The suspense was built up by carefully constructed plot lines in the preceding episodes. There was also an extensive media and public relations campaign. In the UK bookmakers took bets on which character shot him. All of the other characters in the series were filmed carrying out the deed to ensure that none of them could give the game away to the media.

In the UK the shooting scene was shown on national news programmes. It became a major current event. In the USA, the episode that showed the shooting and the one that followed it drew the largest advertising revenue hitherto achieved by any programme.

All of this was undoubtedly an achievement of brand leadership for the sector. It also helped ensure the reputation of the production company Lorimar Inc. The stars of the show became international showbusiness figures, able to command large fees and huge media and public relations coverage.

In all cases, the key to high brand strength and leadership is the ability to reflect customer and consumer requirements rather than (or at least as well as) technological excellence. The product itself is only *commercially* excellent if consumers are confident of the benefits that are to accrue from owning and using it.

Consolidation

Consolidation occurs when an organisation seeks to preserve its position in its markets, niches or sectors, its range of activities and operations, and its customer bases. Consolidation also implies the reinforcement of an existing position. This may be sought through increased marketing and public relations activities, improvements in efficiency, productivity and the cost basis of the organisation, and improvements in quality or delivery targets. It also depends upon the nature of the markets in which operations are being conducted. The major players in the oil sector undertake general marketing campaigns, television advertising, offers and price moves in response to moves by others in the sector, and in this way consolidation may be seen as a form of defence.

Johnson and Scholes also include the concept of consolidation in declining markets. As the fact of the decline becomes apparent, organisations will seek to gain every last possible benefit through 'strategies of harvesting'. These include the sale of the brand themselves and also of licences, franchises, technology, distribution rights and the leasing of premises and facilities, as well as the maximisation of product sales. The purpose is to be left with as few unrealised assets as possible, having gained the maximum possible harvest from the sector before it finally ceased being a profitable area of activity.

Withdrawal, retrenchment and contraction

Withdrawal, retrenchment and contraction strategies take place as a result of decisions to move out of particular activities and/or to concentrate the resources of the organisation and its expertise on a reduced portfolio of offerings.

There is not necessarily a negative connotation to this. Withdrawal from particular spheres may take place as the result of reviews and activities, which arrive at the conclusion that loss-making or resource-consumptive offerings are being carried by the organisation's profitable and positive activities. It may also be a response to economic conditions: for example, where charges and interest rates are sufficiently high to make it worth sub-contracting transport fleets and distribution outlets rather than owning them. This happened in the UK in the late 1980s and early 1990s when both insurance companies and building societies divested themselves of estate agency chains that they had originally acquired when they were seeking additional outlets for their financial offerings, and when general investment in property was considered worthwhile.

Organisations wishing to divest themselves of loss-making activities must, however, first consider the effect on their remaining range and on their continuing image, prestige and confidence. Concentration of resources on a more limited range of activities may lead in time to opportunities for expansion and intervention elsewhere. Within this context withdrawal strategies take one or more of the following forms.

1. Concentration on core business at the expense of niche operations. Much depends on the criteria used to define 'core'. These may relate to volume, profit margins, income or resource consumption. They may also relate to reputation, confidence, image and identity.
2. The sale of assets, liabilities, subsidiaries, patents and brands. These activities raise an instant cash windfall in return for the loss of the opportunities that each is to create in the future. Balances clearly have to be struck between the need to divest on the one hand, and the need to gain a realistic, even credible price, for the asset in question on the other.
3. The end of the useful life of a hitherto profitable product. This normally arises for one or more of the following reasons. It may be that the result of these have been superseded by a superior, more modern or more fashionable alternative, as, for example, in the cosmetics and car sectors. It may be the result of the loss of regard (for example, fur coats and ivory ornaments). It may be the result of changed expectations: for example, it may hitherto have been the norm for a sector to have a six-week delivery time for its offerings, but a new entrant can now deliver in six days. Rather than reinvest or re-engineer in order to be able to compete with this, the player in question withdraws.

The most common circumstance for this is where the organisation is faced with massive investment, transformation, modernisation or rehabilitation bills on which it cannot see an adequate rate of return. It also occurs with trading relations and activities taking place in volatile areas and sectors. Organisations that operate in these areas know that in extreme circumstances they may lose their entire capital investment if it is nationalised or destroyed by the government of the country in question, or if there is a revolution or civil war. The other area where escape is an option is where there is a sudden loss of regard, confidence or demand for the offerings in question (as happened with transatlantic air tickets during the Gulf War of 1990, again as the result of a political crisis).

In the pursuit of withdrawal strategies, full consideration will be given to the exit barriers concerned. Again, having taken the decision to divest or withdraw, the process must be conducted in an orderly and rational manner (whatever the spark that set off the withdrawal, whether rational or irrational).

■ Diversification

Diversification strategies occur where the organisation seeks to extend its current range of offerings or spheres of activity. This may be through means of integration (fully discussed below), or it may be through new product development or new market development. It may arise as a result of the assessments of the current range of products and markets which are deemed to have arrived at maturity and which therefore require development and new introduction.

Diversification may be classified as either related or unrelated.

■ Related diversification

This constitutes the development of the range of offerings and activities within the current ambit or experience of the organisation in question and according to its current expertise. It may be a direct relationship as, for example, where an industrial building company seeks to diversify in the house building sector. It may be a generic relationship as, for example, where an electrical goods company adapts its technology in order to produce electronic calculators and digital wrist watches. It may be related to the market sectors covered: for example, a confectionery company moving into the dog and cat biscuits sector may gain advantage because the product outlet is the same. It may be related to the capacities of the technology and technical expertise that the organisation has: for example, radar was originally invented for military purposes, but now has a variety of commercial uses. It may constitute the development of a complimentary range of products as, for example, moves by dairy companies into the sale of bread (to complement butter), cakes and scones (to complement the cream), and biscuits (to complement the cheese and cream). It may be an extension of the use of the production technology owned by the organisation (for example, the output of components for one sector may easily translate by modification into components that are suitable for others).

■ Unrelated diversification

This is where the organisation treads its own new ground. The best recent UK example of this is the Virgin Group transition from records and music retailing into the airlines business. It represented a complete change of direction on the part of the organisation; a move from the known to the unknown. It recognised the fact that effective performers in the sector made profits and that there was scope for a small, high-quality operation in a field dominated by global and national flag carriers and United States multi-national operators.

It had no previous experience in the field at all.

BOX 9.10 Unrelated Diversification

When the Abbey National changed its status from building society to public limited company, it became a small operator in a global pool – that of banking and finance – as distinct from the largest player in a domestic, quirky and traditional pool (the

UK personal lending sector). This had developed from the cooperative mutual assistance and friendly society movements of the eighteenth and nineteenth centuries. While its customers and orientation remained by and large the same, the rules of the field on which it was now playing were very different.

The range of companies owned by the Hanson organisation and other diversification-oriented holding companies is also held up as an example of unrelated diversification. However, this has to be seen in the context in which such organisations acquire the companies that they then improve, transform and sell on. All the acquisitions of the Hanson Group are made on the basis of the following quotation from James (Lord) Hanson, the company Chairman: 'The principal objective has remained to expand profitably, through careful expansion through acquisitions.' This is supported by the organisation's concentration on famous, established household names, organisations of maturity in relatively stable markets but which nevertheless lend themselves to restructuring, re-engineering and rejuvenation. In this case, therefore, while the organisations themselves and the sectors that they are in may be unrelated, the basis on which they are acquired nevertheless remain the same.

■ Synergy

Any diversification should have this as its driving force: a combination of capacities in both niches and organisation together with the need for change and progress in the existing activities of the organisation. The effect is compounded where there are slack capacities, underutilised production means and technology or surplus cash in the organisation in question.

■ Integration

In order to understand the strategic concept of integration we must look again at Porter's five-force model of competition. The sources of integration are those that lie within the model (see Figure 9.1).

Backwards integration is where organisations buy up or into their suppliers, usually to control the raw materials and components. It may also serve the purpose of limiting the volume or quality of a component or material to competitors. This is especially true where the particular material or component is of critical importance or value.

It also occurs when the organisation purchases the makers of its own production or information technology and the means of transport of the raw materials and supplies. In some cases also organisations buy up scientific research, market research and information and other consulting firms in their sectors to ensure an early supply of new products, ideas and proposals.

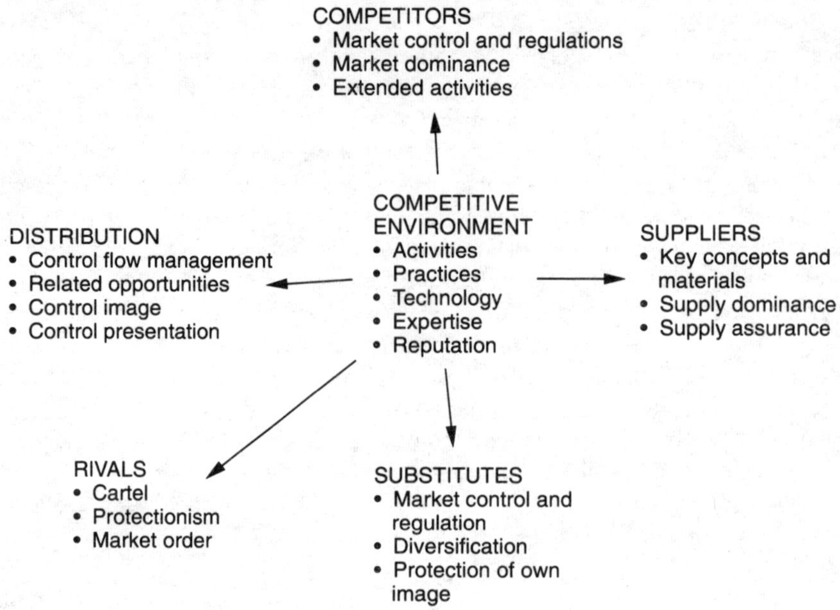

Figure 9.1 Porter's five forces model of competition applied to related diversification and expansion

Finally, organisations may establish their own financial services groups for the purpose of underwriting customer credit, extended payment schemes, loans and charge cards.

Forwards integration is where the organisation in question buys up its customers. This can be extended onwards: to their customers, the means of distribution, transport fleets, retail outlets, the retail chains that service these, and any agencies that provide after-sales or repair activities.

This may also be apparent where component companies require the means of setting up assembly plants; and where assembly plants set up the means of finishing and packaging.

Northern integration occurs where organisations buy up those seeking to enter the market sector in question in order to prevent this from occurring or as an effective move to use the additional capacity that would become available, as part of a drive towards some form of market domination (for example, in terms of size, output, volume, technological capacity or other economies of scale).

Southern integration is where organisations buy up the means of production of critical substitute products. This, again, will be carried out for the purpose of sectoral domination or increased influence, or to preserve and maintain the position of the original offering at the expense of the substitute. It also gives the organisation in question the opportunity to hedge its bets; it has the ability to offer both the original product and the substitute at its disposal and will do this according to the whims and demands of the market.

Integration with sectoral rivals occurs in a variety of forms. It may take the form of a straight merger between two or more organisations in the sector in order to create a dominant or more influential organisation; or for reasons of synergy in regard to the technology, customer base, location, distribution and outlets available at each of the organisations contemplating the merger. It may take the form of joint ventures. It may enable collaboration in specific sectoral projects to take place. It may enable sufficient resources to be put together for the organisations in question to be able to finance and control specific projects and developments. It may also take the form of take-overs.

BOX 9.11 Diversification

Some diversification comes about as the result of the use of spare production and output capacity. For example, a commercial baker may gain entry into new market sectors by producing bread, cakes and confectionery for supermarkets that are distinctively and differently packaged from standard or own brand range of offerings. Airlines try to ensure that their planes fly as full as possible, as often as possible and this is achieved partly through diversifying into the standby and package tour and holiday sectors. Regional soft drinks manufacturers make products under licence for the global players and brands: Coca Cola, Pepsi, Lilt, Schweppes, for example, are all made on a localised basis throughout the world rather than centralised and shipped around the world. The small producer must balance the benefits of this diversification with the consequences of producing a competitor's product for distribution in the same region.

■ Take-overs and acquisitions

These take place for one or more of the reasons indicated under the integration and diversification headings. The major general benefits of pursuing this line (rather than developing an organisation's capacities in the area) are the relative time and speed of operation advantages, economies of scale, and market advantages.

Take-overs and acquisitions may also be contemplated for the purpose of: gaining access to and control of customer bases and portfolios; specialised technology and expertise; high-profile brand names; high-value companies; prime sites; footholds in new markets, sectors, locations and countries; prestige, image, profile and promotional objectives; and to maintain control over capacity, output, price and value in the sector. Take-overs may be either friendly or hostile, the organisation being taken over can go into the new relationship willingly or unwillingly. The latter occurs when the acquiring organisation either buys enough of the other company's equity to control it, or else dominates the existing business relationship to such an extent that take-over is the only option for the dominated organisation. The former occurs where the organisation being taken over agrees to sell a controlling interest to the dominant company because of the advantages that are to be gained from this arrangement, whether perceived or real.

■ Mergers

Mergers tend to be for the same purposes as take-overs. The difference is the way in which the relationship is entered into. A merger is normally much more collaborative, voluntary and mutually entered into than an acquisition, which (however friendly) is normally dominated by the organisation doing the taking over.

Mergers take place for all the reasons indicated under integration and diversification. They also take place for the more general and offensive and defensive reasons of generating a size and strength sufficient to take advantage of opportunities in the sector in question, or to generate sufficient strength to resist and respond to offensive moves by other players in their sector.

■ Collaborative strategies and alliances

■ Joint ventures and consortia

Joint ventures and consortia are lesser versions of the merger approach. They occur where two or more organisations pool their resources for a project, piece of research, offensive strategy or initiative.

The overriding principle behind the joint venture conception is again synergy; that the different organisations concerned pool their resources, expertise and technology in order to carry out the work in hand to the highest standards of each of the joint venture organisations. Joint ventures and consortia are to be found above all in construction, building and civil engineering projects. They also occur in the computer information, medical research and drug sectors, car manufacture, military equipment manufacture, and leisure sectors. It is normal, but by no means universal, for the joint venture to be given its own distinctive identity. In some cases this leads to the formation of a company for the duration of the matter in hand. The advantages of size and resource concentration referred to elsewhere also apply. Some engineering and construction projects are too large and complex for the expertise to be held in one company. The same applies also to computer and information technology and expertise.

It also enables the elements of risk to be shared out between the member companies. Again, this problem is compounded if one organisation not only has to carry the weight and complexity of the project in hand but also the risks of failure.

It is also a way of organisations gaining 'toe in the water' experience of areas in which they may have only a general capacity or expertise.

■ Hook-ups, associations and networks

This is a variation on the same theme as joint ventures and mergers. It occurs in situations where for example one organisation agrees to give prominence to or provide an exclusive outlet for the products of another in its activities (see Box 9.12).

BOX 9.12 Hook-Ups and Associations

There are many examples of this from the leisure sector. At McDonald's the only soft drinks on sale are products of the Coca Cola company. Each of the other major fast food chains – Wimpy, Burger King and Kentucky Fried Chicken – has similar hook-ups. Supermarkets and department stores give prominence to major branded suppliers in their sectors (for example, Boots plc and Rayban sunglasses; Tesco supermarkets and Virgin Cola). Car manufacturers agree to use the in-car entertainment products of one electronics manufacturer.

The overriding concern is the mutual commercial benefit that accrues: by providing the exclusivity and taking a percentage, both organisations benefit. The distributor has a constant and confident source of products that will always be provided by the manufacturer because of the certainty that the outlet will continue to sell it.

Other more general *ad hoc* associations and collaborations may take place where some future mutual advantage or benefit is perceived, again driven by the synergy principle. Collaborations on research tend to occur in the expectation that they will yield mutual benefits more quickly than if each company works on its own.

Licensing and franchising are variations on this theme. In the former case, licences are sold by the holders of patents or blueprints for the right to manufacture, distribute or sell a product under licence in return for a fee or share of the profits. In the case of franchising, the division of activity is more clearly delineated. Again, in return for a fee payable to the main company, the franchisee operates the business in question as if it were his own, to the extent that he has the responsibility for any manufacture, distribution and sales. The franchiser undertakes national advertising and promotion maintaining the brand name. The franchisee carries operational responsibility for quality and service. He may normally sell only the franchiser's products or a range of products agreed with them. If he falls down on any of this, or on related matters of quality, expertise or service, the franchise may be withdrawn.

Sub-contracting

Sub-contracting is akin to the normal general relationship between an organisation and its customers. For a fee (the price) the sub-contractor agrees to provide products and services to the agreed volume, quality, value and deadlines. Any dispute over this is resolved in the same way as any dispute over any purchase at all.

The idea is attractive to organisations as they pursue the identification of core and peripheral activities (the latter are open to sub-contracting). Many organisations sub-contract cleaning, security and canteen services to those companies that specialise in these fields.

Other forms of this relationship exist in the use of recruitment, selection and staff agencies, and technology, business and management consulting services.

Every sector also has its expert sub-contractors. These ply their expertise across its entirety, working at some stage for all organisations within it. For example, in building construction and civil engineering, specialist companies are brought in for specialised jobs, such as draining and earthworks in construction, and the fitting-out of buildings, ships and aircraft in the civil and other engineering activities.

Managerial aspects of joint ventures and collaboration networks

These forms of activity are likely to be fully successful only if the characteristics and expertise of the organisations concerned are effectively blended and harmonised.

Identity

For any collaboration that is to take place over any considerable period of time it is usual to have a distinctive identity for the following reasons. It is necessary to give those working on it in turn a sense of identity and belonging in regard to the venture itself as distinct from that with their parent organisation. Continued reference back to the parent organisation is likely to emphasise differences among those who are actually supposed to be cooperating.

It creates a specific point of reference for all concerned. It becomes 'the project' or 'the venture' – indeed 'the job'. In the case of computer, civil engineering or construction projects, there is also the need to have this point of reference in regard to the client or project commissioner.

More generally, it is part of the process of energising the activities surrounding the project or initiative. It is also part of the process of resource-gathering and allocation that the matter has its own identity.

■ Liaison

Some form of steerage or directorate has to be established. This is to ensure that the basic mutuality of interest and harmony is preserved to establish a review process, and as part of the general aim of giving focus and identity. It is also a problem-solving forum. Again, in the case of commissioned projects, it is likely to include client representatives as well as the partners in the collaboration.

■ Support

The collaboration must be capable of being supported throughout its useful life by the partners. In these cases, it is normal for staff, resources, expertise and technology to be committed to the collaboration and, as a result, away from the partner company. Collaborators must be able to sustain this.

BOX 9.13 Project Strategies

Project work arises from a variety of sources. Overall, the main requirement is for some form of synergy: the combining of distinctive expertise, resources, people, technologies, and (often) organisation in the pursuit of something that is either commissioned, or of commercial value, once it has been completed. Project work normally has a distinctive life: distinctive, that is, from mass or flow production. In some cases it is a form of mega-unit production. Sources of projects are:

- public works and infrastructure: schools, hospitals, bridges, roads, railways, other public buildings and amenities;
- utility projects: energy sources, power stations, water works;
- other infrastructure: power, energy, gas, electricity and water distribution;
- communications: satellite and telecommunications, information technology, super highways;
- private works and infrastructure: airlines, shipping, commissioned and speculative building development;
- social need: hospitals and amenities;
- financial scale: where the matter in hand is too large for one organisation;
- expertise scale: where the matter in hand is too large, or diverse, or complex for the work force of one organisation;
- development paths: involvement in one project is seen to lead to other related opportunities;

- defence projects: because of the global demand for advanced military technology;
- drug research: because of the ever greater expectations placed on medical science;
- project pyramids: where involvement in one project requires involvement in sub-projects and activities that have to be completed before the main matter is undertaken. For example, the builders of the Channel Tunnel had first to develop earth-boring machines of the scale and strength necessary for the particular main project: the tunnel itself.

There are distinctive features of the resource/time/expertise commitment. Once involved, an organisation may not easily be able to pull out. There is also an open-ended commitment; projects invariably gather lives of their own. They are likely to turn up both problems and opportunities during their progress.

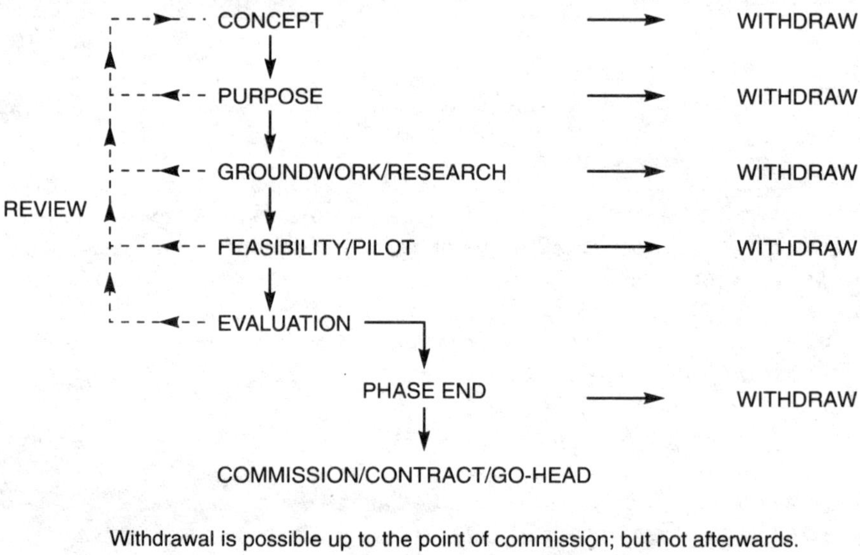

Figure 9.2 A basis for involvement in project work

Acceptability

Joint ventures and networks must be acceptable to everyone directly affected. The matter may arise for a variety of reasons. For example, one of the potential collaborators may be (or may have been) involved in unethical or unacceptable activities elsewhere; it may have a history of bad or controversial employee relations; one company's levels of pay and benefits may be substantially higher than those of the others.

It may also be necessary to take into account the views of existing customers and clients.

☐ *The project approach*

This is currently held in high regard by experts in management as a vehicle for pooling and maximising expertise and resources, and for developing expert managers. Many major projects are now beyond the scope of one organisation's resources. In order to manage a project or initiative successfully, and especially in a joint venture or collaborative situation, the manager must have a range and complexity of skills, qualities and attributes, and must be able to bring these to bear in a great variety of ways. Such managers must be capable of developing and improving this level and range of expertise. The testing ground or microcosm for this is in projects and ventures of this type. The managers concerned will either exhibit this expertise here and therefore indicate their potential for greater things, or else they will not, and may therefore be channelled elsewhere. (See Box 9.13 for a fuller illustration.)

☐ *Contracts and agreements*

It is normal for any form of collaboration or alliance to be subject to some formalised measure of agreement or understanding. For joint ventures and consortia project work, sub-contracting and franchising formal contracts always exist.

Each party involved therefore understands the nature, extent and duration of the commitment undertaken. Specifically, matters related to resource input, financial state, the benefits of success and liabilities of failure are addressed.

■ Other influences

■ The environment

All organisations and their activities interweave with their business environment, customers' environment and the communities within which they operate. They are also subject to general, legal, economic, social, ethical and political pressures and influences. Any strategy to be formulated must therefore have regard to these limitations. It is no use producing something that cannot be delivered for one of these fundamental reasons, for no strategy is any use if the environment in which it is envisaged taking place cannot or will not permit it or allow it.

Related to this is the more general question of the acceptability of the organisation and its products. Part of the strategy of any organisation must therefore consist of the means of addressing this. The basic level of acceptance and mutuality of interest between organisation and environment must first exist if there is to be any chance of success.

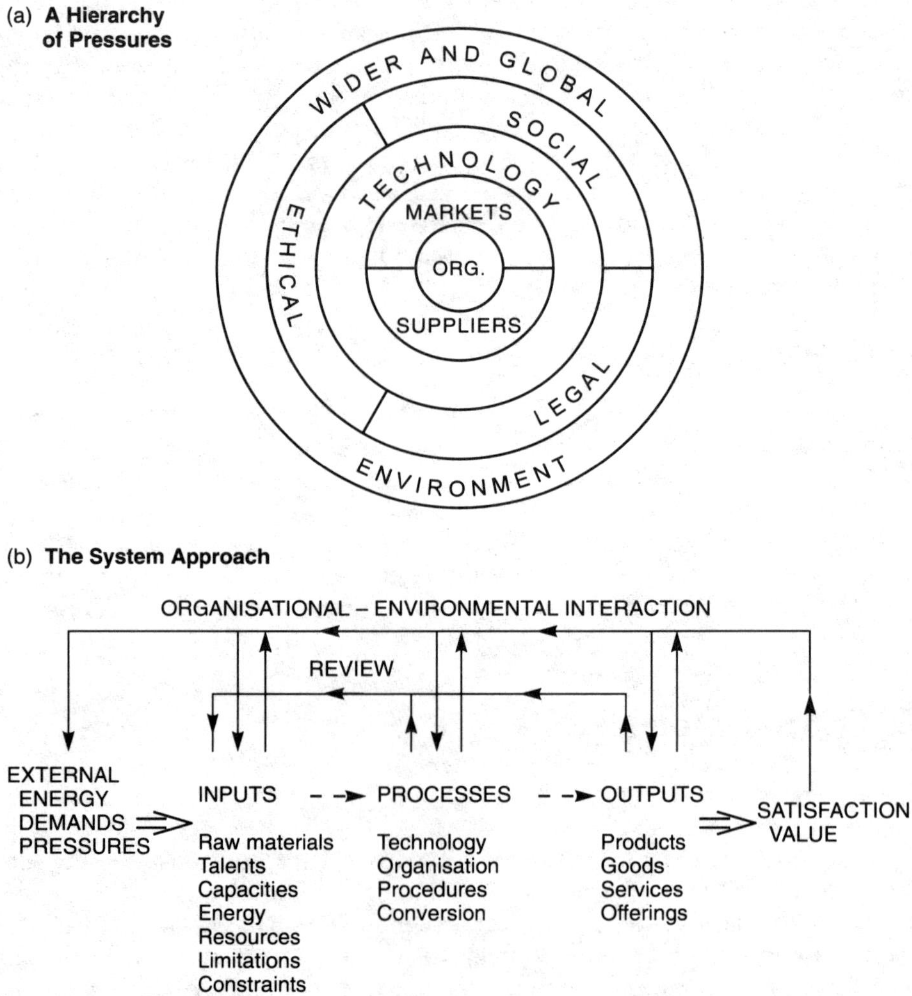

Figure 9.3 The organisation in its environment

Mention should also be made of the extent to which an organisation may influence its environment. In many cases this capacity is very limited. Organisations must therefore work within the constraints imposed. They must also be prepared for any new limitations or hazards that may arise under the legal, economic, social, ethical or political headings to which they would have to respond (again from a position of limited influence).

Once in existence, the capacities of organisations for changing their spheres of operation are limited by the capital and financial liabilities that they have incurred to get to their present position, their real or relative expertise in the current field, and the behavioural or expectational impressions that they have built up, together with their reputation in it.

The point therefore is that organisations tend to be limited to their own area and spheres of operations. They will thus tend to formulate strategies within this context. In sectors where this is heavily dominated by process technology – for example, oil, chemicals and telecommunications – business strategy is likely to be concerned with guaranteeing raw materials, attention to costs and charges, technological improvements, the optimisation of processes, and the search for potential new outlets. The extent of capital investment in such technology ensures that the organisation in question continues to operate in this field. This is quite apart from the extensive effort that would be required to change the wider perceptions of the organisation if it were to move into a new field entirely. It is also necessary to convince the new sector where such a change is made that the organisation has expertise in it, however good it was at business in the previous sphere.

Some organisations do clearly make such transitions, however. The move of the Virgin Group into the airline business is a case in point, although the charges incurred by the organisation in this move consisted of the creation of the airline itself, creating a distinctive image for it, gaining an operator's licence, and obtaining landing spaces at the desired airports. At the outset, the only asset in the organisation's favour was the proven track record of its Chairman, Richard Branson, in the music business, and the continuing high regard and public esteem in which he was held.

■ Commitment

Much is made of the necessity to have full commitment and involvement. It is essential for the success of the strategy that all those involved (which means every employee) understand it. It is unarguable that this is by no means always the case; and some organisations that do not make their strategy clear to all employees may indeed be successful, or at least survive. The counter to this is to imagine how much more successful these organisations would be if everyone involved did understand what they were doing and why, and both subscribed to and 'owned' the direction of the organisation.

BOX 9.14 Commitment and Constant Improvement

1. Output improvement – measured in terms of volume and/or quality and also deadlines. Invariably there is a competitive advantage to be achieved in each of these ways, or in a combination of them (for example, the same volume output but more quickly; the same volume output but with increases in quality and precision due to technological advances in production and technology).
2. Improvements in customer base and volume where this is possible.
3. Improvements in customer service, the perceptions and attitudes of the customers, and the deepening of their loyalty to the organisation and its products. This may also be measured by reductions in complaints.
4. Measures against the previous year/period. These show absolutes in movement. For full effectiveness the full context has also to be addressed and evaluated.
5. Improvements in returns against performance targets (in whatever terms these are set). Also implicit in this are improvements in the accuracy and effectiveness with which these targets are set.
6. Research and development improvements. These include the strike rate (the number of successful and profitable new products as a proportion of the total number of inventions and discoveries made).
7. Procedures. Improvements in this area are measured in the speed and effectiveness of their operation. This includes financial controls, information systems, product/output systems and human resource management and management style.
8. Market research. This leads to the more effective and efficient targeting, both of outputs and also of the marketing campaigns and activities that support them.
9. Manufacturing processes. Improvements in this area lead to more effective usage of more raw materials, better and/or quicker volume and quality of output, packaging and storage. Improvements in manufacturing processes may also be measured in terms of reductions in the number of rejects and reductions in wastage rates. They may also be measured in terms of effectiveness and absolute measures of time usage of the manufacturing processes themselves.
10. Constant improvement in the effectiveness of the output of staff and of their satisfaction in the work and in consideration also of matters of morale, motivation and commitment.
11. Delivery/supply times and flexibility. This is a feature of just-in-time approaches. It leads to better services from suppliers and more effective use of storage space.
12. Response times and deadlines, especially in the meeting of orders and customer responsiveness. The concept of 'time to market' has also to be considered here, covering the entire time span from drawing board to profitable offering.

13. Internal processes, relations and communications, including management style and approach. Improvements are easily measurable and quantifiable through the evaluation of levels of absenteeism, turnover, sickness absence, strikes and disputes, and accidents, as well as the use of attitude surveys.

The theme of constant improvement is important, therefore, for a variety of reasons. It represents the major contribution to be made by all functions and all of the staff within them. Addressed in this way, it also indicates the range of approaches to be taken and complexity of issues that may be addressed in this manner.

■ Conclusion

The purpose of engaging in any of these activities is the strengthening of the organisation as a going concern, and of the directions that it is pursuing. None of the activities outlined are ends in themselves. Whatever is done, must stand up to the tests of feasibility and acceptability.

■ Feasibility

This is a process, a focus for inquiry and judgement, to be undertaken at the point at which such developments are first considered. This is an assessment of the proposal in the terms indicated at the beginning of the chapter. Analysis of risks and potential rewards and returns will also be evaluated at this stage.

The matter will then be seen in the wider context: for example, if an acquisition is contemplated, whether this may lead to an auction with others in the sector for the take-over target, thus inevitably pushing up the initial outlay. This in turn will have an impact on the projections of rewards and returns and may make these less attractive.

■ Acceptability

This is the measure of the outcome of the assessment of feasibility. It then becomes a matter of judgement for those involved.

The acceptability to all stakeholders must be assessed. There are implications for the organisation's managers and staff in all cases. Shareholders and backers need to be convinced of the value of the returns on their investment in the light of the proposals.

Consumers and customers must be satisfied that they are to receive at least the same level and quality of value and service in the new situation. When the organisation expands, they need to be certain that they are not going to lose any feeling of personal relationship now that the establishment is larger. When it contracts they must be satisfied that this is a strategic move, and not one of panic or crisis; confidence must be maintained.

This is the context in which strategic forms are to be seen. They must fit with both current and future expectations and be capable of organisational assimilation, as well as carrying purely operational potentials. All organisations use them in some format at some time, so it is important that a full understanding of all the implications is achieved.

■ Work assignments and discussion questions

1. Outline the feasibility studies that should be conducted by the Skoda Car Company, were it to consider expanding its range to include a high-performance model and a Range Rover-type model.
2. To what extent has the expansion/diversification strategy of the Virgin Group in the soft drinks sector been successful? Outline the means and stages by which this should be evaluated.
3. Why did British Airways divest one of its holiday/tour operation companies in December 1994?
4. A small company that manufactures ladies' clothing sells all its production to one department store group. On both sides, what are the advantages and disadvantages of this arrangement?

CHAPTER 10

Implementation

Introduction

The purpose here is to indicate and explain the range of factors necessary to translate strategy and purpose into productive, effective and profitable activities. This involves a process that consists of:

- assessing whether what is envisaged is feasible or sensible;
- gathering and allocating resources for the purpose;
- creating and developing an organisation that is suitable to the purpose;
- creating and developing sub- and supporting strategies that reinforce and energise the chosen purpose;
- creating suitable coordination and control features, together with effective means of monitoring, review and evaluation of activities.

The foundation of this lies in the commitment of the organisation, its top managers and all its staff to the direction chosen. Priorities and patterns of activities must be determined.

Gaining commitment

In order for this to be effective there must be a universal understanding of the proposed direction and of the part to be played by each department, division and group. This is essential in order to gain a full commitment to purpose and to the activities to be undertaken in its pursuit. This is supported especially by the levels of resources allocated to each activity; a lack of, or inadequacy of, resources is destructive to both strategy and morale.

Priorities

Priorities are set in response to a range of demands and pressures. They may be:

- **internal and organisationally driven** – for example, the need to get activities off the ground because of pressures further down the operational pipeline;
- **time and resource driven** – for example, the need to conduct activities by a certain time in order to beat a price rise in a component;

- **market driven** – the need to get an item to customers before they decide to choose elsewhere, or in order to meet a seasonal deadline (for example, Christmas);
- **operationally driven** – the need to complete one activity because the next cannot be started until this is done;
- **competitive pressures** – the need to respond to the activities and initiatives of other operators in the field or else face losing market share;
- **technology maximisation** – the need to gain maximum usage from equipment during its productive life.

Priorities may also be driven by external forces, such as the pressures from backers to achieve returns by a given deadline, or to use resources by the end of the accounting period.

Prioritisation of activities is achieved through the use of approaches such as critical path planning and analysis, which are discussed below.

The priority system must also have enough space and resource for the handling of problems and crises when these arise.

Assumptions

Assumptions are made about all proposed activities. Problems arise where these take on the appearance of facts or come to be accepted as such. The range of possible outcomes of proposed activities must always be kept in mind. Specific issues may be tested as part of the feasibility or piloting process (these are discussed below).

Activities

Patterns of activities must be decided and determined. The actual mixture varies between organisations. The total coverage is as follows:

- steady state: the daily conduct of ordered activities and operations;
- innovative: the pursuit of research, development and ideas for the future;
- crisis: the ability and capacity to handle problems;
- policy and direction: the creation, development and maintenance of strategy;
- pioneering and invention: creative aspects of organisation and management, wild-carding, 'thinking the unthinkable', and championing.

This is the basis on which sub- and supporting strategies, directions and policies are developed. The overall purpose is to ensure continuing access to the required volumes and quality of staff, technology, supplies, markets and finance. This invariably means considering both a variety of sources and the adoption of creative and imaginative approaches to the problems and issues raised in each area.

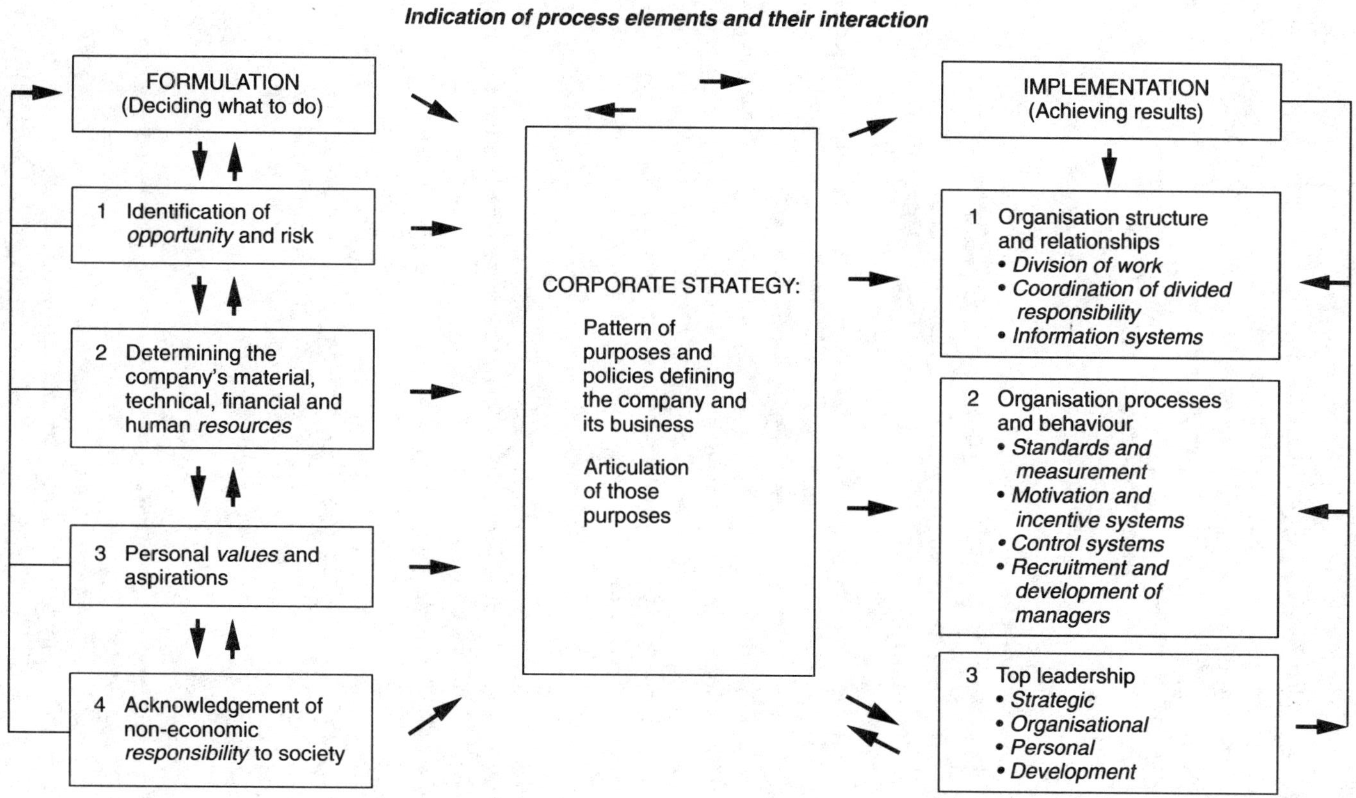

Figure 10.1 The implementation of strategy

From: C. R. Christensen (1987).

Making strategic decisions and choices

Decision-making is both a progression and a process. It is based on:

- initial definitions of the problems and issues to be considered;
- determination of the processes to be used in their resolution;
- the timescales for achievement and completion;
- the gathering of information in order to clarify the issues;
- identification of critical factors;
- definition and evaluation of alternative courses of action;
- the choosing of the preferred alternative;
- the preferred means of implementation, the consequences of this, and the opportunities to which the given choice leads.

Alongside all of this lies a constant process of progress, information, risk and uncertainty review. The purpose of this is to gain maximum possible knowledge and understanding of potential courses of action before a choice is made.

It is also essential to consider the wider pressures and issues. In the management of crises, it is necessary to take quick, precise and effective decisions. In the consideration of major changes or policy initiatives, it is essential to gain the understanding and support of all concerned.

Consultations, as extensive as possible, in the given set of circumstances, will be carried out in order to gain this understanding and support. Ideally, these address all those affected. It is critical to gain the support at least of all those who are to be concerned with the implementation of the direction chosen.

It is also necessary to consider the range of external pressures present. These are:

- market, environmental and global issues as they affect the proposed direction;
- the influence and effects of pressure groups, lobbies, legitimate interest groups, eco-socio-political parties and groups, and the state of public opinion;
- any strong social, ethical or religious factors, elements and beliefs.

These constitute the boundaries within which strategic decisions are taken (see Figure 10.2). It is essential that the support of all concerned is gained if the choice is to be effective, whether the decision is a consensus or the determination of one person.

Critical success and failure factors

'Planning is everything; the plan is nothing' (Dwight D. Eisenhower, 1994). 'Strategy analysis and choice are of little value to any organisation unless the strategies are capable of being implemented' (Johnson and Scholes, 1994). It is therefore essential that these factors are identified and clarified. They are: the size, structure, technology and expertise present; the size, structure, capacity and potential of the markets; the support of the organisation's backers; the reactions of the environment and communities; and the interactions of these with each other. They vary in specific terms dependent upon the type and range of activities proposed. These, in turn, are tested and assessed in one or more of the following ways.

1. Feasibility and pilot studies, often in the form of a mini-launch of a particular product. These occur both with pre-set objectives and criteria in mind, and also with a wider general monitoring brief.
2. Performance forecasting and projections, often based on computer modelling and simulations. These will be subject to intense scrutiny and inquiry and must always be supported by assessing the range of best, medium and worst outcomes.

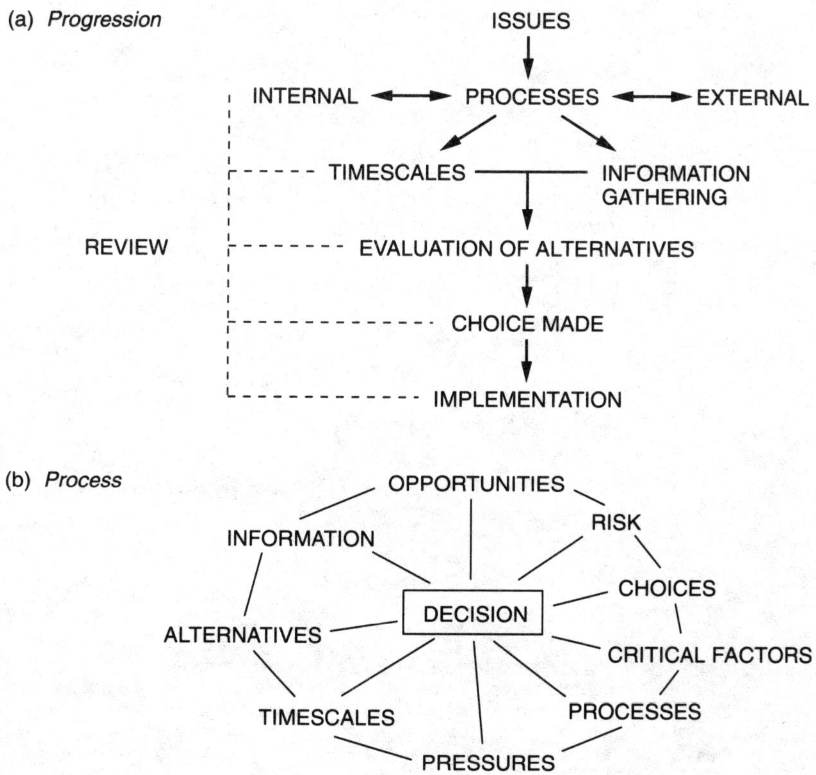

Figure 10.2 Decision-making

(c) *A model of strategic decision-taking*

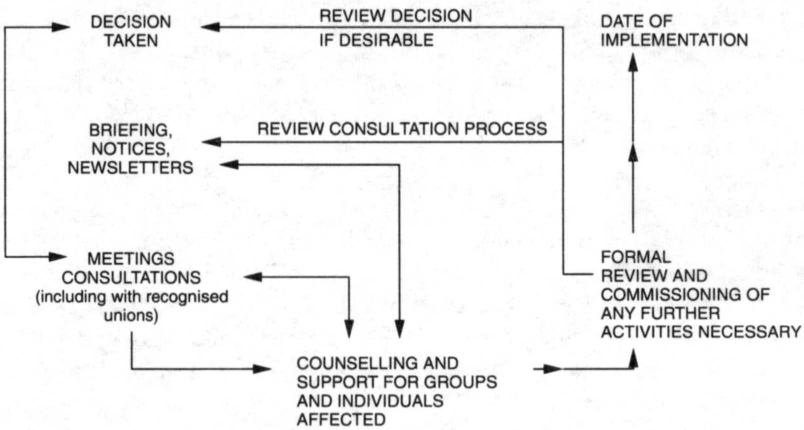

To be used for:
- strategic, directional, operational, technological and locational changes
- behavioural and human relations issues arising
- solving problems (see also below)

(d) *A problem solving model*

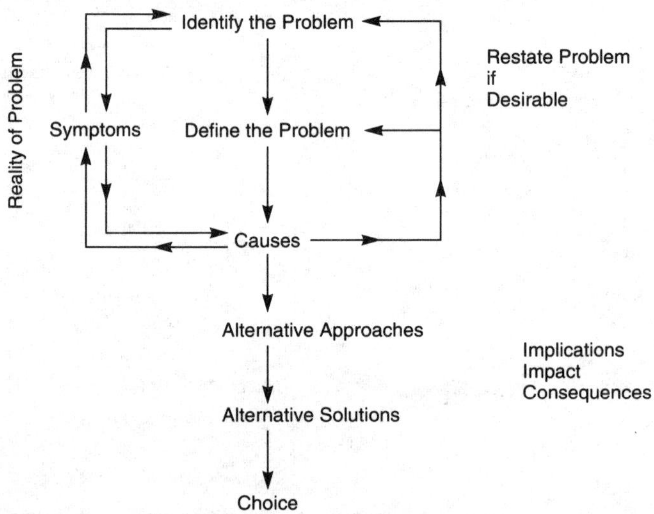

Purpose: to ensure that a rigorous and disciplined approach is recognised and understood as being necessary in all situations; and that it is adopted.

Points for consideration throughout the process must also include: the context and nature; when it is occurring; where it is occurring; why; its impact on the rest of the organisation, department or division; the extent to which it can be avoided; the extent to which it can be controlled; the consequences and opportunities of not tackling it (which is *always* a choice).

Figure 10.2 Decision-making (cont.)

Projections of total success should be considered: in extreme cases for example, this could lead to the inability of customers to gain access to the particular product and ultimately to organisational loss of reputation.

Projections of total failure – 'the nightmare scenario' – should also be assessed so that the organisation is under no illusion as to what the total level of loss might be.

3. Ultimate consideration. Every product has an element that, if it cannot be overcome, means that it is certain to fail (see Box 10.1). Whatever this is must be identified, isolated and tested.

BOX 10.1 Critical Factors

The Chicken Test is carried out on aero engines. These engines have to be strong enough to deal with flocks of birds that unfortunately get sucked into them. The Chicken Test consists of hurling frozen chickens at the prototype engine in a wind tunnel. If it cannot meet the Chicken Test it will not be able to deal with the real situation and has therefore to be redesigned.

The Dover–Calais cross-Channel ships, Fiesta and Fantasia, were introduced in 1989. At the time they were the largest ships on the route. At the end of their first year of operation, they each had to be refitted with more powerful engines and steering systems because of the specific problems of moving around the confined spaces of Dover and Calais harbours and in order to deal with the cross-winds and cross-currents at the entrance to Dover harbour.

The UK Community Charge (Poll Tax) of 1987–91 failed because it was impossible to collect. This was because it was a personal tax targeted at individuals who are mobile, rather than at addresses, outlets or places of work, as is the case with other more successful taxation methods.

4. Profitability and effectiveness assessment. This is an inquiry conducted around the anticipated performance of a product, usually in relation to the others in the portfolio. This is normally carried out as shown in Figure 10.3.
5. Acceptability – the extent to which the particular product meets the customer and consumer requirements of fulfilling expectations, giving satisfaction and value and meeting the customers' price, quality and value expectations. In some cases, ethical and social factors are a part of this. The wider question of confidence may also need to be addressed.

Beyond these, general organisational strength and capability must match the demands of the direction proposed, and be able to reconcile and accommodate these alongside the existing range of activities and obligations.

- **Return on Investment (RoI):** the rewards gained as the result of placing resources and energy into particular areas and activities.
- **Return on Capital Employed (RoCE):** similar to RoI, normally measured against the share capital volume of the organisation.

These are used:

- to measure current, recent and historic returns on activities;
- to assess potential returns based on a combination of projections, forecasts and extrapolation;
- to assess opportunity costs.

They may be used as absolutes. It is useful to include a time frame, either (a) a 'deadline' by which results are to be achieved or (b) a graduated approach.

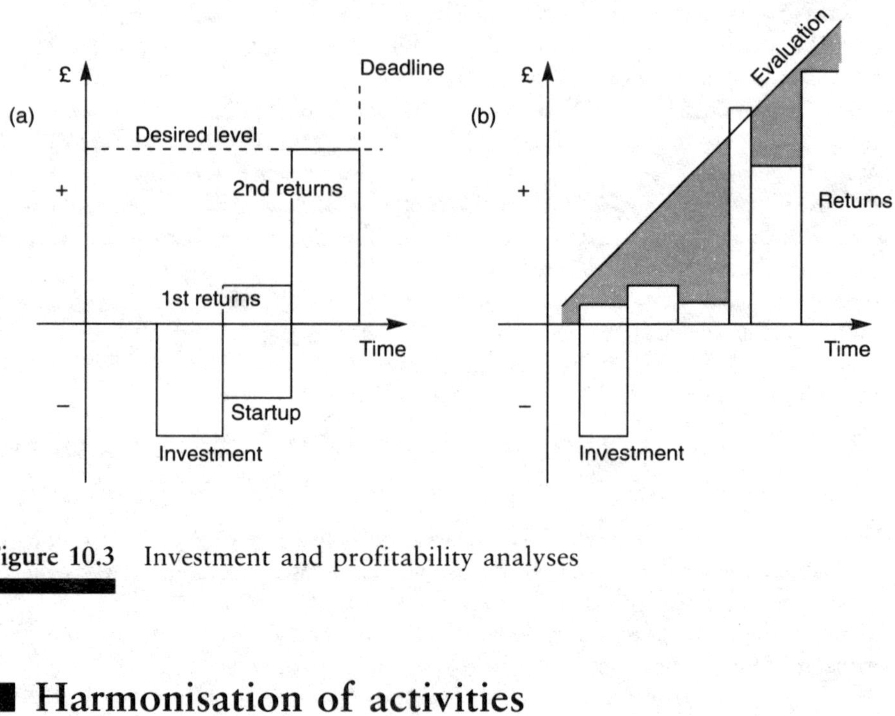

Figure 10.3 Investment and profitability analyses

Harmonisation of activities

This is the establishment of means and fora to ensure that interdepartmental activities are conducted in the pursuit of direction.

Regular meetings are required between managers and within departments, divisions and groups to ensure that this happens. Review processes are organised around this. Effective information systems and channels of communication are essential.

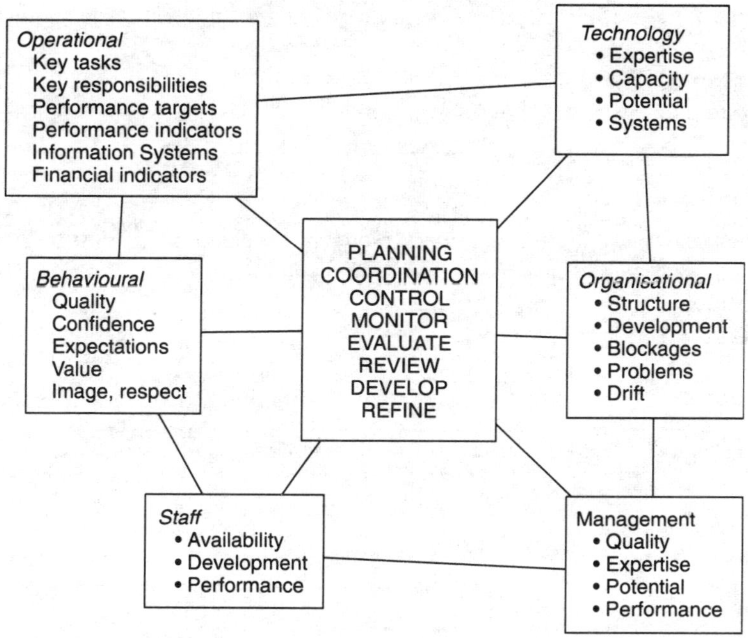

Indicates the ranges, mixture and interaction of activities, and key strategic managerial functions at the centre.

Figure 10.4 Implementation activities

The ideal outcome is a situation of mutual understanding and respect, together with the identification of stresses and strains that can then be put right before they become dramas and crises. Problems are raised and dealt with at an early stage and then again before they become critical. The focus is on organisation direction.

Where this is lost, activities become departmentally and divisionally oriented. Functions set their own agenda. This becomes a breeding ground for inter-departmental conflict and strife. Pecking orders are established and time and resources are spent on lobbying those with influence and control. Those involved concentrate on establishing their own position, normally to the detriment of total organisational performance. Information systems and their outputs are contaminated in order to meet the requirements of the *realpolitik* rather than the needs of the business.

It is essential to recognise that both function and individuals have their own pressures, agenda and objectives. These must be assimilated into the organisation's direction and ways of working so that everyone and everything is satisfied. This can only be achieved if there is clarity and commitment to purpose and if the means and methods of harmonisation are suitable.

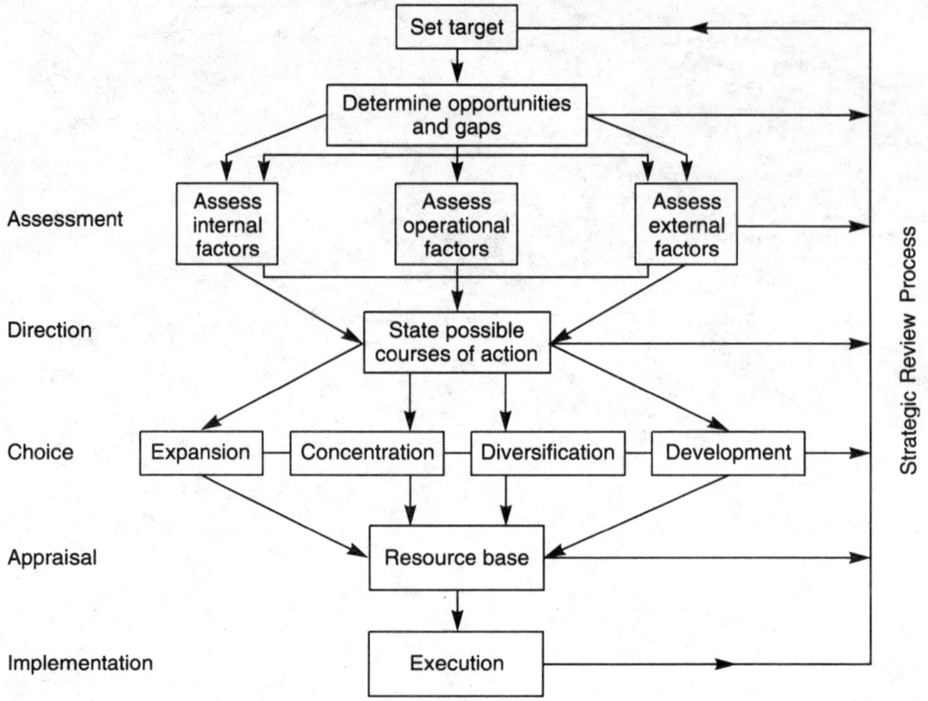

Indicates the stages, factors and process to be considered at the time of strategy determination.

Figure 10.5 The process of choice

BOX 10.2 Functional Pressures

Personnel:	Filling vacancies; settling disciplinary hearings and grievances; legal constraints; equal opportunities; meeting the deadlines of other functions; redundancies.
Marketing:	Sales and profits; repeat business; new business; plans and campaigns; research; customer complaints; public relations.
Production:	Staff and technology maximisation; maintenance; scheduling; supplies and raw materials.
Accounting and information:	Quality, value and volume; usability and utility; confidence.

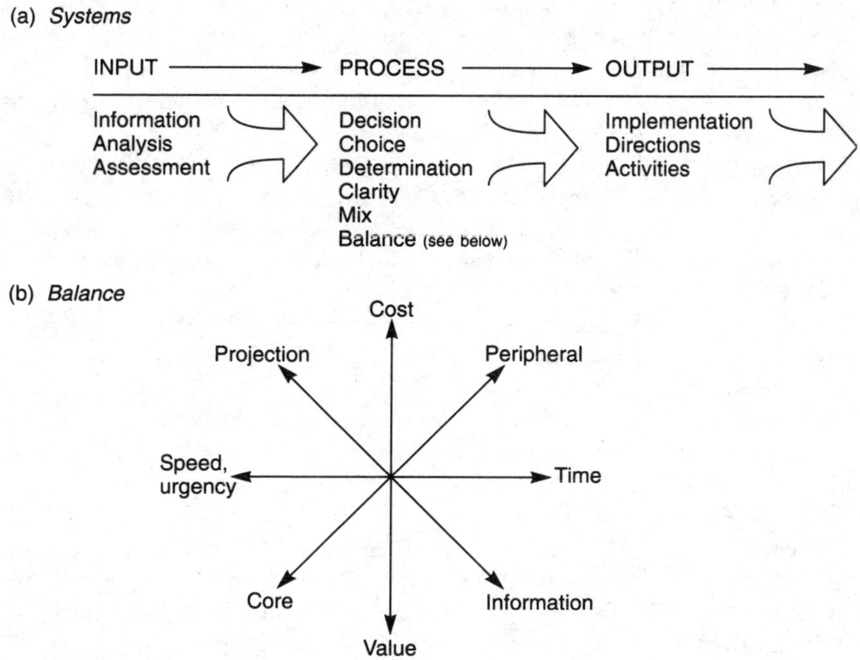

Indicates both (a) key conceptual activities and (b) key elements and considerations.

Figure 10.6 The planning and implementation process

■ Resource allocation

This is carried out ideally on the basis of need. It should be the result of assessing:

- the volume and intensity of work carried out and the implications arising;
- coverage of fixed costs;
- the ability to cover variable costs, as and when these arise;
- the needs of particular activities and situations;
- the handling of crises and problems.

In practice, this is not always the case. The most common faults are as follows.

1. **Fixed budgets:** these lead to activity stoppages when the budget is used up; or in contrast, a spending spree at the end of the accounting period or financial year to ensure that the money is spent if it cannot be carried forward.
2. **Resource bargaining:** this occurs where managers bid for resources in the knowledge that they will not receive everything required. They therefore overbid in order to achieve some form of satisfaction.
3. **Pecking orders:** this is where, for example, Departments X and Y receive all that they require and then whatever is left over is divided up between the others. This is commonly found in resource concentrations at Head Offices to the detriment of far-flung divisions and operations in diversified and dispersed organisations.

The basis of need is determined by decisions taken by the organisation in relation to its range of activities. For example, if it is determined to be the cost leader in its field it must invest in new production technology wherever this becomes available. If it is determined to be a pioneer of new products, research and development functions must be supported. Products that are in decline are either allowed to die, be killed off or else rejuvenated (again, with resource implications in each case).

The relationship and interaction between levels of resources and activity levels should also be indicated. Over- and under-resourcing both lead to waste and inefficiency: in the former case, because it will invariably be at the expense of another function; in the latter, because nothing is ever done properly or completely.

■ Control mechanisms and activities

These exist to ensure that resources are being used in optimum ways in pursuit of the overall direction and the activities that are conducted in their achievement. They provide information on which judgements and assessments can be made. They indicate where and why matters are going well, and where improvements can be identified and implemented.

Control mechanisms and activities are established in the following ways.

1. The management of staff; establishing procedures and patterns of work; through job and task descriptions; discipline and grievance; and health and safety. There may also be control elements in pay and reward systems (the achievement of targets leads to extra pay, or additional time off); accident, absence and sickness procedures and monitoring; training and development activities.
2. The management of finance and budgeting systems, the purpose of which is to provide accurate and assessable information in relation to particular operations.
3. The effectiveness of functional activities such as marketing campaigns; the purchase and use of capital equipment.

4. The effectiveness of budgeting information and communication systems and reporting mechanisms and relationships.
5. The establishment of performance targets and indicators.

These are set in the context of the organisation's given ways of working. Indeed, their output may indicate the need for changes in these as the result of the information gained.

This is especially important where the organisation operates in diversified, devolved or decentralised ways. Means must be established which reconcile the needs for local autonomy with the need for effective reporting relationships with the centre.

The main general issues to be addressed are those of flexibility and rigidity. Functions must be given sufficient leeway to conduct effective operations without constant reference to higher authorities. At the same time, boundaries must be established in order to maintain overall control.

Control is therefore a joint function conducted by individual managers in conjunction with those who determine the size, scale and scope of particular activities and who allocate resources.

■ Critical paths and networks

These are devised as part of the process of harmonising, planning and scheduling activities by breaking them down into their component parts and showing these in the form of a diagram or activity flow chart. They indicate the times and resources needed to complete each activity. They indicate also the interrelationship between all necessary activities and operations.

The result is that a total schedule for the work can be established and a critical path shown which indicates the shortest possible time for completion.

It also indicates critical incident areas where there is a requirement to coordinate many activities at once; where there is an area of high risk; and where potential blockages and hold-ups may occur.

It establishes the priority areas by identifying those activities on which others depend, and it is a summary plan of action which includes an outline or indication of everything and everyone involved.

It is an indication of consequences when activities are not completed on time, and the compounded effects of these. Finally, it establishes an order of work: those activities that must be completed in sequence and those that can be carried out in parallel. It also establishes specific deadlines for everything.

The technique can be adopted for any activity or situation. It is much used on project work where there are normally distinctive and definite start and finish deadlines.

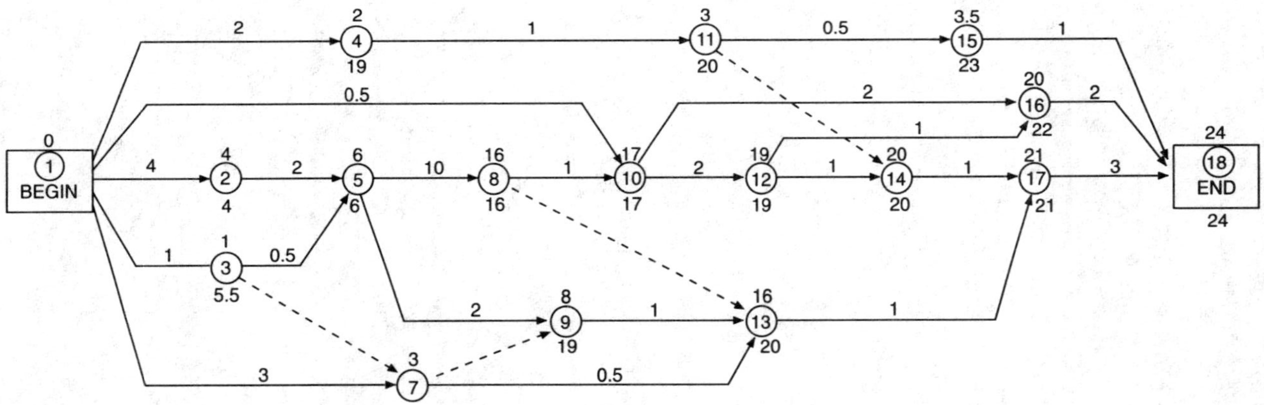

Key

(4) Activity number

4 → Time unit (reactivity)

→ Operational progression

- - → Operational tie-ups

19 ◯ 19 Time completed (cumulative) — The number on top is the earliest point at which the activity can be completed; the number below is the latest point by which it must be completed.

Critical Path (1) – (2) – (5) – (8) – (10) – (12) – (14) – (17) – (24)

Purpose: a project/operational schedule; a planning tool; a model against which to measure actual progress. Identification of critical incidents (those on the critical path). Identification of potential problems, blockages and hold-ups.

It can be used as a wider model of scheduling, design and evaluation of activities. It can also be drawn up as a map of production areas, or of systems and information flows. It is also a fundamental means of planning, coordination and control.

Figure 10.7 Network and critical path plan

■ Monitoring and review processes

The purpose is a continuous, general and formal, regular review of progress and achievement, assessing the reasons, both for success and shortfall, and also for any drift (whether this is beneficial or detrimental).

The boundaries of this are:

- organisational performance, both overall and by department, division and function related to aims and objectives;
- group and staff performance appraisal;
- production, sales and income performance related to stated aims and objectives;
- customer respect and regard;
- relations with the community and environment;
- measurement of particular initiatives (for example, marketing campaigns, research projects, joint ventures, seasonal products);
- product portfolio and life cycle assessments;
- indicators of good and bad performance, such as production faults, customer complaints, staff factors (absence, turnover, and so on);
- suitability of stated aims, objectives and targets.

It is a continuous process, punctuated by regular formal reviews conducted by directors and top managers, and those responsible for particular activities. It should also be conducted within departments, divisions and functions in respect of their own performance in the same way. The process is then developed as part of the assessment and establishment of directions for the future. The outcome is an informed judgement and assessment of the current state of the organisation and a focus for making improvements and adjustments and the means of establishing why success or failure has come about.

■ Organisation design

Suitable forms of organisation must be established. These must be capable of accommodating the financial size and scale envisaged; the technology to be used; and the human resources required. Planning, control, information and maintenance systems must be introduced. A management style must be devised.

It must be capable of maintaining and developing the position (or positions) in the value chain. Supply and purchasing systems, and distribution and outlet methods, are required.

This is the basic context and framework for the design and creation of organisations. The driving force is not therefore that 'We are in activity X, therefore we need organisation format Y', but rather the creation of a structure that supports and enhances the stated purpose.

Conventional approaches must be seen in this context. There will invariably be requirements for recognised and distinctive expertise (for example, marketing, personnel, research and development). These will be established in respect of the particular context, rather than in the uncritical creation of departments and divisions.

Any format adopted must be capable of development and progression, of being flexible, dynamic and responsive. It must be capable of accommodating the directions proposed. It must be able to accommodate changes in technology and activities as these occur. People must be operationally, professionally and technically comfortable with the format of the organisation.

It is apparent that whatever the format or nature of activities, a rigid structure is not likely to be appropriate. Stresses and strains occur where the demands of business and forms of organisation conflict. Means must be found to have these resolved without creating costly administrative superstructures.

The organisation must be capable of constituting think-tanks, creative activities and project groups. These normally operate across functions; where they are from within a given discipline, their activities often push at the boundaries of the function.

The structure adopted also reflects management style, and the attitude and approach to the staff. Dependent upon this are the size and nature of control, support and administrative functions; approaches to discipline and grievance; *realpolitik*; operational systems and formats; and reporting relationships. Again, whatever is used must be suitable to the purpose.

BOX 10.3 The Characteristics of Organisations

The following is a summary of general characteristics:

- product and service range and diversity;
  product and service range interaction and support;
  geographic coverage;
  product and service quality;
- number and nature of market segments served;
  segment interaction;
  distribution channels;
- nature and extent of branding;
  sources of customer confidence;
- primary policy;
  attitude to costs;
  gearing (the balance of shareholders' funds with loans, debentures and other liabilities);
  ownership structure;

- technology;
  research and development, new product and service development;
  potential capacity, use of capacity;
- size, structure of organisation;
  complexity of organisation.

It is useful to consider ways in which these differ between organisations.

BOX 10.4 Organisation Types and Formats

Simple: Functional/entrepreneurial: indicates simple hierarchy and above all the top/central figure as the key.

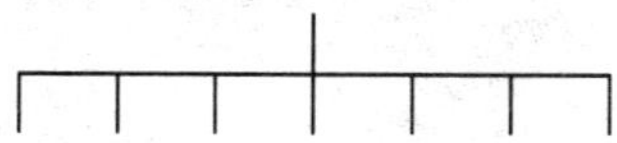

Line: Hierarchical/specialised/functionalised: indicating authority, rank, status, influence, reporting relationships and career paths.

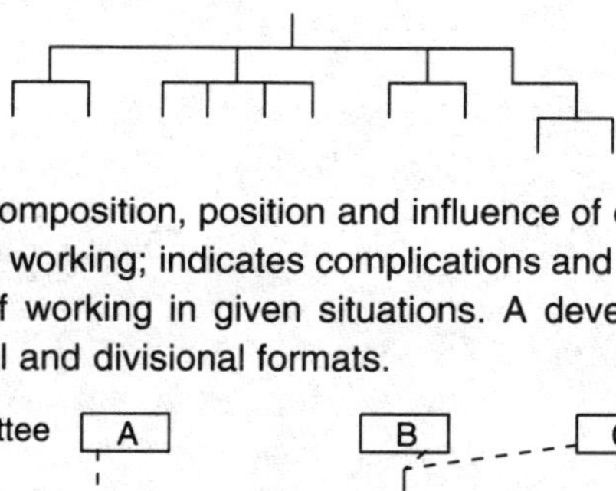

Committee Structures: Indicates composition, position and influence of committees on ways of working; indicates complications and restrictions on ways of working in given situations. A development of hierarchical and divisional formats.

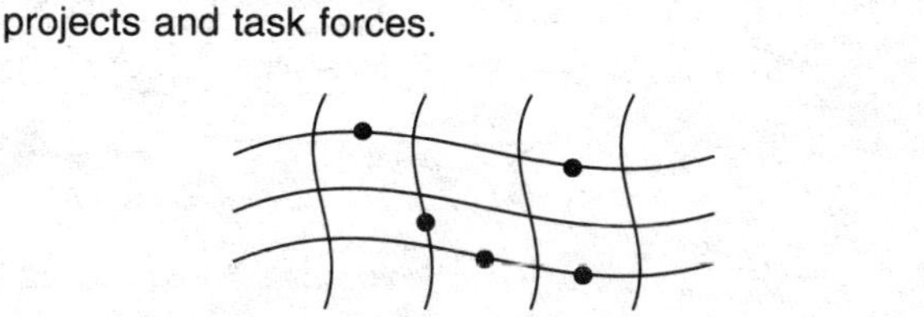

Matrix: Operational/functional: indicating operational relationships, cross-department points of contact; specific activities such as projects and task forces.

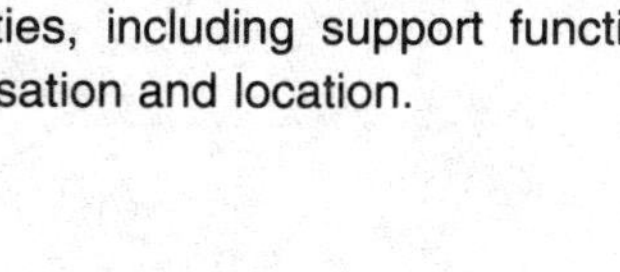

Line/staff: Sophisticated functional/divisional/hierarchical. Indicates the range of activities, including support functions; may also include specialisation and location.

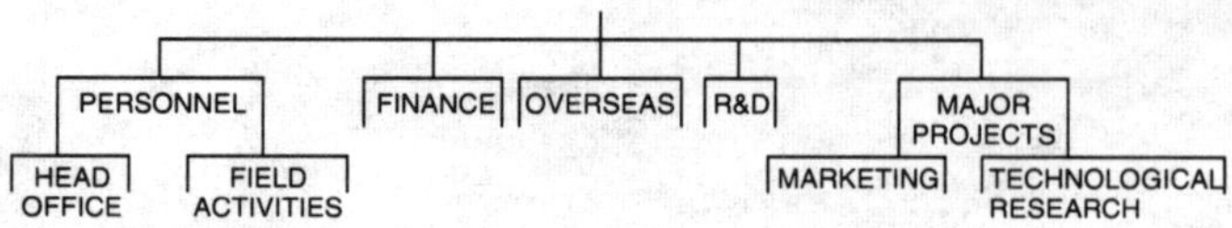

7Ss: Model of the interaction of influences, activities and direction. Indicates areas of behavioural and managerial concern; no indication of function, direction or authority.

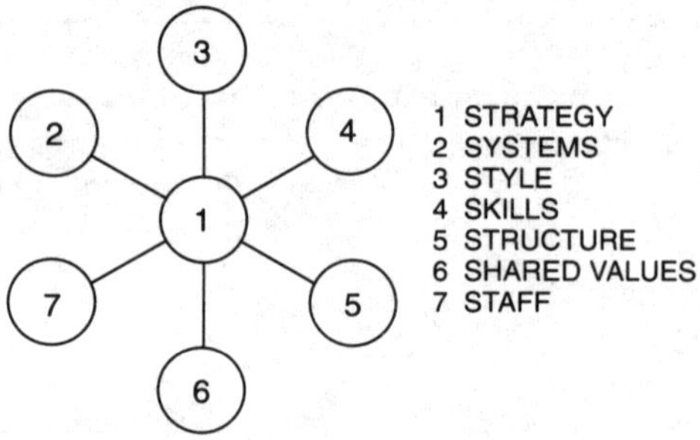

Socio-Technological: Organisational format is driven by physical construction of premises. Based on classical system approach of input–process–output.

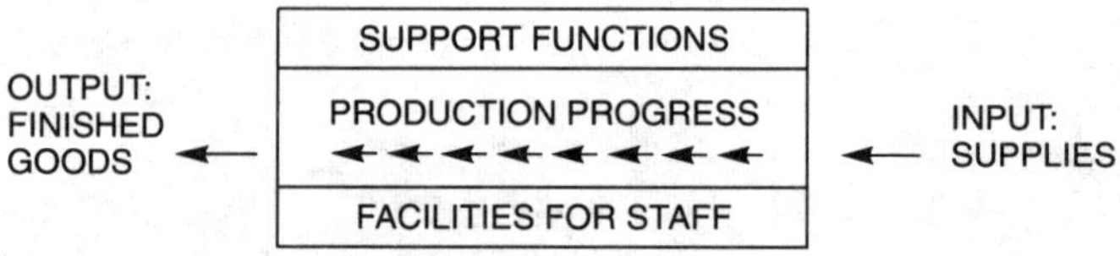

The Mintzberg Model: Indicates operational core (the production area, the shop, the travel agency); the strategic pinnacle (the realm of top management); the middle line (the functional managers and supervisors); the technostructure and support functions; the support staff; and the ideology.

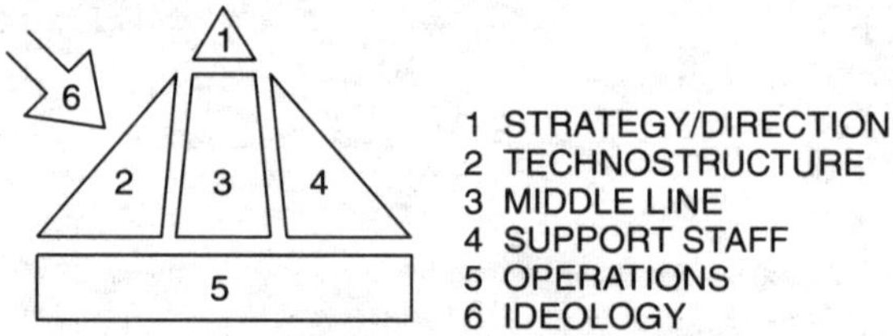

Any format adopted must be able to accommodate the direction that has been determined. The more complicated especially require careful design and assimilation if they are truly to be suitable to the given purpose.

BOX 10.5 The Time Clock

Using the time clock to record staff movements is an industrial tradition and more sophisticated forms of this (for example, electronic clocking on and off) are used extensively in commercial and public services.

It is extremely wasteful and inefficient. Someone checks all the cards at the commencement of each work period. At the end of the day, week or month, someone else adds up all the time worked by all employees. Someone else translates this into wages.

Someone also normally supervises the clocking-in and clocking-out to make sure that nobody clocks in for anyone else.

Someone else is also required to supervise all these supervisory operations.

The alternative is to do away with this altogether. This is achieved by giving people their time to commence work, and requiring their manager to take up the case if someone does not arrive when required.

As this happens with clocking-in anyway, a swathe of costly administrative activities can be removed.

The activity, above all, reflects the attitude and respect in which the staff are held. The more onerous and sophisticated the clocking-on procedures, the lower the respect, and the greater the reflection of a lack of trust and regard. This is compounded where different systems apply to different categories of staff. Its control and supervision is also extremely costly and resource-consumptive. Its perceptions are negative from all points of view. It is a symbol of the total nature of the organisation.

■ Human resource strategies

The design and management of the human resource is critical to the successful implementation of direction. The required approach is a combination of the following elements (all are present in the establishment of a successful, effective and committed body of staff).

1. Identification of those factors that tend to attract people to the organisation, and those that attract people away. This constitutes an understanding of the organisation's strengths and weaknesses as an employer, both absolute and relative to others in the location and in the sector. This is carried out at all levels and for all activities and jobs.
2. Locations of activities and the nature of potential work force present in the area. Potential staff with the required qualities may be readily available on the local labour market. Conversely, they may require extensive retraining and re-orientation (for example, if they work in or have been laid off from, a quite different sector).

3. Developing a distinctive culture that gives the organisation and its staff a strong mutual identity and interest which is suitable to the purpose and activities undertaken.
4. The need and ability to compete with other employers in the area and in the sector on the basis of: wages and salaries; intrinsic job satisfaction; professional and technical development; career paths; mutual loyalty and continuity; opportunities; stability and continuity.
5. The design of pay and reward packages to meet the expectations and aspirations of those who come to work in the organisation. This has to be reconciled with the organisation's requirements.
6. The design of jobs that are interesting, fulfilling and rewarding. This includes recognition of inherent problem areas and taking steps to minimise their effects. This also includes the creation of a functional, comfortable and suitable working environment. This is likely to include patterns and hours of work, and relating the demands of the business to the wider requirements of those coming to work.
7. Training and development strategies designed to enhance and improve all aspects of business performance and involving all staff. Many organisations take the view that training and development is an essential feature of successful business life, and that part of the employment contract is a commitment to train and be trained. Successful training and development strategies integrate organisation and operational requirements with personal and professional needs.
8. Setting clear standards of performance, attitude and behaviour at work and in some cases in the wider conduct of life (for example, Ford executives are not allowed to smoke in their company cars). The normal output of this is that everyone knows where they stand. A strong bond and affinity is established with those who come to work for the organisation. The organisation does not, however, set out to be all things to all people, and rejection does occur; this will ideally be at the pre-employment stage.
9. Integrity and honesty in all dealings between staff and organisation. Equality of opportunity and access to promotion, training and development are absolute. Problems are solved, not institutionalised. Language used is simple and direct. Discipline, grievances and the use of procedures are kept to an absolute minimum. Industrial relations activities are simple and straightforward and not founded in conflict. Pay rises and other rewards are delivered on time and in full. There is full access to all company information. Consultation is continuous and open on all matters that affect the work force.
10. Means of solving problems when they do arise. This covers discipline, grievance and dismissal, arbitration, representation (including relationships with trade unions), redeployment and redundancy. This has to be seen in relation to the paragraphs on standards and integrity. The onus is to resolve such issues as far as possible, quickly and to the satisfaction of all concerned.
11. The core and peripheral organisation. This includes determining which activities are to be retained within the organisation and which are to be contracted out. It also includes consideration of the use and value of sub-contracting, hiring of consultants, seasonal work forces and flexible rostering.

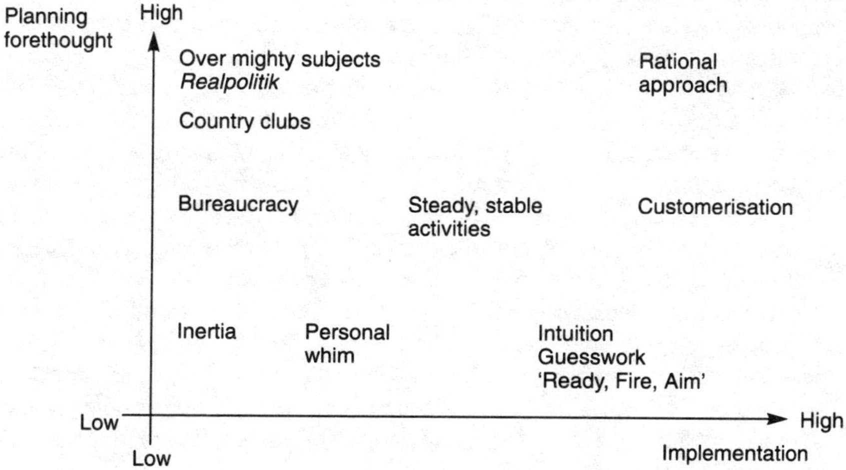

An indication of the mixes of planning and implementation activities, and some influences and conclusions that may be drawn.

Figure 10.8 Planning and implementation mixes

Marketing strategies

Marketing strategies consist of the following.

1. Marketing mixes of all the products to be offered. This is the combination of price; the promotional, presentational and advertising aspects; the properties and benefits that accrue from the product itself; and the nature of locations and outlets where it may be obtained. It also includes the interactions and mutual support that all offerings in the product range afford to each other.
2. Development of the organisation as being safe and steady and the promotion and presentation of confidence and strength. This is directly related to the current range of offerings, and has implications for new products and future activities.
3. Determination of the sectors in which products are to be offered so that the benefit and satisfaction to be accrued through ownership and use may be presented in ways acceptable and positive to those customers and consumers.
4. The creation of activities in support of this, including advertising campaigns, sales teams, brochures, information, help and support lines, sponsorship and public relations activities. Increasingly popular also is the relationship between organisations and their communities, support for local groups, clubs and philanthropic and charitable activities.

5. Joint activities where appropriate, often conducted in conjunction with retail and distribution outlets. These may also be conducted in order to develop the organisation's profile, image and expertise and to gain a foothold in new fields.
6. Market research and investigation to ensure that products are going to be effective and will remain so. This is critical in assessing likely and potential demand, the opportunities to be gained and possible consequences of failure. It is also a critical part of measuring the position of items in the product life cycle.
7. Product life cycle assessment and the implications that arise. This is conducted both for individual items and for the total range. It provides a form of definition (for example, of where products are in relation to the Boston Matrix), as well as the cycle itself, and helps to indicate where marketing priorities may lie and what marketing activities are likely to be suitable.
8. After-sales support and services to ensure that the product in question continues to give good and lasting value. There are also implications for price here, whether a total price or total product and service, or whether there are additional price considerations for each component part.

■ Purchasing and supply strategies

The influence on these are as follows.

1. Command and influence upon sources of supply. This is especially important where a key component or material is difficult to get hold of, or is in short supply. In these cases organisations may choose to use space (and therefore capital resources) in stockpiling and accommodating these in order to be able to guarantee their own successful activities.
2. Purchasing patterns. These tend to be viewed on a continuum of regular purchases at the one extreme, to stockpiling at the other.

   Whatever is determined is driven by organisational requirements, balancing the commitment of resources in this area with other needs.

   'Just-in-time' approaches to purchasing are currently held in high regard because the onus for both storage and regularity of delivery is placed on the supplier. There is therefore no need to commit to further resources in this area provided that deliveries can be guaranteed.

   The organisation may also choose to buy up the entire production of a particular component and then act as its wholesaler (and therefore as its regulator also).
3. Multiplicity of sources. It is usual to be able to turn to a variety of sources of supply so that a relative security of supplies may be ensured. It also avoids or limits any question of dependence or dominance in the relationship. It is also necessary to consider the stability and steadiness of purchases which may occur as the result of being prepared to deal with a single or main supplier. Conversely, it is essential to be able to preserve sources of materials if a supplier gets into difficulties.

Distribution strategies

The following elements have to be considered here.

1. Choice of outlets. This includes the use of the range of shops available, including supermarkets, chain and department stores, mail order and catalogues, warehouse arrangements and cash and carry. It requires the establishment of support for this, which takes the form of staff training and product awareness for those directly involved. Hire purchase, finance plans and credit arrangements may also need to be created.
2. Limitation. Products gain in value through exclusivity. This occurs if it is not universally available. Establishing a distinctive but limited range of outlets may therefore lead to the ability to command premium prices, with increased margins for both producer and distributor.
3. Fleets. There is the question to be addressed of whether to lease, sub-contract or buy up transport fleets (or whether to use a mixture of these). Consideration should also be given to the size of the fleet and whether any spare capacity could become a niche business opportunity.
4. Premises. There is the need to address the question of distribution premises in the same way (whether to lease, sub-contract or own the outlet). Products may also be offered for sale in the outlets of other organisations (again, this is usual for department and chain stores, mail order and supermarkets). Questions of whether to have regional and local distribution centres (warehousing and wholesaling) must also be resolved.

Strategic drift

Strategic drift occurs where purpose and direction are lost, not clearly stated, not clear at all, or not understood.

The normal counter to this is along the lines that 'If we strive for heaven we will at any rate get the earth.' Satisfactory performance tends therefore to be measured in terms of anything that is achieved in pursuit of the desired or stated target.

Strategic drift is recognised and remedied by following critical paths; undertaking criterion reviews and other marker activities; interim performance and turnover reviews; product life cycle monitoring; product portfolio monitoring; and market reviews. There are real answers to be found by paying attention to each of these processes. If the strategy is seen to be adrift, and the directorate and top management appear quite happy with this (or at least to be doing nothing about it), the strategy is prone to lose value and currency in the organisation at large.

Drift may also be caused by changes in circumstances and nature of the markets, or indicated by a lack of responsiveness. Changes in production technology and methods; a sudden boom or faddishness in the market; or product obsolescence all also indicate a lack of direction.

The general behavioural aspects should also be acknowledged. The longer the drift is allowed to go unchecked or unresolved, the harder it is to gain the commitment of everyone to getting the activities under consideration back on track.

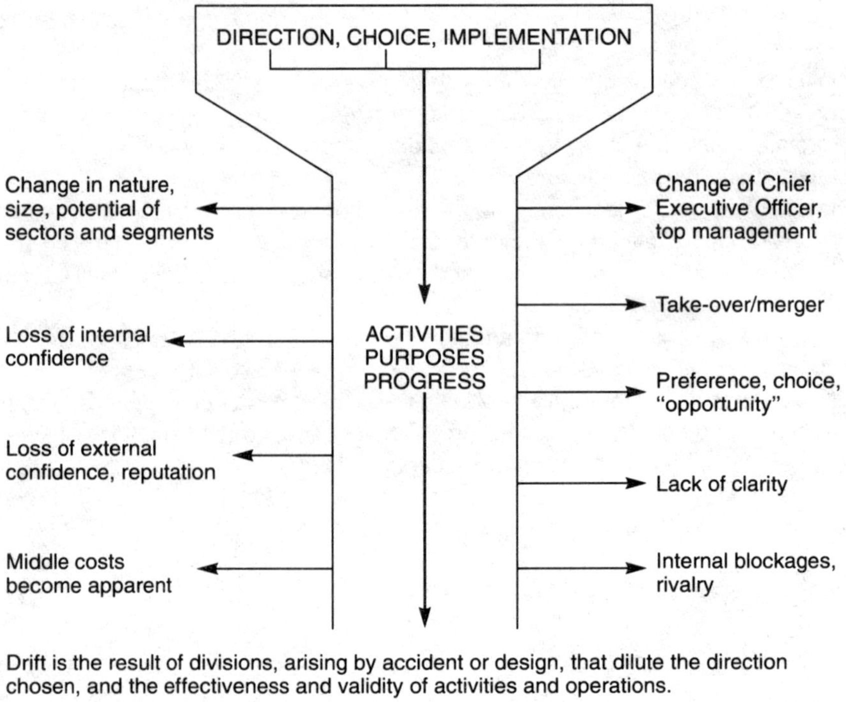

Figure 10.9 Strategic drift

Drift also occurs in operational terms. The most common manifestations of this are wages drift (increases in the wage bill outside the ranges determined upon); income and turnover drift (whereby income and turnover targets that fail to meet projections are nevertheless allowed to pass unchecked and set a new and usually lower standard for satisfactory performance); and marketing drift (which is whereby the activities of marketing and advertising campaigns are not fully evaluated in terms of effectiveness, perceptions or attitudes on the part of the markets or in terms of additional returns).

Drift also has irrational elements. The sudden withdrawal of a product or strategic champion from the scene may lead to a loss of the energy necessary to sustain the activities in question. The champion may have had a key role in getting the matter in hand launched, and those responsible for its development and implementation may place no particular regard or value on it.

Drift also occurs because of *realpolitik*. From the point of view of those working in the organisation the matter under consideration may simply have been an output of the need to be seen to be doing something and again it will lose any impact or impetus once this need has passed. Additionally it may relate to the position of an overmighty subject or vested interest group; and this may be in terms of either the need for a triumph or attachment to a prestigious piece of work; or, conversely, in the ability of either to block something or kill it off altogether.

■ Other problems in development and implementation

■ The opportunity-capability match

Chief among the problems is the ability of those responsible for directing the organisation to match the proposed strategy with the distinctive capacities and capabilities of the organisation. This involves full and continuing appraisal of all the following aspects and their effect and contribution to the overall clarity (or otherwise) of purpose, strategic advance (or drift), and the identification and exploitation of opportunities that become apparent along the way.

■ The flexibility-focus-purpose mixture

This also involves the extent to which a true balance is struck between each. This is so that, on the one hand, the approach is not too blinkered to see and take advantage of opportunities as they unfold, but also so that this is achieved without diverting from central paths. Such opportunities are to be seen in the context of the core strategy and not diversions from the chosen path. Above all, core resources should not be divested away from core purposes and towards faddish or unconsidered activities.

■ The familiarity-pioneering mix

This also includes the effect that ventures into new areas have on the organisation's historic nature and regularised customer bases. Again, there is a balance to be struck between the two. Above all, sticking to the familiar must be seen as a dynamic and purposeful choice, rather than a recipe for stagnation or complacency.

■ The quality of operations, management, operations, production and output technology and operational staff

This concerns not only all of these, but also the maintenance and improvement of each of these and their interaction with each other.

■ Constant improvement

This should additionally be seen in the context of the development and harmonisation of the strategic and operational interface. Each of these feeds off the other. The clarity of the strategy, and the ideal and practical coverage of it becomes ever more apparent the greater the true understanding of operations, management, staff and technology. Or, conversely, the operational aspects refine and make practical and real future strategic proposals.

There is also required a more general reflection on the suitability of operations to the proposed strategy. This concerns the development of and/or investment in the operational capacities of the organisation if the strategy is to be fully realised. The strategy may or may not require this development (it may, for example, require the converse: that is, limiting the present capacities of the organisation).

■ The structure, systems and style mix of the organisation

This has again to be seen in both strategic and operational terms. This includes evaluation of their general suitability in relation to the desired purposes. Where necessary, part of the strategy devised should be a change or transformation initiative that has the purpose of ensuring that a mix between these elements and the strategy is to be achieved. The structure systems and management style of the organisation are servants of the strategy and should have no other purpose. If they were designed or developed for a previous purpose and this no longer holds currency or the original has changed or been lost, then there will be problems of dysfunction.

■ The culture and shared values of the organisation

These are reflected in the prevailing attitudes and levels of identity among the staff, and the extent of their commitment to the organisation and its purposes. This is in turn reflected in general manifestations of motivation and morale. In particular this may be reviewed in terms of levels of strikes, disputes, absence, turnover, accidents and complaints received.

Externally, this is the extent to which the customer is truly at the hub of the organisation's purposes. This aspect is reflected in general levels of satisfaction with the products and services offered (and again in the volume and nature of complaints received).

■ Levels of investment

Japanese and other Far Eastern manufacturing organisations understand this above all, and this is reflected in their success in capturing market share and in the developments and output of high-quality, highly valued products supported by excellent service levels.

BOX 10.6 Investment

The story is told of two factories, one British and one Japanese. Both employed 20 members of staff in their production process. Both purchased a machine that could do the work of the 20 members of staff with only one operator. The British company bought one machine and made 19 members of staff redundant. The Japanese company bought 20 machines.

BOX 10.7 Mitsubishi

In the 1950s, 1960s and 1970s the Mitsubishi Company of Japan employed a large work force in the manufacture and fitting-out of ocean-going ships. When this sector collapsed in the early 1970s, the Mitsubishi Company was able to transform itself from a shipbuilder into a car manufacturer. Part of the reason for this was the extent of investment in technology and the quality and generic nature of the machinery which meant that it could be transformed fairly easily from one manufacturing activity to another. Part of the reason also was the extent of investment in the work force and their identity as Mitsubishi employees rather than as shipbuilders.

■ The softer issues

We must also address the softer issues of creativity, imagination, flexibility, dynamism, happiness, satisfaction and fulfilment. This is to ensure that the right spirit is engendered as a contribution to the long-term effectiveness of the organisation. Those who do not believe that these elements should be present or have any importance or value are invited to consider the success and quality of those organisations where they are missing.

Do not forget, either, the validity, viability and effectiveness of the organisation's sub-strategies which cover the areas indicated elsewhere of supplies, processes, distribution, the human resource, marketing and research and development.

■ Realpolitik

The *realpolitik* of the organisation includes the extent, strength and nature of the internal political system, and the priority and pecking order of the favoured and unfavoured departments and divisions. There are two distinctive elements. Those on the operational side cannot work in isolation from it or in spite of it. Those on the strategic side seek to ensure that operations can be carried out within it, and so devise strategies that match up with it.

■ Ethics

There are ethical elements to be considered that relate either to the nature of the offerings produced, or to the nature and type of the production processes or to the nature of the customer and markets to be served. There are, for example, extremes of this in the defence sectors and in the production of fast moving consumer items through sweated labour (often in the Third World, but also found in parts of the West). There are questions of integrity raised concerning the use of animals, children and women in marketing activities. There are equivalent questions raised by the decision to supply particular markets (for example, South Africa in the 1970s and 1980s; Iraq in the 1980s and 1990s; Iran in the 1980s; the former Yugoslavia in the 1990s).

BOX 10.8 The Involvement of Unions as Stakeholders

One source of capital that has recently been pursued by organisations is that of their representative unions. The purpose is the gaining of financial backing as well as employee representation and commitment on their part. The idea is worth pursuing in theory at least for a variety of reasons.

The union mind is concentrated on overtly commercial lines because it has become a commercial stakeholder in the organisation. It is the joining and matching of the employer and employee interest, the acknowledgement of the extent of the common ground that exists. This can be compared with the preamble to the agreement between the UK Amalgamated Engineering and Electrical Union (AEEU) and Sanyo (UK) Limited that runs as follows:

> Both parties recognise that the well being of the employee is dependent upon the company's success and that the high standards of product, quality and

reliability are essential if the products produced at the establishment are to become, and remain competitive, and that therefore the maximum cooperation support must be given to measures designed to achieve, maintain and improve quality and reliability of standards.

Organisations that do this have taken up a variety of distinctive positions. They have both offered a stake and ceded a measure of influence to distinctive interest. They have sought a source of finance, the interest of which should directly match its own. It is a development of the staff participation concept. It is also a development of the social partnership concept into that of economic partnership.

It may also be seen from the more general point of view of involvement. Peters (1986), quoting the success of the USA Bethlehem Steel Company attributes part of this to the fact that the staff own 40 per cent of the company's equity. There is an extension of this in the involvement of the unions as shareholders. This strategy is open to criticism on the grounds of control (as with all large and institutional or majority shareholders), and on the grounds of distinctive competence (again, as with all large shareholders).

Early examples in the UK where unions were involved in commercial ventures failed, as witness Triumph/Norton/Villiers and Meriden Coventry in the 1970s.

Currently, the process is well advanced in the USA. Activities in the area include the acquisition by unions of large blocks of equity in TWA and North West Airlines.

Projections of success

These may simply be wrong. They may be wildly optimistic or pessimistic, and in either case (though for different reasons) the end result is dysfunction. In the former case the organisation is left with stacks of products that it perhaps cannot sell, or in regard to which it has to bring the price down, or engage in other marketing activities. In the third case, the organisation is beset by orders that it cannot meet, leading to customer dissatisfaction (and often also loss of reputation on the part of the organisation and its output).

This arises from inaccuracies along the line of the strategy process, marketing research, product design and delivery, so that whatever we put into the model used to project and forecast the outcomes and results was wrong.

Much of this is to do with the wrong information being gathered in the first place (the information industry has its own telling phrase RIRO Rubbish In = Rubbish Out). The information may have been corrupted by the product champion (especially if the champion had her own secondary or subversive agenda to pursue, or else was an overmighty subject). Market research and product take-up surveys may indeed have been carried out, but the line of questioning corrupted so that the results were led or pre-empted in a particular direction. An overmighty subject or politician may have instructed such research to produce a particular set of results in support of his own preferred position. Finally, there may be a range of knowledge and research from which to draw conclusions and on which to base strategic proposals and activities, and which shows a variety of possible outcomes; the organisation or individual in question may simply have been highly selective in its choice of tranche of research.

■ *Ad hoc* strategies

Organisations may choose to go in particular directions on the whim of an individual, or on a collective whim. Such initiatives may have little or no bearing on the history, expertise, or recognised capabilities and capacities of the organisation. In such cases organisations simply set off in the direction indicated because 'it seemed like a good idea' to those responsible for the strategy processes of the organisation.

■ Conclusions

Activities, policies and sub-strategies are created in support and pursuit of the organisation's main strategies and directions. The main measure of the success of these is the extent and strength of this support. It provides a point of reference for evaluation and indications of where these activities require development, refinement and change.

Strategy evaluation is not an exact science. It is rather an evaluative process, the result and outcome of which is the continuous harmonisation and re-harmonisation of activities with purpose. Both are invariably affected as the capabilities of the organisation are refined and directed in the pursuit of purpose. As the overall direction chosen progresses and develops, the activities undertaken change and alter emphases and priorities, and also turn up opportunities and problems. The most thorough evaluation and monitoring cannot possibly anticipate all of the problems that occur during the implementation of strategy. It is essential to recognise that there are bound to be pitfalls and crises, and that means of coping with these have to be present in all organisations.

■ Work assignments and discussion questions

1. What are the main factors to be taken into account when deciding to use a major celebrity (for example, Madonna and Michael Jackson with Coca Cola and PepsiCo) to promote a particular product or product range?

2. Why is it often difficult for major changes in emphasis or direction to be achieved fully and successfully in multi-national companies and public service bodies? What proposals could be made to overcome this?
3. Why did the Laker Sky Train service between London and New York fail so spectacularly? Which of the problems and issues could have been foreseen and how might these have been addressed?
4. Why was the Mitsubishi company able to move successfully from shipbuilding to car production (see Box 10.7)?

CHAPTER 11

Strategies for Change and the Management of Change

Introduction

Organisations and managers today recognise the inevitability of change. Change has positive and negative attributes. On the one hand, it presents opportunities, the chance to experiment, to create something new, to diversify, to expand into new areas, to develop new skills and expertise, and a presence and reputation in new areas. On the other, it represents uncertainty, ambiguity, the modification (and in many cases the passing) of existing and comfortable activities and ways of doing things.

Change has no single cause. It is a complex blend of social, global, cultural, economic, political and technological processes, all of which interact and all of which have to be understood, reconciled and harmonised.

There is also a strong human element. Changes and developments in expertise, capacity, attitudes, behaviour and values are all increasingly features of organisational life and essential for organisation effectiveness.

Change is never absolutely predictable. It is not possible, for example, for an organisation to be certain that as a result of investing in new production technology, it will become effective and successful. The decision to invest will have been based on the best analysis of information available and may be an essential step. There will, however, be other factors to be considered, including the state of the market, consumer confidence, the state of the other players in the sector, the availability of expertise to use the new production technology, and so on.

Change is not linear. It should also not be seen as an isolated event or series of events. It is a process caused by the interaction of organisations, their resources, equipment and people with the forces of change that exist in markets, customers and the wider environment.

Forces for change

Competitiveness

Competitiveness has become more intense in virtually every sector due to the globalisation of trade and commerce. It has occurred also as a result of increasing levels of customer expectation, causing people to take a much more informed view of product quality, excellence and value. The consequence, in many sectors, is a greatly expanded range of offerings and a wide variety of price, quality, value, volume and time mixes, leading to a much greater customer choice. In many sectors the size of the total market has not expanded so that the result is an increased number of players chasing a steady consumer base. There are also very few and increasingly fewer sectors that are protected and not subject to the threat or risk of entry.

■ Economic

The explosion of product ranges and their universal availability has coincided with recessions across the major consumer markets of Western Europe, North America and (to a lesser extent) Japan. This has brought a reduced propensity to spend to areas of increased competition. This has resulted in organisations having to invest more heavily in their success, often for reduced results over longer periods of time.

This has caused organisations to review their cost bases and to seek more effective and efficient ways of doing things. It has included job and pay cuts, redeployment and retraining, drives for greater organisation and work force flexibility, and new forms of organisation and structure.

■ Technology

The rate of technological advance is greater now than ever before. This continues to increase, especially in production automation, robotics and information technology. This has brought with it a knowledge and capability explosion. An ever-increasing volume of knowledge is more widely available, adaptable and useful; and the capacity to produce for an ever-increasing range of sectors is also more widely available to more organisations.

This also indicates the need to invest and to be prepared to reinvest in production and information technology whenever required.

■ Product obsolescence

Products and service life cycles are becoming shorter as a result of the increase in their volume and quality. Many of those currently available did not exist in the recent past; many do not remain available for long; and all are subject to potential threat from current and future invention, research and development.

■ Customer satisfaction

Full understanding is required of the needs and wants of customers and how these are actually satisfied, as is an understanding of the particular offerings of organisations in the range of overall priorities of customer bases. Understanding customer confidence and expectation and the propensity to spend is also necessary bith in general, and also concerning particular offerings.

■ Opportunities

Opportunities exist for all organisations in their own familiar fields and in others to which their products and expertise can be adapted. The following questions must be addressed.

1. What else could the technology produce and for whom?
2. Who else could be persuaded to use the product or buy the services?
3. Where else could the offerings be marketed, and how?
4. How else could they be presented, packaged or otherwise differentiated?
5. Where do the absolute strengths and weaknesses lie, and how can the strengths be developed to competitive and commercial advantage?
6. What is the true nature of competitive advantage, and how else could this be developed and expanded?
7. What are the price levels that can be commanded in response to each of the questions?
8. What are the volumes that can be sold in response to each of the questions?
9. Where else may these initiatives lead?

■ Customer gluts and shortages

Customer gluts and shortages occur from time to time in most sectors; they are more likely to occur in some than others. Those that are subject to seasonal fluctuation are especially susceptible (for example, ice cream and soft drink consumption always rises during summer months; extreme cases of this occur during long hot summers).

It also tends to occur in short-term and faddish/fashion sectors. This happened, for example, in the UK with the demand for Teenage Mutant Hero Turtles in the period preceding Christmas 1991.

In these cases the market expands so quickly that the unwary organisation cannot meet the total demand. Market share is therefore lost to chancers and opportunists.

At the opposite extreme, customer shortages occur when products cannot be sold. This may happen in the reverse of the above circumstances, such as a cold summer or the arrival of the next fashion or fad. It may also occur because of the entry of a new competitor into the sector who is able to offer all the benefits of the existing players with some other distinctive advantage, such as price, quality, value or differentiation. It may also occur due to factors outside the control of the organisation: for example, a recession, or the placing of the offering in question under legal restraint.

Labour gluts and shortages

This is especially critical where labour shortages occur, whether in skills, aptitudes, quality or volume terms. There is a balance to be struck between acquiring the required capacities over the short term and assessing the likely development of the situation over the foreseeable future.

The result is an analysis that leads to a range of conclusions. At one extreme the view will be taken that this is a temporary nuisance, while at the other, the particular quality demanded may be in such short supply that the organisation decides either to pay premium and economic rents for it or to find alternative solutions to the problem.

The problem of labour gluts also bears consideration. Overtly, less of a commercial pressure, it is nevertheless essential to ensure that absolute standards of capability within the workplace are maintained. It is also a position of responsibility. It is often necessary to consider divesting parts of the work force.

BOX 11.1 Labour Gluts and Responsibility

There is a short-term advantage perceived to be gained through the depressing of wage levels during periods of high or increasing unemployment. This is often conducted along the lines of 'If you do not like it there are plenty out there who would love your job.' Readers are invited to draw their own conclusions as to the true regard in which the work force in question is being held and the likely nature of the relationship between the staff and the organisation and a wider quality of working life that is likely to exist in an organisation which takes this view. It is an approach that is to be avoided absolutely.

BOX 11.2 The Turbulence of the Business Sphere in the 1990s

A brief summary of this is desirable.

EU and the rest of Western Europe

This area is affected by the creation and development of the EU single market and the development of trading relations between its member states, its neighbours in the rest of Europe and the other trading blocks of the world, especially Japan, the rest of Asia and North America. It is subject to resource demand and priority pressures on public services. It is also subject to extreme market and competitive pressures arising from the volume, quality and utility of products produced by

Japan, Malay, Chinese and Korean manufacturing companies. It is also affected by large volumes of job loss. These have occurred and continued to occur in manufacturing primary industries and public sector services.

The EU is also subject to the pressures of enlargement brought about by the joining of Sweden, Finland, and Austria on 1 January 1995. Members of the ex-USSR also wish to belong.

North America

This region is affected by the manufacturing boom and output of Japan, Malaysia, China and Korea (as with the EU). It is affected also by continuing high levels of unemployment, and is subject to increasing demands for public health, personal social services and wider imperatives of urban renewal in some parts. It is affected by the industrial void left by the ending of the Cold War.

In the case of both Western Europe and North America there is consideration required of recession, retrenchment and loss of confidence.

The Pacific Rim

This area consists principally of Japan, Korea, Indonesia, Malaysia and China. This is the chief global production area. It provides cars, electrical and other consumer goods to the advanced, sophisticated markets of the world. There are particular issues of trading surpluses and dependency to be addressed. There is also the prospect of recession to be considered as the rest of the world becomes unable to consume the volumes of goods hitherto taken up. It is also necessary to consider the hitherto (by Western standards) huge levels of investments made in these industries by the Japanese, Korean, Malay and Chinese companies and their need to be replenished and serviced.

Emergent sectors

In the early to mid-1990s and in global terms the major areas are South America, India, Pakistan, China and the former USSR. This status may also be accorded to parts of the EU, especially Greece, Spain and Portugal; to parts of North America, especially Mexico and the Southern USA and also to Malaysia, Indonesia, Taiwan, and parts of Africa and South America.

Collapse of empires

This concerns especially the ending of the USSR and the problems and issues to be addressed in the wake of the emergence of its former members as distinctive nations. Those wishing to join the EU are going to a great deal of trouble to bring themselves up to the required standards. In general, vast levels of investment are required in their infrastructure.

Compound memberships

This concerns several different trading, defence and Commonwealth-type blocks and spheres of influence, and the resultant complexities of global and national relations that are developed.

Spheres of influence

This relates to the trading relationships drawn up, both general and specific, and principally cars, consumer goods, food and agricultural produce; the spread and proliferation of defence equipment and the usage of nuclear technology for military purposes and the generation of energy; and the sheer volume of business to be gained as the result of entry into such areas as India and China, and the former USSR.

Oil

This remains the core of global energy provision. The sector is dominated by the nations of the Middle East. There is additional provision in varying degrees from North America, South America, Africa and the UK. In future there are to be great contributions from Russia and South-East Asia.

This is illustrative of and indicative of the variety and complexity of the forces at work. Their contribution to the levels of turbulence in the business sphere is in turn compounded by the great rates of global technological advance, the creation of global training agreements and barriers, and political and military imperatives and influences.

■ Barriers to change

These must be identified and considered. They are as follows.

1. **Levels of investment.** Investment as a barrier to change arises when the arrival of a new player or new production (or information) technology give an entirely new complexion. In such cases, it is normally necessary to invest heavily in the new production and output technology in order to continue to compete.

   The question also arises where one player in the sector gains significant advantage through an ability to command large levels of investment. There is also a problem where players are placed at serious disadvantage through their inability to gain access to the levels of investment that are available to other players in the sector or that are now required to remain competitive.

Driving Forces	Restraining Forces
• Change at the top • Powerful external influences • Vision of the future • Powerful leader/key staff • Acceptance of need to change • Externally focused • Crisis/opportunity • Market demands/new market opportunities • Quality • Changes in expectations • Actions of competitors • Technological advance • Obsolescence of existing activities • Declining returns	• Career-based organisation • Organisation structure • Organisation culture • Turnover of staff • Comfort of staff • Success over long period • Stable environment • Stable ways of working • Authority, patterns and reporting relationships • Vested interests • Technology • Image (peronal, professional, organisational) • Identity • Fear of the unknown • Comfort with the known

Both driving and restraining forces require attention. Attention only to the driving forces is likely to cause stresses, strains and disputes as the restraining forces set their own alternative agenda. On the other hand, the restraining forces must be addressed to ensure that they are replaced with something positive and to avoid leaving a vacuum.

Figure 11.1 Force field analysis: drives and restraints

2. **The current state of the organisation.** This is overwhelmingly a barrier to change when there has been a long, successful and profitable past, and when it has been held in high regard and has a general reputation for excellence and quality. In these circumstances it is very difficult to convince everyone concerned of any need to change.
3. **Structures and systems.** These represent the familiar current ways of working. Any change to them is bound to lead to upheaval, dissidence and dissatisfaction. This must be seen from both the organisational and the personal points of view. Staff require convincing that the new is to be superior to the old. This is especially true in the case of historically successful organisations. In personal terms people see the career path that they had mapped out for themselves vanishing overnight. In either case something is needed to replace these and must be made clear; a void must not be left.
4. **Skills and capabilities.** The current skills basis of the organisation is normally a factor. Where this is based on historic activities, extensive retraining and re-orientation is likely to be required and this has to be integrated with market or operational changes. Where this barrier is largely perceptive (that is, for example, where the organisation has hitherto been a supplier of a particular sector and is now to change or diversify) there may simply be questions of minor retraining or a general process of shift in understanding required.

Genuine skills obsolescence is much more traumatic, and the barrier that is to be addressed in this case is the trauma created. People who have invested their whole working lives in following a particular trade or occupation feel very threatened when this is removed. Part of the successful management of change lies in convincing those affected of the worth and value of the future, as well as in the retraining in skills and aptitudes.

5. **Technology.** Technology is a barrier to change from the following points of view:

   (a) usage and recognition of the complete range of uses to which the technology could profitably and effectively be put;
   (b) lifespan, where there is useful life and therefore returns still left in the technology (and measured usually against the opportunity costs of ceasing production, divestment, withdrawal or the sale of it); and where historic levels of investment are high and recent;
   (c) sectors: the inability to recognise the potential to adapt the technology to serve a wider and new range of sectors;
   (d) unit costs: the extent and length of time for which these are likely to remain competitive (this includes consideration of the general price, quality, value and cost mixture);
   (e) maintenance costs;
   (f) replacement costs, timescales and staffing implications (such as training and work methods).

6. **The current behaviour of the organisation.** The following aspects of this should be considered.

   (a) Vested interests. These include those who profit from the current ways of doing things and who may lose influence and respect of the results of any changes made. Restrictive practices, union recognition and influence and distinctive work structures have all to be considered in this regard. This also includes management and professional groups who have profited from current and historic ways of conducting activities.

       Extremes of this are overmighty subjects and overmighty groups that may have great negative influence such as (abilities to block or negate the effects of change or proposals for change).
   (b) Management style. If this is good it becomes a barrier to change in itself. Any change that is proposed must therefore be carried out with the view that this should as far as possible not be disrupted or diluted; that the past effectiveness should be built on and developed.

       If it is bad or if it is inappropriate to the new state of affairs envisaged, it may nevertheless be defended by the management group which again sees loss of opportunities, influence or prestige as the outcome.
   (c) Shared values, and the extent to which these are to be disrupted, perpetuated or developed; the actual and the desired shared values. Where shared value changes are needed this also has to be entwined into the change strategy and the activities devised in pursuit and support of this.

7. **Location.** The extent to which this is a barrier to change is to be considered as follows.

   If the organisation has a distinctive regional identity it may decide that its best future course of action lies in diversification but remaining local.

   If it has a range of outlets in different places, it may consider expanding the variety of offerings being distributed.

   If it requires to expand its range of customers or outlets the potential location of these may carry logistic barriers in relation to transport, time and distance to be addressed.

   If the location question is a major shift – that is, going into entirely unfamiliar territory – there are behavioural (as well as logistical) barriers to be overcome: of fear, trepidation and the unknown. This is all invariably compounded by myths and legends, both positive and negative, of those who have previously made such quantum leaps or who have ventured into these areas.
8. **Entry and exit barriers.** Any of the above constitute barriers to change. More specifically, the entry and exit barriers that pertain to the particular sector are also likely to require analysis and evaluation. They may in themselves constitute barriers to change.

BOX 11.3 End Phasing

The lack of an end phase to activities is also regarded as a barrier to change by some authorities (Owen, 1985; Lessem, 1988). The hypothesis is that people are much happier to move on to the new once they truly believe that the old has ended. Organisations that follow this line of reasoning therefore create celebrations or wakes at the end of projects, activities, phases and initiatives in order to underline and achieve this. Once the celebration has been held, once the ending is truly demonstrated, the staff are then much happier to accept the new and much more likely to do so and to look forward rather than back (because the past has clearly ended).

BOX 11.4 Myths and Legends

Myths and legends arise around larger-than-life characters and major organisational triumphs, successes and disasters. An organisation folklore is generated by these, reflecting the nature of the organisation itself. The stories themselves are likely not to vary all that much, but the standpoint and attitude of their telling is polarised according to the nature of the organisation.

All organisations have stories of disasters. The best organisations tell this with hilarity mixed with a determination that such disasters will never happen again.

The worst organisations tell these with an attitude of blame and recrimination. The genuine positive or negative culture is fed by these, emphasising the positivity or negativity.

Positive or negative, the stories are exaggerated in their telling and become ever more extreme and fanciful. There is a serious positive function played by this. It is the ability of staff members to associate with, or to have the illusion of association with tales of bravery, adventure and excitement. To face the opposite – the humdrum, mundane and uneventful – for the whole of one's working life without the illusion of adventure is in many cases extremely disquieting and unacceptable to those concerned. There is, therefore, an overwhelming reason to allow them to take place and to provide an environment in which they can gather life.

Rites, Rituals and Routines

These are the organisation's punctuation marks: the elements of comfort that everyone needs in order to give measure of familiarity, routine and stability to their working environment. In daily operational terms these consist of the hours of work (for example, 8 till 5), patterns of work (for example, opening the post first or sorting it into piles), breaks ('I always have my break at 10 o'clock') and so on. In organisational operational terms they are reflected, among other things in the presentation of the organisation in its reception area, over the telephone, in its dealings with clients (the extent and nature of the relationship, the extent to which corporate hospitality is available, the extent to which the staff go on outings or have Christmas parties and so on). They are also reflected in ways of working ('No one ever does anything around here until it is too late'). They are reflected in all negotiating meetings, committees, groups and group work. They are reflected in strategy and planning cycles and the required meetings and activities that go into these.

BOX 11.5 Behavioural Barriers to Effective Change

These may be summarised as follows.

1. **It cannot be done.** A barrier both to confidence and understanding. It is based on a lack of true, full and accurate information concerning the matters in hand.
2. **There is no alternative.** This comes in two forms. It is adopted by both the work force and the interest groups in and around it that have a vested interest in the maintenance of the status quo either because it is familiar or because any change will result in loss of influence (as stated in the text). This is especially true where ways of working have been both effective and productive over a long period of time and where people are used to these. The other

side of this is where directorates and managers adopt this as the one and only explanation for a change that is to take place. If this is conducted in isolation it simply becomes a challenge for people to think of alternatives. It also becomes a challenge for overmighty groups and overmighty subjects to devise blocking mechanisms.

3. **Lack of clarity.** This is where organisations have not sorted out their own clarity of purpose or the basis of the changes that are proposed. Neither customers nor staff therefore go along with them with any degree of confidence or understanding. It is a reinforcement of the oft-stated element that aims and objectives and a general clarity of purpose must be worked out in advance of any activities.
4. **Use of language.** Again, this must be the language of those who are being required to make the change proposed (customers, clients, community or staff).
5. **Fear and anxiety.** These are the human responses to concepts and situations that are either unknown or uncertain. They are the initial response to any change that is proposed. If they are allowed to get out of hand, these become exercises in the devising and promulgation of hypothetical scenarios that could, in certain circumstances, become problems on the changing landscape. It is both morale-sapping and wasteful of energy and other organisational resources.
6. **Perfection.** Again, this may be seen from two points of view. The first is that the status quo suddenly becomes a perfect scenario, something with which everybody is happy (whether or not this has indeed been the case in the past).

   It also becomes of itself a barrier to progress; that is, people will see the new scenario as being less than perfect and will work to ensure that as it is less than perfect, no change is actually to go ahead.

■ Change management

Successful and effective management of change is dependent upon the presence of the following.

1. Analysis and recognition of the driving forces and barriers present, and the determination to tackle them.
2. The commitment of the directorate and top managers of the organisations to the proposed change or changes, whatever this is in terms of direction, initiative, reorganisation, restructuring, repositioning.
3. The commitment of resources to this purpose.
4. The definition and promulgation of global aims and objectives and sub-aims and objectives that are to be followed in pursuit of the overall change strategy.

5. A structure for the proposed range of activities and initiatives by which changes required are to be achieved. This should include the establishment of priorities, deadlines and areas of responsibility.
6. An understanding of the range of possible outcomes of the approaches taken. This in particular requires assessment from the standpoint of:

   (a) understanding the effects upon staff, their anxieties, hopes and fears for the future;
   (b) understanding the effects upon customers if there are, for example, to be changes in points of contact, modes of delivery and distribution, product specifications and marketing activities;
   (c) understanding the timescales involved, and timetabling where possible.

BOX 11.6 Staff and Change

Effective change in relation to the staff affected is only achieved if the following rules are obeyed.

1. The language used must be clear, simple and direct. It must be the language of the receivers (rather than the givers) of the information. It must cover:

   > what is to happen; why it is to happen; when it is to happen; the range and nature of the effects that it is to have upon the staff and when these will occur; any specific issues, especially redundancy, retraining, redeployment, relocation; general issues that relate to the future prospects and opportunities; specific timetables – both for the total change process and in regard to specific issues (such as the installation of new production technology or the commencement of any redundancies or redeployment that is to happen).

2. This is followed up by the full range of consultation, briefing, discussion and counselling processes. These take place over the pre-change and change implementation phases.

   The ways in which this is done emphasise the general respect and regard for the staff and the need to create an enduring working relationship for the future. There is the need to address the changing and evolving nature of circumstances. Different opportunities may become apparent during the change processes. The approach indicated is more likely to lead to their successful and effective exploitation.

   There is also the need – where redundancy and redeployment are features – to continue the work of the current circumstances until the changes have been fully effective. This can only take place successfully if this approach is followed.
3. Counselling takes place with individuals in order to address their particular anxieties and uncertainties about the effects of the proposed change. New

working times, new work practices, new work locations and the effects of retraining, redeployment and relocation must be addressed.

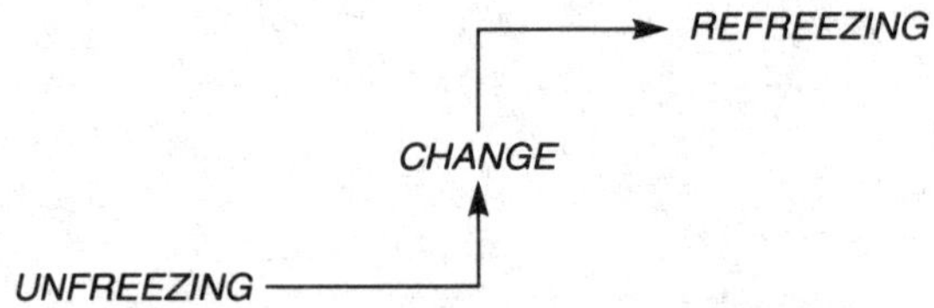

Figure 11.2 Traditional/rational model of change

This is an illustration of the classical change 'step by step' method. It is useful as a simple configuration.

However, it is to be seen in the context that it appears linear, and that change is nearly always more complex. The final element – refreezing – also tends to mislead, as the process is usually required to produce flexibility and dynamism. 'Refreezing' implies that a return to absolute order is to be achieved; this is normally not the case.

MODEL

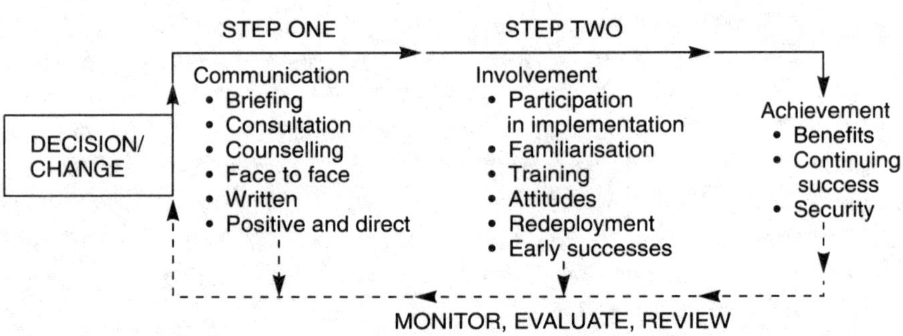

To be used for:

- strategic, directional, operational, technological and locational changes;
- behavioural and human relations issues;
- solving problems;
- introduction of specific matters such as no-smoking, uniform, appraisal, and representation policies

The critical element is the quality of communication.

Figure 11.3 A model for the introduction of change and major contentious issues

BOX 11.7 Consultation and Change

The idea of true consultation has historically been extremely threatening and frightening to Western managers and strategists (see Peters; Lessem; Harvey Jones). True consultation takes place when the organisation has decided upon its direction and when it then goes to its stakeholders (especially staff and customers but all are effective to some extent) with its proposal.

It is not a question of 'what do you think we should do?', but rather 'This is what we are to do. We need your support in its implementation. What are the issues to be addressed in this? Do you foresee any problems in going down this path?'

However, the process of consultation will always indicate the nature and range of issues that those actually affected see as being important.

Consultation is the process by which the proposed path is illuminated.

The importance of this cannot be overstressed. Quite apart from the points made here, we have already identified the extent to which staff and staff groups have the capacity to block or neutralise organisation activities if they do not understand their interest in pursuing them.

BOX 11.8 Consultation and Disasters

Strategic approaches to change also avoid disasters, or at least minimise the possibility of their occurring. In the early 1970s staff at Ford, Vauxhall and British Leyland all found out at different times about proposed high levels of redundancy from the news media before being told initially about it by the companies concerned. Elsewhere adequate communication practice would have been instrumental in avoiding the poll tax/Community Charge of 1986–90. Early full consultation would have proved beyond all doubt that this would not work in its proposed format.

This also applies to the 'Abbey Endings' marketing strategy of the Abbey National plc following its transition from building society to bank (see pp. 000).

■ Customers

Customers also expect convenience and satisfaction, confidence and continuity, of service in their dealings with organisations. Any change in the relationship with the customer must not have any adverse or negative effects.

Points of contact

If these are to be changed there is a clear potential inconvenience for the customer. When the change is first proposed it must be presented in terms of either an equivalent range of benefits that meet the convenience criterion in different ways, or else as a clear and distinctive advantage over the previous arrangement.

Edge-of-town superstores, supermarkets and shopping centres are clear examples of this. Originally the stores had to woo people away from the traditions of going into town centres where they had done their shopping. The approach taken was to emphasise the positive qualities of the new rather than the loss of the old. The emphasis was placed on: ease of access, adequate car parking, the convenience of the one stop for all items style of shopping, availability of cafeteria and rest facilities. The success is so great that for many town centres a collective move is now required on the part of those that still remain in them to change and recharge their attraction in other ways.

All changes will be preceded by extensive consultation and other general public relations activities to prepare those affected for the new ways of working. The prerequisite for the success of this is clearly that at the point of change, the new arrangement is in place and working effectively, and any teething troubles which might occur are quickly resolved.

Culture change

The culture of the organisation – 'the ways in which things are done' – is certain to be affected by any change. The culture which currently exists is either wrong, needs developing or improving, or is somehow otherwise incomplete in regard to that which is desired or required. There are a variety of reasons why this may be so.

The organisation may have been in the steady state for a long period of time. This may have arisen for both positive and negative reasons. At its most positive it may have been effective and highly regarded in markets and sectors which have themselves been steady and stable for long periods of time and which only now are being shaken up by technological advances, new players and changes in customer expectations.

The negative occurs where such stability has allowed the emergence of illusions of infallibility, permanence and other outputs of complacency. There are also likely to be specific additional outputs: for example, bad customer service on the part of a utility monopoly; quality that is technologically or process drives rather than demanded by customers.

Culture is the repetition of the ways in which groups of people think, believe and act. This is based on the shared values of the organisation. The result of culture change must be to reflect this in the ways desired by the organisation.

Culture is not therefore to be allowed to emerge. It is to be positively created as part of the organisation, development and strategy formulation process.

Transition from the old to the new, from the existing to the desired, must carry with it positive expectations on the part of those who are to be affected. People will cling to the old until given positive reasons for switching to the new. A great part of this is to be achieved in the use of high-quality positive and continuous communication.

Other factors

It is essential to establish what staff, customers and other stakeholders actually think, believe and feel about the organisation, its works and its products.

This works best if the organisation has an ideal in mind. This ideal can then be compared with the reality. Part of the change process will then concern itself with moving from one to the other. This normally includes attention to the following:

1. Changes in standards. These occur in all aspects of the organisation and its processes:

   (a) supervision, communication, customer awareness, quality of output, the standard of commitment of the staff and parts, sectors and divisions of it;
   (b) particular measures of commitment, to the organisation, its products, customers and markets.

2. Changes in attitudes: where a negative attitude exists among the staff or parts of it; where the prevailing attitude has been allowed to develop and form without positive intervention from the organisation. In any case, the outcome is detrimental to organisation and individual performance. Specific attitudes – to different departments, to other staff and above all, to customers and clients – have also to be considered.
3. Changes in values and shared values: the commonality of purpose and identity that is the reason (or reasons) for the staff to be there. Where they have been allowed to form or emerge without reference from the organisation is a major cause for concern.
4. Changes in behaviour: this is necessary in specific ways of working. Other more general elements, such as health and safety and the standards and nature of the ways in which colleagues, customers and clients are handled, are also important. It includes establishing trust and honesty.
5. Changes in beliefs: this is the most difficult aspect of all. Beliefs are formed over considerable periods of time. Enforced changes in beliefs are usually traumatic. Again, they are concerned with absolutes of trust, honesty, respect, loyalty and

commitment. Some staff give their allegiance to their department; to their division; to trade unions; to professional associations; to an overmighty subject. Others use the organisation as a sponsoring vehicle for outside interests (such as voluntary work). Cases where these are legitimate beliefs may still require harmonisation within the organisation.

6. Motivation and morale, especially where these are negative. The indicators here are the levels of strikes, disputes, accidents, absenteeism and turnover, and the nature and volume of customer complaints.
7. Public acceptance, based on the fact that 'Everyone likes to be liked, needed and valued.' Where this is not present there is an extremely destructive effect upon general morale. It also affects recruitment and retention of staff. This is exacerbated where potential members of staff have also been customers and clients of the organisations concerned: particular examples of this in the UK in the 1990s include British Rail and the National Health Service.
8. The presence and potential of catalysts and agents of change (see Boxes 11.15 and 11.16).

Changes in these areas require the organisation to assume responsibility for them (rather than allowing them to emerge and gain whatever form they develop). This, in turn, requires a recognition that they are important and fundamental to both strategic and operational success. The following can then be considered:

1. The required standards, attitudes, values, behaviour, beliefs; the levels and outputs of each that are required in the pursuit of a harmonious, productive and profitable working environment for all concerned.
2. The opportunities and limitations placed on motivation and morale by the work itself, the technology used, the styles of management, supervision and organisation adopted; it also requires assessment of specific issues such as strikes, disputes, absenteeism and accidents.
3. The nature and extent of the wider public and community esteem in which the organisation is held.

Change is only truly effective where the organisation is genuinely committed to it and has some vision of the required outcome. This is reflected in:

- the nature of the activities undertaken;
- the extent to which they address all issues and factors;
- the extent of commitment of top managers, the resources put into it and the general approaches to the staff in pursuit of it;
- the overall clarity of purpose which the matter is given.

Attitudes and values may also be formed (especially among new staff) through the assumption and promulgation of particular obligations and responsibilities by the organisation in question at the point of induction. In the same way levels of motivation and morale may also be addressed.

Beliefs, however, are deep rooted. Belief change requires all concerned to acknowledge that something at the core of their psyche, something in which they have had faith, with which they have been comfortable for years, is either wrong or inadequate or else has come to the end of its useful life. There is a clear obligation to recognise this, and not simply to destroy the old belief which leaves a void. The old has to be succeeded by the beginnings of the new: something positive for the future.

BOX 11.9 Bone-Deep Beliefs

Part of the key to this lies in the findings of the Affluent Worker studies of the 1950s and 1960s. In particular, implicit in the nature of the wage–work bargain illustrated in the course of the studies is the permanence of it. Carried on for the period of time that it was, it inevitably took on the form of an act of faith.

The consequence is that a form of identity partnership of mutual dependency is generated. This becomes the means to the ends on both sides: the output required by the factory, the economic support for life outside work for the staff. Whole communities all over the Western and industrialised world were established on this basis.

It is thus easy to see where the notion of belief is formed and where it sits in situations such as these. It can also be seen to be reflected in the trauma that occurs when this form of working arrangement comes to an end. Not only is the economic arrangement determined, but also the whole act of faith as represented by the lifestyle, the community, the permanence and the wage–work bargain itself.

Part of the understanding of the collapse of hitherto enduring industrial sectors has to be seen in this way. It applies in the UK to the docks, mines, shipyards and domestic engineering and car firms.

It also underlines the importance placed by the best new organisations – Nissan, Toyota, Toshiba, The Body Shop, Virgin – on the creation of their own distinctive culture, a part of which is the foundation and formulation of beliefs.

■ Changes in technology and production

These occur in the pursuit of improvements in quality and volume of output. There have also been implications among production companies for staffing levels: in the great majority of cases, the technology has replaced human jobs, leading to general community and organisational destabilisation and rises in unemployment among those who hitherto followed occupations in these sectors.

There are also implications for new markets and sector entry. New and improved standards of quality, presentation and packaging, for example, may give access to sectors hitherto not available. This in turn implies more general considerations of expectation and confidence. The new sector may be initially receptive to the quality of product; it will subsequently require the nature and level of service from the entering organisation to equal that which it has always been used to from previous players.

There are implications also for training, development, retraining and redeployment, some or all of which are likely as the result of changes in production methods. Supervision structures and reporting relationships are also likely to be affected. These activities are to be structured as part of the total change process. They are likely to have an impact upon timescales for change.

A general part of the technological change process is concerned with getting the staff used to this. This includes familiarising them with the new situation and any practical and environmental changes that go with it. This is especially true where there are fundamental activity changes (for example, from manual work to machine minding), or where the work force has been completely redesigned. In rational terms, the benefits of both may be clear. At the level of behaviour and expectation and confidence however, the staff may have to be convinced of this and then eased into it.

Advances in production technology have themselves contributed to the general climate of change. The nature and rate of technological advance is certain to increase in the foreseeable future. The nature of production-oriented work, investment in production technology and the skills, capabilities and qualities that go with it are all also certain to change.

■ Changes in name

The name of an organisation is the short-hand summary by which it is known. It summarises the whole of its reputation, confidence, product and output range, image and identity. It also summarises general perceptions of quality and strength in each of these elements. The question of the names of brands is discussed fully elsewhere: see Chapter 9.

■ Reasons for name changes

1. Mergers and acquisitions. In these circumstances the name is changed when there is some overriding need for a distinctive new identity (that is, a summary) to be generated.

BOX 11.10 Name Change (1): Merger

An example of this was the merger of the two computer and electronic information systems firms, Sperry and Burroughs, into Unisys in 1986. The new name was chosen to indicate that a new organisation was to be formed, and that it would be greater than either of the two previous companies. It would also have its own distinctive identity for the future. This was the approach chosen. It was done in this way rather than calling the new company Sperry Burroughs (or Burroughs Sperry) which would have preserved the old, and perhaps also some distinctive pre-existing identities. The purpose was to create a company for the future and not a reminder of the past.

2. Divestment of the old. In these circumstances a new name is given as part of the process of getting over a previous disaster, bad reputation or other crisis or hiatus (see Box 11.11).

BOX 11.11 Name Change (2): Divestment

An example of this is the Sellafield Nuclear Plant. Originally called Windscale (after the nearest village), it found itself with overwhelming pressure to change because of the bad national and media reputation generated by persistent leakages and pollution scares. The name Sellafield was used to hasten this process.

In 1987, the P&O company took over Townsend Thoresen Car Ferries, the cross-Channel ferry company operating between various ports on the south and east coast of England and ports on the north coast of France, Belgium and Holland. Following the Zeebrugge disaster of March 1987 the name of Townsend Thoresen was dropped by the new owners, P&O, and this was reinforced by the adoption of the P&O name, logo and colour scheme.

Boots and Timothy Whites, two department store companies, merged in 1970. At first the stores continued under their existing names. However, they ran into the problem of identity, among both staff and customers. The next idea entailed Boots carrying the range of drugs, health products, cosmetic and other domestic products, while Timothy Whites concentrated on hardware and appliances. Again the problems of confusion and lack of distinctiveness occurred. Timothy Whites was finally dropped, first in favour of a differentiated Boots Cook Shop, and then finally everything was brought under the distinctive Boots brand name and logo in 1980.

3. Differentiation. This is where the name is changed in order to accentuate the uniqueness (real or perceived) of a product in relation either to near competitors or because of a name nearness to some other (completely different) offering.

BOX 11.12 Name Change (3): Accentuation

An example of this is to be found in the name Poundstretcher. Originally the British Airways name for economy class and late booking discounted fares, the company extended it to cover one of their holiday subsidiaries. It was then dropped, first for the latter and subsequently for the former, because of the confusion that thus arose.

An example of the second may be found in Wimpy, the burger bar, and Wimpey, the building company. The burger bar chain has been taken over by Burger King and is to lose its identity and Wimpy name in favour of the global brand name of Burger King.

This does not happen in all cases. An example is Parka, the clothing manufacturers, and Parker, the fountain-pen manufacturers. In each case, the company concerned is sufficiently confident of its brand name, existing strength and sufficient difference of activities to be able to exist alongside the other.

4. Rejuvenation. This is a variation on the differentiation theme. It is likely to occur as an integral part of the total product or organisational rejuvenation process. It occurs for example where a product retains its integrity but requires a new name. Alongside this it also often requires new packaging, appearance and design features to keep it up to date or bring it up to date in the eyes of the market. It may also require this as part of the process of new market entry.

   It may also be a variation on the theme of breaking with the past (see Box 11.13), and the name change may be muted to address this particular aspect.

BOX 11.13 Name Change (4): Rejuvenation

Thus, for example, BT arose out of British Telecom which, in turn, was given an identity separate from the UK Post Office of which it was originally a part before privatisation.

Similarly, National Power, Powergen and Nuclear Electric were all created as part of the process of breaking with the past, again alongside privatisation. They were also created as part of the process of rejuvenating their activities, style, structures, focus and outputs which were supposed to be the distinctive benefits to accrue in the wake of their privatisation and break-up.

5. Globalisation. This is where there is a pressure to use a universal name rather than one which is localised. Thus, for example, while General Motors keep up their distinctive European brands of Vauxhall and Opel, the brand names of each are gradually being harmonised: Astra and Corsa are now the same for both product ranges.
6. Localisation. This is the reverse of the above. It occurs when a product requires a distinctive name for a particular locality. This may be because the original global name has the wrong connotations (or an unfortunate translation) in particular languages. It also occurs where what is distinctive in one country or locality does not easily translate into others.

   This originally happened in the General Motors case indicated above. When General Motors adopted the Vauxhall and Opel names they develop them as having distinctive identities.
7. Image. A part of the process of name change is concerned with the recreation, re-orientation and repositioning of the organisation's image or images. This may also be achieved to an extent either by changing the company's features, logo, distinctive style, colours and colour combinations; or by updating those that already exist.

BOX 11.14 Logo

Organisations that have gone down the change route include BT. When it was privatised it had a distinctive yellow and turquoise colour mix and turquoise logo. In 1989 it changed its logo to a figure of Mercury (the messenger of the gods) and its colour scheme to a two-tone grey. Its distinctive colours became red and blue (rather than turquoise), as did its lettering.

An example of an organisation that has gone down the update route is BP. It has simply changed the balance of yellow and green in its logo and in its style and presentation of its retail outlets and delivery tankers.

8. Joint ventures. It is worth noting that in the interests of the effective management of joint ventures, it is often necessary to give them a distinctive title and identity. Much of this is behavioural; the purpose is to ensure that both the staff and members of the public who come into contact with it have a positive identity with it rather than a nebulous or negative identity or harking back in relation either to the component companies of the joint venture or some mythical past with which they are associated. There is a clear advantage in giving a distinctive and positive identity.

In all cases, and whatever the reason underlying the name change, there are impacts on staff, customers, clients and community to be recognised. Much of this is, as we have seen, related to the overwhelming need and drive for high general levels of confidence. It should always be remembered that a measure of comfort, understanding and familiarity existed with the previous name and images (however bad these may have been). What is proposed or envisaged as the outcome of the new name and image must therefore ultimately be at least as strong as the previous one and associated with the desired positive qualities.

■ Conclusions

Change is carried out on the basis that the result is a better organisation. Activities are also improved. There are also specific impacts upon both staff and customers. There are more general matters of comfort, consistency and stability, leading to enhanced confidence on the part of all concerned.

Change is a process, not an action (or series of actions). There are mazes, sophistications and complexities involved. Organisational change is not linear. It is multi-faceted, whatever the matters in hand are.

Organising the design, implementation and management of change is integral and critical to success. They should address each of the elements to which reference has been made, and are to be monitored, reviewed and evaluated in the same way as everything else.

An understanding of the process, and its components, is essential on the part of all concerned. This affects those managers and supervisors who are to be responsible for implementation, and everyone – internal and external – who is affected.

BOX 11.15 Catalysts for Change

Catalysts crystallise the need for change. They may usefully be summarised as follows.

1. Loss of economic and competitive advantage. This is overwhelmingly where costs rise or where they do not fall as fast as those of the other players in the field. It also has an impact on many other elements, as indicated below.
2. Production technology. This concerns the ability to command the price level afforded by the latest and most effective production technology, the levels of investment required and the rate and timescales of returns. It also relates to the extent, diversity and multiplicity of uses to which it could be put.
3. Marketing activities, especially when it is apparent that initiatives are required; the currency–obsolescence mix of present marketing activities; the currency–obsolescence mix of offerings.
4. Blockages and dysfunctions, including communications, decision-making processes, managerial style, prevailing attitudes, values and levels of motivation and morale.
5. Strategic confidence, and a full understanding on the part of all those involved, about the overall corporate purpose and their part in it.

6. Expansion and contraction, entry and withdrawal, especially by key or dominant players (in the case of entry by potential key or dominant players). There are considerations here for continuing market stability and confidence.
7. Complacency: in this case the catalyst for change is the recognition of the extent to which this is present and its outputs in the particular organisation (normally illusions of infallibility or permanence).
8. Spare capacity. This is the drive not to have machinery, equipment, technology and expertise standing idle. The drive towards optimising its usage may lead to other outlets and new sectors being sought.
9. Specific experience. This is where new key appointments and technology bring with them expertise, contacts and other forms of opportunity that may be useful to the particular organisation in the future.
10. Opportunism and pioneering. This is the recognition of general opportunities as they arise subject to the evaluation processes referred to throughout the text.

The following should also be noted:

In the wake of a major hiatus – loss of a major customer, or a strike or disaster – there arises the opportunity to evaluate, reform and reposition old ways of working, approaches, attitudes and practices.

Take-overs, mergers, divestments and de-mergers are all likely to carry some implications for change.

The activities of government, in particular economic changes, trade barriers and legal constraints, all have effects on the ways in which organisations are able to carry out their work.

BOX 11.16 Agents of Change

Agents of change come under two distinctive headings. They may either be **external**, brought in or retained to carry out (or at least energise) the change required; or they may be **internal**, where this life and energy comes from persons, departments, divisions, groups and teams within the organisation.

Consultants

These are normally external, although some organisations do use their own internal specialist functions on a consultancy basis (especially marketing, human resource and technology). Consultants are brought in for a variety of reasons, including:

- to give an external validity to a direction that has already been decided;

- to remove the bearing of controversial or bad tidings from within the organisation (or, if internal, from its mainstream);
- to come up with the required answer: that is, the one that the organisation needs but which again it is impossible to present as its own for reasons of *realpolitik*;
- an independent view of proposals and initiatives, in which the consultants may be used simply to identify the way forward. In these cases the organisation assumes responsibility for implementation.

However, consultants may assume responsibility for the implementation also, in which case they will continue to be involved as strategy is translated into action. The latter may then become the basis of a continuing relationship. This is then likely to include addressing specific opportunities, problems and spin-offs that may be encountered during the change process.

Key players and key appointments

These occur where particular characters are brought in who have special qualities, expertise and experience, in order to give particular direction to a set of activities. This is likely to occur in most spheres and activities over a period of time.

The opportunities themselves

A business opportunity that becomes apparent may itself act as the key change agent in that it requires both the organisation and its staff members to recognise it and take advantage.

Technology

This may also act as a change agent as it usually brings requirements for retraining, redesign, restructuring and reorganisation.

Project and development work

This may be carried out in order to open up new markets and areas of expertise or of developing a reputation which may, in turn, enable these areas to be opened up. Consideration should also be given to the opportunities generated by the availability of joint venture and sub-contracting work.

Work assignments and discussion questions

1. What were the key features of the successful transition of the Virgin Group into the airline and air travel industries?
2. Outline a change strategy for a London-based domestic and motor insurance organisation that seeks to:

   (a) relocate to Milton Keynes;
   (b) replace its databases and information systems with more modern technology;
   (c) reduce its total work force from 6000 to 2500;
   (d) increase its market share from 3 per cent to 5 per cent (domestic); and from 10 per cent to 15 per cent (motor).

   What key factors must be considered? What are realistic total time frames for each, and for the whole?
3. Discuss the changes in approach attitudes and behaviour that are required by the UK–France cross-Channel ferry services in the light of the opening of the Channel Tunnel.
4. How should the problems and issues surrounding the M25 London orbital motorway have been addressed in order for the project to have been fully successful when it was first conceived? What actions should now be taken in order to ensure that it is eventually successful in the future?

CHAPTER 12

Conclusion: The Future

The future

The purpose of this final chapter is to identify those matters that are important or are likely to become so in the business sphere of the late twentieth century and beyond.

The business sphere is in a state of flux. Great change, turbulence and instability is the context in which activities are set to take place for the foreseeable future. There is a technological revolution driving this, and there are global operational and distribution capabilities reinforcing this. Also to be considered are the global sources and nature of finance and other resources, revolutions in telecommunications and the availability, quantity and quality of information, and distinctive developments in these areas that are likely to have an impact as well.

Changes

Changes that have affected the business sphere since the end of the Second World War may be summarised as follows.

Technological Affecting all social, economic and business activities; rendering many occupations obsolete; creating and opening up new spheres of activity.

Social The changing of people's lives from the fundamentals of life expectancy and lifestyle choice; to travel; to be educated; to receive ever-increasing standards of expertise in health care; to be fed; to enjoy increased standards of social security and stability.

Eco-political Resulting in changes in all governmental forms; the state of flux of the EC and the adoption of supernational laws and directives and the single market; the collapse of the Communist Bloc and the USSR (to which reference has been constantly made throughout this book); the emergence of Taiwan, China, Korea, Vietnam and Malaysia as spheres of economic influence; and the potential emergence of South Africa and South America in the same way.

Expectational In which changes may be expressed as from stability to a state of change itself; the change from the expectation of working for one company or organisation to working for many; changes in occupation, training and profession, especially in the West; changes in political governments and the instruments of state (to which reference was also made above in the examples of the EC); the general regard of the business sphere and the public service sectors which operate within it that change and turbulence are the norm rather than stability.

Legal That is, legal constraints upon activities and operations which apply to particular sectors (for example, in the matter of animal testing in the pharmaceutical sector), advertising (for example, in the use and exploitation of women, children and animals), the human resource (for example, in the requirement to offer equality of opportunity to all members of staff in most Western countries). Other legal constraints to be considered arise from dealings in particular nations or in places where particular trade and other treaties have been signed.

Ethical In terms of what is considered to be right and wrong and a more genuine regard and knowledge of the effects of particular business actions on the world, the environment and the future. This includes greater awareness of the true constitution of dominant and dependency relationships and obligations in this regard.

Stakeholders A greater regard of the true position of organisations' stakeholders and the nature of the stakes that they hold. This has a particular implication for the role of business as a supporter of the wider community and the mutuality of this wider relationship. The converse of this is the process of redlining to which reference has been made elsewhere.

Profit The shift in regard of this from a concept of pure and short-term surplus to a state of long-termism and a relative reflection of the permanence of the organisation and its continuity in the pursuit of customer satisfaction. This can be seen reflected in the commercial and operational successes of the Japanese car and electrical goods businesses of the 1980s and 1990s. It is also a function of this way of regarding profit that both the levels and nature of investment required to achieve this for the future have had to be completely reconsidered.

Mind set This is the way of thinking about organisations, their strategies, activities and operations. A complete change is required away from formalised structure, systems, order and methods, and the acceptance of the turbulent, fluid, ever-changing background as the basis for success. A whole new way of business, operational and strategic thinking is necessary, and must be accepted.

The maximisation and optimisation of resources, returns on investment and performance outputs are paramount. Levels of satisfactory performance based on historic activity schemes and the returns on them are no longer acceptable or tenable; neither, increasingly are they competitive, profitable or effective. There is an ever-growing awareness that resources have been underutilised; that levels of waste are profligate. There is a dawning realisation that attention to these elements is in itself a source of profitable and cost-effective activity.

Information

Information is a commodity. It therefore has a distinctive value. It is the oil that lubricates and facilitates the great majority of other business activity.

It is available in ever-greater quantities. Its most effective usage will clearly be by those who have the technology to process it quickly and effectively. It must be capable of being stored and retrieved in marketable and usable ways and measures. It is necessary to understand its full range of applications and uses also.

There are competitive and commercial advantages to be gained from the effective and continuous gathering and analysis of information. The full potential of this is only now being assessed and realised. Sources of information and the speed at which the information itself can be gathered will greatly expand in the future.

Technology

Technology is seen in terms of its versatility and adaptability. It is also measured in terms of the value and quality of its outputs. It requires the ability to produce commodities and offerings that with some slight adjustment or realignment (for example, repackaging and relabelling) can be offered to a variety of sectors. There must also be the ability to produce items to absolute standards of volume, quality, cost and time. The best technology is also increasingly being regarded as that which can be re-tuned to produce widely differing items from the same basis.

Global organisations, multi-nationals and international companies

In the sectors dominated by these organisations the following changes are set to take place. New markets are to be sought. There is virtually no barrier to the global operator. There is no area that is genuinely closed (though restrictions may be placed by quota systems and restricting rights of entry by particular countries or regions or by placing particular legal constraints on sectors). Economies of scale, the command of resources and production/output technology, and the need to maximise the returns on these drives any organisation in this position to reconfigure itself and enter new markets making new offerings (as, for example, with the use of digital and electrical goods technology to produce wrist watches). The levels of investment required also make it very difficult for any organisation that is not of this size, or cannot command this level of resource, to compete on this scale. It is much more likely that smaller organisations will rather find more specialised, localised or otherwise distinctive sectors and niches in which to operate.

Global projects

An output of the ability to command this level of resource technology is the ability to participate in global projects. These are as follows.

1. **Construction projects:** of the size and scale of the Channel Tunnel, Scheldt Barrage and Arabian water desalination schemes, and the experience and expertise in these activities that lead to related opportunities elsewhere in the world. Tunnelling operations are likely to become available between the North American mainland and offshore islands (for example, Vancouver Island); both tunnel and bridge projects are envisaged for the linking up of different parts of Northern Europe, Scandinavia, America, Southern Europe and North Africa (for example, between Spain/Gibraltar and Algeria). Desalination is seen as a long term opportunity for agriculture and settlement, and also in the pursuit of alternative sources of drinking, domestic, residential water supplies in many parts of the world.
2. **Oil, gas and energy exploration and development projects:** as demand for energy grows, oil and gas fields hitherto considered uneconomic to exploit are now subject to serious scrutiny. There are large oil and gas resources in the former USSR and on the South American continental shelf.
3. **Transport:** the next generation of global public transport is envisaged to be a super jumbo jet, able to take up to 1000 passengers. Its progress, however, is dependent upon the ability of global companies in the various fields of airliner design, jet engines, steel and electronics (among others) to cooperate. One consortium looking at one particular design consisted of companies from the UK, France, USA, Japan and Korea; the complexities involved, cultural shifts and differences required, quite apart from the expertise to be harnessed, are phenomenal.

   The other aspect of the transport sector is in the development of the next generation of personal transport that meets current requirements in terms of convenience, expectation, habit and comfort in ways that are to be resource- and fuel-effective and efficient. Both water and electrical technologies are currently being explored and investigated.
4. **Information:** this is the development of global information systems and the satellite, fibre optic and personal transmission and receiving systems. Communications are to be conducted on a personal rather than installation basis; audio, visual and information technology are to be personal, unique and global rather than installed, pre-set and pre-tuned.

Such projects require distinctive expertise and global scale resources. These projects are simply too large for single organisations to contemplate.

By their very global nature, the rewards to be accrued from effective and successful activities are enormous. A radical rethink of the nature of activity, competition and competitive positioning in the pursuit of projects such as these is required. It is clearly necessary to recognise that there is a prospect of organisations (as well as countries) creating their own trading blocks (especially in regard to these sectors and the resource and technology levels commanded by them). This has implications for competition, for the ability of communities to make progress and for the commissioning, design, usage and potential in all fields.

Different approaches to globalisation and internationalisation

It is possible to envisage the expansion and diversification of activities. Five approaches may be illustrated. They all interact with each other.

The Eurotunnel model This is the bringing together of a range of companies, with distinctive expertise and also with large financial resources, for the purpose of creating an enterprise that is both large and sophisticated enough to carry out the required activities. In the particular case of Eurotunnel the organisation was created by ten construction and civil engineering companies (five British, five French) and a financial resource base provided by 200 banks drawn from all over the world. This structure has implications for future projects of this nature, and for the creation of 'commercial nations'.

The Japanese model This is the creation of overseas and globalised subsidiaries in the image of the parent company. It involves high levels of investment and the creation of a relationship between the distinctive advantages of the offerings to be made with the needs and wants of the communities in which these are now to be made.

The Japanese model and example of Japanese companies are worth studying because of their worldwide successes, particularly in competition with established Western organisations. Overwhelmingly, this is the result of the generation of supreme levels of satisfaction in the broadest and most sophisticated sense of the car, electrical and consumer goods sectors. This is being developed by companies in the food sector (Aldi, Costco) and computer sector (Apple Macintosh). It is also being developed by Marks & Spencer as it takes its distinctive quality, branding and status mix into France and New Zealand (among others).

The traditional multi-national corporation model This has to be studied in the context that more and more organisations are trading outside the country of their own domicile in the pursuit of new markets and competitive advantage, and also as they find alternative outlets for existing products. Multi-national-type operations are being carried out by hitherto local, regional and national operators and in sectors that have up till now been regarded as being localised, regionalised and confined to within national boundaries. Thus, for example, in the highly localised Western banking sector (where overwhelmingly, banks of the country in question hold the money and financial obligations of the people of the country in question) the UK Midland Bank is now a part of the Hong Kong and Shanghai banking group. We have already referred to the food supermarket sector above – which has also hitherto been highly localised. Manufacturing, banking, construction and distribution organisations are making forays into the emerging nations of the former USSR.

The acquisition model This is where the globalisation process is undertaken through the acquisition of a local company. The buying organisation brings its product range to bear through an outlet that is likely to be already well established and (as long as the acquisition was successful) well regarded. An example of this clearly is the Hong Kong and Shanghai banking group acquisition of Midland indicated above. In cars, examples are to be found in the acquisition by BMW, the German car company, of the UK Rover Group; and through the acquisition by Volkswagen, the German mass car producer, of Skoda, the Czechoslovakian manufacturer.

A variation on this is the sale of licences and franchises in new areas in order to generate familiarity and possible competitive advantage but without the levels of investment that are necessary in full-scale acquisitions.

Joint ventures These have traditionally been a familiar way of working in the construction, civil and other engineering sectors. They are now to be found in a range of global activities and the concept is expanding (see Box 12.1).

BOX 12.1 Joint Ventures

In the airline sector there is a hook-up between British Airways and US Air that gives each an inlet into the other's sectors. For British Airways this is the ability to penetrate the highly regulated and restrictive internal US air transport and travel sectors. For US Air, this is the ability to open up a through booking system from all the primary and secondary air travel destinations in the USA (approximately 300 outlets) to the BA global network.

It is clear from this that a great potential for these developments still exists. The examples given are deliberately of emerging global sectors and new nations and of those sectors where internationalisation and globalisation has yet to be fully realised. The general lesson to be drawn is of the potential for almost any sector to become globalised. However localised, protected or insulated they may traditionally be or appear to be, they are nonetheless, when viewed in this way, relatively open to the incursion and acquisition processes indicated and to the changes also brought on by technological advance.

■ Contractors and specialists

The role and function of contractors and specialists are set to develop in all sectors along the lines where such a relationship has traditionally been established (for example, in engineering and construction). Both the nature and expertise of the contractor is likely to vary, however. This depends on the view taken by organisations of the distinctive competence that they require all the time and on their payroll. We have already seen how, in some sectors, services such as security, cleaning and catering have been divested. Other areas may be considered.

1. Legal services, in which the organisation retains firms of lawyers specialising in their own particular sphere and in general matters of business and employment law rather than holding on to expensive legal departments.
2. New product developments and general research services on a fee/contract basis rather than as a department or division of the organisation. This may take on the status of wholly owned or partly own subsidiary in some circumstances.
3. Management services (the contracting-out of specialist executive functions).
4. Clerical services sub-contracted on the basis that there will be peaks and troughs in the workflow that may need attention. The requirement is for the work to be done when necessary; however this necessity may not warrant the retention of a permanent work force.
5. Specific activities, such as software design.

Variations on this exist in the commercial endowment of university research departments and in the commissioning of prizes and competitions.

■ Agencies

Another variation exists in the hiving out to agencies of certain distinctive functions rather than holding these in-house. The purpose as always is synergy: in this case the creation of a working relationship that uses the strengths of the agency to best advantage while freeing up organisation resources for areas of its own strength.

Again, there are traditional areas of agency activity, such as recruitment, public relations, advertising design and quality control, and these spheres of activity are likely to develop as organisations themselves better understand their own core/peripheral activities. This may include finance, clerical and secretarial services, specialist production and component manufacturing and maintenance contracts also.

■ Management as a distinctive field of expertise

Many organisations still promote staff into managerial ranks on the basis of technical competence or past performance rather than on the basis of any assessment of managerial aptitude or talent. Many organisations also still do not train their staff either for their first or subsequent managerial and supervisory posts.

There is still a need therefore to change attitudes and approaches. Organisation commitment in this sphere is essential, both initially and in the continuous development of managers in the necessary skills, knowledge, attitudes and aptitudes. The professionalisation of management and the requirement and the harnessing of qualities of energy, enthusiasm, personal commitment, drive and ambition; and the ability to lead, motivate, communicate, solve problems and take decisions is critical to organisation success. High-quality management is a central part of the investment required in the pursuit of competitive advantage.

Closely related to this is the development of management styles and organisation types suitable to the particular operations. This plainly varies between organisations and sectors. However, absolute qualities of openness, honesty, accessibility, truth and trust and the quality of communications and decision-making processes that are required do not.

■ Employee relations

On the specific question of employee relations, the requirement is to move away from adversarial approaches and from the institutionalisation of problems. The need is to generate a cooperative and harmonious approach and orientation towards problem-solving. This then frees up otherwise unproductive time and resources for better usage elsewhere.

Staff management style must also be developed. At present much of this is based on distrust, pecking orders, *realpolitik*, organisational infighting, and jockeying for position, resources and the eyes and ears of powerful people.

All of this divides people and dilutes efforts. The whole becomes less than the sum of its parts. Organisations become fragmented and disjointed.

Superstructures have therefore to be created to manage the distrust and conflict generated. These consist of trade union and other staff negotiation and consultative activities, and departments and functions to manage these. Extensive rules, regulations and procedures are written in support of all this and these have to be constantly referred to, interpreted and updated. Committee and cluster group systems have also to be established.

Again, all of this commands organisational resources that could otherwise be used more effectively elsewhere.

The alternative is the evolution of organisations that have none of this. This involves the creation of a management style and positive attitudes and shared values, freeing up for productive and positive purposes the resources used hitherto in managing these adverse situations.

■ Changing structures

Organisation structures are being devised that reflect this reappraisal of the ways in which they are required to work. The purpose is to establish lean form, streamlining and flatness, cost-effectiveness and efficiency and simplicity of communication and decision-making processes. This itself frees resources for other positive purposes. Those responsible find that what is required is an effective balance of the key aspects of control, permanence and direction, and flexibility and dynamism. The ways in which organisations are to be constituted and reviewed for the future reflect this. The permanent establishment of organisations and organisational functions is likely, increasingly, to become a thing of the past. Organisations will rather have a fluidity and flexibility (ad hocracy) rather than rigid and unresponsive structures.

■ The future of public services

The future of public services is tied in with the reappraisal and reassessment of what these should be, how they should be provided, who should provide them, who should pay for them and who they should be aimed at. This is more complex than might first appear. There are conflicting pressures.

Those in greatest need of the services are not always visible, yet their numbers are growing. Political elements now include media coverage, especially consequences of bad stories and the need to be both seen to be doing something and also the ability to have stories placed in the media which prove that something is being done. There are pressures to raise standards of service by such bodies as the EC; yet such pressures bring with them the need to find additional resources for these at a time when the great majority of governments, especially in the West, are having ever greater demands placed upon them. The wider question of government responsibility for all of its citizens and the nature of this responsibility is also something that needs to be addressed in this context.

■ Health and education

The particular fields of health and education carry the additional burden of ever-increasing awareness and expectation on the part of ever-widening sections of the population and ever-increasing numbers of people. In each case today's provision will not be sufficient for tomorrow, either in fact, or to meet expectations.

■ Health

Expectations for health service and health care expand as cures and treatments are found for hitherto fatal accidents or diseases. Diseases can be tackled at source or by inoculation or immunisation. Parts of the human body that fail or wear out can be replaced or rejuvenated through the transplanting of organs and also the use of artificial limbs, veins and skin.

There is, in addition, an extremely profitable cosmetic health and surgery sector. While much of this is dedicated to the whims and facies of a rich clientele, many of the techniques developed for it have application and usage in the treatment of emergencies and injuries: for example, skin grafting is extensively used in the treatment of burns.

There is a question or morality here also. This is the extent to which such a fundamental human need as health care and well-being should be dependent upon the ability of the individual – or, for that matter, the community or the nation – to pay. It is often, in the case of Third World and emerging nations, tied up in the complexities and convolutions that accompany regional aid.

■ Education

The demand for education also grows alongside the state of technology, knowledge, understanding, awareness and enlightenment. An adequate education today is quickly obsolete.

The grounding that people receive as a basic necessity to be able to understand, survive, progress and work is therefore increasingly a start only. It requires constant updating and development throughout life. It therefore becomes something that is an integral part of all life. This idea is neither developed nor resourced anywhere except among Western and Japanese academia and intelligentsia.

■ Other public sector services

As the numbers of population increase, so does the sheer volume of those who require some form of social support or security. At its most basic this is itself a reflection of basic health and education needs: the ability to support and look after the people, to provide shelter, food and some capabilities. In the West the problems have to be tackled in relation to lack of money on the part of individuals and the prevalence of health, medical and social disadvantage that goes with this.

In the emerging nations this should be seen in similar terms. It is also complicated in these cases by population explosions and the need to find new methods of support and service provision.

This is a sketch and summary of the state of public sector services and the pressures on them. Several clear conclusions can be drawn, however.

■ Resources

There is an absolute level of resources required in order that the services to be provided are both useful and adequate. Those who have alternative means of delivery have found that short-term resource advantage is not available. Resource advantage is only to be gained through more radical and therefore longer-term restructuring (as with all other activities). It is also essential to invest in the skills, qualities and technology required by public services. Again this is as with any other field of activity; and again, the best services are to be found where this happens; and again, the converse is also always true: lack of investment leads to a lower volume of services badly delivered.

■ Focus

This is the ability to truly target public services where they are required, to the right people and with absolute quality and volume. Efficiency and effectiveness of resource utilisation can only occur if this is done.

It is also to be achieved only if a true equivalent of the profit motive that exists in commercial sectors is found. The best approach to the profit motive in this regard is the creation of the energetic, driven – and focused – organisations that would have to exist if such an output was actually required. The measure of success, however, is to be found in the effectiveness and quality of service. Performance targets are therefore clearly required to be set and assessed in this way; rather than assessment by financial or market analysts, this would ideally be carried out by public service analysts.

■ Providers

It is clear from this that the nature and quality of service is much more important than who provides it. There is no reason why public services need to remain in the national or local government domain provided that they are free at the point of delivery to all those who require them, and underpinned by an absolute commitment in terms of volume, quality, continuity and reliability.

If the current instruments of service are to remain in place they require overhauling and repositioning. They are both resource-inefficient and unfocused. They have created for themselves bureaucratic, managerial and administrative jungles which dissipate the efforts made on the part of the client groups.

Social responsibility

There is also the question of social responsibility. The nature of this requires both absolute definition and also setting in the context of the particular part of society. Governments constantly reposition their priorities in regard to the communities that they seek to serve. During the period 1945 –90, for example, this positioning task took its cue entirely from the need to spend enough money on defence in perpetuating the Cold War. Elsewhere, there is the need to reconcile a general responsibility for the health, education, social stability and well-being of all members of the society with the implications for what this actually means for the particular society in its particular situation and in regard both to the activities of that society and the resources which are available as the result. There are also questions of absolute political positioning, absolute moral and ethical standards and the stated priorities of the society or community in question to be addressed and reconciled.

Traditional and accepted ways of carrying out these services have to be questioned in all cases and radically restructured in many if there is to be any prospect of public-sector services continuing for the foreseeable future. The instruments of service plainly do not, and cannot, work in many places. They require radical redesign and repositioning. The services themselves require refocusing and repositioning to ensure operational effectiveness, resource efficiency and maximisation and the management structures which are truly needed rather than those that actually exist. In the UK, this is likely to be a long and painful process as the different interest groups involved come to terms with the fact that the old ways no longer work. The special difficulty is that no consensus exists as to what should be put in their place.

Those responsible for public policy invention and direction, and those who are charged with translating it into practice, must reposition themselves. Overwhelmingly, this requires that they make the complex shift from short term to long term, from expediency to strategy, from cash surplus and budget domination to investment. If this were to happen, there is a much greater chance that top-quality public services will indeed become available to all and at much greater cost-effectiveness.

Conclusions

The general conclusion is the necessity to reconcile the turbulent environment and business sphere, and the great advances in technology and expertise with the conception of organisational stability, permanence and clarity of strategic purpose to ensure that this can be achieved. The strength of organisations and the directions and strategies chosen must reconcile these if they are to be successful. In the past, the best organisations have managed to do this and to generate activities within this framework. In the future, additional complexity is implicit in the size and the nature of those markets, the scale and scope of investment, technology, production methods and activities and the increasing globalisation and sophistication of markets and sectors. Also, as we have seen, the concept of product and service quality related to the raising of expectations are now firmly in place. There is a relationship between levels of investment and technological excellence.

Beyond this, the main general lesson to be learned is this: that effective business and public strategies are not optional. Any organisation that does not have clarity of purpose will not compete successfully. No public policy, no public services or health or education services can be effective (and certainly not cost-effective or resource-efficient) unless a true clarity of purpose is first articulated.

The overriding obligation of organisations to their stakeholders is to remain in business. They can only do this if they make a profit and thus ensure their own relative permanence and stability, either by continuing to produce that which customers need and want; or, if they are public services, if they continue to provide effective and quality outputs that enhance and alleviate in turn the quality of the life of the client groups.

Above all, business, public and competitive strategy is a process. Each of the elements identified and analysed, illustrated and discussed in these pages is either a part of that process or a different slant on, or insight into it. As a process, above all it requires process controls. These are the 'hands on the tiller', maintenance, operational adjustments; and the identification and assessment of new horizons as they become visible. Most fundamental of all, however, is the entwining of the elements of flexibility, responsiveness, dynamism and creativity with the essential clarity of purpose.

Bibliography

D. Abell (1980) *Defining the Business*, Prentice-Hall.
I. Adams, S. Hamil and A. Carruthers (1991) *Changing Corporate Values*, Prentice-Hall.
I. Adams, S. Hamil and A. Carruthers (1992) *Corporate Strategy*, Prentice-Hall.
H. I. Ansoff (1979) *Strategic Management*, Pelican.
H. I. Ansoff (1984a) *Business Strategy*, Pelican.
H. I. Ansoff (1984b) *Corporate Strategy*, Pelican.
H. I. Ansoff (1984c) *Implementing Strategic Thinking*, Prentice-Hall.
D. Asch and C. Bowman (eds) (1986) *Readings in Strategic Management*, Macmillan.
M. K. Ash (1984) *On People Management*, Warner.
M. Baker (1983) *Market Development*, Penguin.
G. Binney and C. Williams (1995) *Leaning into the Future*, Brealey.
Boston Consulting Group (1970) *The Product Portfolio in Concept*, BCG.
C. Bowman and D. Asch (eds) (1992) *Strategic Management*, Macmillan.
V. Buell (1985) *New Product Development*, Sage.
R. Buzzell and B. Gale (1987) *The PIMS Principles*, Free Press.
A. Chattell (1995) *Managing for the Future*, Macmillan.
W. Clark (1988) *The Want Makers*, Corgi.
C. R. Christensen (1986) *Business Policy*, Irwin.
G. Cohen (1988) *Marketing Strategies*, Routledge.
S. Cooke and N. Slack (1991) *Making Management Decisions*, Prentice-Hall.
P. Doyle (1989) *The Strategic Importance of Brands*, Economist Intelligence Unit.
P. Drucker (1964) *Managing for Results*, Heinemann.
P. F. Drucker (1981) *Towards the Next Economics*, Heinemann.
P. F. Drucker (1985) *Innovation and Entrepreneurship*, Pan.
P. F. Drucker (1986) *The Practice of Management*, Heinemann.
W. Duncan (1994) *Manufacturing 2000*, Amacom.
D. Francis and A. Woodcock (1979) *Unblocking Your Organisation*, Routledge.
M. W. E. Glautier and B. Underdown (1991) *Accounting Theory and Practice*, Pitman.
W. Goldsmith and G. Clutterbuck (1986) *The Winning Streak*, Heinemann.
J. Goldthorpe *et al.* (1963) *The Affluent Worker*, vols 1–4, Cambridge University Press.
M. Goold and A. Campbell (1987) *Strategies and Styles*, Blackwell.
A. N. Grundy (1992) *Corporate Strategy and Financial Decisions*, Kogan Page.
R. G. Hamermesh (1986) *Making Strategy Work*, Wiley.
G. Hamel and C. Prahalad (1994) *Competing for the Future*, Harvard.
C. B. Handy (1993) *Understanding Organisations*, Pelican.
J. Harvey-Jones (1990) *Making it Happen*, Pan.
J. Harvey-Jones (1994) *All Together Now*, Heinemann.
G. Hofstede (1980) *Culture's Consequences*, Sage.
M. Hudson (1995) *Managing without Profit*, Penguin.
G. Johnson and K. Scholes (1994) *Exploring Corporate Strategy*, Prentice-Hall.

A. Kakabadse (1991) *The Wealth Creators*, Kogan Page.
R. M. Kanter (1986) *The Change Masters*, Free Press.
R. M. Kanter (1988) *When Giants Learn to Dance*, Free Press.
P. Kotler (1980) *Marketing Management*, Prentice-Hall.
P. Kotler (1991) *Analysis, Planning and Control*, Prentice-Hall.
J. Kotter (1982) *The General Managers*, Free Press.
R. S. Lessem (1986a) *The Roots of Excellence*, Pan.
R. S. Lessem (1986b) *Intrapreneurship*, Wildwood House.
R. S. Lessem (1988) *Transforming Management*, Prentice-Hall.
C. Macray (1991) *World Class Brands*, Addison-Wesley.
H. Mintzberg, (1979) *The Structure of Organizations*, Prentice-Hall.
H. Mintzberg, J. Quinn and S. Goshal (1995) *The Strategy Process*, Prentice-Hall.
R. Monks and N. Minnow (1994) *Corporate Governance*, Blackwell.
V. Packard (1957) *The Hidden Persuaders*, Penguin.
V. Packard (1960) *The Waste Makers*, Pelican.
R. Pascale (1990) *Managing on the Edge*, Viking.
R. Pascale and A. Athos (1981) *The Art of Japanese Management*, Pan.
T. Peters (1990) *Thriving on Chaos*, Macmillan.
T. Peters and N. Austin (1992) *Liberation Management*, Macmillan.
T. Peters (1982) *In Search of Excellence*, Free Press.
A. Pettigrew and R. Whipp (1991) *Managing Change for Competitive Success*, Blackwell.
M. E. Porter (1981) *Competitive Strategy*, Free Press.
M. E. Porter (1986) *Competitive Advantage*, Free Press.
M. E. Porter (1990) *The Competitive Advantage of Nations*, Free Press.
G. Randall (1990) *Marketing to the Retail Trade*, Heinemann.
G. Randall (1992) *Principles of Marketing*, Routledge.
W. J. Reddin (1970) *Managerial Effectiveness*, McGraw-Hill.
A. Ries and J. Trout (1982) *Positioning*, McGraw-Hill.
E. Schein (1985) *Organization Culture and Leadership*, Jossey-Bass.
E. Sternberg (1994) *Just Business*, Warner.
A. Toffler (1980) *The Third Wave*, Collins.
M. Tushman and W. Moore (eds) (1984) *The Management of Innovation*, Pitman.
J. Ward (1984) *Profitable Product Management*, Heinemann.
P. Warr (1986) *Psychology at Work*, Pelican.
B. A. Weitz and R. Wensley (1988) *Readings in Strategic Management*, Dryden.
P. Wickens (1995) *The Ascendant Organisation*, Macmillan.
A. Williams, P. Dobson and M. Walters (1987) *Changing Culture*, IPM/IPD.
J. Woodward (1964) *Industrial Organisation*, Oxford University Press.
M. G. Wright (1980) *Financial Management*, Routledge.

Index